Contest for California

BEFORE GOLD
California under Spain and Mexico
VOLUME 2

ROSE MARIE BEEBE & ROBERT M. SENKEWICZ
Series Editors

Contest for California

From Spanish Colonization to the American Conquest

Stephen G. Hyslop

THE ARTHUR H. CLARK COMPANY
An imprint of the University of Oklahoma Press
Norman, Oklahoma
2012

Publication of this book is made possible through the generosity of Edith Kinney Gaylord.

LIBRARY OF CONGRESS CATALOGING-IN-PUBLICATION DATA
Hyslop, Stephen G. (Stephen Garrison), 1950–
　Contest for California : from Spanish colonization to the American conquest / Stephen G. Hyslop.
　　p. cm. — (Before gold : California under Spain and Mexico ; v. 2)
　Includes bibliographical references and index.
　ISBN 978-0-87062-411-7 (hardcover : alk. paper) 1. California—History—to 1846. 2. California—History—1846–1850. 3. California—Discovery and exploration—Spanish. 4. Spaniards—California—History. 5. Missions, Spanish—California—History. 6. Indians of North America—Missions—California. 7. Mexican War, 1846–1848—Campaigns—California. I. Title.
　F864.H97 2012
　979.4′01—dc23

　　　　　　　　　　　2011037977

Conquest for California: From Spanish Colonization to the American Conquest is Volume 2 in the series Before Gold: California under Spain and Mexico.

The paper in this book meets the guidelines for permanence and durability of the Committee on Production Guidelines for Book Longevity of the Council on Library Resources, Inc. ∞

Copyright © 2012 by the University of Oklahoma Press, Norman, Publishing Division of the University. Manufactured in the U.S.A.

All rights reserved. No part of this publication may be reproduced, stored in a retrieval system, or transmitted, in any form or by any means, electronic, mechanical, photocopying, recording, or otherwise—except as permitted under Section 107 or 108 of the United States Copyright Act—without the prior written permission of the University of Oklahoma Press.

1 2 3 4 5 6 7 8 9 10

*In memory of my father and mother,
who brought me into California*

Contents

List of Illustrations	9
Introduction	11
Prologue: Alfred Sully's Fall from Grace	19
PART ONE: SPANISH COLONIZATION (1769–1784)	31
1. Spiritual Conquest	33
2. Cross and Crown	59
3. The Anza Expedition	75
4. Settlement and Strife	93
PART TWO: EXPOSED TO THE WORLD (1785–1825)	111
5. Overtures from Abroad	113
6. The Smugglers' Coast	145
7. Imperial Sunset	175
PART THREE: TRADERS AND TRESPASSERS (1826–1841)	207
8. Paths of Subversion	209
9. Revolutionary California	243
10. The Emigrant Tide	281
PART FOUR: THE AMERICAN CONQUEST (1842–1848)	303
11. Intervention at Monterey	305
12. Frémont's Forays	319

13. The Bear Flag Revolt	349
14. Occupation and Resistance	369
Conclusion: The Illusion of Innocence	401
Bibliography	409
Acknowledgments	423
Index	427

Illustrations

FIGURES

Portrait of Junípero Serra	32
Junípero Serra preaching to Indians	37
Reception of La Pérouse at Mission San Carlos, 1786	112
View of Monterey presidio, 1792	131
Indians in tule canoe, San Francisco Bay, 1806	132
Dance of Indians at Mission San José, 1806	159
View of Fort Ross, 1828	168
"Scene on an Old Californian Cattle Ranch, in Early Spring," ca. 1870	249
Richard H. Dana, Jr., 1842	252
Yerba Buena (San Francisco), 1837	263
Juan Bautista Alvarado	266
John A. Sutter	280
"Sutter's Fort—New Helvetia," ca. 1846	287
"A Parley: Prepared for an Emergency," ca. 1866	295
"Taking of Monterey," 1842	308
John C. Frémont	318
"Pass in the Sierra Nevada of California," 1844	325
Monterey, California, ca. 1846	354
General Mariano Vallejo	363

Andrés Pico 392
"Battle of San Gabriel, California," 1847 397

Maps

Map of the California coast, 1791–92 46
Frémont's map of his explorations in 1842 and 1843–44 322–23
Map of Mexico, 1846 332–33

Introduction

This book examines the taking and remaking of California from the Spanish conquest launched in 1769 to the American conquest that concluded in 1848, drawing extensively on the accounts of soldiers, settlers, missionaries, merchants, and others who made history there and reflected on it. Some significant accounts by early Californians have been uncovered in recent times, but much of the available testimony was compiled by Hubert Howe Bancroft and his staff in the late 1800s as they produced their epic, multivolume history of early California. Theirs was an achievement of biblical proportions, but like the Bible those volumes are not easily read from start to finish. Readers seeking something less massive and monumental but unwilling to settle for a mere survey of these fateful and eventful years when Spanish imperialism gave way to its American equivalent will, I hope, find this interpretive narrative of early California, based on firsthand accounts, accessible and revealing.

To cover so large a field within a single volume means leaving out much of importance that does not relate to the central historical theme here—the contest for California, meaning not only power struggles between Spanish colonists and Indians or later between Mexicans and Anglo-Americans but also disputes over matters of principle between members of the same group. Spanish officials and missionaries, for example, sometimes blamed each other for exploiting Indians or ignoring their rights. Such arguments were of consequence then and still resonate today. What were the legal and moral obligations of colonizers or conquerors to those under their authority? Was freedom a natural and universal right, never to be denied, or was it a privilege that authorities could properly limit or revoke in the larger interests of an orderly, obedient society? Did a promising land like California belong rightfully to those native to the country or to those strong and resourceful enough to take possession and make the most of it? These and other questions were fundamental to the contest for California and preoccupied those who vied for supremacy there in words and deeds. Their accounts form an impressive body of historical literature with recurring themes that bear on our enduring conceptions of liberty, justice, destiny, and redemption.

Many books went into the making of this one, and scholars whose works helped guide me are credited later in the acknowledgments. My main sources, however, are those who witnessed the events described here. (Quotations from primary accounts conform to the editions or manuscripts cited in all essentials, and no attempt has been made to regularize spelling or punctuation.) I have examined the testimony of those witnesses critically, sometimes questioning their assertions and assumptions, but I have tried to deal with them on their own terms and avoid imposing on them concepts or theories alien to their world and way of thinking. Central to the worldview of many Spaniards who colonized California were lessons drawn from the Bible. Biblical precepts also shaped the thoughts of many Anglo-Americans as they expanded westward, whether they spoke plainly of God's will or more loosely of Providence or manifest destiny. When Pedro Font, a Franciscan friar who set out across the Sonoran Desert to California in 1775 with Juan Bautista de Anza and his colonists, likened that trek to "the crossing of the people of Israel through the Red Sea over to the promised land," he was sounding a theme that would long resonate among California's pioneers.[1] To reckon with them on their own terms means exploring such themes and their historical implications.

Special attention is paid here to the trying and often contentious journeys that brought to California people of various nationalities, including not just Spaniards, Mexicans, and Americans but also Russians, Britons, and other foreigners who were not destined to rule this country but helped shape its future. Traders and colonists who endured those taxing journeys often felt they had a purchase there or a right to exploit the opportunities they found in California by virtue of the sacrifices they made getting there. They came into this country as one might come into an inheritance, feeling fully entitled to it, regardless of the prior claims of other parties.

As its title suggests, this work is largely concerned with those who laid claim to California as colonizers or conquerors. To evaluate their actions and assertions, however, we must consider the claims of people native to the country who were colonized or conquered, including Indians and Californios, meaning people of Spanish heritage who were born in California or settled there during the Mexican era. My aim is not to present a comprehensive history of the Californios or the Indians among whom they lived, which would require far more space than this volume provides, but to examine how they responded to the challenges posed by foreigners who infringed on their domain. The annals of early California contain some compelling testimony from Indians and a treasure trove of reminiscences from Californios. Their vivid impressions and reflections, incorporated selectively here, serve to correct or place in context the subjective accounts of the conquerors, who often justified their intrusions by misrepresenting those they imposed on and demeaning their accomplishments.

Conquerors and colonizers have always claimed superiority over people they subjugated, but the tendency of those imposing on others to claim moral authority for doing so has increased over the centuries. The Spanish and American takeovers examined in

---

1. Pedro Font, *With Anza to California, 1775–1776: The Journal of Pedro Font, O.F.M.*, 83.

these chapters occurred at a time when conquest was no longer considered inherently virtuous and had to be justified. This was the result of a revolution in Western thought that culminated with the Enlightenment, which was at its height when Spanish colonists first came to California (a term used in this book to refer to what Spaniards called Alta California as distinguished from Baja California, colonized earlier). The intellectual and moral ferment of the Enlightenment coincided with the expansion of European empires around the globe and raised questions about the responsibilities of colonizers to those under their authority. In ancient times, conquerors often claimed to be serving some divine purpose or bringing order to the world by taming savages or scourging evildoers. But few people then doubted that conquest for whatever purpose was virtuous—a word of Latin origin meaning manly or possessed of courage, fortitude, and other qualities considered stereotypically masculine, whether exhibited by a man or a woman. To conquer was to prove one's manliness and debase one's foes so thoroughly that they were no longer considered men, or truly human, and could rightfully be killed or enslaved. That attitude was still prevalent when Christopher Columbus and his followers reached the New World and killed or enslaved Indians of the Caribbean. It took a reform movement within the Catholic Church, led by the Spanish Dominican friar Bartolomé de las Casas, to establish the principle that Indians were indeed humans who had souls and could be converted to Christianity and that they were not to be killed or enslaved unless they rejected salvation and defied God and king.

This and similar efforts by Protestant missionaries and reformers to temper the cruelty of colonization did not end the brutalization of Native peoples in the Americas or elsewhere. By 1769, however, when Spanish colonists founded San Diego, conquerors were considered truly virtuous only if they helped redeem the country they claimed by converting or civilizing its inhabitants and respecting their rights, which Enlightenment philosophers saw not as conditional rights due those who embraced Christianity and obeyed the Crown but as inalienable human rights, derived from natural law. Junípero Serra and other Franciscan missionaries who came to California considered the Enlightenment concept of natural law godless and sacrilegious; but Spanish officials in their day were influenced by such philosophical ideals, and the padres too saw themselves as defenders of Indians and their rights. Spanish colonists and missionaries sometimes mistreated Indians in ways that violated their own laws or principles, but this should be no more shocking or surprising to us today than the fact that American occupiers who later promised Californios justice and equal rights failed to deliver on that pledge. Human expectations may have risen over time, but human nature remained much the same. Dreams of power and preeminence that were older than civilization and scripture had to contend with the requirement that conquest be rationalized and justified as never before.

This project began as an attempt to understand the process by which Americans infiltrated and took control of California, following the same line of inquiry as my earlier book, *Bound for Santa Fe*, which deals with the American infiltration and conquest of New Mexico. It soon became clear, however, that the American experience in California was so thoroughly intertwined with the experience of Spanish colonizers, Mexican settlers, and Russian, British, and other foreign interlopers that it must be treated here initially as a subplot, which gradually came to dominate the region's history. Some American settlers married Californios and adopted their customs and beliefs, while others remained apart. But all who entered this country and laid claim to it became actors in a drama that Spanish colonists initiated and played roles anticipated by the deeds of their imperial predecessors. To separate the American story in California from the story of those who came before would be like separating the New Testament from the Old, where the great biblical themes of promise, ruin, and redemption are laid out.

This is not a story that lends weight to the argument for American exceptionalism or the idea that Americans had—and still have—a unique role to play in the world as moral exemplars and liberators. To be sure, Americans showed exceptional enterprise and initiative in pursuing the opportunities awaiting them in California and acted with a freedom and independence that distinguished what Thomas Jefferson, in a letter to James Madison in 1809, called their "empire for liberty" from imperial regimes that placed stifling restraints on their subjects.[2] Americans were indeed fortunate in the rights they enjoyed and exercised, but that led American expansionists to assume they were doing those less fortunate a special favor by imposing on them. Editor John O'Sullivan, who promulgated the term "manifest destiny," summed up that spirit of expansive exceptionalism when he wrote in 1839 that the United States had a "blessed mission to the nations of the world, which are shut out from the life-giving light of truth . . . and her high example shall smite unto death the tyranny of kings, hierarchs, and oligarchs, and carry the glad tidings of peace and good will where myriads now endure an existence scarcely more enviable than that of beasts of the field. Who, then, can doubt that our country is destined to be *the great nation* of futurity?"[3]

A number of Americans engaged in the takeover of California subscribed to that theory and claimed that they were liberating this land of promise from Mexican or "Spanish" tyranny. (Such expansionists often referred to Mexicans as Spaniards and made little distinction between the Mexican Republic and the Spanish empire of old.) To view the American conquest against the backdrop of Spanish colonization and Mexican independence, however, is to recognize that it was at best a mixed blessing for a country that was not nearly as oppressed and benighted as those expansionists asserted. Indians of California would fare worse under American authority than under the overbearing paternalism

---

2. Jefferson to Madison, April 27, 1809, in Joseph J. Ellis et al., *Thomas Jefferson: Genius of Liberty*, 118, 133.
3. John O'Sullivan, "The Great Nation of Futurity," 430.

of the Spanish mission system. And annexation by a nation that reserved democracy for white men only and relegated millions of black slaves to an existence "scarcely more enviable than that of beasts of the field," in O'Sullivan's words, was no great boon for a racially mixed Mexican society where slavery had been abolished if not yet eradicated.

If Americans in California were not exceptionally virtuous as conquerors, neither were they particularly cruel or exploitive by the standards of their time. Many who arrived overland from the United States brought with them a defiant frontier mentality—sharpened by their struggles with Indians and their self-reliant disdain for higher authority—which led them to exaggerate their grievances against Mexican officials and inclined them when challenged to shoot first and ask questions later. But that defensive attitude was not limited to Americans and could be found on Spanish, British, French, and other colonial frontiers around the world. If anything distinguished Americans as colonizers and conquerors, it was the fervor and conviction with which they protested their innocence while trespassing on others. In the words of Josiah Royce, one of the first historians to examine the American conquest of California critically, "The American wants to persuade not only the world but himself that he is doing God service in a peaceable spirit, even when he violently takes what he has determined to get."[4]

Spanish priests and soldiers also felt they were serving God when they imposed on Indians in California and claimed their country. But Spanish colonization—which began there with the so-called spiritual conquest of Indians by Franciscan friars, aided by soldiers who accompanied them—differed from American colonization in stressing the acknowledgment of one's sins as a prerequisite for redemption. In order to convert Indians, Franciscans had to make them conscious of sins unknown to them before they were exposed to Christianity. Spanish California had no place for those who clung to the illusion of innocence. Conquerors as well those they conquered had to admit guilt before receiving absolution. If they

---

4. Josiah Royce, *California: A Study of American Character*, 119.

failed to do so, they had no chance of entering a promised land that lay beyond this earthly realm of strife and suffering.

That pious hope was not enough to satisfy Californios who sought fulfillment in this life and found much to admire in those enterprising Americans who settled among them peacefully during the Mexican era and held out the promise of worldly redemption in the form of a free, fair, and prosperous society. But few American expansionists acknowledged how far their nation was from realizing that dream and how impure their motives were in seeking to annex Mexican territory. Although a sense of guilt lay deep within the Protestant heritage of many Anglo-Americans, it had been largely externalized by the time they reached California. They had learned to absolve themselves by casting blame on their opponents. In justifying their conquest, they denied the biblical lesson of humanity's fall from grace—the knowledge of good and evil as inseparable strands of our moral fiber—and maintained their innocence, a dangerous illusion to which expansive Americans would long cling when seeking to fulfill what O'Sullivan called their "blessed mission to the nations of the world."

PROLOGUE

Alfred Sully's Fall from Grace

Alfred Sully was not born to conquer, but as a young man seeking distinction in an era of relentless American expansion he found that path laid out for him. The son of painter Thomas Sully of Philadelphia, one of the nation's leading portraitists, he entered West Point in 1837 at the age of sixteen, hoping to put his creative talents to constructive use as a draftsman and engineer. A decade later, however, during the Mexican War, he took part as an infantry commander in the shattering American assault on Veracruz, which fell to forces led by General Winfield Scott in March 1847 after being blasted by artillery fire. "Such a place of destruction I never again wish to witness," Lieutenant Sully wrote. He was sorry to say that women and children were among the victims but faulted the populace for not fleeing the city in advance: "General Scott gave them warnings of his intentions, but, Mexican-like, they depended too much on the strength of the place."[1] That was mild criticism compared with the aspersions cast on Mexicans by some Americans who invaded their homeland and wrought destruction without regret. Sully seemed better suited for the role of reconstructing

---

1. Alfred Sully in Langdon Sully, *No Tears for the General: The Life of Alfred Sully, 1821–1879*, 23–24.

a defeated country and reconciling its people to conquest. Such was the task that awaited American occupation forces when he landed in Monterey, California, in April 1849 as quartermaster.

Sully soon made the acquaintance there of Angustias de la Guerra, whose Spanish-born father, José de la Guerra y Noriega, had commanded the presidio at Santa Bárbara and whose husband, Manuel Jimeno Casarín, had served as an official in Monterey before the American takeover in 1846. She had long and close ties to Anglos. Among her in-laws were American merchant Alfred Robinson and English trader William Hartnell, both of whom had become Catholics and Mexican citizens before entering her family. Annexation by the United States, she concluded, was a better fate for California than continuing "on the road to utter ruin" under a poor and politically unstable Mexico. Monterey was spared bombardment by American forces, who took the town unopposed, and she and other prominent residents saw no reason to spurn polite American officers like Lieutenant Edward Ord, the brother of Dr. James Ord, an army physician whom she would later marry following the death of her husband Jimeno. In her wartime diary, she referred to Edward Ord fondly as "Don Eduardo," observing that "he looks like one of us. He is very charming and dances divinely." But her friendship with him and with other American officers did not ease her fears that this new regime might bring wrenching changes to her country. "Putting the laughter and dancing aside," she wrote, "we are all ill at ease because we do not know how we, the owners of all this, will end up! May God be with us!"[2]

Señora de la Guerra's ambivalence toward the occupiers was aptly summarized by an American acquaintance, merchant William Heath Davis, who married into this society and wrote that prior to the Mexican War the women of California "were wholly loyal to their own government and hated the idea of any change; although they respected the Americans, treated them with great cordiality and politeness, and entertained them hospitably at their homes, they would not countenance the suggestion that the United

---

2. Angustias de la Guerra in Rose Marie Beebe and Robert M. Senkewicz, trans. and eds., *Testimonios: Early California through the Eyes of Women, 1815–1848*, 265, 277–78.

States or any foreign power should assume control of the country." Angustias de la Guerra—who followed Spanish tradition by retaining her maiden name but was referred to by Davis as Mrs. Jimeno—shared those sentiments and was initially hostile to invading Americans. "In a patriotic outburst," Davis related, she "exclaimed one day that she would delight to have the ears of the officers of the United States squadron for a necklace, such was her hatred of the new rulers of her country." But whenever an American officer was taken sick, he added, "Mrs. Jimeno was the first to visit the patient and bestow on him the known kindness so characteristic of the native California ladies."³

Señora de la Guerra's policy of dealing charitably with Americans in the hope that they would respond in kind continued after the war, affording Sully and other officers a gracious hostess to look after them. In a letter written to his family not long after he reached Monterey, he described her as "a tall majestic looking woman, about 30 or 35, remarkably handsome . . . very agreeable, very good natured & very smart. In fact she is a well read woman & would grace any circle of society." With her husband away at his ranch and there "being no male in the house," he added, "Me Madre (that is the name she calls herself though she is rather young & handsome to have so old a boy as me) requested me to make her house my home." This might have been considered improper if she lived alone, but the house was brimming with servants and family members, including her eldest daughter, Manuela, who was fifteen and hence of marriageable age there. Manuela was "remarkably pretty & gay," he wrote, and "like all Spanish girls, monstrous fond of a flirtation. I fear she finds this rather a hard job with me, for my bad Spanish always sets her a laughing."⁴

Sully was captivated by Manuela and eventually proposed marriage. But until he made his intentions clear he remained quite close to her mother, who served officially as godmother to many

---

3. William Heath Davis, *Seventy-five Years in California*, 37, 66–67; Susanna Bryant Dakin, *The Lives of William Hartnell*, 280–81.
4. Alfred Sully Papers, Western Americana Collection, Beinecke Rare Book and Manuscript Library, letter of June 14, 1849; Sully, *No Tears for the General*, 41–42; Beebe and Senkewicz, *Testimonios*, 193–97.

youngsters in California and carried on in that capacity informally by taking Sully under her wing. She was only six years older than he was, and he at first found her a more congenial companion than Manuela, who struck him initially as too young and impulsive for an officer approaching thirty. In letters home, he mentioned the mother more often than the daughter and used language that caused family members to worry that he was straying into an affair. "Could I come across another Doña Angustias de la Guerra," he wrote in August 1849, "I don't think I would long be an old bachelor. She has given me a piece of gold from which I wish you to have made a ring." To ease the concerns of his family, he later explained that he wanted the ring "to adorn my person & at the same time show my respect for the lady (who is by-the-by a married lady with 7 children)." There was in fact nothing improper in his relationship with Angustias, but he was less than truthful when he claimed that he had "not yet seen anybody in this country good enough for me."[5] Indeed, when later deprived of the company of Angustias and Manuela he found that they had been almost too kind and too good for him and left a void in his life that he could not fill.

When Angustias befriended Sully, her marriage was strained. (She and Jimeno were at odds over financial and family matters and would separate before he died in 1853.) She found solace in the attention this courtly young American paid her, but she allowed Manuela to enjoy his company as well. On one occasion when Manuela asked to attend a dance with friends, Angustias suggested that Sully serve as her chaperon: "If my son Don Alfredo will take my daughter to the ball," she declared, "she can go."[6] Angustias trusted Sully and must have been shocked when he asked for Manuela's hand in marriage a short time later, but she and her husband did not rule out the match. Their chief concern was that Sully was not a Catholic. They told him that they would have to consult relatives, including Antonio and José Joaquín Jimeno, who served as padres to small communities of Christian Indians still living at California's decaying missions.

---

5. Alfred Sully Papers, letters of August 19, 1849, and December 29, 1849.
6. Alfred Sully Papers, letter of May 1, 1850; Sully, *No Tears for the General*, 57, 85, 239–40 n. 5.

Unlike Robinson, Hartnell, and other foreign settlers who adopted the customs and creed of their hosts, Sully had no intention of converting to Catholicism. Fearing that he would never gain parental consent and would lose the popular Manuela to another suitor, he took strong measures that he admitted were "not altogether according to Hoyle." He sent a friend off to San Francisco to seek a dispensation allowing him as a non-Catholic to marry a member of the faith. Then he had the wife of a fellow officer, Captain Elias Kane, invite Manuela to their home, where she arrived in the company of an admirer, a "young gentleman" of Monterey who was favored by her mother. While another officer distracted that unfortunate suitor, Mrs. Kane escorted Manuela into the kitchen, where she and Sully were promptly married by the local priest. He was later removed from his post for performing this ceremony without parental consent. Sully appeared unaware that his actions might have compromised the priest and insulted the young admirer who unwittingly escorted Manuela to her wedding, but he could not ignore the offense he caused her parents. "The old folks are as mad as well can be," he wrote. "I went to see them & was invited never to show my face again."[7]

Both of Manuela's parents had reason to feel cheated, but for Angustias the betrayal was deeply personal, coming as it did from someone she had treated as a member of her family. The betrayal was symbolized by the gold ring that Sully had intended to wear in her honor. In June 1850, a month after his furtive wedding, he wrote home to thank his family for sending it: "The steamer of yesterday brought me two letters & the ring, which is pronounced beautiful. Manuela has it."[8]

Angustias was slower than her husband to forgive Sully. She too reconciled with him when she learned that Manuela was pregnant. By imposing on this proud family and violating the code by which they lived, however, Sully had set the stage for tragedy. In late March 1851, less than two weeks after giving birth, Manuela fell

---

7. Alfred Sully Papers, letters of May 28, 1850, and August 28, 1850; Sully, *No Tears for the General*, 61–63, 237 n. 3.
8. Alfred Sully Papers, letter of June 23, 1850.

violently ill and died after eating what Sully called a "fatal orange," sent to her as a present. It was rumored afterward that the gift came from a disappointed suitor in town, who poisoned the fruit. Sully had urged her not to eat the orange, fearing that it might be bad for her, but her mother thought it would do her no harm and consulted the physician (her future husband, James Ord), who gave his consent. "Thus by the ignorance of a doctor I have been robbed of a treasure that can never be replaced," Sully lamented. His black servant, Sam, was devoted to Manuela and became so distraught after her death that he killed himself, believing "that in the world to come we would all be united once more together." The final blow for Sully came a short time later when Angustias, who had recently given birth, took Manuela's infant to bed with her to nurse the boy and fell asleep with him in her arms. "When she woke up he was dead," Sully wrote. "She had strangled it in her sleep. The doctor persuaded her it died of a convulsion, but to me alone he told the true story."[9]

In his shock and grief, Sully may have misinterpreted these terrible events. The "fatal orange" was just one possible cause of the sudden intestinal torments that Manuela suffered before she died (she may have contracted cholera). And Sully's assertion that Angustias "strangled" the infant in her sleep hinted perhaps at an unconscious motive on her part—lingering hostility toward him—that existed only in his imagination. But whether those deaths and the demise of Sam were the result of "ignorance & violence," as he put it, or of random misfortunes beyond anyone's control, Sully had reason to feel that dreadful punishment was being visited on him and his in-laws. "It appears like a judgment from God for some crime that I or her family have committed," he wrote.[10]

Sully was surely aware that the act he believed set this tragedy in motion—eating a forbidden fruit—was like the original sin that brought God's judgment on Adam and Eve. His new family's devastating fall from grace occurred in California, a bountiful

---

9. Alfred Sully Papers, letter of April 30, 1851; Sully, *No Tears for the General*, 69–71.
10. Alfred Sully Papers, letter of April 30, 1851.

land likened to Eden, which made that biblical precedent hard to ignore. But Sully had other reasons, rooted not in myth but in history, to feel that he as a representative of the expanding American empire and his in-laws as heirs to the old Spanish imperial order were being punished for their sins. Taking Manuela was a personal conquest for him, achieved in defiance of the values and customs of people over whom he had authority as an occupying officer. And they and their ancestors had committed similar deeds or misdeeds in colonizing California and claiming Indians as mistresses or menial laborers. Sully compared their way of life to that of a "rich Southern planter, only in place of Negroes they have Indians for servants."[11] Although not a slaveholder, Sully had a black servant. The death of Sam added to the burden of guilt he bore as a master and conqueror and shared with those of Spanish heritage who once dominated this country.

The bitterness and resentment that overcame Sully when the seemingly safe harbor he found in California was shattered gradually receded, allowing him to resume cordial relations with his in-laws. He and Angustias grew even closer than they had been before, linked now by a sense of loss that was too great for either to bear alone. Before leaving for Benicia at the northern end of San Francisco Bay—a transfer he sought in order to distance himself from Monterey and its painful associations—he visited Santa Bárbara with Angustias to pay his respects to her father. Sully characterized that venerable figure as a "queer old specimen of an old Spanish gentleman, very polite, very dignified & very hospitable, but very bigoted & very tyrannical but not unkind." As indicated by that ambivalent assessment, Sully found saving graces in the old colonial regime of Cross and Crown that his late wife's grandfather represented. Wishing to see the church where Manuela had been confirmed, Sully visited the hilltop mission overlooking the town and admired "the altar at which she had as a child so often knelt, & at the foot of the altar the tomb of her grandmother, who was more than a mother to her." Saddened, he left the sanctuary and

---

11. Alfred Sully Papers, letter of June 14, 1849; Sully, *No Tears for the General*, 42.

walked behind the mission, where an aqueduct built by Indians under the supervision of padres now lay in ruins. "It is wonderful what those old Spanish priests were able to accomplish with the means at hand," he wrote. "How they civilized the Indians & taught them every branch of useful knowledge & then with the workmen of their own creation erected works that would do credit to any part of the world."[12]

This appreciative view of the mission system echoed that of Alfred Robinson and other foreigners with close ties to this society and contrasted sharply with the skeptical assessments of American visitors who remained aloof from Hispanic California and saw little to admire in the spiritual conquest of the padres, dismissed by some critics as slave drivers. Were the missions good or evil? This question, which remains with us today, was being hotly argued long before the American takeover of California. That in turn contributed to a larger historical debate about the virtue of conquest in general, whether intended to assimilate Indians and save their souls or to further democracy and extend what Jefferson called an empire for liberty across the continent. For Alfred Sully, praising the missionaries was a way of paying tribute to Manuela and the world that nurtured her. He did not stop to consider that the good done by the padres might be linked to evils such as placing Indians under demoralizing restraint and punishing them bodily if they defied those strictures. Nor did he dwell on the moral complexities of his own position as a conqueror. Good might have come from the offense he caused by abducting Manuela had she and her child survived and his ties to her family lengthened and deepened, making him a bridge between the old regime there and the new. But the tragic consequences of that elopement prevented him from remaining long in Monterey as a guest of Angustias de la Guerra—who kept Manuela's room just as it was before she married—and sent him into exile. He ended up on the Great Plains, that vast field of toil and strife east of Eden, where he served out his days in uniform as a hardened Indian fighter.

---

12. Alfred Sully Papers, letter of June 1851; Sully, *No Tears for the General*, 72–75.

Alfred Sully's career resembled that of Spanish officers sent to California in the early years of colonization—men who sometimes found the burdens of expanding and defending their empire greater than any pleasure, profit, or prestige they derived from that task. As latter-day conquistadors who shared power in California with Franciscan missionaries quick to remind them of their legal and moral obligations, they operated under constraints unknown to predecessors such as Hernán Cortés, the conqueror of Mexico. Those ruthless adventurers were Christians who hoped to gain eternal credit by enlarging the Catholic domain, but they were also seeking heaven on earth by pursuing wealth and glory on a fabulous scale that would make them gods among men like Alexander the Great and other legendary conquerors. Such soaring ambitions helped fuel explorations that first brought California to the attention of Europeans in the mid-sixteenth century and prompted efforts to colonize that country, sometimes imagined as paradise on earth.

Paradise was not an innately Christian concept, and California often inspired dreams of profit and delight that owed more to pagan mythology than to biblical precedents. It derived its name from a Spanish romance written in the early 1500s by Garci Rodríguez de Montalvo, who told of an epic struggle between good and evil in which the hero Esplandián successfully defended Christian Constantinople against pagan enemies, including Queen Calafia, "ruler of California Island, where an amazing abundance of gold and precious stones are found." Situated "on the right-hand side of the Indies," California was "very close to the region of the Earthly Paradise" and inhabited by "black women," who lived like Amazons.[13] Periodically those warlike women of California, clad in gold armor, went abroad to fight and brought back male captives for procreation, raising any girls they conceived as a result and dispensing with the boys by feeding them to ravenous

---

13. Rodríguez de Montalvo in Rose Marie Beebe and Robert M. Senkewicz, eds., *Lands of Promise and Despair: Chronicles of Early California, 1535–1846*, 9–11.

griffins guarding the island and its riches. Ultimately, Queen Calafia was transformed—and Constantinople saved—when she fell for Esplandián and ordered her forces not to attack the city. Afterward, she converted to Christianity, wed Esplandián's cousin, and returned with him to California, thus opening its wealth and wonders to Christian civilization.

This romance drew on ancient legends about fabled islands where promise mingled with peril, including the land of the Sirens, whose enchanting song lured sailors to their doom; and the isle of the Hesperides, nymphs who tended a tree bearing golden apples, guarded by a serpent that never slept (a myth resembling the biblical story of Eden with its serpent and forbidden fruit). The realm of the Hesperides was sometimes described as far to the west in the direction of the setting sun, much like California. The Greek playwright Euripides evoked its charms in his drama *Hippolytus*: "And O for that quiet garden by the Western sea / Where the daughters of Evening sing / Under the golden apple-tree."[14] In Greek legend, the hero Hercules—a mythic prototype for conquerors and colonizers of all descriptions—was given the task of penetrating that garden, slaying the serpent, and carrying off the golden apples. In the pagan as opposed to the biblical worldview, to violate a garden paradise and seize its forbidden fruit was regarded as a virtuous exploit (in the root sense of virtue as manly and imposing) rather than a shameful act of disobedience. That pagan adventurousness was shared to some degree by most colonizers who came to California throughout its history, including Alfred Sully, who took pride in penetrating the defenses shielding his beloved Manuela from the outside world and claiming the prize. Rodríguez de Montalvo brought that same venturesome spirit to his legend of California, while framing the tale in suitably Christian terms. In the process, he defined the terms by which this as-yet-undiscovered country would be imagined—as an island of sharply contrasting possibilities, where profit and doom, glory and infamy, ruin and redemption, lay forever entwined.

---

14. Euripides in Dora Beale Polk, *The Island of California: A History of the Myth*, 24.

Spanish explorers thought that California was an island and persisted in the belief for some time as they continued to search for a terrestrial paradise, often envisioned as an island rich in gold and occupied by Amazons. Cortés, in exploring the western coast of Mexico and sending colonists to Baja California, hoped to discover an island harboring Amazons and their presumed treasures. Only gradually did such legends of California give way to reality. For centuries, it remained an island for all intents and purposes, cut off from the rest of North America by forbidding mountains and severe desert that shielded the bountiful Central Valley—the great garden that later attracted American settlers—more effectively than the stormiest of seas. And though Spanish colonists did not find Amazons there or much in the way of mineral wealth, they continued to think of themselves as heroic civilizers like Esplandián, boldly confronting the godless Natives of California and winning them over body and soul. In 1785 soldiers guarding Mission San Gabriel put down an Indian uprising there inspired in part by a shaman or medicine woman named Toypurina. She confessed under questioning that she had encouraged the revolt because she was angry with the Spaniards for imposing on her people and "living on their land."[15] Placed under the supervision of missionaries, she converted to Christianity, took the name Regina (queen), and wed a Spanish soldier. Much like Queen Calafia, who emerged from the "darkness of evil, rebellion and paganism," in the words of one Franciscan historian, she embraced her former enemies and their faith.[16]

Despite such apparent gains for California's colonizers, they had little cause for celebration. Theirs was a "world of trial," as one early American visitor to California, Harrison Rogers, put it, filled with perils for those who sought its rewards.[17] Ultimately, Americans would claim the prize, and many of them rejoiced at their good fortune. But some concluded that in grasping the fruits

---

15. Toypurina quoted by her interrogator, Sergeant José Olivera, in Beebe and Senkewicz, *Lands of Promise and Despair*, 248.
16. Francis J. Weber, ed., *The Pride of the Missions: A Documentary History of San Gabriel Mission*, 17.
17. Rogers in Harrison Clifford Dale, ed., *The Explorations of William H. Ashley and Jedediah Smith, 1822–1829*, 210.

of victory they lost their innocence and forfeited their presumed right to California. That dissenting view of the American conquest was reinforced by the mistreatment of Mexicans and Indians by Anglo prospectors and settlers, whose sweeping claims left little room for the country's earlier inhabitants. "The American wanted every rod of his land, every drop of water on it," wrote reformer and novelist Helen Hunt Jackson in the late 1800s; "his schemes were boundless; his greed insatiable; he had no use for Indians. His plan did not embrace them, and could not enlarge itself to take them in. They must go." In her view, such rapacious expansionism was a lamentable fall from grace for a land once guided by the benign paternalism of the Franciscans, whose methods were "wise and humane." She looked back on Spanish California as paradise lost and saw the ruined cloisters of its missions, where boughs that once bore fruit in abundance stood "gaunt and shrivelled," as hallowed gardens whose blessings had been forsaken by the profane inheritors of this land.[18]

This was a nostalgic reading of the past, one that overlooked the extent to which the realities of the Franciscan regimen fell short of its ideals. Nonetheless, by contrasting Spanish efforts to draw Indians into their imperial system with the Anglo-American tendency to shove dispossessed tribes aside, Jackson refuted the claim that Americans were salvaging a country that their profligate Hispanic predecessors had sadly neglected. Through such debate, California remained an arena for conflicting values and ideals long after its fate was seemingly resolved. This contest did not end with annexation in 1848; nor did it begin with the first visits by Yankee coastal merchants several decades earlier. To understand the process by which Americans like Alfred Sully infiltrated this country and laid claim to it in word and deed, we must first examine the Spanish conquest that prefigured their takeover and set the stage for subsequent efforts to redeem this land and fulfill its promise—a problematic goal that could not be pursued without deeply unsettling consequences.

18. Helen Hunt Jackson, *Glimpses of California and the Missions*, 35, 94, 112.

Part One
SPANISH COLONIZATION (1769–1784)

Portrait of Junípero Serra by Father José Mosqueda, early 1900s, based on an older painting that was lost during the Mexican Revolution. *Courtesy Santa Bárbara Mission Archive-Library.*

CHAPTER I

Spiritual Conquest

For Father Junípero Serra, the spiritual conquest began in earnest in May 1769 at Velicatá, a campsite in Baja California that served as a staging ground for efforts to extend Spanish California northward to the harbors of San Diego and Monterey. Born on the Spanish island of Mallorca, Serra had served as a missionary in Mexico (New Spain) since 1750, but his efforts had been among tribes with some exposure to Christian teachings. Now, as president of Franciscan missions in California, he was seeking out Indians known as pagans or gentiles, who were strangers to his faith. As he wrote in his diary, he was eager to answer "the call of so many thousands of pagans who are waiting in California on the threshold of holy Baptism."[1]

Serra journeyed north to Velicatá from Loreto, the capital of California, accompanied by Indians from existing missions there and soldiers commanded by Governor Gaspar de Portolá. He and Serra were the civil and religious leaders of this so-called Sacred Expedition, responsible respectively for establishing presidios and missions in the newly colonized territory, but they would be the last to reach San Diego. Earlier in the year two Spanish ships, *San Carlos* and *San Antonio* (also known as *El Príncipe*), had embarked

---

1. Junípero Serra, *Writings of Junípero Serra*, 1:33.

for that harbor with men and supplies, while a third ship assigned to the expedition, the ill-fated *San José*, underwent repairs. In late March a party led by Captain Fernando Javier de Rivera y Moncada and Father Juan Crespí—who like Serra and other Franciscans serving in California was both a friar and a priest—had set out northward from Velicatá to pioneer an overland route. By the time Serra and Portolá reached San Diego, it was hoped, a base would be safely established there so that the work of colonization could begin. Serra was fifty-five and troubled by an infected leg that made it painful for him to walk or ride; but when Portolá suggested that he forgo the journey, he responded firmly: "I trust in God that He will give me strength."[2]

Far from lagging behind, Serra urged Portolá to pick up the pace as they neared Velicatá on May 13. The next day was Pentecost, marking the occasion when the Holy Spirit descended on the apostles and allowed them to prophesy in many tongues. Serra hoped to reach Velicatá in time to perform Mass on that auspicious occasion and found a mission there. Only an incurable optimist would have rushed to seek fresh converts in country that could barely support its existing missions, established by Jesuits, who had recently been expelled from New Spain by King Charles III (a Bourbon monarch of French heritage known to his Spanish subjects as Carlos III). The Jesuits were considered disloyal to the Crown and accused of amassing wealth and power, but their California missions had never been very prosperous. When Portolá arrived in late 1767 to take control of the colony, one Jesuit related, he was "rudely shaken out of his dreams of California treasures, of the wealth of the missionaries, and of other such things."[3] Severe drought and plagues of locusts had ravaged crops planted by Indian converts, and many were off foraging for subsistence. Nonetheless, the depleted missions that Franciscans inherited from the Jesuits were asked to contribute food, livestock, devotional objects, and Indian servants to the Sacred Expedition in 1769. The campaign

---

2. Serra in Maynard J. Geiger, *The Life and Times of Fray Junípero Serra*, O.F.M., 1:211.
3. Johann Jakob Baegert in Harry W. Crosby, *Gateway to Alta California: The Expedition to San Diego, 1769*, 18.

Spiritual Conquest

placed a heavy burden on friars there and the Indians under their care, Serra acknowledged, but "they had to endure it for God and the King."[4]

Serra himself did not have everything he needed to perform Mass properly at Velicatá on Pentecost. "While the celebration lasted," he wrote, "repeated discharges of firearms by the soldiers added to the solemnity: and for once the smoke of powder took the place of burning incense, which we could not use because we had none with us." Mission Indians accompanying the expedition joined in the service, he added, but no pagans "dared come near, frightened perhaps by so much shooting."[5]

A day later, however, Serra received word that Indians were approaching and "gave praise to the Lord, kissing the ground." This first encounter with those who knew nothing of Christianity was a defining moment for Serra and a prophetic one for the mission work that lay ahead of him. It came as a shock, for the dozen Indians who confronted him were all males: Native men and boys in the warmer parts of California who had not yet been taught by missionaries to be ashamed of exposing their bodies sometimes wore nothing at all. "I saw something I could not believe when I had read of it, or had been told about it," he related. "It was this: they were entirely naked, as Adam in the garden, before sin . . . not for one moment, while they saw us clothed, could you notice the least sign of shame in them for their own lack of dress." Serra laid his hands on the head of each man, "in sign of affection," and offered them "dried figs, which they immediately began to eat."[6]

By reaching out to these naked Indians and blessing them, Serra accepted them as they were. Yet his goal and that of his fellow friars was not to confirm Indians in their seeming innocence, like "Adam in the garden, before sin," but to make them aware of their sins and move them to repent. The doctrine of original sin taught that the guilt incurred when Adam and Eve disobeyed God and fell from grace afflicted all humanity, staining every child from

---

4. Serra, *Writings*, 1:41.
5. Ibid., 1:61.
6. Ibid., 1:63.

birth. Original sin was absolved through baptism; but once baptized, mission Indians were expected to confess any fresh sins they committed, including acts such as premarital sex that were not considered misdeeds in tribal society. Those who failed to confess and receive absolution risked damnation. "In order for you to gain eternal life," Franciscans taught mission Indians, "it is necessary that you know and remember that you are a sinner in the eyes of our Lord."[7] In effect, Serra and his brethren reenacted the fall of Adam and Eve by offering Indians food and other tantalizing gifts so that they might eat of the tree of the knowledge of good and evil, in scriptural terms, and feel shame. This was necessary, missionaries believed, if pagans were to acknowledge their presumed sins and seek forgiveness. In the words of Serra's colleague and biographer, Father Francisco Palóu, spiritual conquest meant enticing Indians with food and clothing, by which means they could be indoctrinated as Christians and "gradually acquire a knowledge of what is spiritually good and evil."[8]

Serra saw nothing wrong in using gifts to lure Indians into what he called the "apostolic and evangelical net."[9] Other missionaries called this spiritual fishing and felt justified in acting as fishers of men in imitation of Christ. The very fact that Native Californians were targets of proselytizing was a tribute to sixteenth-century Spanish friars who argued that Indians had souls worth saving at a time when some considered them less than human. But once they were caught in the apostolic net or snared on the hook, would they perish or find new life? Although missionaries promised them salvation, the road to redemption could be harrowing. For many California Indians, mission life was neither heaven nor hell but a kind of purgatory, where they performed penitential labors of the sort that fell to Adam when God cast him from Eden: "cursed is the ground because of you; in toil you shall eat of it all the days of your life" (Genesis 3:17). Franciscans believed that those who toiled for Christ were blessed, not cursed, and saw the mission

---

7. Quoted in Christopher Vecsey, *On the Padres' Trail*, 23.
8. Francisco Palóu, *Palóu's Life of Fray Junípero Serra*, 232.
9. Serra, *Writings*, 1:63.

Junípero Serra preaching to Indians,
from Palóu's biography of Serra, 1787; reprint 1913.
*Courtesy Library of Congress, Prints and Photographs
Division* (LC-USZ62-132753).

regimen they instituted as redeeming, much like the training they themselves had undergone as novices. But for Indians who spent their entire lives as neophytes (meaning those newly baptized or recently inducted into a religious order) it was often hard to see beyond the thorns in their path to the promised rewards awaiting them in the next world.

Serra viewed the spiritual conquest he engaged in as a battle with Satan for the souls of Indians, but he did not share the dismal view of some missionaries that tribespeople were devilish by nature. As he journeyed northward from Velicatá with Portolá and company, they encountered some Indians who were hostile, but most appeared friendly. In late May Serra came upon the first pagan women he had yet encountered on the trail—a moment that he had dreaded because he "feared that they went as naked as the men." Instead, he found them "decently covered." (Native women in California often wore a short skirt of woven fibers and a mantle of fur over their shoulders.) One of those women, the wife of the local chief, offered him a gift "the like of which I had never seen—a great pancake of a thing like dough, but full of thick fibres. I went to lay my hands upon her head, and she left the cake in my hands." Like Serra, these Indians seemed more eager to give than to receive. "May God bless them," he wrote. "We bade them farewell and they left, satisfied and content, but saying that they wanted to go farther with us, and follow us as friends."[10]

Serra was there to convert Indians, but they too had a redeeming effect on him by reminding him that pagans were no strangers to charity and other virtues prized by Christians. He offered his blessings, but these Indians and their country were already blessed, a realization borne home to him as the expedition moved from the arid interior of Baja California in late May and entered more promising country near the west coast. It was a "paradise of beauty," he wrote, imagining missions there with cattle roaming the hills and wheat growing in the valleys. "When we came to our stopping place, we met the queen of flowers—the Rose of Castile,"

---

10. Ibid., 1:77–79.

he added. "While I write this, I have in front of me a cutting from a rose-tree with three roses in full bloom, others opening out, and more than six unpetaled: blessed be He who created them!"[11]

Like the founder of his order, Saint Francis, Serra believed that poor people who lived close to nature and the wonders of God's creation made better Christians than those who were wealthy and materialistic. In that spirit, Franciscans took vows of poverty and tried to prevent Indians they ministered to in the Americas from becoming worldly and possessive. "There is hardly anything to hinder the Indians from reaching heaven," wrote one sixteenth-century Franciscan of those he encountered as pagans in New Spain. "The Indians live in contentment, though what they possess is so little that they have hardly enough to clothe and nourish themselves."[12]

Serra shared this view that Indians in their native state were well suited for salvation. Not even the tribal dances he witnessed on his journey—rituals that some missionaries viewed as demonic—shook his conviction that these Indians could easily be coaxed into the Christian fold. On one occasion, he met a man carrying a stick and a rattle who would not eat food offered by the Spaniards until he had placed it on the ground and danced around it. It was his way of saying grace, and Serra had no objection to the ceremony. This same man wished to accompany the Spaniards to San Diego, Serra related, on condition "that we allow him to dance all the way. We agreed to his suggestions with the greatest pleasure. For my own part I cherished a lively hope of baptizing him there." Something frightened the man, though, and he ran off a short time later with "only his timbrel and stick just as he came."[13]

As Serra and company neared what is now the Mexican-U.S. border, they encountered large numbers of Indians. At first, he was delighted to meet with so many potential Christians. "Their fine stature, deportment, conversation and gaiety won the hearts of all

---

11. Ibid., 1:81–83.
12. Toribio de Benavente Motolinía in Edwin Edward Sylvest, Jr., *Motifs of Franciscan Mission Theory in Sixteenth Century New Spain*, 51.
13. Serra, *Writings*, 1:91.

of us," he wrote of villagers encountered near the Pacific on June 23. In days to come, however, Serra found the Indians who flocked around his party less appealing. "Their friendliness degenerated into familiarity," he complained. Possessed of a "mania for clothes or trinkets," they ran off with his spectacles at one point and tugged at his sleeve, hoping to divest him of his habit: "If I had given the habit to all who wanted it, there would be by this time a pretty large community of gentile friars." Some even pestered Portolá and tried to make him part with "his leather jacket, his waistcoat, breeches: in short everything he wore."[14] Franciscans would later exploit this "mania" by using gifts of clothing to draw Indians into missions and teach them modesty. Yet Indians prized clothing because they knew it was a source of pride to men of the world like Portolá, whose outfit defined and distinguished him. Serra's seemingly humble habit was a matter of some pride to him as well, for he had worn it as a sign of his beloved vocation ever since undergoing his yearlong novitiate as a youth. Such distinctions of costume and rank were not lost on Indians and heightened their desire for clothing, beads, and other status symbols purveyed by Spaniards.

That hankering for material possessions belied the notion that Indians cared little for such things and would easily adapt to a Franciscan regimen that discouraged them from coveting goods or yielding to the tempting offers that Spanish soldiers and civilians made to them for their labor or sexual favors. Such deals were not always initiated by Spaniards. Shortly before his party reached San Diego, Serra reported, Indians at one village tried to obtain clothing from soldiers by offering them women to consort with. When the soldiers refused, they were threatened and got away only by giving the Indians "whatever articles they had with them such as napkins, handkerchiefs, etc."[15]

The lesson Serra drew from such incidents was that Indians were easily led astray by contact with colonists and their offerings. These gentiles were descendants of Adam and Eve like the rest of

---

14. Ibid., 1:107, 111–15.
15. Ibid., 1:119.

the wayward human race, subject to temptation however innocent they might appear. Serra's solution, like that of other missionaries, was to make Indians aware of the consequences of indulging their sinful passions while isolating them as much as possible from the corrupting influences of society. In a time-honored policy known as *reducción*, Indians from a wide area would be reduced or concentrated at California missions. The isolation of mission Indians was far from absolute, for friars would often grant them leave and would allow some to live with non-Christians in tribal villages. But Serra did all he could to shelter neophytes from worldly temptations in emulation of Saint Francis, who by his own account had found the path to salvation only after he turned his back on the comfortable surroundings in which he was raised and "left the world."[16] The otherworldliness at the heart of Franciscan mission efforts set friars at odds not only with Indian converts who wanted greater freedom of movement but also with Spanish officials who hoped that when the missions disbanded—as they were supposed to after ten years or so—former neophytes would join colonial society and serve its purposes. Even as Franciscans furthered the goals of the Spanish empire through spiritual conquest, they erected barriers between mission Indians and Spanish colonists that ran counter to the interests of the state.

Serra's determination to build a new world for California Indians within a protective mission framework was evident in a letter he wrote to his Franciscan superior, Father Juan Andrés, on July 3, two days after arriving in San Diego. The grim circumstances that he encountered there seemingly offered little cause for hope. "The expedition by sea was a disaster," he reported. Many who had embarked for San Diego aboard the *San Carlos* and *San Antonio* succumbed to scurvy and other ailments. Perhaps because they were better nourished, all the officers survived, as did three friars who arrived by ship, but more than two-thirds of the ninety sailors and soldiers who came by sea perished. To make matters worse, several of the mission Indians with Rivera y Moncada and Crespí

---

16. Saint Francis in William J. Short, *The Franciscans*, 8.

had died before that first overland party reached San Diego in May, and all of those with Portolá and Serra had deserted before their party arrived. "I visited the sick who were many," Serra wrote of his bittersweet reunion with Crespí and others, "mingling compassion for so many poor people with the consolation of our safe arrival."[17]

Amid such desolation, Serra remained hopeful about the prospects for spiritual conquest. "I consider that the missions to be founded in these parts will enjoy many advantages over the old ones, as the land is much better and the water supply is more plentiful," he declared. "The Indians especially of the west coast seem to me much more gifted; they are well set up, and the Governor looks upon most of them as likely Grenadier Guards because they are such stoutly built and tall fellows."[18] Portolá's dream would never be realized. Although some California Indians would campaign with Spanish or Mexican forces as scouts or auxiliaries, they would not serve as regular troops. The aims of Franciscan friars would long clash with those of officials who hoped to secularize missions and assimilate Indians, and secularization when it finally arrived would not bring most Indians the rights and opportunities that transformed objects of colonization into loyal subjects or citizens.

Seeds of conflict were already being sown at San Diego, where rampant sickness and death among the Spaniards left them vulnerable to attack by Indians who had reason to regard them as bad medicine. For California Indians, the spiritual cure that Serra and his colleagues offered was hard to distinguish from the grievous ills that attended their arrival and later proliferated in their missions. Native people new to Christianity might be forgiven for wondering if these white shamans whose God suffered agonies on a cross were themselves agents of suffering, akin to witches in tribal society whose spells were thought to cause disease, sterility, and death.

That, of course, was not Serra's purpose. His faith brought him joy in this life as well as hope of eternal life, and he did not foresee that imparting that faith to Indians through spiritual conquest

---

17. Serra, *Writings*, 1:123, 133, 135; Hubert Howe Bancroft, *History of California*, 1:126–31.
18. Serra, *Writings*, 1:139.

might sap them of the vitality he witnessed on his journey. That tragic outcome was not simply the result of extraneous factors such as the spread of disease over which Serra and his followers had little control, however. Mission Indians often remained attached to their ancestral customs and beliefs and found being subjected to a regimen hostile to rival forms of spirituality disorienting and demoralizing. Europeans who entered holy orders and found the discipline unbearable were free to end their novitiate and rejoin the world, but Indian neophytes did not have that option.

Many Indians eluded Serra's evangelical net; but few fared better in Spanish colonial society, for the restraints placed on them were not just religious but cultural. Spaniards were meant to serve God and king, and Indians were meant to serve Spaniards. By that logic, Native Californians were a long way from heaven, but at least they had a place on the ladder. Many Anglo-Americans who would later colonize this country felt that Indians served no purpose at all and would sweep them aside with a contempt that made their earlier handling by Spanish colonists seem almost saintly by comparison.

Natives of New California

The Indians encountered around San Diego—referred to by Spaniards as Diegueños and known today as Kumeyaays—were just one of many tribal groups encountered in the newly colonized territory. Officials had yet to distinguish Alta California from Baja California, but Serra was aware of having entered a promising new land, which he deemed "distinctly better than Old California."[19] Culturally, this New California was not one country but many, home to an astonishing variety of tribespeople. No other region in North America could rival its linguistic diversity, which reflected the diverse landscape, riven by earthquakes and volcanism and gouged by myriad rivers and streams descending from the Coastal Ranges and the Sierra Nevada. Indians belonging to at least a half-dozen major language groups were drawn to what is

---

19. Ibid., 1:145.

now the state of California, where they subdivided amid its fractured terrain into some one hundred linguistically distinct tribal groups. Among Native Californians, wrote the observant Father Gerónimo Boscana in the early 1800s, the diversity of language was so great "that almost every 15 or 20 leagues, you find a distinct dialect; so different, that in no way does one resemble the other."[20]

That linguistic diversity greatly complicated mission efforts. It would have taken a miracle—a second Pentecost—to enable Serra and his Franciscan apostles to speak in the tongues of all the Indians gathered at their missions. Many padres learned Native languages eventually, but until then they relied on Indian interpreters and remained at some remove from neophytes who were not conversant in Spanish. In other respects, however, the diversity of California Indians aided colonization efforts. The various tribal groups were in turn divided into small tribes, typically consisting of a few villages. Politically and militarily, they were not very formidable. War parties in California were generally small, like the one that shadowed Rivera y Moncada and Crespí as they neared San Diego in May. Crespí counted twenty-nine warriors, "with large quivers on their backs and bows and arrows in their hands."[21] They shouted at the Spaniards and shot arrows at them but retreated when soldiers fired their muskets. A few tribes in and around California, notably the Mohaves and Yumas (Quechans) along the lower Colorado River, were larger and better organized, with powerful chiefs capable of mustering hundreds of warriors. But most California Indians subject to Spanish colonization, which was largely confined to the southern and central coastal areas, were more easily conquered because they were already divided into small tribal units and found it hard to contend with companies of soldiers on horseback armed with muskets, swords, and lances.

---

20. Gerónimo Boscana, *Chinigchinich: A Historical Account of the Origins, Customs, and Traditions of the Indians at the Missionary Establishment of St. Juan Capistrano, Alta California*, 3.
21. Juan Crespí, *A Description of Distant Roads: Original Journals of the First Expedition into California, 1769–1770*, final revision, 233 (this edition offers the Spanish text and English translation of various versions of Crespí's journals, including the field draft, the first revision, and the final revision); Crosby, *Gateway to Alta California*, 93.

The larger tribal groups to which those bands belonged were sometimes named for missions founded within their territory, as in the case of the Dieguenos living around Mission San Diego, founded by Serra soon after he arrived. To their north along the coast lived the Luiseños, who congregated in years to come at Missions San Luis Rey and San Juan Capistrano, and the Gabrielinos (Tongvas) near the future Mission San Gabriel. Tribal groups of the central coast impacted by Spanish colonization included the Chumash, whose territory extended northward from the Santa Bárbara Channel to around Morro Bay; the Salinans living between the upper Salinas River and the nearby coast; the Esselens of the rugged Big Sur region; the Ohlones between Monterey and San Francisco Bay; and the Miwoks along the northern rim of that bay. Over time, Indians from other tribal groups would be drawn into missions, among them the Serranos and Cahuillas of the arid southern interior, the Yokuts of the San Joaquín Valley, and the Pomos of the Napa Valley.

As of July 1769, Spanish knowledge of those tribal groups was largely confined to the Dieguenos. Ensign Miguel Costansó of the Royal Corps of Engineers, who arrived aboard the *San Carlos*, observed in his informative journal that those Indians lived in "huts of a pyramidal shape covered with earth," wore scanty clothing woven of "very fine maguey fiber," carried arrows in quivers fashioned from animal hide, and wielded a wooden war club called a *macana*.[22] The effect of such accumulating observations was to show that Indians at first perceived as little more than naked savages were in fact people of some craft and ingenuity whose technology was better adapted to this environment, in certain respects, than the implements of the Spaniards.

Much more would be learned about California Indians during the overland expedition that Governor Portolá launched from San Diego in mid-July in pursuit of Monterey Bay. Despite the heavy losses suffered recently by his party, he pushed ahead with that task because Monterey was considered a more important objective

---

22. Costansó in Crosby, *Gateway to Alta California*, 105–106.

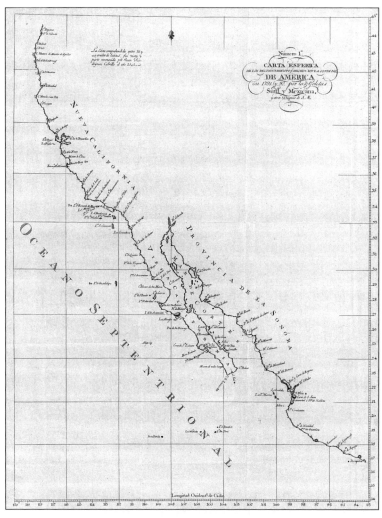

Map of the California coast based on the reconnaissance
of the Spanish ships *Sutil* and *Mexicana*, 1791–92.
Courtesy David Rumsey Map Collection (www.davidrumsey.com).

than San Diego. Spanish interest in Monterey was based partly on a misconception fostered by mariner Sebastián Vizcaíno, who had explored Monterey Bay in late 1602 and described it as a fine harbor. In fact, it was far inferior as an anchorage to San Diego Bay, reconnoitered by Juan Rodríguez Cabrillo in 1542. Monterey Bay was too exposed to wind and waves to become a great port, but it still had strategic significance. Spain was intent on advancing its American frontier northward to prevent Russians from venturing south from Alaska and occupying California, which served as a buffer, shielding the Mexican heartland and its mineral wealth. Furthermore, Manila galleons returning from Asia laden with silk, spices, and other treasures followed ocean currents and prevailing winds that often brought them to the California coast near Monterey before they turned south and made for Acapulco, where their goods were unloaded and hauled overland to the Atlantic. The voyage, which lasted six months or more and exposed those aboard to scurvy and other diseases, was described by one passenger in the late 1600s as "the longest, and most dreadful of any in the World."[23] By the late 1700s advances in ship construction and navigation had reduced the perils of that journey and lessened the need for a way station in California. But Spanish officials still hoped that Monterey would play a part in that lucrative trade, and they would order galleons to stop there for supplies in years to come.

Another factor impelling Spanish colonists and explorers northward up the Pacific Coast was the growing imperial threat from England—known officially as Great Britain following its union with Scotland in 1707. In 1763 Britain had sealed its victory over France in the Seven Years' War by gaining control of Canada and former French territory between the Mississippi River and the British colonies along the Atlantic. Prior to that settlement,

---

23. Gemelli Careri in Charles E. Chapman, *A History of California: The Spanish Period*, 91; John L. Kessell, *Spain in the Southwest: A Narrative History of Colonial New Mexico, Arizona, Texas, and California*, 64; Steven W. Hackel, *Children of Coyote, Missionaries of Saint Francis: Indian-Spanish Relations in Colonial California, 1769–1850*, 36–42; Iris H. W. Engstrand, "Seekers of the 'Northern Mystery': European Exploration of California and the Pacific," in Ramón A. Gutiérrez and Richard J. Orsi, eds., *Contested Eden: California before the Gold Rush*, 86–92.

France had ceded to its ally Spain the province of Louisiana, which included the port of New Orleans and a vast area west of the Mississippi over which France had little control. On balance, Britain gained more than Spain did from the French withdrawal from North America and emerged as a formidable threat to Spanish interests. In 1768 Captain James Cook launched the first of three explorations that would enhance Britain's status as the world's leading naval power and give it access or claim to many places around the Pacific, including the Sandwich (Hawaiian) Islands and Nootka Sound off what is now British Columbia. Cook's visit to Nootka Sound prompted keen international competition for the precious sea-otter pelts obtained there and elsewhere along the Pacific Coast, from California north.

Faced with such challenges, King Carlos III and his advisors sought to bolster the Spanish-American empire by colonizing California as far north as Monterey and launching naval expeditions to Nootka Sound and beyond to counter Russian or British claims to the Pacific Northwest. This ambitious program was carried out at a time when that empire was no longer highly profitable. Guarding the northern frontier of New Spain with a chain of presidios extending from Tubac in what is now Arizona to Natchitoches on the Texas-Louisiana border was in fact draining the royal treasury. To make ends meet, the Crown proposed shifting some of the financial burden of defending and extending the empire to existing colonies. Depleting the old missions in California to support the new was one such expedient devised by José de Gálvez, sent to New Spain as inspector general to implement reforms that included raising revenues to help cover the costs of imperial expansion. Without the impetus provided by Gálvez, the dream of a greater California inspired by the tantalizing reports of Cabrillo and Vizcaíno might never have been realized.

The strains of achieving that momentous objective with minimal resources drove Gálvez to his wit's end—he went temporarily insane in late 1769—and weighed heavily on Governor Portolá and his successors. Ultimately, resentment toward a mother country that could no longer afford its vast imperial ambitions would contribute to rebellions against Spanish rule in the New World. For now, however, disobedience and dissent were nipped in the bud. In 1767 Gálvez had cracked down on those in New Spain who protested taxation, conscription, and the expulsion of the Jesuits by executing scores of dissidents and issuing a decree that made it clear imperial reform did not mean freeing colonists from subservience to the Crown: "Vassals of the throne were born to be silent and obey—not to debate or discuss the affairs of the government."[24]

Until resentful Spanish colonists began openly challenging the Crown in the early 1800s, officers like Portolá and men under their command would dutifully meet the demands placed on them. They were loyal to the king, and some did well enough in his service to raise families on the frontier and retire in dignity. But their greatest incentive was to win the respect of the men they campaigned with. As Miguel Costansó, who joined the Portolá expedition that departed San Diego in pursuit of Monterey on July 14, 1769, wrote of the presidial troops who persevered on that hard journey: "They are men of much endurance and long-suffering under fatigue, obedient, resolute, agile, and, we do not hesitate to say, the finest troopers in the world and among those soldiers who best deserve the bread of the August Monarch whom they serve."[25]

In Search of Monterey

Portolá left behind at San Diego fewer than a dozen healthy soldiers to guard colonists who were convalescing and protect Serra's fledgling mission effort there. Then he headed north to find Monterey Bay and establish a presidio there with the aid of supplies delivered by sea. Finding an overland route was essential, given the perils of ocean travel and the limited capacity of the few ships available for colonization efforts. Portolá's expedition included more than sixty men, including Ensign Costansó; Juan Crespí

---

24. Gálvez in Crosby, *Gateway to Alta California*, 11.
25. Costansó in ibid., 117.

and another Franciscan, Father Francisco Gómez; Lieutenant Pedro Fages from the Spanish province of Catalonia and six of his Catalonian volunteers; and Captain Rivera y Moncada, Sergeant José Francisco de Ortega, and twenty-six other *soldados de cuera* (leather jackets), who had marched overland to San Diego from the presidio at Loreto. Among those soldiers were members of families such as the Ortegas, Carrillos, and Alvarados that would later gain prominence in California. Their distinctive leather jackets, worn by many presidial troops on the Spanish-American frontier, were "made of six or seven plies of white tanned deerskin," Costansó noted, and were "proof against the arrows of the Indians, except at very short range."[26] Portolá and his followers seldom covered more than four leagues a day (about ten miles). Yet they made steady progress, delaying their departure on Sundays only long enough for the friars to say Mass.

By evening on July 18 they had reached the future site of Mission San Luis Rey. "This is a grand spot," wrote Crespí, "the best of any that we have come across." Abounding in wild grapes and lush grass that offered fine pasture, it seemed to him a perfect place to "convert over to our holy faith all of the numerous heathen folk." Shortly after they arrived, he noted, forty naked men, "painted in all colors," approached and laid down their bows in a gesture of goodwill.[27] Women and children followed the men into camp, a sure sign to Costansó that these Indians were "certain of our friendship." Portolá's men camped there through the following day, offering the Luiseños gifts of glass beads and ribbons. Those novelties made such an impression on the Indians that "they did not want to leave us, however much we tried to get rid of them," Costansó related, "and they remained until very late watching and observing us."[28] Among the Luiseños, Portolá's company experienced none of the hostility that marred Spanish relations with the Diegueños around San Diego. There the colonists came to stay,

---

26. Miguel Costansó, *The Discovery of San Francisco Bay: The Portolá Expedition of 1769–1770*, xxi.
27. Crespí, *A Description of Distant Roads*, field draft, 275–79.
28. Costansó, *Discovery of San Francisco Bay*, 7, 9.

Spiritual Conquest

built a fort (a forbidding act that often aroused suspicion and hostility), and suffered grievous ills that made them look cursed and vulnerable. Here they appeared strong and confident, opened their camp to visitors and showered them with presents, and prudently moved on before they outstayed their welcome.

On July 28, approaching what is now the city of Los Angeles, the company experienced a violent earthquake followed by strong aftershocks. The first and most violent tremor, Crespí wrote, "must have lasted the length of a Creed, the other two less than a Hail Mary."[29] The Gabrielinos who lived here were no strangers to earthquakes, but this one was frightening enough to elicit prayers from Indians and Spaniards alike. As Costansó related, one Indian who appeared to be a holy man "began, with horrible cries and great manifestations of terror, to entreat the heavens, turning in all directions, and acting as though he would exorcise the elements."[30] Portolá's men christened the river by which they were camped Río de los Temblores (River of Earthquakes), known subsequently as the Santa Ana. Near its mouth lay the exposed bay of San Pedro, which would later serve as an anchorage for merchant ships.

By August 1 Portolá and company were passing through the heart of the future Los Angeles. Antelope bounded across the valley, and scouts returned that evening to report spotting another river a mile or two ahead. The next day, Costansó reported, the entire expedition reached that "beautiful river," flowing through "an extensive canyon containing many poplars and alders."[31] They dubbed it Río Porciúncula in honor of the chapel of Saint Francis, to which the second day of August was dedicated on their calendar. The fertile site surrounding it became known as Nuestra Señora de los Angeles de la Porciúncula (Our Lady of the Angels of Porciúncula). Crespí envisioned it as home to a mission, but it became instead the site of Spanish California's largest pueblo.

After fording the river on August 3, Costansó related, the company traversed country that "appeared to us most suitable for the

---
29. Crespí, *Description of Distant Roads*, field draft, 317.
30. Costansó, *Discovery of San Francisco Bay*, 15.
31. Ibid., 19.

production of all kinds of grain and fruits. On our way we met the entire population of an Indian village engaged in harvesting seeds on the plain."[32] Some Anglo settlers would later deride California Indians as Diggers or grass-eaters for gathering wild seeds, grains, or roots in this way, but such subsistence activities required diligence and know-how. Once harvested, seeds and grains were roasted, ground in mortars, and baked into loaves that were as nourishing as the bread or tortillas that Spaniards made from wheat or corn.

Aside from harvesting and hunting, Gabrielinos there engaged in trade with nearby groups like the Chumash and distant tribes like the Mohaves and Yumas, who kept them informed of Spanish ventures. On August 6 Indians visiting Portolá's encampment in the San Fernando Valley drew a map on the ground of the Santa Bárbara Channel and its islands and, using sign language, told of ships that had been sighted there recently and of past visits by bearded men dressed like Spaniards. They informed Crespí that far off to the east lived "people like us (pointing to the soldiers), with swords, guns and horses; that they had houses, and that there were also three Fathers (pointing to ourselves)."[33] The Indians were probably referring to the Spanish outpost of Tubac and the nearby mission of San Xavier del Bac, in what is now Tucson.

In the days to come, Portolá and company made their way through San Fernando Pass to the Santa Clara River, which they followed down to the sea near present-day Ventura. This brought them into the territory of the Chumash, who impressed Costansó as "alert, diligent and skillful." They lived in large, dome-shaped lodges that housed several related families, with partitions between bedrooms. Their sturdy wooden canoes were caulked with tar from springs in the area and carried up to ten men, who wielded paddles "with indescribable agility and swiftness" as they traveled back and forth between villages on the mainland and the Channel Islands. Chumash women, Costansó added, wove baskets "of a thousand different forms and graceful patterns." Shell beads served these

---
32. Ibid., 21.
33. Crespí, *Description of Distant Roads*, field draft, 357–59.

Spiritual Conquest 53

Indians as currency, but like other tribal groups in California they valued "more highly the glass beads that the Spaniards gave them," offering in exchange "all they possess, such as baskets, otter skins, bowls, and wooden dishes."[34]

In time, an infusion of glass beads and other European goods would disrupt the economy of Native Californians, rendering them increasingly dependent on Spaniards and their offerings. For now, however, the appearance of strangers with wondrous possessions was cause for joy. On the night of August 15 Chumash flocked to the Spanish encampment and serenaded the men with bone pipes and whistles, which "only served to annoy us and keep us awake," Costansó complained.[35] The raucous celebration "had our Captain somewhat worried," Crespí remarked, "but plainly it was all done in order to entertain us."[36]

As they progressed up the coast, practical-minded soldiers vied with the friars in devising names for landmarks. The troops called one Chumash village along the channel Carpintería because Indian carpenters were crafting a canoe there. Farther along, they dubbed a ravine where a stream rushed down to the sea La Gaviota after killing a seagull there. For the most part, however, the place-names that Portolá's company and later Spanish colonists bequeathed to California reflected the shared devotion of priests, soldiers, and settlers to the saints. In their view, God was a distant and majestic figure who could not be expected to attend personally to every petition from his earthly subjects. But he graciously appointed the Virgin Mary and other saints as intercessors to hear their prayers and plead for mercy on their behalf. By conferring saints' names on the landscape, pioneering Spaniards expressed a hope shared by later settlers of other faiths—that in this land of promise and peril their prayers would be answered.

From La Gaviota the company proceeded due westward along the Pacific to Point Conception (Concepción), where the coast turns sharply northward. Indians they encountered there were not as

---

34. Costansó, *Discovery of San Francisco Bay*, xxvii–xxxi, 33.
35. Ibid., 37.
36. Crespí, *Description of Distant Roads*, first revision, 401.

well-off as those along the Santa Bárbara Channel. Some had no houses at all and were probably engaged in fishing expeditions or other subsistence activities that often carried California Indians far from their home villages. Although they stored food they harvested for later consumption, lean times were part of the seasonal round for many tribes there. Even the seemingly prosperous Chumash along the channel were short of food when Portolá's company returned that way in winter. Such hardships, aggravated by the disruptive impact of colonization, would make the food and shelter offered at Franciscan missions hard for some Indians to resist.

Among the dangers faced by Native Californians as they fished, hunted, or harvested were deadly run-ins with grizzly bears, encountered by Portolá's men as they left the relatively dry southern coast for the lush central coast, where bears frequented streams visited by spawning fish and fields laden with roots and berries. At one spot dubbed Los Osos (the bears), soldiers targeted a grizzly that took nine bullets before collapsing. Another bear withstood nearly as many shots and mauled two of the expedition's mules before slinking off to die.

In mid-September, after passing Morro Bay, the company came up against a rugged, mountainous stretch of the coast that looked impassable. (They had reached Ragged Point, where the Santa Lucía Range meets the sea.) Turning inland at San Carpoforo Creek, they made slow progress through its narrow canyon, clearing a path for the animals as they went. After a week's toil, they gladly entered the broad Salinas River Valley, whose oak trees, Costansó noted, were "loaded with acorns, as yet unripe," used by Indians to make bread or gruel, "of which we have partaken in various places." Until the acorns ripened, Salinans there were living on seeds and pine nuts, which they offered the Spaniards, despite Costansó's impression that these "wandering Indians" had little to spare.[37]

Reaching the marshy mouth of the Salinas at month's end, Portolá and company heard the murmur of the ocean nearby

---

37. Costansó, *Discovery of San Francisco Bay*, 79–81.

Spiritual Conquest

and hoped they had reached Monterey Bay. Rations were dwindling and men were coming down with scurvy, which made their expected rendezvous with the supply ship *San José* at Monterey a matter of some urgency. They had no way of knowing that the ship had been lost at sea—or that the broad, surf-swept bay into which the Salinas entered, exposed to winds from the northwest, was in fact the Monterey of legend. On October 4 Portolá convened his officers. They agreed this was not the "much desired port of Monterey" and resolved to continue northward in pursuit of that goal and the hoped-for *San José*.[38]

Failure to recognize Monterey Bay opened new fields of discovery to the company. Several days after resuming their journey, near what is now Watsonville, they came upon the largest trees they had ever seen, up to five yards in diameter, Costansó reckoned, with wood of a "dull, dark, reddish color."[39] He and Crespí were the first Europeans to witness and describe the California redwood. What a pleasure it was, the friar wrote, "to view this blessing of timber."[40] The greatest blessings for the ailing men of the company were the food and comfort offered them by Ohlones as they moved north up the coast from Point Año Nuevo. "There was a large village of very fine, well-behaved heathens who greeted us with much hubbub and rejoiced a great deal over our coming," Crespí reported on October 23. At the center of the village stood a circular, grass-thatched council house, spacious enough to "hold the entire village," surrounded by many smaller lodges of similar design. The inhabitants offered their Spanish guests tamales made from acorn meal and a paste that tasted like honey, wrapped in cane leaves. The hills in the vicinity were covered with good soil, Crespí observed, "though the grasses had almost all been burnt."[41] That burning was deliberate, performed by Native Californians of various tribes to kill off weeds and promote fresh growth, thus improving prospects for hunting and harvesting in seasons to come.

---

38. Ibid., 91.
39. Ibid., 99.
40. Crespí, *Description of Distant Roads*, first revision, 553.
41. Ibid., first revision, 577–79.

The men with scurvy were fast recovering, which Costansó attributed to a change in the weather—the first autumn rains had swept in from sea along with fresh winds—but had more to do with their improved diet. At month's end the skies cleared. From high ground near the coast, Costansó and others could see off to the north and west distant landmarks consistent with mariners' accounts of the Farallon Islands (Farallones) and Drakes Bay (known then to Spaniards as the port of San Francisco for Saint Francis). Clearly, they had missed Monterey, which by all accounts lay well south of Drakes Bay.

At this moment of great disappointment for the company, fortune redeemed their expedition. On November 2, Costansó related, soldiers went off hunting deer and reached the summit of the coastal ridge that culminates at what is now the city of San Francisco. From that vantage point they beheld "an immense arm of the sea or estuary, which extended inland as far as they could see."[42] Two days later the entire company ascended the ridge and beheld the magnificent expanse of San Francisco Bay. They were the first party of European Americans to bear witness to that great harbor, which had eluded discovery by mariners because its entrance was narrow and often fog-shrouded.

Monterey Bay bore no comparison to that outstanding anchorage, but the company remained intent on finding Monterey, the assigned goal. They spent barely a week reconnoitering San Francisco Bay and environs, camping in the vicinity of present-day Palo Alto amid hospitable Ohlones. Crespí saw fine prospects there for colonization: "a grand spot, this, for a very large plenteous mission with vast amounts of good soil . . . and vast numbers of heathen folk, the finest and best-mannered that have been met with in the entire journey."[43] Indians visiting the encampment came from three different villages, and Crespí reckoned that the area had many more settlements, judging by the smoke rising from distant campfires or scorched fields. This was no wilderness that

---

42. Costansó, *Discovery of San Francisco Bay*, 119.
43. Crespí, *Description of Distant Roads*, first revision, 605.

Spiritual Conquest

the Spaniards were laying claim to but well-developed tribal territory, managed and improved by its numerous occupants.

On November 11 Portolá again convened his officers, who agreed that Monterey lay somewhere behind them to the south. Two weeks later they were back at the mouth of the Salinas River. They saw no ship in the bay and no reason to set aside their earlier conclusion that this was not the celebrated port of Monterey. Before departing, they erected a cross with an inscription instructing any Spaniard who might land there to dig for a letter buried below. They had searched in vain for Monterey, the letter declared: "Finally, now disappointed and despairing of finding the port, after so many endeavors, labors, and hardships, and without other provisions than fourteen sacks of flour, the expedition sets out today from this bay for San Diego. Pray thou Almighty God to guide it, and, sailor, may his Divine Providence take thee to a port of safety."[44]

Retreating southward, the company endured damp days, frosty nights, and dwindling rations. In late December Portolá divided up the remaining flour among the soldiers to keep hungry men from stealing it. That was not quite all the company had left, it turned out. As usual, the officers and friars fared somewhat better than the troops, receiving ham, biscuits, and chocolate, which when mixed with hot water and sugar provided Spanish colonists with their favorite beverage. (Among the supplies hauled overland from Loreto to San Diego earlier in the year were 600 pounds of sugar and 1,150 pounds of chocolate.) As the weary company traveled south, Indians whose own provisions were running low in this lean season nonetheless offered food and guidance that eased Portolá's return to San Diego. Here as elsewhere, they often received beads in return, but these transactions were conducted as exchanges of gifts and viewed as such by the grateful Spaniards. "There were days on which we missed the comfort of seeing natives," wrote Costansó. He knew that Indians had salvaged his party, as they would sustain colonists there with their labors in years to come.[45]

---

44. Costansó, *Discovery of San Francisco Bay*, 147–49.
45. Ibid., 103, 155; Crosby, *Gateway to Alta California*, 54; Hackel, *Children of Coyote*, 45–50.

Yet many Spaniards would continue to view the Indians on whom they relied as the ones in need of salvation, to be achieved through conquest.

Nearing San Diego, Portolá and his hungry men began butchering their mules, and the stench clung to them. In a brief account of the expedition, he remarked that by the time they reached their destination in late January 1770 they smelled "frightfully of mules." Upon learning that they had failed to locate Monterey, Serra told Portolá: "You come from Rome without having seen the pope."[46] Grim, gaunt, and downcast, the governor and his men were in no condition to savor what they had accomplished—an extraordinary journey of discovery that revealed both the great harbor of San Francisco Bay and the great resources of the intervening country and its tribal inhabitants. Those hospitable Indians had instilled in perceptive pioneers like Costansó an appreciation for Native Californians that would not long survive the convulsive process of colonization already underway in San Diego.

---

46. Portolá in Chapman, *A History of California*, 226.

CHAPTER 2

Cross and Crown

The past six months had been far from rewarding for Junípero Serra, who had remained in San Diego while Governor Portolá went in search of Monterey. On Sunday, July 16, 1769, two days after the overland expedition departed, Serra had consecrated Mission San Diego de Alcalá by blessing a cross raised by soldiers on Presidio Hill (above what is now Old Town) and performing Mass in a makeshift chapel there built of poles and brush. He could not hope to baptize Indians at this point, for that required some understanding of Christianity on their part and he had no "interpreter to communicate in any proper fashion with these poor naked gentiles."[1] Gifts of the sort used to lure Indians elsewhere had little effect here. The Diegueños would not eat food offered by the sickly Spaniards, and they became less grateful for beads, clothing, and other presents when they found that such articles could be stolen. Attempts by the few healthy troops remaining at San Diego to discourage theft only increased the Indians' hostility toward these uninvited guests, who showed no signs of leaving.

On August 15, while several soldiers were off attending to other duties, Diegueños attacked the infant mission. "They imagined

---
1. Serra, *Writings*, 1:149–51; Geiger, *Life and Times*, 1:232–33.

they could kill us all very easily," Serra wrote afterward.² But the four men on guard took up their muskets and repulsed the assault with the help of the expedition's carpenter and a blacksmith named Chacón, who had just received communion and let out a crusader's war cry: "Long live the faith of Jesus Christ, and may these dogs, enemies of that faith, die!"³ Serra remained in his hut during the battle, holding images of Christ in one hand and the Virgin Mary in the other and praying that "with such defense either I would not have to die, or that I would die well, great sinner that I am." As it turned out, the only Spaniard to perish was his young servant, José María Vergerano, struck by an arrow. "At the first shot he darted into my hut," Serra related, "spouting so much blood at the mouth and from his temples, that I had hardly time to absolve him and help him to meet his end."⁴

Afterward, soldiers built a stockade around the mission, which made Serra's task of reaching out to wary Diegueños no easier. Like other padres with linguistic and cultural barriers to overcome, he sought out youngsters who were more outgoing than their elders and quicker to learn a new language. A boy of about fifteen became his intermediary and arranged for him to baptize a child from a nearby village. According to Serra, the child's parents had "given their free consent to the Baptism," but the meaning of the ritual may well have escaped them.⁵ He offered the child clothing, which likely served as an incentive for those who brought the little boy to the mission, where the corporal of the guards was called on to serve as the boy's godfather. But as Serra was about to pour water from the baptismal shell, related his biographer Palóu, "pagans snatched the child and carried it away to their village." Serra would not allow soldiers to pursue and punish them, recognizing that they had acted in ignorance, which he had not dispelled. As he confided to Palóu, he attributed the sorry outcome "to his own sins."⁶

---

2. Serra, *Writings*, 1:151.
3. Chacón in Palóu, *Palóu's Life*, 77; Geiger, *Life and Times*, 1:234.
4. Serra, *Writings*, 1:151–55.
5. Ibid., 1:151.
6. Palóu, *Palóu's Life*, 78; Geiger, *Life and Times*, 1:235–36; Bancroft, *History of California*, 1:137–39.

The prospects for spiritual conquest looked even worse when Portolá returned in January 1770 to San Diego, where colonists were subsisting on provisions they brought with them or crops they cultivated. "We have tortillas on the table and vegetables in the garden," Serra wrote. "What more could we wish?"[7] With the addition of Portolá and his men, however, the colony had only enough food to last a few months unless resupplied by the *San Antonio*, which had returned to San Blas for provisions and reinforcements in late 1769. Portolá decided that if the ship did not arrive by March 19, the feast of San José, patron saint of the expedition, he would abandon San Diego and head south.

Serra had no intention of leaving and sought divine assistance by leading the colonists in a novena to San José—nine days of prayer in which they asked the saint to intercede for them and hasten the arrival of their supplies. On the day of decision, their prayers were seemingly answered when a ship appeared offshore. But the *San Antonio* did not enter San Diego harbor, as hoped, but instead continued up the coast toward Monterey. Captain Juan Pérez mistakenly presumed that Portolá and his company were still encamped there. Crewmen of the *San Antonio* soon learned of Portolá's whereabouts when they went ashore for water along the Santa Bárbara Channel and encountered Chumash, who indicated that Spaniards had recently returned south through their country. Pérez promptly reversed course, and the ship reached San Diego with sorely needed provisions on March 23. Once again, California Indians had provided vital assistance to colonists, but the credit went to the Spaniards' patron saint.

This reprieve enabled Portolá to leave a small complement of soldiers at San Diego as guards for the mission (a presidio would later be established nearby) and proceed with the settlement of Monterey. Although Portolá still had doubts as to the location of the fine harbor described by Vizcaíno, the exposed bay he had left behind in December was the only likely candidate. He made plans to return there overland in April with Father Crespí, Lieutenant

---

7. Serra, *Writings*, 1:159; Geiger, *Life and Times*, 1:239–42; Bancroft, *History of California*, 1:164–67.

Fages, and nineteen soldiers. Serra was no less intent on founding a mission at Monterey and left two friars in charge at San Diego before sailing for Monterey aboard the *San Antonio*—a trip that took longer than the overland expedition because of adverse winds.

Reaching their objective in late May, Portolá and Crespí stood in calm weather at Point Pinos and saw the bay at its finest. Basking sea lions covered the shore like "cobblestone pavement," Crespí observed, and two whales breached nearby. On such a day, the placid anchorage nestled between the headland on which they were standing and the mainland to the east looked like a mariner's delight. They exclaimed in one voice: "This is Monterey Harbor!" Crespí, a prolific diarist, was almost at a loss for words after finally realizing that goal: "I know not how to describe the joy and happiness we felt at seeing the end of all the steps we had spent upon finding it."[8]

Nearby they found the cross they had raised in December amid ceremonial objects left there by Indians, including staffs adorned with feathers and bundles of food. Elsewhere, Crespí noted, Indians had placed "small staffs with feathers on them at all of the places where we made camp during the first voyage."[9] This may have been the Indians' way of purifying places that had been profaned by strangers. Serra performed a similar ritual after landing at Monterey. On Pentecost, June 3, 1770, he consecrated the ground by sprinkling it with holy water, thus banishing all "infernal enemies."[10] Then the assembled members of Portolá's expedition took possession by raising a cross, followed by the Spanish flag, and shouting in unison: "Long live the Faith! Long live the King!"[11]

Portolá had decreed that the cross should be raised before the flag because the king's chief purpose in colonizing this country was to spread the faith. That pious assertion gratified Serra, but the worldly interests of Spanish officials were sometimes at odds with the goals of missionaries. When Portolá departed Monterey in early July aboard the *San Antonio*, leaving Pedro Fages

---

8. Crespí, *Description of Distant Roads*, final revision, 733.
9. Ibid., field draft, 735.
10. Quoted in Bancroft, *History of California*, 1:170.
11. Serra, *Writings*, 1:169; Geiger, *Life and Times*, 1:247–48; Hackel, *Children of Coyote*, 27.

as commandant at Monterey, the thorny issue of who had precedence—Serra as man of the Cross or Fages as representative of the Crown—remained unresolved. Known as the Stormy Catalan, Fages stirred up more than a few tempests in Monterey and left others there besides Serra praying for his departure. Sergeant Mariano Carrillo, a leather jacket born at Loreto, penned a lengthy complaint to his superiors, portraying Fages as a pitiless taskmaster. Not until Serra insisted that soldiers be allowed to rest on the Sabbath did Fages free them from domestic chores like fetching water or washing clothing, which he wanted done on Sundays so they could devote the remainder of the week to other duties.

Fages was in a difficult position, for the few mission Indians who accompanied the expedition to Monterey were under Serra's direction. The commandant was left without laborers to whom he could assign tasks that his soldiers found demeaning, such as mixing mud with straw to form adobe bricks for the presidio. Some resentment was inevitable, but Fages compounded the grievances of subordinates like Carrillo by constantly berating them. On one occasion, he lit into Carrillo for using the corral rather than the latrine for an urgent call of nature. "I replied that it had not been a case of intentionally disobeying his orders," Carrillo wrote, "but that the emergency had come upon me then and there. He then gave vent to his wrath with other insulting remarks, and threatened that if he caught me another time, he would hang a chain around my neck." Some of the sergeant's complaints were seemingly petty. Fages, he wrote, reserved "fine chocolate" for his Catalonian Volunteers from Spain while dispensing "ordinary chocolate" to Carrillo and others from Loreto.[12] Favoritism shown to Spanish-born soldiers on the frontier was no small matter, however, for native-born recruits who received scant praise from superiors and infrequent promotions. From the start, life here was marked by tensions between full-fledged Spaniards in high positions like Fages and those raised in California who served under them and felt their best efforts on behalf of the Crown went unrewarded.

---

12. Carrillo in Thomas Workman Temple, ed., "Three Early California Letters," 32, 40, 43, 47; Geiger, *Life and Times*, 1:253.

Authorities at Odds

More pronounced in California's early years was the contest between Cross and Crown personified by the growing rift between Serra and Fages. The two men lived at close quarters in the newly constructed presidio in Monterey until Serra and Crespí could find a better site for their purposes. No Indians lived near the presidio, and the area lacked fertile soil and fresh water. Serra saw brighter prospects for a mission a short distance south, near the mouth of the Carmel River, whose waters could be used for irrigation. His work there would begin in 1771. In the meantime, he and Crespí tried to communicate with curious young Indians who visited the presidio. It was not easy for the friars to impress them while living as wards of Fages, who wanted the key to their quarters "so as to lock us in and out when he pleased," Serra complained, and insisted that they were not to discipline Indians "except by his authorization."[13] As yet, Serra had few Indians under his care and did not press the matter with Fages. The commandant, for his part, served as godfather when Serra performed his first baptism at Monterey in December 1770, christening a five-year-old Indian boy there Bernardino de Jesús.

Serra and Fages had more to argue over as the mission system expanded. News that Monterey had been colonized prompted a celebration in Mexico City, where church bells tolled and Viceroy Antonio María de Bucareli hailed Serra for his efforts as "Reverend Father President of those missions."[14] Plans were underway to send additional missionaries to California. Serra had declared that he could employ a hundred friars there "and still have work for more."[15] But his Franciscan superior at the College of San Fernando in Mexico City, Father Rafael Verger, considered him overzealous in his plans for expansion and could spare only ten missionaries for the newly colonized territory. (Demands on the college would be lessened in 1772 when Franciscans turned the Baja California missions over to Dominican friars, a move that marked the first formal distinction between Baja and Alta California.)

---

13. Serra, *Writings*, 1:241; Geiger, *Life and Times*, 1:279.
14. Bucareli in Geiger, *Life and Times*, 1:265, 273.
15. Serra, *Writings*, 1:213.

Theoretically, the arrival of ten more Franciscans would allow Serra to establish five additional missions, with two friars assigned to each. But some of the newcomers would be needed to relieve missionaries already in place, and each new mission required a half dozen or more soldiers to serve as guards. Fages did not have many troops at his disposal and did not want those he assigned to missions to be tasked with constructing them. Unlike the substantial mission compounds of later times, the early mission buildings were temporary structures framed of logs or poles, roofed with thatch, and plastered with mud. But erecting those buildings was no easy chore for the friars and the few mission Indians and Mexican artisans at their disposal. Serra felt that the guards should help bear that cross by aiding in construction, as some in fact did.

With the limited resources available, Serra succeeded in founding Mission San Carlos Borromeo at Carmel in June 1771, where he and Crespí presided, and three more missions over the next few years: San Antonio de Padua, on a tributary of the Salinas River; San Gabriel Arcángel, near the future pueblo of Los Angeles; and San Luis Obispo de Tolosa, inland from Morro Bay. To lure Indians, the friars employed not only gifts of food, clothing, and beads but also religious symbols and pageantry with strong sensory appeal for people who did not understand Spanish. Serra founded Mission San Antonio in July 1771 by ringing bells hung from an oak tree and calling out: "Come, come to receive the Faith of Jesus Christ!"[16] Only a single Indian responded; but Serra lavished him with gifts, and the man later brought others to the site.

For Franciscans who had yet to overcome language barriers, sacred images were a vital form of communication. Mission San Gabriel, founded on September 8, 1771, the Feast of the Nativity of the Blessed Virgin, reportedly owed its existence to a painting of Our Lady of Sorrows displayed by Father Pedro Benito Cambón and others in his party. According to Cambón, Indians were about to attack them that day when they unfurled the canvas. Transfixed by the image, the warriors threw down their bows, and two chiefs

---

16. Serra in Geiger, *Life and Times*, 1:280.

"took from around their necks the necklaces they value so highly ... and placed them at the feet of the Sovereign Queen of the Angels."[17] Perhaps the sheer novelty of the painting impressed those warriors more than its subject matter, but other reports confirm that Indians drawn to the missions were entranced by images of the Virgin Mary. When women visiting San Gabriel saw the painting, Serra related, they brought food "to the holy image leaving their offerings in front of the altar."[18] The cult of Virgin and Child had innate appeal for California Indians, who revered female as well as male deities, honored certain gifted women as healers or shamans, and showed a devotion to their children that some padres thought overindulgent. "Their parents love them to such an extent that we might say they are their little idols," wrote one Franciscan.[19]

The painting of Our Lady of Sorrows may have postponed hostilities at San Gabriel, but it did not prevent them. Here as elsewhere in the budding mission system, the presence of soldiers who had long been without female companionship led to assaults on Indian women and violent reprisals. Soon after Mission San Gabriel was founded, a chief was shot dead by soldiers while retaliating for an assault on a woman who may have been his wife. The corporal of the guards then had the chief's head severed and placed atop a pole. That grim trophy was taken down at the padres' request, but it would be some time before they regained the trust of the surrounding Gabrielinos. Hoping to curb sexual assaults and the resulting hostilities, Serra encouraged soldiers to wed Indian women; but most refrained, evidently concluding that marriage to a full-blooded Indian was not a good match.

Sexual abuse of Indian women was chronic around Mission San Diego, according to a blistering report written in 1772 by Father Luis Jayme. "With reference to the Indians," he declared, "great

---

17. Cambón in Weber, *Pride of the Missions*, 30; Geiger, *Life and Times*, 1:302–303.
18. Serra, *Writings*, 1:359.
19. Quoted in Maynard J. Geiger and Clement W. Meighan, trans. and eds., *As the Padres Saw Them: Californian Indian Life and Customs as Reported by the Franciscan Missionaries, 1813–1815*, 23; Hackel, *Children of Coyote*, 164–65.

progress would be made if there were anything to eat and the soldiers would set a good example." Food was scarce because little rain fell there and Presidio Hill was ill suited for irrigation—one factor that led to the relocation of the mission in 1774 to a new site several miles up the San Diego River. Another reason for that move was to distance neophytes from soldiers at the presidio. "No doubt some of them are good exemplars and deserve to be treated accordingly," Jayme said of those troops, "but very many of them deserve to be hanged on account of the continuous outrages which they are committing in seizing and raping the women." In one instance, he reported, three soldiers raped and impregnated an Indian woman, who killed the infant "without my being able to baptize it." Another woman was dragged into a corral and assaulted by four soldiers in succession, the last of whom offered her as compensation "two tortillas and some red ribbons." Such acts so enraged Indians living near the mission, Jayme declared, that they were "on the point of coming here to kill us all."[20]

Jayme blamed Fages for punishing only some of the wrongdoers and commuting their sentences to hard labor at the presidio. Serra also considered the commandant lax when it came to protecting Indians and padres. Yet when Fages tried to prevent hostilities by limiting the access of Indians to newly constructed Mission San Gabriel, Serra objected that he was driving would-be Christians away. The exacting commandant could do little to please the demanding father-president. Serra faulted Fages for preventing soldiers from laboring on missions—and for overtaxing them with labor at the presidio and treating them so harshly that some deserted. Fages, for his part, complained that Serra was baptizing more Indians than he could feed at a time when both missions and presidios relied largely on provisions shipped from the south. Serra and Fages were bound to disagree, for they were competing for the limited resources committed by the Crown to this costly undertaking. By 1772 they were no longer on speaking terms and communicated only by letter. Although their dispute

---

20. Jayme in Beebe and Senkewicz, *Lands of Promise and Despair*, 156–60.

was sometimes petty, it went to the heart of a question that would haunt the colony for decades to come: would the missions here serve the state, or would the state serve the missions?

In 1773 Fages was removed from command at the request of Serra, who had traveled to Mexico City to press his case before Viceroy Bucareli. Serra prevailed in part because Bucareli could ill afford to overlook the hefty contributions to colonization made by Franciscans, whose expenses were paid out of an endowment called the Pious Fund confiscated from the Jesuits. Yet Serra's victory was far from absolute. The officer who succeeded Fages as commandant—Captain Rivera y Moncada, a veteran of the 1769 colonizing expedition—proved no easier for him to get along with, insisting like Fages on maintaining authority over the mission guards. Serra had seemingly solidified his own authority by obtaining from the viceroy a decree that the "management, control, punishment, and education of baptized Indians" belonged exclusively to the missionaries.[21] But how could they educate Indians whose languages they had not yet fully mastered? And without relying on the commandant and his troops, how could they control those neophytes who rebelled or ran off?

In relation to each other, Franciscans were friars (brothers). But in relation to mission Indians, they were padres (fathers) and saw it as their duty to pursue and punish errant neophytes, whom Spanish colonists regarded as children, not yet ready to look after themselves. Padres expected help from soldiers in retrieving runaways, for Spanish law required that Indians, once baptized and concentrated at missions, must remain there under the supervision of their padres. Rivera y Moncada and his successors, however, sometimes declined to send troops after fugitives to avoid provoking hostilities with Indians harboring them, who feared that they too might be inducted into the mission system, as captives sometimes were.

In July 1775 Serra dispatched a party of neophytes from Mission San Carlos to retrieve fugitives after Rivera y Moncada had

---

21. Quoted in James A. Sandos, *Converting California: Indians and Franciscans in the Missions*, 53; Geiger, *Life and Times*, 1:383.

failed to act on his request to use troops for that purpose. Those "wayward sheep are my burden," Serra wrote of the runaways, "and I am responsible for them." Nine fugitives were apprehended. He sent four of them to the Monterey presidio to be dealt with by the commandant, explaining by letter that three of the four had "deserted a number of times" and been punished without showing any "sign of amendment." It was the first such offense for the other fugitive, but he had been absent a long time and Serra feared that he might stir up more trouble. "I am sending them to you," he wrote Rivera y Moncada, "so that a period of exile and two or three whippings which Your Lordship may order applied to them on different days may serve, for them and for the rest, for a warning, and may be of spiritual benefit to all." The freedom to come and go as they pleased and commune with friends and relatives in their villages evidently meant more to these Indians than any benefits they derived from Serra's regimen. Their cases called for special treatment at the presidio, he concluded. But he was prepared to continue meting out punishments—usually administered by Indians under the supervision of padres—as required at San Carlos. "If Your Lordship does not have shackles," he wrote the commandant, "with your permission they may be sent from here."[22]

Martyrdom at San Diego

In late 1775 the explosive issues of restraint and punishment convulsed Mission San Diego, resulting in a deadly uprising that demonstrated the extent to which mission fathers remained dependent on Spanish troops. Diegueños were already alarmed by assaults on their women of the kind reported earlier by Father Jayme. Attempts by Jayme and Father Vicente Fuster to discipline neophytes made matters worse. Those who lived at the mission or in clusters of huts surrounding it could not leave without permission from the padres. In early October a chief called Carlos left

---

22. Serra, *Writings*, 2:285, 4:425; Randall Milliken, *A Time of Little Choice: The Disintegration of Tribal Culture in the San Francisco Bay Area, 1769–1810*, 4–5.

without approval, accompanied by his brother Francisco and other neophytes, all of whom failed to return. The brothers had been accused of theft and feared punishment.

At Jayme's request, Lieutenant José Ortega, commander of the San Diego presidio, sent out soldiers but failed to apprehend the fugitives. Ortega did not pursue the matter further because he had a more pressing task—to help construct Mission San Juan Capistrano, in keeping with recent orders from Viceroy Bucareli. Soldiers at San Diego did not care for that duty and at first refused to accompany Ortega, forcing him to bring all his weight to bear. "Am I commanding here loyal servants of the king or traitors?" he railed. "Are you servants of His Majesty?"[23] He reinforced his point by drawing his sword, and the men he chose for the task were soon hard at work on the new mission.

Without resort to the sword, friars like Jayme and Fuster hoped to instill in neophytes a similar dutifulness toward God and the priesthood. They themselves had taken vows of obedience. But the Diegueños, like other California Indians, cherished their freedom and found the idea of taking orders alien and mystifying. Their chiefs led largely by example and relied more on persuasion than on compulsion. Tribal leaders like the fugitive Carlos could ill afford to submit to galling punishment at the hands of Spaniards lest they lose face in the eyes of people who were free to reject their leadership and follow others. Unwittingly, the friars strengthened Carlos as a rebel leader by sending troops after him and bolstered his cause by ordering neophytes flogged for taking part in a pagan dance. It appeared to disaffected Diegueños that the padres were in league with the despised soldiers, whose excesses Jayme had protested. Warned by Carlos and his confederates that they would all be forced to become Christians, several hundred men set out in two groups to destroy the mission and the presidio while Ortega and many of his troops were away.

Well before dawn on November 5, warriors descended on the mission, setting fire to buildings whose thatch roofs easily ignited.

---

23. Ortega in Geiger, *Life and Times*, 2:59.

Others on their way to attack the presidio heard the commotion in the distance and saw flames and smoke billowing from the mission. They pulled back from their target, fearing that troops at the presidio must now be alert to the danger. In fact, those troops remained unaware of the fighting—or claimed ignorance—until messengers reached them belatedly around daybreak. Father Fuster reported that the force attacking the mission included "both gentiles and Christians." It pained him to hear some "who until recently had been my trusted children, giving orders that now they should once and for all make an end of us." The corporal of the guards had only three soldiers at his disposal, two of whom were seriously wounded during the attack, which claimed the lives of Father Jayme as well as a blacksmith and a carpenter. The survivors took shelter in a dilapidated adobe cookhouse, where they came under a barrage of arrows, rocks, and firebrands, which threatened to ignite a sack of gunpowder from which those still fit to fight were loading muskets. Fuster prayed to Mary, promising to "fast nine Saturdays and offer up my Mass in her honor nine times" if she delivered them from this ordeal. "That night seemed to us as long as the pains of Purgatory," he wrote. Finally, around dawn, the attackers retreated. Jayme's body was found battered beyond recognition. "His chest and body were riddled through with countless jabs they had given him," Fuster lamented, "and his face was one great bruise from the clubbing and stoning it had suffered."[24]

Serra saw Jayme's martyrdom as God's way of furthering the spiritual conquest. Now that the land had been watered with blood, he declared according to Palóu, "the conversion of the San Diego Indians will take place." This idea of redemptive sacrifice was central to Christian teachings. Not until Christ and the martyrs who followed in his path poured out their blood like water on parched soil were repentant sinners shown the way to a new Eden in the world to come. Serra and his colleagues believed that they could help prepare neophytes for that heavenly order by subjecting them to rules of the Franciscan order, including poverty (or

---
24. Fuster in Beebe and Senkewicz, *Lands of Promise and Despair*, 187–91.

forsaking individual gain for the good of the mission community), chastity (or abstinence before marriage and fidelity thereafter), and obedience. To the padres, California was no paradise. This land and its inhabitants were doomed unless redeemed, they believed, and that task required men of militant faith who would impose on others to save them. As Palóu saw it, the uprising at San Diego was inspired by Satan, who hated the missionaries for capturing the souls of "pagans over whom he held sway."[25]

Such militancy aroused resistance in California Indians, who lost their tolerance for alternate forms of spirituality when their freedom and well-being were at stake. They believed that the power shamans possessed could be turned from good to evil purposes and feared holy men who brandished their faith like a sword. Inevitably, spiritual conquest and the constant threat of force that made it possible embroiled Spaniards in a prolonged struggle with Indians, which overshadowed the international contest that prompted this colonization effort. Spanish commanders could hardly be expected to fend off Russian or British intrusions along the coast if their few available forces were busy guarding missions and pacifying Indians. For California to serve successfully as a buffer against rival powers, it needed not just more troops but more settlers who could support the colony with their labor and help defend it if called upon.

Seven women had reached San Diego as colonists by ship in 1773, and several families had arrived overland from the south with Rivera y Moncada when he took command later that year. But the Spanish population of California was still overwhelmingly male. According to Serra, Indians wondered where this strange breed of men without women came from and concluded that they were the offspring of the mules they rode. Fortunately for this struggling colony of fewer than two hundred people, reinforcements in the form of settlers and soldiers with wives and children were on their way to California from Sonora in 1775 under the leadership of Juan Bautista de Anza.

---

25. Palóu, *Palóu's Life*, 160, 167; Geiger, *Life and Times*, 2:68.

Word of Anza's expedition was welcome to Serra, because it meant it that the San Francisco Bay area with its wealth of potential converts could now be colonized, a project that had been deferred pending the arrival of more resources. A less zealous father-president might have been appalled by the tribal resistance encountered at San Diego and dreaded the prospect of sending out friars two by two to proselytize among so many potentially hostile Indians. But Serra was the prototypical California dreamer, and the high hopes this country inspired in him withstood repeated setbacks, convulsions, and contradictions. He had been there for only six of his sixty-one years, but all that he was and ever wished for now lay in California. "There is my life," he had written from Mexico City in 1773 before returning to Monterey, "and there, God willing, I hope to die."[26]

26. Serra, *Writings*, 1:389; Geiger, *Life and Times*, 1:397.

CHAPTER 3

The Anza Expedition

On Sunday, October 22, 1775, a party of 240 Spanish soldiers and colonists, including 29 women and more than 100 children, assembled at the presidio of Tubac in what is now southern Arizona to celebrate Mass before setting out across the Sonoran Desert for California. Among those present was the expedition's commander, Lieutenant Colonel Juan Bautista de Anza, born in Sonora in 1736. (His father, a captain of the same name, died three years later fighting Apaches.) Presiding over the ceremony was Father Pedro Font, a Spanish-born Franciscan who kept a revealing journal of the expedition. Font used this occasion to urge colonists to prepare for an ordeal that would test them body and soul. "I exhorted everyone to perseverance, and to bear up under the hardships of so long a journey, and to hold themselves lucky and happy that God had chosen them for that undertaking," he related. "And by drawing a parallel between the crossing of the people of Israel through the Red Sea over to the promised land and the present expedition's journey to Monterey and their crossing over the Colorado River, I proclaimed to them what punishments God might put upon them, if they misbehaved with the Gentiles along the way or scandalized them with their actions, as He did with the Israelites."[1]

---

1. Pedro Font, *With Anza to California*, 83.

In years to come, many pilgrims bound for California would look forward to entering that promised land, but few would recognize as Font did that such golden opportunities placed them under solemn obligations. Steeped in scripture, he knew that those favored by God were held to high standards and subjected to harsh trials. To help colonists through their ordeal, he chose as patroness of the expedition the dark-skinned Virgin of Guadalupe, who had appeared miraculously to a young Indian soon after Spaniards conquered Mexico City. Font knew of no one better to inspire Anza's recruits, consisting largely of mestizos (people of mixed Spanish and Indian ancestry), than Our Lady of Guadalupe, spiritual guardian "of the Indians and of this our America." He hoped that pagan Indians encountered on this journey would soon be among her followers. God and "the Most Holy Virgin Mary of Guadalupe," he told the colonists, would see them safely across the desert if they behaved as good Christians and dealt justly with those Indians. And at the end of life's journey, he assured them, they would know "the happiness of eternal rest in the land of promise."[2]

Font's words may have disappointed those colonists who hoped to enter the promised land in this world rather than the next. The land of Canaan awaiting the biblical Israelites was real enough. Why should those who followed Anza on this hazardous errand into the wilderness have to wait until they died to enter the land of milk and honey? To Font and his fellow missionaries, no earthly Canaan with its fleeting pleasures could compare with the everlasting delights of heaven. But others who joined these holy men in strenuous efforts to colonize the northern reaches of New Spain hoped that somewhere on the frontier—perhaps in that beckoning country called California—they would find a more rewarding existence on this side of the grave.

Among those who differed with Font on such matters was the commander of this expedition. Ambitious and energetic, Anza was not one to look forward to the "happiness of eternal rest" and did not share Font's view that colonization was all about saving souls.

---
2. Ibid., 73, 83.

In 1772, as part of an official inquiry into Franciscan mission efforts in Sonora, Anza had reported to Viceroy Bucareli that friars there were doing Indians more harm than good by making them labor for mission communities in which they had no real stake. "I believe that they should be left in complete possession of what is theirs to work for themselves for their own benefit," he wrote. Indians who had their own property and were not confined to "wretched" missions would trade and intermingle with Spanish settlers, he argued, and the frontier would be more peaceful and prosperous as a result.³

Despite Anza's dim view of mission efforts, he collaborated fruitfully with Franciscans who shared his desire to open an overland route between Sonora and California. In 1774 he had reconnoitered that route by traveling from Tubac to Mission San Gabriel and back with a small party of soldiers, mission Indians, and friars, including Father Francisco Garcés, who had come to Sonora in 1767 to take charge of Mission San Xavier del Bac, founded by the accomplished Jesuit friar-explorer Eusebio Kino. Like Kino, Garcés ventured out frequently from San Xavier, searching for Indians to convert. Many missionaries born in Spain as he was found this distant frontier forbidding and the Indians fearsome. But Garcés was in his element. "I am glad that I have no Spaniards in my care," he wrote. "There are plenty of Indians. I like them and they like me."⁴

Neither Garcés nor Anza had broken new ground in these explorations, for Indians had long been traversing the desert between Sonora and California. Yumas living near the junction of the Gila and Colorado Rivers occupied a central position in the region. Paths to the west linked them to the Diegueños and other California Indians near the coast, while trails to the east brought them in contact and conflict with Papagos and Pimas along the Gila. Anza and Garcés were guided in 1774 by Sebastián Taraval, a mission Indian from Baja California who had accompanied colonists

---

3. Anza in John L. Kessell, ed., "Anza Damns the Missions: A Spanish Soldier's Criticism of Indian Policy, 1772," 58–59; David J. Weber, *The Spanish Frontier in North America*, 248–53; J.N. Bowman and Robert F. Heizer, *Anza and the Northwest Frontier of New Spain*, 27–39.
4. Garcés in John L. Kessell, "The Making of a Martyr: The Young Francisco Garcés," 190; Vladimir Guerrero, *The Anza Trail and the Settling of California*, xii, 3–7.

to San Diego in 1769 and settled at Mission San Gabriel before fleeing to the Yuma villages. Anza valued his services and retained him as guide and interpreter for the colonizing expedition of 1775. Garcés would accompany the colonists as well, but only as far as the villages of the Yumas and neighboring tribes along the Colorado.

Anza had not found colonists for this expedition on the desolate and dangerous Sonoran frontier, where Apaches remained hostile. Instead, he had looked for recruits in the more populous district of Sinaloa, which then formed the southern part of Sonora. Settlers there were "submerged in the direst poverty and misery," he wrote Viceroy Bucareli, "and so I have no doubt they would most willingly and gladly embrace the advantages which your Excellency may deign to afford them."[5] Anza enlisted married men as soldiers to emigrate with their families and establish a military colony on San Francisco Bay to shield that strategic area and serve "as a base and beginning for successive establishments," in Bucareli's words.[6] Anza's expedition would more than double the Spanish population of California. But his roster included just four civilian families compared to some thirty soldiers and their kin. That would do little to alter the contentious nature of a colony whose military and religious factions were often at odds.

That factionalism was not confined to California. Commanders in New Mexico had long feuded with Franciscans who oversaw mission efforts among Pueblo Indians. As in California, the disputes there often came down to the question of who had ultimate authority over Indians and their indispensable labor. By the late 1700s the quarrel between Cross and Crown on the northern frontier had expanded to include a larger moral issue—whether the mission system violated the rights of Indians as defined under Spanish law or more broadly by Enlightenment philosophers who saw liberty as a natural right to which all were entitled. When Anza stated that Indians should "be left in complete possession of what is theirs," he was echoing principles of the Enlightenment that spread from European courts and salons to reform-minded

---

5. Anza in Herbert Eugene Bolton, *Anza's California Expeditions*, 1:206.
6. Bucareli in ibid., 1:210.

officials in distant colonies. Missionaries like Junípero Serra, for their part, dismissed the Enlightenment conception of liberty as heresy—a devilish deception that undermined obedience to God and king.

As yet, the pursuit of liberty had not transformed New Spain as it had New England, where in 1775 colonists launched a rebellion against King George III. Anza and like-minded Spanish commanders who found fault with the mission system did so as loyalists, not rebels. And in faithfully serving the Crown they sometimes found common ground with missionaries like Garcés, whose affection for Indians and skill in dealing with them helped avert hostilities. A friar like Font, in contrast, who loved Indians in spirit but disdained them in the flesh—and held Anza and his hard-pressed colonists to biblical standards of morality that few people could live up to in such trying circumstances—was bound to clash with his commander. In the end, Anza's colonizing expedition exemplified both the heroic communal efforts that enabled Spaniards to occupy remote California in the face of enormous obstacles and the tensions and divisions that undermined Spanish resolve and weakened California from within.

Bound for Canaan

On October 23 Anza left Tubac and led colonists northward toward Mission San Xavier del Bac. Decamping was laborious, for they started out with more than a thousand animals, including horses, pack mules, and cattle. Anza's long train was vulnerable to attack by Apaches, notorious for raiding Spanish herds. With the exception of ten veterans from the Tubac presidio, his soldiers were inexperienced and preoccupied with their families. Font considered it miraculous that Apaches "have not attacked us" and thanked the Virgin of Guadalupe, without whose protection "we would have suffered losses, as our few soldiers were raw and inexperienced."[7] Some had two or three youngsters with them on horseback, he added, and most rode with at least one child.

---

7. Font, *With Anza to California*, 89.

Several women were pregnant when the expedition started out, and one of them came to grief the first night. She "successfully gave birth to a very lusty boy," Anza reported, but died early the next day despite his efforts to save her with medicine he carried.[8] Her newborn and six other children survived the expedition—as did every other colonist under Anza's command. On October 25 they reached Mission San Xavier, where Font solemnized the marriages of three soldiers. (Unconsecrated marriages were common in northern New Spain, where many settlers lived far from missions and their priests.) Font described San Xavier as "brought very low by the hostile actions of the Apaches."[9] Some converted Pimas lived there, but more resided nearby at a mission outpost called Tucson. Soldiers would soon abandon Tubac and establish a presidio at Tucson, which would in turn attract settlers. Colonization of the northern frontier took three forms—mission, presidio, and pueblo (civilian settlement)—but missions and presidios fostered their own enduring settlements at sites such as Tucson, San Diego, Monterey, and San Francisco.

From Tucson, the colonists moved northwestward through Picacho Pass to the Gila River, passing the ruins called Casa Grande. Built around 1300 by Indians known to posterity as the Hohokams, that multistory adobe building was mistaken by Spanish explorers for a relic of the Aztecs, the original Mexicans. As Font wrote, "It appears that it was established by the Mexicans during the time they were led by the demon in their migration through several countries before reaching their promised land of Mexico."[10] Font had no doubt the Aztecs were led by the devil, because they made human sacrifices to their gods; but Christians too died for their God or put heretics to death in God's name.

For much of November, colonists bound for the promised land of California traveled westward along the Gila through country that looked irredeemably bleak to Font, who saw "nothing worth praising." The river vanished in places, and soldiers had to dig

---

8. Anza in Bolton, *Anza's California Expeditions*, 3:7.
9. Font, *With Anza to California*, 87.
10. Ibid., 94.

into the sand for a few sips of brackish water. By mid-month the nights were freezing, compounding the ordeal for Font, who suffered from fever, chills, and intestinal torments. He continued to conduct Mass, but the Pimas and Papagos he met along the way showed more interest in his services than the colonists did. In one sermon, he scolded soldiers who were so jealous and possessive of their wives "that in addition to not letting them talk with anyone else, they had forbidden them to come to Mass." At night, Font noted, the colonists sang hymns and "prayed the Rosary in their family groups," but they seemed understandably wary of confessing their sins to so strict a father.[11]

In late November they reached the Yuma villages along the Colorado. Anza counted on a warm reception there because he and Garcés had befriended a chief called Salvador Palma, who prized the gifts he received from Spaniards seeking to bring the Yuma and nearby tribes under their influence or authority. "As soon he saw me he began to embrace me," Anza wrote.[12] Palma received a special present from Viceroy Bucareli, Font noted: an elegant outfit that included "a cape or cabriole of blue cloth decorated with gold braid, and a cap of black velvet adorned with imitation jewels and a crest like a palm." Font felt that he should have been present when such gifts were offered to the Yumas, for "the Indians show favor and respect to those who give to them."[13]

Font concluded that Anza was intent on denying him any distinction among these status-conscious Indians. He had been asked by the commander to bring along his harplike psaltery "to attract Indians, especially the Yumas, who are very fond of celebrating." But since the journey began, Font complained, Anza had "said nothing more to me about it, nor suggested my playing it nor desired to hear it nor wished any people to gather in my tent; while I have been dragging this useless burden along without its doing any good for the Yumas, or anyone." Font was further offended when Indians visiting the Spanish camp failed

---

11. Ibid., 91, 114, 86.
12. Anza in Bolton, *Anza's California Expeditions*, 3:38.
13. Font, *With Anza to California*, 122.

to maintain a respectful distance and pressed in on him with such curiosity that they became "importunate and tedious." They "stink from their windiness," he added. When they crowded around, he found it hard to breathe and used a stick to keep them away, provoking an angry response. He concluded that if they had to submit to religious instruction and discipline, "all of their friendliness, which is more due to the gift of beads than to their docility, might turn to arrogance." Yet none of this seemed to bother Garcés, who was "so well suited to getting along with the Indians and going among them that he seems to be very much like an Indian himself." He could sit happily with Yumas around the fire for hours, Font marveled, and eat with gusto foods "as unclean as they themselves are . . . In sum, as I see it, God has created him wholly suited to seek out these unfortunate, ignorant, and rustic people."[14]

Unlike Font, Garcés recognized that these Indians had much to offer Spaniards. Yumas were vital to Spanish hopes of linking Sonora with California. The corn, wheat, and melons they cultivated with water diverted from the Colorado helped sustain Anza's colonists and later parties. And Yumas offered them crucial assistance in crossing the river. "Three Yumas carried Father Garcés across on their shoulders," Font related, "stretched out face upward like a dead man."[15]

Font's task was not to remain there among Indians like Garcés but to accompany Anza to California and back and minister to his recruits. Yet he did not get along much better with the colonists than he did with the Yumas. Soon after departing the Yuma villages in early December, Anza allowed the colonists some liquor (*aguardiente*), Font related, as a result of which there was much "drunkenness and shouting among that crowd." Font confronted Anza the next day and told him that drunkards and those like him who enable drunkenness "both sin."[16]

Font and Anza clashed again two weeks later during the most trying stretch of their journey, which took them over severe desert and snow-capped mountains to coastal California. Before crossing

---
14. Ibid., 123, 119, 135, 129, 144.
15. Ibid., 121.
16. Ibid., 131.

that desert, Anza divided his party, anticipating that potential campsites ahead would not have enough water to sustain all the colonists and their animals as a group. He and Font went forward with the first division, and Sergeant Juan Pablo Grijalva and Lieutenant José Joaquín Moraga followed with the second and third divisions, respectively. On December 13, after struggling across sandy terrain, Anza's division reached a campsite called San Sebastián on San Felipe Creek, running down from the mountains, which were "more deeply covered with snow than we had ever imagined would be the case," Anza observed.[17] For colonists from warmer climes to the south, it was a fearful sight. Even at low-lying San Sebastián, snow fell the next day, and weary, half-starved animals died from the cold in the night.

Anza and company waited at San Sebastián for the trailing divisions to catch up. On December 15 Sergeant Grijalva and his party limped in. Some were "crippled by the storm," Anza noted, and one man was so badly frozen "that in order to save his life it was necessary to bundle him up for two hours between four fires."[18] Two days later, Lieutenant Moraga's division reached camp in similar condition. Glad to be back together, colonists held a fandango to celebrate. "Some rather unruly partying broke out," wrote Font, who added: "a widow who was traveling with the expedition quite brazenly sang some *glosas* [improvised verses] that were not so nice. Her singing was acknowledged by the applause and shouting from the rabble. Her companion, that is, the man with whom she was traveling, became angered at this and punished her." Anza ran from his tent to restrain the man, who in Font's opinion was giving the widow, María Feliciana Arballo, what she deserved. "Let it be, sir, he is doing the right thing," he said. "No, Father," Anza replied, "I must not allow these excesses in my presence."[19]

Font faulted Anza for allowing a greater offense, "the excess of the party," to continue late into the night. The next morning at Mass, he condemned the colonists and implicitly censured their commander. They should have thanked God for "not having died,

---

17. Anza in Bolton, *Anza's California Expeditions*, 3:56–57.
18. Ibid. 3: 58.
19. Font, *With Anza to California*, 154.

as the animals did, during all those hardships," he told them. Instead, "it seemed they were thanking the devil with that kind of festivity." Anza was too angry to speak with Font afterward. His silent fury confirmed Font's view that Anza was an excessively proud man and that any little thing "served to annoy" him.[20] But this was no small matter. Font was challenging Anza's moral authority by demanding that he and his colonists honor rules of conduct better suited for a monastery than for this harsh frontier, where the shared joys of song, dance, laughter, and *aguardiente* were secular forms of communion that few people could live without. Not all friars were as severe as Font, but the questions raised by his uncivil sermonizing lingered. Could priests trained to the monastic life serve the needs of colonists or Indians who were not prepared to live like monks? Could they help build the strong, secular California that Spanish authorities hoped for?

Font kept up his moral crusade in the days ahead. On Christmas Eve, at their camp in desolate Coyote Canyon, a pregnant woman whose birth pangs were so severe that Font was called to hear her confession so she could die in grace rallied and "successfully gave birth to a boy child." This could have inspired a joyous Christmas sermon, but Font chose to dwell instead on the "Christmas Eve refreshments" that Anza allowed the soldiers. "I am well aware of what small profit I shall gain from speaking," he began bitterly, "given how I have no role to perform here." Christmas, he went on, was no time for "eating and drinking, dancing and drunkenness, uproar and shamelessness." His stern words did not sit well with the commander, who remained "vexed with me during the entire day," Font observed.[21]

A Promise Fulfilled

Ailing, disconsolate, and friendless, Font himself was sorely in need of a Christmas blessing that would raise his spirits. Something like that came to him belatedly on December 27 when he

---

20. Ibid., 154.
21. Ibid., 161–62.

stood with the colonists at San Carlos Pass—their gateway to coastal California—and saw a new world before him. It was "like a change of scene on a stage," he wrote. The far side of what he called the "main California range" was "green and lush with good grass and trees." This was promising country, if not the promised land of his prayers, and it had an invigorating effect on him. He felt "considerably better" in these new surroundings, and his rift with Anza began to heal as well. "The commander was a bit agreeable with me today," he wrote on December 30, "and we talked some along the way (whole days used to pass without our saying anything to each other except what was strictly necessary)."[22] Anza regained his earlier respect for the fortitude of this friar, "who by force of his spirit and zeal has come battling with great ills all the way."[23] The two men continued to quarrel on occasion, but tensions were eased by their delight at coming into this fruitful Canaan, which reminded Font of his native land. On New Year's Day, 1776, the colonists crossed the Santa Ana River on a makeshift bridge. This was "a moist and fertile land," Font observed, "very similar to Spain" in its plants and flowers and in "the fact that the rains come in the winter."[24]

On January 4 they arrived at Mission San Gabriel, set in a valley "with a good deal of water and very good soil," Font observed. He reckoned that 500 Christian Indians were living in huts near the mission buildings. This was not the impressive adobe compound that later visitors would admire, but the site offered "such fine advantages for agriculture and such fine grazing for livestock and horses that nothing better might be wished for," Font wrote. The country indeed looked "like a promised land," he allowed, "although the fathers have undergone a great deal of want and hardship in it." The neophytes struck him as "mild mannered and more or less well inclined." Conversion was voluntary, but the padres used meals of *atole* (corn-meal gruel) and *pozole* (a porridge of grain and vegetables to which meat was sometimes added) to

---
22. Ibid., 168, 170, 172.
23. Anza in Bolton, *Anza's California Expeditions*, 3:25.
24. Font, *With Anza to California*, 175.

attract Indians and lure them back when they were granted leave to visit relatives or forage in the mountains. "Normally they do not fail to return," Font remarked, "and sometimes they come back with a gentile relative who remains for instruction, either because of the others' example or else attracted by the pozole, which they like better than their plants and wild foods, and thus those Indians are usually 'caught by the mouth.'"[25]

Font approved of this regimen, but he was well aware that a system of indoctrination based on catching and controlling Indians could breed violent resistance. News of the bloody uprising at Mission San Diego in November 1775 caused Anza to delay the last phase of his expedition, which would take him to San Francisco Bay. Awaiting Anza at Mission San Gabriel was Captain Rivera y Moncada, commandant at Monterey and the acting governor of Alta California. (He reported to Governor Felipe de Neve at Loreto, but Neve's practical authority was limited to Baja California.) Anza complied with the commandant's request for help in pursuing and punishing the leaders of the San Diego revolt, but their relationship was strained. Anza was a higher-ranking officer with closer ties to Viceroy Bucareli. And his plan to colonize San Francisco Bay was regarded skeptically by Rivera y Moncada, who had reconnoitered that area and concluded that the northern end of the peninsula, overlooking the strategic entrance to the harbor, was not well suited for settlement. He told Font that they might spare themselves the journey, "as we would not attain the goal for which we came."[26] Rivera y Moncada's resistance to expansion stemmed largely from the fact that he had fewer than a hundred soldiers at his command before Anza arrived and was hard-pressed to defend the existing missions and presidios.

Anza and Font found common ground in their disdain for Rivera y Moncada, whom Font considered unsympathetic to the friars and their mission efforts. On January 6, as Anza prepared to depart with troops for San Diego, leaving the colonists behind

---
25. Ibid., 177, 179–80.
26. Ibid., 205.

at San Gabriel, Font expressed disappointment at not being asked to accompany him. He had vowed from the start that he would "not depart from Anza's side" but wished to be treated by him as an equal, who came on this expedition "by higher command."[27] Anza begged Font's pardon, and the friar went with him to San Diego and remained at his side for the duration of the expedition. As it turned out, Anza and his troops had little to do in San Diego. Although Chief Carlos, the suspected leader of the uprising, was still at large, there appeared to be little danger of renewed hostilities and Anza could not linger. By February Mission San Gabriel could no longer afford to support the colonists. Anza left San Diego and headed north.

In March Carlos tired of life as a fugitive and sought asylum in a chapel at the San Diego presidio, only to be arrested there by Rivera y Moncada a short time later. For violating the fugitive's right of asylum without permission from Father Fuster, the presiding priest, the commandant was excommunicated and barred from attending Mass until he freed Carlos and returned him to the chapel. Both sides compromised in the end: Rivera y Moncada restored Carlos to asylum in the chapel, and Fuster then agreed to surrender him. But this latest episode in the ongoing contest between Cross and Crown left the commandant, a devout Catholic, near the end of his tether. "I am thinking of no other thing but retiring," he wrote. "I want to regain my peace of mind and contemplate eternity."[28]

Meanwhile, Anza had journeyed northward to Monterey with the colonists at a pace that Font found grueling. Anza's custom on the trail was to eat nothing after breakfast until he camped in the evening. Font had endured this silently for months, but he now felt confident enough in dealing with Anza to complain. One afternoon he asked if they might stop soon to eat. Anza replied that the eggs they had for breakfast were enough to last him until nightfall. "But what are a couple of eggs?" Font protested. "I'm forced to admit I'm a man and I need to eat when I'm hungry. Isn't

---

27. Ibid., 182.
28. Rivera y Moncada in Geiger, *Life and Times*, 2:94.

there anything at hand?"²⁹ Anza was taken aback, but thereafter he paused each day at noon for a bite.

Their route up the coast followed the path pioneered by Portolá in 1769 until they turned inland near Mission San Luis Obispo. Along Santa Bárbara Channel, Chumash Indians who had welcomed Portolá's party were now sullen and withdrawn. Soldiers passing through recently had perpetrated "seizures and acts of violence," Font explained, causing women to hide in their lodges and men to block the doors.³⁰ Given the potential for hostilities, plans to colonize this area would have to wait until enough Spanish troops were available to man a presidio and guard new missions. To repair the damage caused by soldiers there required more soldiers, preferably men with wives like those recruited by Anza, who vowed to punish severely anyone in his party who assaulted or provoked Indians.

Five missions had been established in California since the arrival of Portolá and Serra. (Work on a sixth, San Juan Capistrano, had been delayed by the uprising at San Diego.) The distance between those missions placed an emotional burden on friars. "Living so alone and far from each other as they do, the day they see any company is an unusual one," Font related. By "company," he meant fellow Spaniards. Friars were surrounded by neophytes but had difficulty communicating with them. One notable exception was Father Buenaventura Sitjar at Mission San Antonio, who had mastered the language of surrounding Salinans. Their dialect was "hard to pronounce because of all the clicking in it," Font noted, but Sitjar approximated it phonetically and wrote a catechism in the language.³¹ Salinans, for their part, had learned to recite prayers in Spanish.

On March 10 the colonists reached Monterey, drenched by rain but overjoyed to have found safe harbor. The trail into town ran through "lovely country," Font rhapsodized, "green, lush, flowery, fertile, handsome, and splendid." By comparison, the presidio looked dismal. Font spent the night there "in a dirty little room full of lime."

---

29. Font, *With Anza to California*, 210.
30. Ibid., 220.
31. Ibid., 235, 238.

Nearby San Carlos struck him as far more promising—the best of the colony's missions, he judged, and a fitting tribute to their president, Serra, who presided there with Juan Crespí. With them were Francisco Palóu and three other friars, awaiting assignment to the two new missions planned for San Francisco Bay. Such a gathering of brothers was rare on the frontier and a joyous occasion for Font, who had the honor of delivering a sermon at the presidio chapel and spoke with greater charity than he had summoned earlier in the desert, paying tribute to Anza "for the patience, wisdom, and courtesy which he as a leader has had in guiding this expedition."[32]

On March 23 Anza and Font left the colonists at Monterey and proceeded to San Francisco Bay to select sites for settlement. Four days later, they stood and looked out across the Golden Gate. In all his travels, Font had seen no place that "pleased me so much as this one." If it were ever as well-populated as Europe, he added, "nothing in the world could be finer." Anza and Font arrived in fine spring weather, when the hills were green and covered with flowers. Had they come instead in late summer to find the grass withered and the coast shrouded in fog, they might have been less hopeful about the prospects for colonization here. The soil was poor, and neither Spaniards from the south nor California Indians from sunnier areas less exposed to the sea would find the climate congenial. Anza might have learned from the observations of Fathers Crespí and Palóu, who had explored the area and entrusted their journals to Font. But much to his dismay, Anza took no interest in their work, saying that he "would do whatever he thought best."[33] In truth, he had little choice but to locate the presidio near the entrance to the harbor for defensive purposes.

Although the peninsula was not ideal for settlement, it offered good grazing for livestock and fresh streams and lakes that could be used to irrigate crops. On Friday, March 29, Anza's party came upon a stream that Font christened Arroyo de los Dolores, for Our Lady of Sorrows, whose feast was celebrated on that day, a week before Good Friday. He found it "a very lovely spot" and judged it

---
32. Ibid., 243, 247.
33. Ibid., 277, 279.

the best site in the vicinity for the first of the two missions planned for the bay.[34] Mission San Francisco de Asís, known informally as Mission Dolores, would be founded there later that year. It was left to Rivera y Moncada to select a site for the second mission— Santa Clara de Asís, founded in January 1777 on the Guadalupe River near the southern end of San Francisco Bay. That was small compensation for the commandant, who saw Anza reaping glory while he cleaned up the mess in San Diego. The simmering rivalry between the two men came to a boil shortly after Anza left Monterey in April, having handed responsibility for the colonists to Lieutenant Moraga, who would conduct them to San Francisco and oversee construction of the presidio. As Anza mounted his horse in Monterey to return home, appreciative colonists, especially those of "the feminine sex," he wrote, "came to me sobbing with tears . . . They showered me with embraces, best wishes, and praises which I do not merit."[35]

One man who was not sorry to see Anza go was Rivera y Moncada, who informed him by letter that he refused to "permit the establishment of the fort of San Francisco."[36] They had a chance to resolve their dispute in late April when both were at Mission San Gabriel. But by then they were so deeply at odds that they could not bear to be in the same room. As Font related on April 30: "We remained here at this mission and the two commanders communicated with each other in writing . . . one of them from out of his room and the other from out of his tent. Each man relayed his messages by means of his own soldier."[37] Serra and Pedro Fages had come to a similar impasse a few years earlier, and many such quarrels would occur in the future. Rancor at high levels came naturally to California, where the overlapping claims of religious, military, and civil appointees and their distance from higher authorities in remote capitals allowed minor jurisdictional disputes to mushroom into poisonous power struggles.

---

34. Ibid., 283.
35. Anza in Bolton, *Anza's California Expeditions*, 3:155.
36. Ibid., 3:157.
37. Font, *With Anza to California*, 368; Guerrero, *The Anza Trail*, 202–10.

Ultimately, Rivera y Moncada accepted the colonization of San Francisco as decreed by the viceroy. But the quarrel brought Anza's sojourn in California to a bitter end and served as a reminder that this latter-day promised land, like the biblical Canaan, was a highly contentious place. Anza's relations with Font deteriorated as well as they headed east. Font's thoughts turned somber as they made their way back through San Carlos Pass, where Indians hid from them among the rocks. He called them "children of fear and of night."[38] With their California idyll behind them, Font and Anza soon lost sight of what they held in common.

By June 1 they were back in Sonora at Anza's hometown of San Miguel de Horcasitas. Font was invited to a fandango at Anza's house to mark their safe return and would have liked to attend, to show that he too was "happy that we have completed our journey so successfully." But Anza had turned down his proposal for a thanksgiving Mass, and in response Font declined to attend the fandango. He did not wish to take part in festivities "without first having publicly given thanks to God."[39] The inability of these two proud men to join in celebrating one of Spain's proudest feats on the northern frontier testified to deeply divided loyalties among those serving God and king on the contested margins of this overburdened empire.

---

38. Font, *With Anza to California*, 376.
39. Ibid., 404.

CHAPTER 4

Settlement and Strife

The discord between Anza and Font during their colonizing expedition was a passing squall compared to the storm brewing in California between Father-President Junípero Serra and Governor Felipe de Neve. In July 1776 Neve was ordered by Viceroy Bucareli to leave Loreto and take up residence in Monterey, which would now serve as the capital of California. This coincided with the appointment of Teodoro de Croix as commander general of the Internal Provinces, a new department embracing California, Sonora, New Mexico, Texas, and other northern territories. The goal was to unite the frontier administratively, improve its defenses, and promote settlement and economic self-sufficiency within a troubled region that continued to drain the royal treasury. Croix communicated with Viceroy Bucareli and drew on him for supplies but ran his sprawling department largely as he saw he fit, with guidance from King Carlos III and his ministers.

These changes spelled trouble for Serra, who had won major concessions from the devout Bucareli but would now have to reckon with two men, Neve and his superior Croix, who were less inclined to defer to missionaries. Like Croix, Neve, born in Spain in 1727, had been instrumental in expelling the Jesuits from New Spain and worried that the Franciscans too might become a power unto themselves, challenging the Crown's authority. Serra had clashed repeatedly with Fages and Rivera y Moncada over jurisdictional matters, but he had never faced an antagonist like Neve, the first man to rule officially as governor in Monterey and the first to challenge Serra's plan for California by advancing a program of his own, in which padres would play a reduced role.

Neve did not reach Monterey until February 1777. In the interim, the settlement of San Francisco moved forward. Colonists took formal possession of the newly built presidio there on September 17, 1776, and Mission San Francisco was dedicated a few weeks later. For Father Francisco Palóu, who had long been awaiting this assignment, the ceremony was marred by the absence of any potential converts. Indians living in the area had recently been attacked by another band and fled. Some returned to the peninsula in the fall but clashed with Spanish soldiers and hurriedly withdrew. Not until the following spring did they dare approach the mission. "They were attracted by trinkets and presents," Palóu wrote. Some found it better to accept those gifts and the obligations that came with them than to remain in exile and risk further hostilities with rival Indians or intruding colonists. Neophytes who once went about naked like "so many Adamites... without the slightest embarrassment," Palóu observed, received clothing at the mission and like the fallen Adam learned to be ashamed of their bare bodies: "Now they do not undress before others, least of all before the priest."[1]

Serra welcomed the founding of the San Francisco presidio, from which troops were dispatched to guard Missions San Francisco and Santa Clara. He had given impetus to the Anza expedition by urging Viceroy Bucareli to send married soldiers to California as a way of improving morale and reducing assaults by soldiers on Indian women. But he did not want pueblos established there, an objective to which Neve turned his attention soon after arriving in Monterey in order to reduce the colony's reliance on imported

---

1. Palóu, *Palóu's Life*, 192–95.

supplies. The missions still faced occasional food shortages, and the presidios were heavily dependent on provisions shipped from the south at great expense. Neve proposed to supply the presidios with food produced at pueblos settled by experienced Mexican farmers. This too would involve some expense. Settlers would receive rations and a small salary and would be granted livestock and tools as loans, to be repaid in the form of produce for the presidios. In the long run, Neve reckoned, the investment would pay off by making California less of a burden for the Crown financially and fostering towns whose able-bodied men could serve as a militia in support of regular troops.

Serra saw this as a dangerous diversion for a colony whose main purpose, in his view, was to convert Indians. He drove home his point in a letter to Croix: "Missions, Señor, missions are what this land needs and they will provide not only the principal thing, which is the light of the Holy Gospel, but also food for themselves and for the royal presidios better than these towns which have no resident priests."[2] Serra proved prophetic in stating that missions would one day help feed presidios, but Croix could not be sure of this and shared Neve's hope that establishing pueblos would be a first step on the path to a self-sustaining, secular colony. Serra found the idea of secularizing California appalling. It meant exposing neophytes to a frontier society whose temptations might prevent them from entering a better world to come. The pueblos Neve instituted with Croix's approval struck Serra as godforsaken places, without even secular (parish) priests in residence, and he saw no place for them in a colonizing effort that he continued to regard as a Sacred Expedition.

For California's first pueblo, Neve chose a fertile site on the east bank of the Guadalupe River, across from Mission Santa Clara. So eager was he to establish the town, known as San José de Guadalupe, that he took nine soldiers from the presidios of San Francisco and Monterey and made them *pobladores* (villagers) along with their wives and children. The first census of San

---

2. Serra in Geiger, *Life and Times*, 2:165.

José, taken shortly after the town was dedicated on November 29, 1777, listed several couples who had come there from Sonora under Anza with growing families, including Gabriel Peralta and Francisca Valenzuela (who kept her maiden name according to Spanish custom) with three children; Manuel Gonzales and Micaela Ruiz with five children; Joaquín de Castro and María Botiller with five children and a young Indian farmhand; Valerio Mesa and María Leonor Borboa with seven children; and Felipe Santiago Tapia and Juana María Cárdenas with eight children. These families made up more than half the town's original population of sixty-eight, among whom were other veterans of Anza's expedition. Some of those settlers were identified as Spaniards, while others were listed as mestizos or *mulatos*, a term applied to dark-skinned Hispanics known or presumed to be partly of African heritage.[3] One settler, Manuel Gonzales, was identified as an Apache Indian—most likely captured as a boy and raised by settlers in Sonora. Overall, the pioneers of San José were representative of a racially diverse Mexican or New Spanish society epitomized by the patroness of the Anza expedition, Our Lady of Guadalupe, whose name is no longer attached to the city that grew up there but still graces the river that runs through it.

Like most early structures in Spanish California, the first houses in San José were temporary shelters of poles and brush, covered with clay and roofed with thatch. In time, settlers would build more durable homes using adobe bricks, but living arrangements remained spartan. Floors were of packed earth, and cooking was usually done in an adobe oven detached from the house, which reduced the risk of fire and kept homes cooler in summer. As elsewhere in New Spain, houses were set close together around the town plaza. This fortlike arrangement was partly defensive and partly a matter of a cultural preference. By living close together, Spanish colonists signaled that they were sociable, civilized, and rational—and thus distinguished themselves from Indians who roamed the countryside. The policy of *reducción* (concentrating

---

3. Oscar Osburn Winther, "The Story of San Jose, 1777–1869," 4–6.

Indians at missions) reflected the assumption that a close, communal, settled life had a civilizing effect on Native peoples (whose strong communal bonds in their traditional societies were largely overlooked by colonists). Through this process, it was hoped, some California Indians would follow the same path as the Apache Manuel Gonzales and become *gente de razón*: rational people equipped to live in towns and join colonial society.

After initial setbacks, San José began to prosper. In 1781 Neve reported proudly that San José provided the San Francisco and Monterey presidios with all the food they needed. For surrounding Indians, however, this seemingly successful experiment was a mixed blessing. Some worked for the *pobladores*, but they were not always fairly compensated in goods or coins, which were scarce in California. Lieutenant Moraga, who served as commandant at San Francisco and oversaw the pueblo, worried that resentful Indians would attack San José and issued an edict governing their employment: "In no case are they to be brought in by force. Those who want to come are to be paid according to the work that they have done, so that they will return to their villages content."[4]

The padres at nearby Mission Santa Clara saw the pueblo as a threat to the welfare of Indians living in the area and an obstacle to their own efforts to attract converts. When cattle and other livestock strayed beyond the pueblo, some Indians responded by killing the animals, which in turn brought reprisals. The padres blamed settlers at San José for failing to restrain their animals and defended the right of Indians to "slaughter such livestock as trespass onto their lands, without being subject to any penalty whatever."[5] But missions like San Gabriel that were further along in their development than Santa Clara also had large herds of cattle and sheep that ranged widely and caused similar problems. In years to come, the vast herds amassed by colonists would have a devastating impact on the traditional subsistence activities of California Indians, prompting some to raid for livestock and others

---

4. Moraga in Milliken, *Time of Little Choice*, 75.
5. José Murguía and Tomás de la Peña in ibid., 73.

to enter missions or seek work at presidios or pueblos. Colonization had a ruthless momentum that overrode the scruples of civil and religious authorities in California who claimed to have the interests of Indians at heart and were in fact more conscientious in dealing with Native peoples than many colonizers of their day. Their mutual recriminations served to divert them from the realization that they were partners in a conquest that proved deeply unsettling for Native Californians.

One point on which Neve and Serra agreed was that Indian offenders should not be treated too harshly by European standards. Neve had Indians found guilty of stealing or killing livestock flogged and placed in stocks. Like Serra—who sometimes flogged himself to mortify his flesh and atone for sins—he considered such corporal punishment salutary and deemed it appropriate for wayward children or dependents, a category embracing Indian offenders of all ages. As the padres at one mission declared in defense of the penalties they imposed on neophytes, bodily punishment was a right that "God concedes to parents, for the good education of their children."[6] Spaniards found it hard to imagine how shameful such treatment was for California Indians, who disciplined children by scolding rather than striking them and punished most crimes by requiring offenders to pay restitution. Neve tried to soften the blow by offering Indians subjected to corporal punishment kind words and gifts before releasing them, but such mixed messages may have been more confusing than consoling.

Even those who attacked Spaniards or plotted uprisings did not know what to expect if captured. The rebel Carlos, for example, who helped organized the assault on Mission San Diego in 1775, was released after a term of imprisonment and later took part in other disturbances. Neve eventually banished him and several of his confederates, despite Serra's appeals on their behalf. "I have a particular affection for them and long for the salvation of their souls," Serra wrote.[7] Carlos was released from banishment after

---

6. Estevan Tapis and Juan Cortés in Hackel, *Children of Coyote*, 322, 359–64.
7. Serra in Geiger, *Life and Times*, 2:308.

six years at the urging of Fermín Francisco de Lasuén, Serra's successor as father-president.

Several other rebel chiefs were pardoned by Neve in 1777 after they were arrested for planning an uprising. When they continued to plot against the colonists, Sergeant Mariano Carrillo—who had earlier complained of harsh treatment by former commandant Fages—was sent out with a detachment from San Diego by Lieutenant Ortega to bring them in. One chief had boasted that he "hoped the soldiers would come so the Indians could get their hands on them and kill them." Carrillo and his men surprised the rebels in their village before dawn, Ortega reported: "The soldiers overpowered the chiefs and tied them up. They killed two Indians and burned a few in a hut when they would not surrender." Four chiefs hauled back to San Diego confessed that they had "planned to kill the Christians in spite of the pardon they had got in the King's name." Ortega condemned them to be shot to death in the presence of neophytes from Mission San Diego, hoping that the grim spectacle would "stimulate them to live right." He asked the two friars there to offer the condemned men one last chance to convert: "I trust that you will cooperate for the good of their souls, with the understanding that if they accept the saving waters of Holy Baptism they die next Saturday, the 11th, in the morning; and if not, likewise."[8]

This was not the sort of duty that Serra and his Franciscan brethren relished. They wanted to be seen by Indians as guardians, standing between them and the soldiers, whom padres regarded as the chief cause of unrest in California. Governor Neve, for his part, suspected that ill treatment of neophytes by the mission fathers lay at the root of the colony's persistent Indian problems. The plight of neophytes, he charged, was "worse than that of slaves." His attempts to remedy the situation, he added, were frustrated by Franciscans who insisted on remaining "independent and sovereign in their control over the Indians and the Indians' wealth, without recognizing any other authority than that of their own religious

---

8. Ortega in Edwin A. Beilharz, *Felipe de Neve: First Governor of California*, 71–72.

superiors." Serra would not submit annual reports on conditions at the missions to Neve as requested because he was under orders to submit them only to his superior in Mexico City. Nor would he stop performing confirmations until Neve could inspect and approve the papal document authorizing Serra to administer that sacrament, as required by law. "I know the unspeakable artifice and cleverness of this reverend father," Neve wrote Croix. "There is no mischief these religious will not attempt if exasperated, such is their boundless unbelievable pride."[9]

Reform Resisted

All this reinforced Neve's conviction that Franciscans had too much power over Indians and too little respect for civil authority. His proposed solution was to increase the number of missions while reducing the number of padres at most sites from two to one—the exception being missions near presidios, where the second father would serve as presidio chaplain. The restructured missions would need only one missionary because he would not oversee the daily lives of neophytes, who would live and work in their own villages on mission land and rely on the padre only for religious instruction and services.

Neve's plan was ingenious, enlightened, and impractical. Some mission Indians were learning Spanish and agricultural skills, but few would be ready to join colonial society any time soon, whether neophytes remained under strict Franciscan supervision or achieved greater autonomy under Neve's plan. Tribal customs such as polygamy as practiced by chiefs were not easily rooted out in missions overseen by two friars and would surely persist in the largely unsupervised neophyte villages that Neve envisioned. His plan embodied the wishful thinking of Spanish imperial reformers of the day, who hoped that by liberalizing the mission system they could accelerate the laborious process of eradicating tribal traditions and transforming Indians into dutiful Christians and

---

9. Neve in ibid., 52, 60.

loyal Spanish subjects. Converting people to suit the requirements of an imperial culture was not a liberal undertaking, and placing mission Indians under less restraint might only make them less inclined to serve Spaniards and conform to their demands.

Neve's plan was never put to a test because Franciscans would not stand for it. Those at the College of San Fernando in Mexico City appealed directly to the king. Two friars were needed at each mission not just to supervise neophytes, they argued, but to keep up each other's morale. A missionary living alone among Indians might forget his vows, they warned: "Even if the religious on leaving their college were saints, they would cease to be such."[10] The Crown heeded such arguments and ruled that no friar could preside alone over a mission and that padres would remain in charge of "temporalities" (the land and labor of Indians). Neve believed that Franciscans wanted this to enhance their authority at the Crown's expense. Serra feared that if he lost control of temporalities Indians and their property would fall into the uncharitable grasp of soldiers and settlers.

Neve succeeded in limiting the temporal authority of missionaries somewhat by issuing a decree in December 1778 requiring that neophytes elect their own leaders, including *regidores* (councilmen) and *alcaldes* (magistrates), who would oversee the punishment of other neophytes and could not be punished themselves except by military tribunal. Serra worried that this would make neophytes less obedient to the padres. After a heated argument in which he shouted at Neve, he spent a sleepless night and became so agitated that he was unable to pray. "What is the matter with me, O Lord?" he asked aloud, at which point a gospel verse came to him: "Be prudent as serpents and simple as doves." As he explained in a letter to Father Lasuén at Mission San Diego, this meant that it was "best to put into execution what the governor asks, but in such a way that it cannot cause the least change among the Indians nor in the system of the mission." Padres should select the candidates and manage the elections, he explained, so that Indians would behold

---

10. Quoted in Geiger, *Life and Times*, 2:259.

in them "no less authority than they did before."[11] Those elected under this system did not always behave as the padres wished—one was accused of supplying Indian women "to as many soldiers as wanted them."[12] But missionaries retained greater control over neophytes and their elected leaders than Neve intended.

Although largely thwarted in his efforts to reform the mission system, Neve had a powerful impact on California in other respects. He arranged for soldiers who had been compensated only in goods to be paid partly in coin, providing a helpful infusion of cash for an economy that relied largely on barter. And he increased the civilian and military presence in California by founding a second pueblo, at Los Angeles, and a fourth presidio, at Santa Bárbara. That fort would provide guards for new missions among the Chumash and protect a fragile link in the emerging Mission Trail (known officially as El Camino Real) between San Francisco and San Diego, a road used by colonists, couriers, and mule trains as well as friars. Around Santa Bárbara, the trail ran along the beach in places, and travelers were vulnerable to attack from the cliffs above. Neve had reason to fear resistance from the Chumash, who had suffered abuses by soldiers. The Santa Bárbara presidio would further enhance California by developing into a community of some importance as soldiers settled there and raised families.

To provide soldiers for Santa Bárbara and existing presidios, and civilians for Los Angeles, two expeditions to California were launched in 1781. Both were organized by Captain Rivera y Moncada, who had hoped to retire several years earlier but was still serving dutifully under Neve as commandant at Loreto. He recruited colonists in Sonora and Sinaloa and formed them into two parties. He himself would lead the main party of soldiers and their kin to California by the route Anza pioneered. They would stop along the Colorado River, where two Spanish colonies had recently been established among the Yumas that brought together missionaries, soldiers, and settlers in a way never before attempted

---

11. Serra in ibid., 2:246–47; Hackel, *Children of Coyote*, 235–39.
12. Quoted in Sandos, *Converting California*, 73.

on the frontier. A smaller party led by Lieutenant José de Zúñiga, including eleven civilian families bound for Los Angeles, would sail for Baja California and travel overland to Mission San Gabriel. That was a harrowing journey for people who dreaded going to sea, but the path the main party followed was perilous as well.

Few if any colonists would have undergone such ordeals without incentives, notably the promise of pay and rations. (Civilians received compensation for several years, while soldiers remained on the payroll permanently.) One civilian who enlisted—a widow in Zúñiga's party named Nicolasa Ramírez—may have been seeking a husband, for eligible Mexican women were much in demand in California. She soon caught the eye of Guillermo Soto, a soldier who helped escort the settlers to Mission San Gabriel, where the two were married. Meanwhile, Neve was reaching out to Indians living near the site he chose for the new pueblo. Meeting with tribespeople in a village along what is now the Los Angeles River, the governor did some proselytizing, as if to show the friars that they were not the only ones who could convert Indians. He acted as godfather to a dozen boys and girls from the village, who were baptized at San Gabriel, and lent his surname to a young Indian couple who were formally united there "in the eyes of the Church."[13] He hoped that residents of the pueblo he founded would deal amicably with surrounding Indians and hasten their conversion, thus providing an alternative to the missions, which he viewed in much the same light as Franciscans regarded the pueblos: as threats to the welfare of Indians and the security of the colony.

Some of those in Zúñiga's party were suffering from smallpox—one of several diseases that spread from colonists to California Indians with dire effect—and were held in quarantine before traveling to the site of the pueblo. Founded on September 4, 1781, Los Angeles had much the same makeup as San José. Among the forty-four civilians and four soldiers present were settlers classified as Spaniards, Indians, *mulatos*, or *negros* (blacks), such as 55-year-old

---

13. Neve in Harry Kelsey, "A New Look at the Founding of Old Los Angeles," 328; J. Gregg Layne, "Annals of Los Angeles," 198–201.

Luis Quintero, who arrived with his wife, María Petra Rubio, and five children. Within a year, the population of Los Angeles had been reduced to eight families, numbering thirty-two people in all, and they struggled to get by. Through neglect, Neve reported, "they lost their first crop of corn. The plants, already sprouted, dried up because of their carelessness in not opening up the irrigation ditch soon enough to water them." What was needed was "an active and exacting man there who will bestir the settlers to cultivate their crops."[14] The pioneers found such an overseer in José Vicente Feliz, who served as the pueblo's *comisionado* (a soldier appointed to oversee the town and its chosen alcalde). Within a decade of its founding, Los Angeles had 139 inhabitants, living in adobe houses and storing harvests from their well-irrigated fields in a granary.

The Yuma Uprising

For Neve, the founding of Los Angeles was overshadowed by devastating news that reached him in late August 1781. On July 17 Yumas had attacked the Spanish colonies on the Colorado and obliterated them. Most of the party led by Rivera y Moncada had passed through safely to California by then, but he himself had stayed behind with more than a dozen soldiers on the east bank to allow horses and other livestock that were too weak to cross the river to recuperate. He and his men died in the uprising along with most of the male colonists at the Colorado settlements—among them Father Francisco Garcés, whose cordial relations with Yumas in past years did not shield him from retribution.

The Yuma uprising had its origins in the relationship that Garcés and Anza forged with the Yuma chief Salvador Palma, who traveled with Anza to Mexico City to urge Spanish authorities to establish a mission or settlement among his people. Arriving there in early 1777, he underwent baptism and presented to Viceroy Bucareli a petition transcribed and edited by Anza. Palma claimed

---

14. Neve in Beebe and Senkewicz, *Lands of Promise and Despair*, 225; Kelsey, "New Look at the Founding of Old Los Angeles," 331; Jean Bruce Poole and Tevvy Ball, *El Pueblo: The Historic Heart of Los Angeles*, 8–11.

that from the moment Anza informed him "of the Supreme Being ... I resolved to be a Christian, even if it should be at a cost of my life." When he learned later that "polygamy was condemned by the Catholic Church," Palma added, he outlawed the practice: "and today there is not a single example of it, for I did not exempt my own brother, from whom I took away seven of the wives which he had."[15] If, indeed, he forced Ygnacio Palma to give up polygamy, it may have cost Ygnacio support among tribal traditionalists, who respected men wealthy and generous enough to support several wives. Ygnacio later figured prominently in the Yuma uprising.

Prompted by Palma's petition and a desire to secure the route to California that Anza pioneered, Spanish authorities made plans to settle soldiers and missionaries among the Yumas. Both Anza and Garcés recommended that two presidios be established in the region. But Croix, as commander general of the Internal Provinces, could not afford to maintain presidios as well as missions or pueblos in such remote locations. Instead he came up with a plan that would be less expensive for the Crown and would give missionaries less control over Indians, a goal he shared with Neve. Two settlements that he called "pueblos or military colonies" would be established along the Colorado.[16] Each would have two friars who would minister to any Yumas desiring their services but would not control the land or labor of Indians and would not be allowed to punish them, a task left to the commandant. The friars would function more like parish priests, serving both the Indians and the 160 or so Spanish soldiers and settlers at the two colonies, roughly two-thirds of whom were women and children.

Croix urged the inexperienced commandant of this expedition, Santiago Islas, who held the rank of *alférez* (ensign), to use moderation in dealing with the Yumas. But even a seasoned officer like Anza, who was now serving as governor of New Mexico, would have had difficulty reconciling Indians to the presence of so many colonists. Croix's efforts to economize meant that Salvador Palma

---

15. Palma in Bowman and Heizer, *Anza and the Northwest Frontier*, 150–53.
16. Croix in Jack D. Forbes, *Warriors of the Colorado: The Yumas of the Quechan Nation and Their Neighbors*, 185.

did not receive the lavish gifts he hoped for when the colonists arrived in late 1780. Instead the poorly provisioned newcomers relied on Yumas for food and antagonized them by allowing livestock to roam free and trample their fields. Islas made things worse by prevailing on Palma to flog defiant Yumas and by placing his brother Ygnacio in the stocks for insulting Garcés, who lost his good opinion of these Indians when they resisted conversion, dismissing them in writing as "much too stupid to be attracted by spiritual things."[17] (In fact, Yumas were deeply concerned with spirit power, which they derived from dreams that guided warfare and other activities.) The arrival of Rivera y Moncada and his California-bound colonists in June 1781 was the last straw for exasperated Yumas. Even Salvador Palma forsook the Spaniards and joined in the hostilities, hoping to regain prestige among his disenchanted followers.

María Montielo, the wife of Santiago Islas, lived through the fiery uprising in July that claimed the life of her husband and many others. "Realizing that the whole Yuma nation had risen up against us," she wrote afterward, "I gathered the women together and we fled for our lives to the church," where they argued bitterly over who was to blame for their plight. "Let's forget now whose fault it is," Garcés told them, "and simply consider it God's punishment for our sins." Soon Yumas began to burn their houses, Montielo related, "and kill as many of our people as they could. That was the night my heart was broken, when my beloved husband was clubbed to death before my very eyes."[18]

Rivera y Moncada and his soldiers were of no help in this crisis. Stranded on the east bank of the Colorado, across from the settlements, they were overwhelmed and annihilated there. Montielo and other survivors managed to slip away with Garcés and another friar, Father Juan Barraneche. The two missionaries then left her and others by a lagoon. "Stay together," they urged the women and children, "do not resist capture, and the Yumas will not harm you."

---

17. Garcés in ibid., 193–94.
18. María Montielo, "The Colorado Massacre of 1781: María Montielo's Report," 223.

Indeed, nearly half the colonists, most of them women and children, survived as captives and were later ransomed. The priests, for their part, expected no mercy. A Yuma whose wife had converted to Christianity took them in, but they were seized a few days later. "The enemy fell upon them as they sat in the Yuma's dwelling, drinking chocolate," wrote Montielo, who learned of their fate from a fellow captive who witnessed the scene. "Come outside," the priests were ordered by their assailants. "We're going to kill you." Garcés asked if he and Barraneche could have a moment's respite to "finish our chocolate," but they were denied that last request. "Time and again I heard that many of the Yumas did not want to see the fathers killed," Montielo stated. "Nevertheless, their blood was spilled, and the woman who told me of this was close enough to hear their pitiful moans as they lay dying."[19]

The damage this uprising did to Spanish interests on the frontier was never repaired. In September 1782, after overseeing construction of the Santa Bárbara presidio, Neve led troops to the Colorado, where he linked up with forces from Sonora in a punitive campaign against the Yumas. Hoping for a decisive victory that would allow Spain to recolonize the area, they succeeded only in putting the Yumas to flight after attacking one of their villages. The troops were not equipped to stay long, and as soon as they left Yumas reclaimed their homeland. Spanish relations with these indispensable Indians had been severed, and the promising route pioneered by Anza was abandoned.

This ominous setback signaled the end of Spain's last great burst of imperial expansion in America, embracing the entire southern tier of what is now the United States, from California to Florida, which Spain regained from Britain by siding with rebellious American colonists in 1779. That was purely an alliance of convenience, for Spanish royalists abhorred revolution and recognized the Americans as a growing threat to their empire. In 1783, shortly after Neve succeeded Croix as commander general of the Internal Provinces, he received a prophetic warning about the United States from an

---

19. Ibid., 224–25.

aide, Juan Gassiot. "A new and independent power has arisen on our continent," Gassiot wrote. "Its people are active, industrious, and aggressive." It would be "culpable negligence on our part," he added, not to "thwart their schemes for conquest."[20] Land-hungry Americans were already eyeing Florida, Louisiana, and east Texas, and soon American ships would begin prowling the coast of California.

The Yuma uprising weakened Spain's hold on California by depriving that isolated colony of a land bridge to the Mexican heartland. There would be no more Spanish colonizing expeditions to California, no more presidios built there, and only one more town established. California's non-Indian population would amount to only about three thousand by the end of the Spanish era. In that respect it was like Texas, which never had enough Spanish settlers to convince American expansionists that Spain, or later Mexico, had any real claim to the place. The situation was different in New Mexico, where there were more Spanish colonists (nearly twenty thousand) than Pueblo Indians by the late 1700s. Strenuous efforts had been made to open a route between New Mexico and California by Garcés and two other Franciscan explorers, Francisco Domínguez and Silvestre Escalante, who in 1776 explored much of what is now Utah in a circuitous and unsuccessful effort to establish a trail from Santa Fe to Monterey. The desert and mountains separating the two colonies were forbidding obstacles, and neither Yumas nor the Mohaves to their north could be counted on to welcome Spaniards at the Colorado and help them across.

Neve did not have long to lament the Yuma uprising or its consequences for California. By the time he took charge of the Internal Provinces, he was in failing health. He had not seen his wife since leaving Spain in 1764. In 1777, before moving to Monterey, he had asked to be relieved so he could return home to Seville. His request had been denied, much to California's benefit. Like Serra, he spent far more time than he liked writing letters and reports. He had no secretary and often copied his correspondence three or four times for record-keeping purposes. As governor he earned 4,000

---

20. Gassiot in Weber, *Spanish Frontier in North America*, 271, 273.

pesos a year, roughly ten times as much as the average soldier, but part of that went to pay for gifts he distributed to Indians he encountered. He died on August 21, 1784, after drawing up a last testament in which he begged forgiveness of God and man and offered all forgiveness in return. Perhaps he had Serra in mind.

A week later, on August 28, Serra died at Mission San Carlos, at the age of sixty-nine. With him at the time were Francisco Palóu and two visitors who had arrived recently by sea, the Spanish naval captain José Cañizares and chaplain Cristóbal Díaz. In his last hours, Serra thanked them for coming so far "to throw a little earth upon me." He then asked to be buried in the mission church beside Juan Crespí, his "companion of many years" at San Carlos, who had died in 1782. A short time later, Serra grew anxious. "Great fear has come upon me," he told Palóu. "I have a great fear. Read me the Commendation for a Departing Soul."[21]

It was not death that worried Serra but the fate of his soul. He had often referred to himself as a sinner and had been denied martyrdom, which according to Catholic doctrine would have assured him of salvation. Among the faults he acknowledged was that he and the friars under his supervision had not always been as charitable in dealing with Indians as they might have been. "I am aware that we are men and as such we can err," he wrote Croix on one occasion. But he expressed no doubts about the virtue of his mission system or the necessity of exercising strict control over neophytes. What mattered to him ultimately was not whether Indians were happier or healthier under his regimen than in their original state, although he hoped that they would be, but whether they were saved in the next life as a result of his efforts. When he entered California, he told Croix, "there was not a single Christian among the natives of this land. Now, thanks be to God, some thousands have been baptized and hundreds of them are enjoying God in heaven."[22]

Even in his own lifetime, Serra was a controversial figure, whose insistence that Indians must be assimilated through spiritual

---

21. Serra in Palóu, *Palóu's Life*, 247; Geiger, *Life and Times*, 2:238.
22. Serra in Geiger, *Life and Times*, 2:165, 224.

conquest and priestly supervision drew strong opposition from Neve and other authorities. This contest of principles, this earnest argument over how Native peoples should be treated, emerged from within the Spanish empire and became part of California's legacy, as reflected in the debate over whether Serra should properly be recognized as a saint. He himself simply hoped to enter heaven, and he felt more confident that he would after Palóu read the reassuring commendation. "Thanks be to God," he said, "I have no more fear."[23]

Cañizares thought that Serra might yet pull through and hoped aloud that he would be able to make "more journeys for the good of the poor Indians." Serra said nothing in response, Palóu noted, "but with a little smile made it very clear to us that he did not expect this, nor did he hope to get well." Then he lay down to rest, and a short time later Palóu found him "asleep in the Lord."[24]

---

23. Serra in Palóu, *Palóu's Life*, 247.
24. Palóu, *Palóu's Life*, 248.

Part Two
EXPOSED TO THE WORLD (1785–1825)

Reception of La Pérouse at Mission San Carlos, 1786.
Courtesy The Bancroft Library, University of California, Berkeley
(BANC PIC 1963.002:1311-FR).

CHAPTER 5

Overtures from Abroad

On September 14, 1786, two French ships approached Monterey in dense fog. Had their intentions been hostile they might have taken the town by surprise, but their arrival was in fact eagerly anticipated. France and Spain were on good terms. Pedro Fages, back in Monterey as governor after a troubled term there as commandant during the colony's infancy, had orders to welcome this pioneering French expedition, led by Captain Jean-François de Galaup, comte de La Pérouse. These were the first foreign ships granted entry to Spanish California.

Although privileged by birth, La Pérouse had earned this prestigious command by entering the French navy as a midshipman at fifteen and spending the better part of thirty years at sea. His expedition—which was intended to circumnavigate the globe but would end disastrously in the South Pacific—was prompted in part by the explorations of Captain James Cook, who had died in 1779 in a clash with Hawaiian islanders. Accounts of Cook's last voyage revealed that some of his men had profited greatly by selling in China sea-otter furs they obtained from Indians while visiting Nootka Sound along what is now Vancouver Island, territory claimed by Spain. Unlike the British and Russians, the French were not challenging Spanish claims to the Pacific Northwest, but they wanted to know more about the region and its economic potential. The voyage of La Pérouse, who stopped in Alaska before visiting Monterey, was part of an emerging international contest for resources, markets, and bases around the Pacific that would expose California to foreign pressures and intrusions.

As the French ships neared port, two Spanish vessels in the harbor fired their guns periodically to guide La Pérouse to anchorage through the fog, which was slowly lifting. Before sighting the town, he and his men were greeted by whales feeding in the bountiful waters of Monterey Bay. "They spouted every half minute within half a pistol shot of our frigates, and caused a most annoying stench," wrote La Pérouse, who saw pelicans in abundance here as well: "It appears that these birds never fly more than five or six leagues from land, and navigators who encounter them during a fog may be certain of being no further distant from it . . . The Spaniards call them *alcatraz*."[1]

Once in port, the French received royal treatment from Governor Fages and Captain Esteban José Martínez, commander of the visiting Spanish ships. (Two-ship expeditions of the sort led by Martínez and La Pérouse were common during this period, with the senior officer serving as captain of one vessel and commander of both.) "Cattle, garden vegetables, and milk were sent on board in abundance," wrote La Pérouse. Much of that was free, and the rest was billed to him at low prices only because he insisted on it. When it came to making the French welcome, Fages would not be outdone. "His house was our home, and all his people were at our disposal," La Pérouse observed.[2] He was the first of many foreign visitors to remark on the courtesy of California's residents to newcomers, which stemmed partly from their isolation and their yearning for company and news of distant events but also owed much to strong traditions of hospitality among Spaniards and Indians they assimilated.

---

1. Jean-François de Galaup, comte de La Pérouse, *Monterey in 1786: The Journals of Jean François de La Pérouse*, 54–55; Bancroft, *History of California*, 1:426–38.
2. La Pérouse, *Monterey in 1786*, 75–76.

Overtures from Abroad

Soon after arriving, La Pérouse and others in his party visited nearby Mission San Carlos, where Serra's successor, Father-President Fermín Lasuén, greeted them in his vestments and "chanted the *Te Deum* in thanksgiving for the happy outcome of our voyage." La Pérouse paid him generous tribute: "His mildness, charity, and affection for the Indians are beyond expression."[3] Yet Lasuén harbored doubts about his spiritual qualifications to succeed Serra. "This land is for apostles only," he wrote. "Loneliness in this work is for me a savage and cruel enemy." At one point, he had asked to be relieved so that he could return to the companionship of his Franciscan college, San Fernando. But Serra had insisted that Lasuén shoulder the hardest of tasks—supervising Mission San Diego in the aftermath of the revolt there in 1775. Obedience took its toll on Lasuén. When he succeeded Serra in 1785, he was not yet fifty but "already an old man," by his own account, "and completely gray." His awareness that duty and devotion required painful personal sacrifices made him sensitive to the discontents of Indians under his supervision. "The majority of our neophytes have not yet acquired much love for our way of life," he wrote, "and they see and meet their pagan relatives in the forest, fat, and robust, and enjoying complete liberty."[4] An Enlightenment philosopher could not have summed up the malaise of mission Indians any more eloquently.

When La Pérouse, a man of the Enlightenment, toured Mission San Carlos, he saw an institution that denied Indians liberty in ways that reminded him of slave plantations in the West Indies. The regimentation of the workday by the tolling of bells, the punishment of various sins or misdeeds "by irons and the stocks," the pursuit of fugitives by soldiers and the flogging of those brought back all ran counter to what his countryman Jean-Jacques Rousseau had defined as humanity's birthright: freedom.[5] Yet as La Pérouse knew from his journeys, few if any people around the

---

3. Ibid., 77, 87.
4. Lasuén in Francis F. Guest, *Fermín Francisco de Lasuén (1736–1803): A Biography*, 65, 67, 121, 207.
5. La Pérouse, *Monterey in 1786*, 82.

world enjoyed that right in full. "Man was born free," Rousseau wrote memorably, "and everywhere he is in chains."⁶

The question that La Pérouse and other lovers of liberty wrestled with was whether it was just to deny freedom to people considered primitive or backward until they were deemed capable of exercising that right. Parents, after all, kept their children under restraint until they were mature enough to act responsibly. La Pérouse believed that some regimentation and indoctrination of Indians was warranted if it taught them Christian morality and discipline. He felt that a picture in the church at San Carlos showing the torments of hell was a crude but effective lesson for neophytes. "I am persuaded that such a representation was never more useful in any country," he wrote. It would be impossible, he added, for Protestants who disdained sacred images and religious pageantry "to make any progress with this people."⁷

La Pérouse faulted Franciscans, however, for cloistering Indians and being "more attentive to their heavenly than their earthly concerns." Neophytes, he argued, needed more training in the "common arts." At the urging of Governor Fages, Mexican artisans would soon be sent to California to instruct neophytes in weaving, winemaking, ceramics, painting, and other skills. Schooling, however, would progress little beyond what he observed in 1786. Many neophytes learned to recite prayers in Spanish, and some learned to read and write, mastered musical instruments, or performed in choirs. But most gained little educationally to relieve what La Pérouse called "this state of ignorance, in which everything is directed to the recompenses of another life."⁸

For a visitor who remained in Monterey for little over a week, La Pérouse shrewdly assessed the state of affairs there. He recognized that mission Indians were not entirely without liberty. They often went off "to hunt and fish for their own benefit," he noted, "and upon their return they generally make a present to the missionaries of a part of their fish or game." He understood as

---

6. Jean-Jacques Rousseau, *The Social Contract and the First and Second Discourses*, 156.
7. La Pérouse, *Monterey in 1786*, 78.
8. Ibid., 87, 97.

well that the late Governor Neve and other Spanish officials had attempted to reform the mission system and make it "less monastic, affording more civil liberty to the Indians." Yet the election of neophyte alcaldes had done little to lessen the padres' authority, he observed. Those elected were "like the overseers of a plantation: passive beings, blind performers of the will of their superiors."[9] The acknowledgment that Indians had certain rights made California something of an exception, however, in a world where many colonizers exploited Native peoples with utter disregard for the high ideals of moral philosophers.

Some Europeans deplored the ruthless treatment of slaves or peons in far-flung colonies and hoped that their lot would improve as imperial powers pursued less-invasive forms of exploitation. British officials, for example, were now more interested in securing trade routes than in acquiring territory. Trading ventures sometimes led to colonization and conquest, as happened in British India and Russian Alaska. But trade was a quicker and potentially more profitable way of infiltrating and exploiting remote areas than wholesale colonization efforts like the Spanish occupation of California. There and elsewhere along the northern frontier of New Spain, the imperial policy of mercantilism, based on strictly controlled commerce that funneled precious metals and other raw materials from colonies to the motherland, proved unprofitable. Little mineral wealth had been discovered in the region and tribal resistance remained high, forcing the Crown to maintain troops in places where settlers were hard-pressed to meet their own needs. Hoping to make California less of a burden to the Crown financially, Spanish officials granted an entrepreneur named Vicente Vasadre y Vega—who was in Monterey when La Pérouse arrived—the exclusive right to trade in California for sea-otter skins, to be exported to China. Fages told La Pérouse that 20,000 skins "might be collected annually" in California between San Diego and San Francisco and even more north of that bay.[10]

---

9. Ibid., 84, 89–90.
10. Ibid., 100–103; Robert Archibald, *The Economic Aspects of the California Missions*, 116–18; Adele Ogden, *The California Sea Otter Trade, 1784–1848*, 15–31.

Such a haul could not have been sustained for long without depleting the species, as happened in later years.

The glittering hopes of Fages went unfulfilled. Vasadre managed to collect over 1,000 sea-otter pelts in Alta and Baja California in 1786, most of them gathered by Indians. But that was less than some ships engaged in the fur trade along the Northwest Coast obtained in one sailing, and Vasadre's business did not go smoothly. Padres received goods for the missions in exchange for pelts taken by their Indians but complained that the compensation was inadequate and did not like having neophytes absent on lengthy hunting expeditions. Soldiers and civilians soon muscled in on the trade by obtaining furs from Indians for little or nothing—some simply stole the hides—and selling them as the fruit of their own labor. Beyond California, the trade was even more problematic. The pelts went first to Mexico City for treatment before being shipped to China by way of Manila, where merchants of the Philippines Company resented competition from Vasadre and did all they could to thwart him. In 1790 the Crown withdrew his charter.

Success in the fur trade required greater flexibility than the hidebound Spanish mercantile system allowed. A few Spanish merchants received permission to trade in sea-otter pelts after Vasadre's business closed down, but most of the profits to be had along the California coast went to foreigners. Their visits were not legal, but Spain lacked the naval power to prevent ships from entering coastal inlets in pursuit of sea-otter skins and sealskins, which were less valuable but helped offset the costs of voyages that took years.

La Pérouse could not foresee the fate of Vasadre's initiative in 1786, but he would not have been surprised by the outcome. The development of California was being hindered, he concluded, by restrictive Spanish policies and a mission system that was not preparing neophytes to live free and enterprising lives. He believed that "good laws, particularly freedom of trade," would encourage settlement and bolster the colony more effectively than further infusions of troops or missionaries.[11] If those responsible for the

---

11. La Pérouse, *Monterey in 1786*, 103.

colony had shared his views and managed to implement them, California might have been better equipped to withstand the foreign incursions that undermined Spanish and later Mexican authority and left this land of incalculable promise up for grabs.

A Discerning Governor

The choice of Pedro Fages to succeed Governor Neve restored to authority a man who knew more about California than any other Spanish officer. That he had clashed with Serra as commandant was no blot on his record, for his successors had done the same. He dealt so cordially now with Lasuén that some called Fages *frailero* (friar lover).[12] He had taken part in the Portolá expedition to San Francisco Bay in 1769 and had later explored the San Joaquín Valley. Before returning to Monterey as governor, he drew on his reports to write the first comprehensive account of California and its people.

Fages doubted that Spanish colonists would easily assimilate California Indians. Those living between Missions San Diego and San Juan Capistrano, he reported, were "evil-looking, suspicious, treacherous, and have scant friendship for the Spaniards."[13] This uncharitable assessment, quite unlike that of Miguel Costansó and others who met with those Indians in 1769, reflected a hardening of attitudes as Native Californians resisted colonization. But in recognizing their powers of resistance, Fages showed greater appreciation for tribes as organized societies than did most early observers. Even Lasuén, who knew how hard it was to convert and control Indians, believed that they opposed mission efforts simply because they wanted to be free and return to their natural state, "without government, religion, or respect for authority."[14] Fages understood that California Indians had their own rules, beliefs, and traditions of leadership that would not easily be eradicated. Like other Spanish observers, he was particularly impressed with the Chumash, whom he found industrious and enterprising. In

---

12. Fages in Guest, *Fermín Francisco de Lasuén*, 155.
13. Pedro Fages, *A Historical, Political, and Natural Description of California*, 11.
14. Lasuén in Guest, *Fermín Francisco de Lasuén*, 278.

their "inclination to traffic and barter," he wrote, "it may be said in a way that they are the Chinese of California... They receive the Spaniards well, and make them welcome; but they are very warlike among themselves, living at almost incessant war, village against village."[15]

As commandant, Fages worried that his small force of soldiers would not be able to defend the mission system if it expanded too rapidly, and he guarded against that by stressing in his reports that the Chumash and other California Indians were armed and dangerous. Clashes between tribes or villages may not have been "almost incessant," but they were common enough. As Fages observed, California Indians had frequent disputes over "fruits of the earth" (natural resources) and over women. Most marriages were consensual, but some men stole wives in raids on rival bands. For prominent men, acquiring more than one wife was a sign of distinction. Among the Chumash, Fages noted, chiefs or captains "commonly enjoy the privilege of taking two or three wives, and putting them away at will."[16] By enforcing monogamy, missionaries undermined the prestige of tribal leaders, and some resisted their efforts. In one case, a neophyte serving as alcalde at Mission San Luis Obispo ran off with another man's wife. He was acting in a manner befitting captains in his society, but missionaries were appalled and concluded that these Indians had no conception of leadership and no respect for authority.

Even more shocking to missionaries was a practice that Fages observed among the Chumash and other tribes—the presence of a few men in each village who took on the "clothing and character" of women and acted as such with other men. They were called *joyas* (jewels), he noted, and were "held in great esteem."[17] Some chiefs had a regular wife or two in addition to a *joya*, prized because he was strong and good at housework. But *joyas* were not limited to

---

15. Fages, *Historical, Political, and Natural Description of California*, 31.
16. Ibid., 12, 33; Sandos, *Converting California*, 73.
17. Fages, *Historical, Political, and Natural Description of California*, 18; Sandos, *Converting California*, 23–26; Albert L. Hurtado, *Intimate Frontiers: Sex, Gender, and Culture in Old California*, 4–8.

relations with other men or domestic tasks. Some fathered children and played prominent roles outside the home. In 1785 Fages led an expedition inland from the coast near San Diego in the hope of opening a new route to the Colorado River and beyond. His aide sought a guide from local Indians and was offended when they offered him a woman for that task. But no offense was intended. As they explained, this woman was in fact a man, a *joya* who was esteemed for his knowledge of the country and "knew the road well."[18] *Joyas* were honored because they had special traits or powers that set them apart. Conceivably, that high regard for those set apart by nature or the spirits who controlled nature inclined California Indians to respect Catholic missionaries, who dressed and acted differently than other men.

In one way, at least, the mores of Spaniards and Indians here were similar. Among both groups, prominent men or captains often had more than one woman. Fages was no exception. When he returned to Monterey, he brought with him his wife, Eulalia Callis, the daughter of his former commander. She was in her mid-twenties, and he was nearly thirty years older. After giving birth to their second child in August 1784—earlier she had suffered a miscarriage and lost another child in infancy—she told Fages that she did not wish to remain in California. There were still relatively few Spanish women there, most of them mestizos. They faced the trials of childbirth and child-rearing with little or no medical assistance except that provided by midwives. For long periods, Monterey had no physician. People seeking cures relied largely on folk remedies, including herbal medicines provided by Indians. When doctors were present, they did not inspire much confidence. As Mexican chronicler Antonio María Osio wrote in later years of the military surgeon at Monterey, he "wanted to kill some more people before he died, but he could no longer find patients who had faith in him."[19]

18. Quoted in Forbes, *Warriors of the Colorado*, 222–23.
19. Antonio María Osio, *The History of Alta California: A Memoir of Mexican California*, 186; Antonia I. Castañeda, "Engendering the History of Alta California, 1769–1848," in Gutiérrez and Orsi, *Contested Eden*, 245–49.

The determination of Eulalia Callis to leave California caused a rift between her and Fages that widened into a scandalous breach. One day in early 1785, she testified, "I found my husband physically on top of one of his servants, a very young Yuma Indian girl." Fages may have acquired the servant while campaigning against the rebellious Yumas. A wife betrayed in this way might berate her husband privately, but she was not supposed to publicize his misdeeds, particularly if he was governor. "Even though prudence should have prevailed," she related, "I was overcome by passion, which fueled the flames of my rage, which caused me to cry out publicly against this infamy."[20]

When Callis failed to retract her accusations and forgive her husband, she was called before Father Matías Antonio de Noriega of Mission San Carlos. This was evidently not the first time Fages had been unfaithful to her, for when pressured by Noriega she refused to recant and "restore her husband's reputation (as if he had lost it with just that one woman)." She complained later that no testimony was taken from witnesses at the presidio, "such as midwives or others who have knowledge of the situation." Noriega denounced her on Ash Wednesday in the presidio chapel, she added, "and had the soldiers throw me out of church." Lent was a time of penance for all, but her ordeal was just beginning: "On my saint's day they tied me up and transferred me to Mission San Carlos," where Noriega threatened to have her "flogged and placed in shackles."[21]

The task of reconciling husband and wife fell to Captain Nicolás Soler, who came to California as an inspector for the viceroy and served as commandant at Monterey. Like Neve, Soler thought that missionaries had too much influence over civil affairs in California and saw the harsh confinement of Eulalia Callis at San Carlos as no less scandalous than her public dispute with her husband. He sympathized with the *señora gobernadora* (madam governor) but advised her to bear her punishment without protest. He warned Fages in turn that "behavior by a Governor who publicly offends

---

20. Callis in Beebe and Senkewicz, *Lands of Promise and Despair*, 237.
21. Ibid., 237–38.

Overtures from Abroad

his wife cannot be tolerated."[22] Soler's intervention may have done some good, for Callis was released and went back to Fages, gaining a reputation in Monterey for charity and good works.

Soler figured in another controversy around this same time by accusing Father Tomás de la Peña of violently mistreating Indians at Mission Santa Clara. Franciscan authorities considered Soler biased and dismissed his charges against Peña. A short time later, however, Fages saw Peña rebuke two Indian boys who were scuffling in church and pull their ears, drawing blood. With that in mind, he was inclined to believe the Indians who accused Peña in 1876 of beating four neophytes at Santa Clara to death. After lengthy inquiries, Peña was declared innocent, but Fages remained convinced that he was cruel to neophytes and punished them severely with "his own hand."[23] In a letter to Lasuén, Peña insisted that the ear-pulling incident was one of the few times he had ever treated Indians roughly and stated that he had once witnessed Fages striking with greater severity an Indian servant "who was his godchild."[24]

As this controversy underscored, the ongoing contest between Cross and Crown in California was not just about jurisdiction or control but about moral responsibility. Each side faulted the other for mistreating or manipulating Indians when in reality they were partners in the process of exploiting neophytes or making them serve Spaniards and their God and king. Nagging disputes between the two sides over issues such as whether the padres should have to perform services at presidios without compensation—Lasuén ordered friars to resume services at the San Francisco presidio in 1786 after what amounted to a three-year strike there—obscured the fact that missionaries and officials were cooperating in managing Indians and maximizing their output.

Missions were growing more populous and productive, and presidios were increasingly dependent on them for food. Between 1785 and 1795 the number of neophytes in the system more than

---

22. Soler in ibid., 239.
23. Fages in Hackel, *Children of Coyote*, 326–29.
24. Peña in Guest, *Fermín Francisco de Lasuén*, 171; Milliken, *Time of Little Choice*, 93–95.

doubled, to over 11,000. That figure represented only a small portion of California Indians as a whole but dwarfed the colony's Spanish population, which amounted to barely 1,000 in the census of 1790. The increase in the mission population did not mean that neophytes were thriving. To the contrary, death rates in missions exceeded birth rates. The worst epidemics were yet to come, but already diseases such as dysentery were taking a grim toll, particularly among infants. Venereal infections were also spreading rapidly and causing neophytes to become sterile or infecting children born to them. Spanish soldiers were partly responsible for that, as were Indians who accompanied the Franciscans there from Baja California, where the missions were in "decadent condition" because of syphilis, according to Fages.[25] Even padres were subject to infection through procedures such as bloodletting that Indians performed on them or, in some cases, through sexual contact, for not all honored their vow of chastity.

Franciscans kept the neophyte population growing despite high death rates and low birth rates by seeking more converts and founding new missions. During the 1780s more than a thousand Chumash entered the system at Missions San Buenaventura (1782), Santa Bárbara (1786), and La Purísima Concepción (1787). Those new missions benefited from hard lessons learned elsewhere in earlier years, when crops withered and neophytes went hungry. The irrigation works at Santa Bárbara, for example, featured a two-mile-long stone aqueduct that carried water from a dam high in the hills above. Irrigation and the introduction of new crops such as winter wheat led to impressive gains in production. Between 1785 and 1790, according to Franciscan records, the amount of wheat harvested at the missions doubled. The total number of cattle, horses, sheep, and other livestock in mission herds, meanwhile, was approaching 50,000. Occasional shortages caused by drought, blight, or floods that ruined dams still occurred, but in most years the missions raised enough food to meet their own needs and provide surpluses for sale to presidios. As Francisco Palóu wrote

---

25. Fages in Sherburne F. Cook, *The Conflict between the California Indian and White Civilization*, 26; Sandos, *Converting California*, 122–24; Archibald, *Economic Aspects of the California Missions*, 154; Donald C. Cutter, *Malaspina in California*, appendix D.

in 1787: "Would to God that the missions would be able to help the presidios at all times."[26] The padres were glad to see missions outproducing the pueblos, whose occupants they regarded as bad influences on Indians.

Presidios were literally indebted to the missions. In 1797 the presidio at Monterey ran up a debt of nearly 3,000 pesos to Mission San Carlos. Padres collected on their debts by purchasing much-needed goods such as iron tools, nails, and cloth, shipped from the south. That purchasing power caused some resentment toward Franciscans among soldiers and settlers who had little cash to spare. The missionaries did allow themselves a few imported luxuries such as tobacco, snuff, and chocolate, but most of what they purchased went to supply mission communities as a whole.

The growing indebtedness of presidios to missions gave Franciscans greater leverage in California economically and politically. Commandants and governors could ill afford to challenge a mission system on which they now depended. Fages was more of a pragmatist than a reformer, in any case, and his accommodation with Lasuén set a pattern followed by most governors who came after him. Economic considerations had a compromising effect on the padres as well. Although they feared contact between mission Indians and soldiers, they hired out neophytes to labor at presidios, where they often had to work longer and harder than they did at the missions. Although some were paid for their efforts, much of what they earned was credited to the padres and helped them sustain their missions and recruit new converts. Serra had sought control of the land and labor of Indians to ensure that neophytes remained under spiritual authority. But making profitable use of Indian land and labor had become an overriding concern on which the future of the missions and the colony they supported now depended. Soldiers and civilians wanted greater access to the labor and skills of neophytes, and Lasuén had to defend Franciscans against complaints that they were not hiring them out often enough. "Every time the presidios and private individuals ask for

---

26. Palóu in Archibald, *Economic Aspects of the California Missions*, 97–98; Steven W. Hackel, "Land, Labor, and Production: The Colonial Economy of Spanish and Mexican California," in Gutiérrez and Orsi, *Contested Eden*, 116–17.

Indians," he wrote, "as a rule they are given to them; and this does not happen rarely but very, very often."[27]

Although missions became the mainstay of the colony, the pueblos of San José and Los Angeles also produced surpluses in good years and helped support the presidios. Some *pobladores* of modest means in those towns hired Indian laborers who were not neophytes, paying them with food or clothing, often at less expense than it cost to employ mission Indians. This practice contributed to the emerging legend of the leisurely colonist, gadding about on horseback while his Indian peons grubbed in the dirt. Father Isidro Alonso Salazar, after retiring from California, wrote a letter to the viceroy in 1796 in which he portrayed the *pobladores* in the worst possible light. "The residents are a group of laggards," he asserted. "The Indian is errand boy, cowboy and manual laborer for them—in fact, general factotum ... the young men ride on horseback through the Indian villages, soliciting the women for immoral acts."[28] Like other missionaries, Salazar disdained the *pobladores* and may have overstated their faults. Colonists of all descriptions—priests, settlers, and soldiers—worked hard at times but relied substantially on Indian labor. These Indians were too uncivilized to control their own land and labor, it was argued. But any claim to refinement that California possessed, and any hope it had of thriving as Spain's imperial fortunes declined, rested on their efforts.

Spanish Surveys

During the 1790s mounting interest in the fur trade and the Pacific Northwest brought more than a few ships to California's shores, including several from Spain. Facing possible conflict with Great Britain over Nootka Sound and the trade for sea-otter pelts there, Spain made a major concession in 1790 by releasing two British ships seized at Nootka a year earlier and agreeing in principle to share the Pacific Northwest with Britain. This provisional accord, known as the Nootka Convention, was the first formal admission

---

27. Lasuén in Guest, *Fermín Francisco de Lasuén*, 235.
28. Salazar in Archibald, *Economic Aspects of the California Missions*, 94–95.

by Spain that it could not monopolize the Pacific Coast simply on the basis of prior visits by Spanish navigators. Britain and other nations recognized Spanish right of possession from Baja California to San Francisco Bay but regarded uncolonized areas to the north as open to international competition.

The Crown's desire to protect its interests in California and the Pacific Northwest brought one of the Spanish empire's leading navigators, Italian-born Alejandro Malaspina, to Monterey in 1791. Like the earlier voyage of La Pérouse, Malaspina's five-year expedition around the world was a scientific undertaking with strategic significance. Before visiting Monterey, two ships under Malaspina and Captain José Bustamante y Guerra, who was named co-commander with Malaspina but recognized him as chief, surveyed the Pacific Coast from Yakutat Bay in Alaska southward, stopping at Nootka Sound. Malaspina's far-reaching expedition kept alive Spain's hopes of competing in the Pacific with rivals such as Britain, whose naval and economic resources were greater.

Malaspina's crews were ailing and short of supplies when they reached Monterey in September 1791. This was an opportunity for them to rest and refit and for Malaspina to assess the progress of California and its capital, founded in part to offer refuge and provisions to galleons returning from Manila. As it turned out, the captains of those galleons generally avoided Monterey unless desperate for supplies and made directly for Acapulco. They were subject to a fine if they did so, but they could not profit by stopping at Monterey, for they were not allowed to engage in any trade there other than purchasing provisions. Furthermore, their ships were not very maneuverable and had difficulty entering this exposed and often fog-shrouded harbor. Captain Bustamante y Guerra concluded that it was foolish to oblige galleons to stop there but commended Monterey as a fine place for crews to recuperate, being a "healthful country, without vices," offering "the finest meats and sufficient vegetables."[29]

29. Bustamante y Guerra in Cutter, *Malaspina in California*, 47–48; Weber, *Spanish Frontier in North America*, 285–89; Warren L. Cook, *Flood Tide of Empire: Spain and the Pacific Northwest, 1543–1819*, 117–19, 306–20.

One sick crewman with the Malaspina expedition was past recovery, however. John Green, a sailor from Boston who had signed on with Malaspina in Spain as an artilleryman, died soon after the expedition reached Monterey and was buried at the presidio chapel on September 14. The first Anglo-American known to have entered California, he had converted to Catholicism before he died. As recorded in the ship's log: "The sailor Juan Grean, American, a member of our church, and suffering from dropsy, ended his days in the late afternoon, as a result a funeral was held, giving him burial the following morning in the chapel of the barracks."[30]

Monterey proved even more hospitable to Malaspina than it had been to La Pérouse. Lasuén sent neophytes out to hunt and fish for the visitors and gather specimens for Malaspina's natural history collection. In return for gifts such as abalone shells—prized by Indians of the Pacific Northwest, who offered sea-otter pelts for them in exchange—Malaspina gave Lasuén sugar, chocolate, wine, and a profuse letter of thanks that he had framed. He disclaimed any thought of profiting by his services to an officer who had done so much for "our sovereign and the glory of our nation."[31] But other colonists there were eager to do business with the visitors. Residents of San José traveled to Monterey to sell them fruit, Malaspina reported. Their offerings were welcome as antidotes to scurvy and demonstrated that some *pobladores* were more enterprising than their critics acknowledged.

This was Malaspina's only visit to California, but he sent two small ships, *Sutil* and *Mexicana*, back to the Pacific Northwest the following year to explore the Strait of Juan de Fuca, below Vancouver Island. Afterward, the two vessels stopped in Monterey in August 1792. Chronicling this visit was pilot and artist José Cardero, who sketched the town and its residents and contributed to the expedition's official report, most likely serving as its author. That report included high praise for the presidial troops, disparaged by some later foreign visitors. Those soldiers were "as good as they are neglected," the author observed, and did not spend their

---

30. Quoted in Cutter, *Malaspina in California*, 29.
31. Lasuén in ibid., 38.

days lounging about while Indians did all the work: "one can be seen acting as sentinel of the guard; another herding livestock, roping an animal, or driving a cart; still another building a wall, making a door, or sewing shoes; yet another arming himself to go into the interior." These troops were not sufficiently rewarded for their services, the report concluded, and had little opportunity to "build up an estate" for retirement and "give comfort to their families."[32]

Beginning in 1784, a few retired soldiers had in fact received provisional land grants around San Diego and Monterey, where they raised cattle and other livestock—the first such ranchos in the colony. Officially, that land still belonged to the Crown, but in most cases their ownership was eventually recognized. Some of the grants were extensive, but these were not the prosperous California ranches of later days. José del Carmen Lugo—whose father, Corporal Antonio María Lugo, was granted Rancho San Antonio near Mission San Gabriel—recalled that the typical ranch house in colonial times "was of rough timber roofed with tules. It rarely had more than two rooms." The door was never locked or barred, he added, "because there was no one who would enter to steal, and nothing which would be worth taking."[33] However humble, these ranches offered rare opportunities for private initiative. Of the hundreds of soldiers who served in colonial California, only about thirty received such grants. Franciscans did not welcome ranches near their missions and expanded their own domain by establishing *asistencias:* mission outposts where neophytes herded cattle and sheep. Spanish authorities never put to the test the report's prediction that if land were granted liberally to veterans, "in a very few years one would see a flourishing colony created on this fertile landscape."[34]

The report also offered suggestions for improving the mission system and the instruction of neophytes. Lasuén had repeatedly asked that a grindstone be sent there by supply ship for a mill that La Pérouse had presented as a gift to Mission San Carlos, but the

---

32. Quoted in Donald C. Cutter, *California in 1792: A Spanish Naval Visit*, 121, 128.
33. José del Carmen Lugo, "Life of a Rancher," 216–17; Beebe and Senkewicz, *Lands of Promise and Despair*, 434–42; W. W. Robinson, *Land in California*, 45–58.
34. Quoted in Cutter, *California in 1792*, 128.

"humble pleas of the president have not been enough to obtain this benefit." Missionaries should be better equipped, the visitors recommended, and better educated in Native languages and other subjects. Missionaries at San Carlos had composed a catechism in the two main Indian languages spoken around Monterey. But teaching Indians rote responses to perplexing theological questions ("When Jesus Christ died on the cross, did he die as God or as man?") was not enough of an education to make neophytes "useful to society and the state." Finally, the report urged that missionaries reconsider their practice of instilling in neophytes the communal spirit of the Franciscan order by making them "work for everyone, without permitting property to anyone."[35] Neophytes might work harder and be better prepared to join Spanish colonial society if they had property of their own to look after.

These were similar to the conclusions reached by La Pérouse, but they were stated more cautiously and courteously in this report, reflecting the views of visitors who had much in common with the hard-pressed colonists of California, serving their king dutifully on a distant frontier. Malaspina and his officers had faith in the Crown's ability to address the problems they identified, but that faith was misplaced. King Carlos III, the last monarch to attempt to reform and revive the faltering Spanish-American empire, had died in 1788 and been succeeded by the irresolute Carlos IV. Far from court, the spirit of reform lived on in thoughtful reports like this one, but they had little or no impact. Official neglect left California exposed to harsh scrutiny by foreigners, who saw openings there to exploit.

Vancouver's View

The visit of George Vancouver to California in late 1792 heralded a new era in which this remote Spanish colony would face ever-greater challenges from representatives of rival nations. Unlike La Pérouse, a sympathetic observer from a friendly Catholic country, this accomplished British navigator served an imperial power often

---

35. Ibid., 133, 137–39, 153.

View of Monterey presidio, 1792, by José Cardero.
Courtesy The Bancroft Library, University of California, Berkeley (BANC PIC 1963.002:1308-FR).

at odds with Spain and composed a thoroughgoing critique of the colony that offered a rationale for conquest echoed in later times by Anglo-American expansionists. Vancouver had served under Cook and was now leading an ambitious expedition of his own, one that would take him to many lands around the Pacific before he completed his circumnavigation in 1795. Like other such voyages, this was a projection of national might, asserting Britain's right to explore the globe and exploit areas unoccupied by rival colonizers.

Before reaching California, Vancouver visited Nootka Sound and met with Spanish commander Juan Francisco de la Bodega y Quadra, a seasoned explorer in his own right who had reconnoitered the Pacific Coast from San Francisco Bay to Vancouver Island. The two officers tried to work out unresolved details of the Nootka Convention and reconcile the competing interests of Britain and Spain in the Pacific Northwest. Bodega y Quadra knew that Spain would be hard-pressed to defend its claims against British naval might if the deal unraveled. (When Vancouver encountered the diminutive *Sutil* and *Mexicana* during his voyage, he judged them the "most ill calculated and unfit vessels that could possibly be

Indians in tule canoe, San Francisco Bay, 1806.
Courtesy The Bancroft Library, University of California, Berkeley (BANC PIC 1963:002:1021-FR).

imagined for such an expedition.")[36] Bodega y Quadra charmed and flattered Vancouver but made no concessions to him in talks. He wanted the British, in exchange for free access to Nootka Sound and the return of property confiscated there, to recognize the Strait of Juan de Fuca as the northern boundary of Spanish territory. Finding themselves at an impasse, he and Vancouver agreed to refer the issue to their superiors and parted amicably in September 1792. Bodega y Quadra arranged to meet Vancouver again in Monterey and made sure that he received cordial treatment in California.

On his way to Monterey, Vancouver stopped in San Francisco Bay to take on supplies and assess the progress of Spanish colonization. In mid-November, after passing the inlet known as Bodega

---

36. George Vancouver, *A Voyage of Discovery to the North Pacific Ocean and round the World, 1791–1795*, 1:93; 2:593, 678; Cook, *Flood Tide of Empire*, 389–92.

Bay (after Bodega y Quadra), he threaded the Golden Gate in his ship *Discovery* and entered "a very spacious sound, which had the appearance of containing a variety of as excellent harbours as the known world affords." Sheep and cattle were grazing on the hills near the presidio, where he was soon enjoying the hospitality of Ensign Hermenegildo Sal, acting commandant. Vancouver likened the presidio to a "pound for cattle" and noted that it was protected by only two small cannons. Such was "the inactive state of the people," he concluded, that they left this strategic bastion, guarding one of the world's finest ports, virtually defenseless.[37]

Vancouver was much given to such sweeping pronouncements, but his assessment of California and its inhabitants was not entirely bleak or unforgiving. He appreciated the courtesy of the commandant and his wife, who greeted him at the door to her house "seated cross-legged on a mat ... with two daughters and a son, clean and decently dressed, seated by her." The house had dirt floors and little furniture to speak of, but the occupants had a dignity and grace that disarmed Vancouver's sharply critical instincts and "rendered their lowly residence no longer an object of our attention."[38]

Similarly, Vancouver offered insights into the culture and capacities of California Indians that sometimes ran counter to his unflattering assessments of them. He dismissed the tule canoes that Indians used to cross San Francisco Bay, for example, as "the most rude and sorry contrivances for embarkation I had ever beheld," but noted later how Indians set out to fish in those buoyant canoes amid high winds and waves, "without seeming to entertain the least apprehension for their safety." He characterized neophytes at Mission San Francisco as among the most miserable people he ever saw in terms of "the faculty of human reason," but observed that women and girls there had learned to weave on looms and were turning out cloth that "was by no means despicable."[39]

Later, while visiting Mission Santa Clara, Vancouver saw neophytes carrying out chores "with a mechanical, lifeless, careless

---

37. Vancouver, *Voyage of Discovery*, 2:702, 708, 711.
38. Ibid., 2:710.
39. Ibid., 2:707, 712, 714.

indifference." Since Spaniards reportedly found Indians "in the same state of inactivity and ignorance on their earliest visits," he added, "this disposition is probably inherited from their forefathers." In fact, early Spanish visitors described California Indians as lively and active. Vancouver himself discerned such admirable traits in Native peoples living outside the mission system and in some neophytes at Santa Clara who had adapted to the regimen there—"intelligent, tractable, and industrious persons," who were building "comfortable and convenient habitations."[40] The dullness that Vancouver and other witnesses observed in colonized Indians may well have been a product of their historical circumstances. People who were conquered, spiritually or otherwise, often responded bleakly and mechanically to the demands of their overseers. Some neophytes emerged from that torpor to serve as loyal adherents of the regime or determined opponents. Others remained in a state of listless disaffection. They grudgingly obeyed the rules; but as Lasuén recognized, they did not much care for this way of life. Their wit and vitality went dormant and sometimes never revived.

In late November Vancouver left San Francisco for Monterey, after thanking his hosts for "our hospitable reception, and the excellent refreshments, which in a few days had entirely eradicated every apparent symptom of the scurvy."[41] The hospitality was renewed at Monterey, where Bodega y Quadra arranged a fandango at the presidio. Vancouver said nothing about it in his journal, but surgeon and naturalist Archibald Menzies described the affair in detail. It was supposed to start at seven, he wrote, "but the Ladies had such unusual preparations to make that they could not be got together till near ten, & as they entered they seated themselves on Cushions placed on a Carpet spread out at one end of the room . . . most of them had their Hair in long queues reaching down to their waist." The term "fandango" referred to such festivities in general and to a particular dance, performed by

---

40. Ibid., 2:721–22; James J. Rawls, *Indians of California: The Changing Image*, 25–34.
41. Vancouver, *Voyage of Discovery*, 2:726.

a couple to the accompaniment of guitar or voice. "Sometimes they dance close to each other," Menzies observed, "then retire, then approach again, with such wanton attitudes & motions, such leering looks, sparkling eyes & trembling limbs, as would decompose the gravity of a Stoic." Afterward, Vancouver asked two Polynesian women from Hawaii—who were returning home with his expedition after being carried off to Nootka in a British merchant ship—to exhibit "their manner of singing & dancing." This did not "afford much entertainment to the Spanish Ladies," reported Menzies, who added: "indeed I believe they thought this crude performance was introduced by way of ridiculing their favourite dance the Fandango, as they soon after departed."[42]

Vancouver's visit linked California not only to Hawaii and other Polynesian islands but also to distant Australia. While visiting Monterey, he obtained cattle and sheep for delivery on his storeship *Daedalus* to the fledgling British penal colony at Botany Bay. Bodega y Quadra would not accept payment for the livestock or other supplies furnished to the British, Vancouver noted, and "gave strict orders that no account whatever should be rendered."[43] Menzies later learned that Bodega y Quadra had accepted personal responsibility for expenditures "to the amount of 1800 dollars ... without giving us the least intimation of the Sum to which his public spirited generosity had thus made him liable."[44]

Relations between this generous host and his guests were strained briefly when armorer's mate James Etchinson deserted the *Chatham*, the companion ship to Vancouver's *Discovery*, as they prepared to depart in early 1793. Etchinson was "a very ingenious Mechanic," wrote midshipman Thomas Manby, and "had done a great many Jobs for the Spaniards."[45] Manby and others believed that Etchinson had been enticed to desert, but Bodega y Quadra offered a reward for Etchinson's return and induced the only blacksmith in Monterey, José de los Santos, to replace Etchinson aboard

---

42. Menzies in ibid., 2:732–33 n. 2.
43. Vancouver in ibid., 2:742–43.
44. Menzies in ibid., 2:742–43 n. 1.
45. Manby in ibid., 2:788 n. 1; see also 4:1417 n. 2.

the *Chatham* when that fugitive failed to appear. (Two other men deserted from the *Daedalus* and remained in California, among them a stowaway from Australia named Thomas Smith.)

Bodega y Quadra's unfailing generosity was a matter of principle as well as policy. He may well have hoped that placing Vancouver in debt to him might work to Spain's advantage diplomatically, but he also seemed intent on instilling in this visitor an appreciation for the values of his hosts, whose lives were enriched by exchanges of gifts and courtesies that brought them little profit but much satisfaction. Vancouver hailed him on parting for his "benevolence and disinterested conduct" and held him in "the highest esteem."[46] But that did not alter Vancouver's low opinion of Spanish California, which he regarded in sum as a losing proposition that would be better off under new ownership.

When Vancouver returned to California in November 1793 to survey the coast from Monterey southward, he had to contend with another host who was far less obliging, interim governor José Joaquín de Arrillaga. Ordered to guard against British intrusions, Arrillaga was duly skeptical when Vancouver claimed grandly that his expedition was for the "benefit of mankind, and that under these circumstances, we ought rather to be considered as labouring for the good of the world in general, than for the advantage of any particular sovereign." Irked by the restrictions that Arrillaga placed on British movements in Monterey, Vancouver found his tone "sneering, forbidding, and ungracious."[47]

Vancouver later dropped his indignant stance when Commandant Felipe de Goycoechea at the Santa Bárbara presidio proved more hospitable and allowed the visitors free movement during the day. Gratified, Vancouver ordered his men to stay within sight of the presidio or mission and not ramble about as they did on their first visit to Monterey, where they had perhaps "made too free with the liberty then granted." Vancouver was charmed by Santa Bárbara, the youngest and most populous of the presidio communities, with 235 colonists in residence as of 1790. It was a

---

46. Vancouver in ibid., 3:792.
47. Ibid., 3:1083, 1085 n. 1.

"far more civilized place than any other of the Spanish settlements," he judged. "The buildings appeared to be regular and well constructed, the walls clean and white, and the roofs of the houses were covered with a bright red tile." Some Chumash there lived as neophytes at Mission Santa Bárbara, but many others resided in villages by the bay and struck him as quite different from the mission Indians at Monterey or San Francisco: "They seemed to possess great sensibility, and much vivacity, yet they conducted themselves with the most perfect decorum and good order."[48]

Although Vancouver felt that mission efforts in California had not done much to improve Indians, he admired Franciscans for trying. He described Lasuén, now in his mid-fifties, as a venerable old man of about seventy-two, with a "tranquillized state of mind, that fitted him in an eminent degree for presiding over so benevolent an institution." While in Santa Bárbara, Vancouver met one of the most gifted missionaries in California, Father Vicente Santa María, who arrived from nearby Mission San Buenaventura with ten sheep and twenty mule loads of roots and vegetables for Vancouver and his men. "Having crossed the ocean more than once himself, he was well aware how valuable the fresh productions of the shores were to persons in our position," wrote the grateful Vancouver, who offered to take the priest south by ship to a landing near his mission.[49]

Santa María had been in California for nearly two decades. In 1775, as chaplain of the *San Carlos*, which was surveying San Francisco Bay, he had gone off "hunting for our Indians," as he put it, to introduce them to Christianity. Those he encountered struck him as genial and quick-witted, able to pick up his own words faster than he could learn theirs. At one point, he related, a chief "came up to where I was reciting my prayers, and placing himself at my side on his kneecaps, began to imitate me in my manner of praying, so that I could not keep from laughing."[50] The ability to laugh

---

48. Ibid., 3:1091–92, 1095.
49. Ibid., 2:730, 3:1096.
50. Santa María in Joshua Paddison, ed., *A World Transformed: Firsthand Accounts of California before the Gold Rush*, 32, 40.

when others in his position might have taken offense was among the gifts that made Santa María an exemplary padre. He had a devoted following among the Chumash and spoke their language fluently. Those who accompanied him to Santa Bárbara urged him not to go aboard the *Discovery* with Vancouver, fearing that he might come to harm. When he returned to San Buenaventura, neophytes ran to him and kissed his hand. Vancouver found the mission buildings, fields, and gardens there to be far superior "to any of the new settlements I had yet seen."[51] Of the four missions established in Chumash territory, this was the only one not embroiled later in the Chumash Revolt of 1824.

Continuing south down the coast, Vancouver stopped briefly at San Diego. The hilltop presidio struck him as "dreary and lonesome, in the midst of a barren uncultivated country." Soldiers there, he reported, drew provisions from Mission San Juan Capistrano up the coast, "one of the most fertile establishments in the country." As at San Francisco, he saw little to stop foreign ships from intruding or attacking and boasted of entering San Diego harbor unchallenged by "any of His Catholic Majesty's subjects."[52]

Vancouver expanded on that theme of Spanish neglect in his general remarks on California, which were revised for publication along with the rest of his journal after his final visit to California in late 1794. At that juncture, Spain and Britain were allied against revolutionary France, and a final resolution of the Nootka dispute was imminent. Vancouver was glad to find that the demanding Arrillaga had been "ordered to some inferior establishment" and replaced by the newly arrived Governor Diego de Borica, who received the visitors cordially.[53] By the time Vancouver returned home in September 1795, however, Spaniards were no longer his allies. King Carlos IV had abruptly switched sides and joined France against Britain. He did so to avoid defeat by an invading French army, but the Royal Navy would later shatter Spain's fleet. In summing up his impressions of California for publication,

---

51. Vancouver, *Voyage of Discovery*, 3:1101.
52. Ibid., 3:1107, 1128.
53. Ibid., 4:1416.

Vancouver was likely influenced by the renewal of an old and bitter Anglo-Hispanic rivalry.

Vancouver concluded that Spain had not turned California "to any profitable advantage" and would inevitably lose the colony to a stronger and more enterprising power. He saw little chance of Spanish settlements ever prospering or expanding in California, for the colonists led "a confined, and in most respects a very indolent life." The soldiers, he added, "do nothing, in the strictest sense of the expression; for they neither till, sow, nor reap, but wholly depend upon the labour of the inhabitants of the missions and pueblos for their subsistence."[54] This sweeping indictment ran counter to the testimony of Archibald Menzies, who observed that the soldiers were "generally Stout Men capable of bearing great fatigue, & without any exaggeration the most dextrous & nimble Horsemen we ever saw."[55]

Vancouver could not argue that Spanish efforts in California had been entirely fruitless. Instead he claimed that what Spaniards had achieved—the discovery and colonization of two great harbors at San Diego and San Francisco, the cultivation of fertile areas and building up of large herds of livestock, and the indoctrination of Indians "practiced in many domestic occupations"—was worse than doing nothing without adequate defenses against rivals lured by such temptations: "All these circumstances are valuable considerations to new masters, from whose power, if properly employed, the Spaniards would have no alternative but that of submissively yielding."[56] Vancouver did not call for Britain to seize California, but he clearly believed that Britons could do better than Spaniards at exploiting what he called New Albion, the old English proprietary title for California that harked back to the forays of Francis Drake. Vancouver's utilitarian argument—that undeveloped countries should go to those who could profit most from them—would later be echoed by Anglo-Americans seeking to justify their own imperial designs on California and other remnants

---

54. Ibid., 3:1126, 1129.
55. Menzies in ibid., 2:741 n. 1.
56. Vancouver in ibid., 3:1135.

of the once-mighty Spanish empire. Long before they set out to claim this country, Anglos began preparing the way for conquest by surveying and subverting Hispanic California in writing.

An American Incursion

Spain was not quite as neglectful of California and its defenses as Vancouver suggested. During the 1790s San Francisco, San Diego, and other ports were fortified with *castillos* (coastal batteries). They would not withstand concerted attack by enemy warships, but it was hoped that they would deter pirates and smugglers. Merely enforcing trade restrictions, however, would do nothing to foster economic development. The opportunities that Spain had left largely unexploited along California's coast were now attracting foreign merchants. In 1796 the first American vessel received at a California port, the *Otter* out of Boston, was granted permission to anchor at Monterey and take on fresh water and other necessities. As its name implied, the ship was involved in the sea-otter trade, among other profitable pursuits. Such vessels sometimes stopped furtively along the California coast to bargain with Indians or colonists for pelts. At Monterey, however, Captain Ebenezer Dorr was allowed only to purchase needed supplies, as permitted under Spanish law. Governor Borica put Indians to work in Monterey grinding flour for the *Otter* by hand. The ship's first mate, Pierre Péron, watched them as they labored and "could not understand why a mill was not established like the ones in Europe."[57]

Dorr should have been grateful for obtaining supplies, a courtesy often extended to foreign merchant ships in California even when officials suspected them of smuggling. Instead, he defied his hosts by ridding his vessel of unwanted crew members, among them ex-convicts who had boarded the *Otter* in Australia. They had been useful in the Pacific Northwest, where ships that were not well manned risked attack, but Dorr would have to pay them a

---

57. Péron in Richard Batman, *The Outer Coast: A Narrative about California before the World Rushed In*, 119; Odgen, *California Sea Otter Trade*, 32–33; Bancroft, *History of California*, 1:534–40.

share of the profits if they returned with him to Boston. When his request to unload them in Monterey was denied, he did so anyway, leaving behind ten men and one woman, a stowaway from Botany Bay named Jane Lambert.

As first mate Péron put it, Governor Borica had "a great deal to complain about."[58] But he soon discovered that the castoffs had useful skills such as carpentry and put them gainfully to work in Monterey until 1797, when they were deported to Spain. The need for skilled labor would make California a haven in years to come for sailors of various nationalities who jumped ship. Slowly but surely, foreigners infiltrated the colony and filled positions for which Spanish colonists lacked training, even as foreign captains prowled the coast and pursued trade for which Spanish merchants lacked authorization.

Colonial authorities made a fitful effort to bolster California against foreign intrusions by founding a third town there in 1797. Known as Branciforte for the viceroy who sponsored the plan, it was situated near Mission Santa Cruz and designated a *villa* (a town under military authority) rather than a pueblo. When Lasuén learned that it would be within "three or four gunshots of Santa Cruz," he protested that Spanish law did not allow for a town so near a mission.[59] He feared disputes over boundaries and grazing rights of the sort that arose between Mission Santa Clara and nearby San José. He also worried that the colonists would be a bad influence on neophytes, and the first recruits who arrived by sea did not reassure him. Some were convicts, found guilty of petty crimes. Most had skills or trades, but few were adept at farming. They struggled to make a living. Unlike San José and Los Angeles, both of which grew slowly through the colonial era, Branciforte languished and eventually lost its identity.

The failure of Branciforte underscored California's dependence on the missions, seven of which were founded in the 1790s, bringing the total to eighteen and coming close to realizing the goal of a

---

58. Péron in Batman, *Outer Coast*, 119.
59. Lasuén in Guest, *Fermín Francisco de Lasuén*, 325; Francis F. Guest, "Establishment of the Villa de Branciforte"; Bancroft, *History of California*, 1:564–72.

chain of missions situated roughly a day's journey apart, stretching from San Diego to San Francisco. That rapid expansion posed problems for Lasuén, who had to contend with resistance from Indians new to the mission system, many of whom sought food and shelter rather than indoctrination and discipline. He also faced scrutiny from officials who worried that stern Franciscan measures violated the rights of Indians and would provoke hostilities, straining California's fragile defenses.

Such were the concerns of Governor Borica, who ordered padres not to punish neophytes with more than twenty-five lashes and not to send mission Indians in pursuit of fugitives. In 1797 two friars at Mission San Francisco—one of the weakest links in the chain, plagued by hunger and disease—dispatched a party of neophytes to retrieve fugitives from that mission in violation of Borica's order. A third friar there, Father José María Fernández, informed Borica in writing of that foray and blamed his fellow padres for mistreating neophytes and causing them to flee. Fernández had denounced those abuses earlier and been branded a troublemaker, "entangled with secular elements who had sinister goals." He insisted that he was only trying to help his neophytes, whose sufferings he shared like an anxious parent. "I love the Indians very much and will feel their misfortunes even more if they are to be treated like this," he wrote. "I repeat, I love them very much, because they have caused me great sorrow, very bad days, many sleepless nights, some tears, and ultimately my shattered health."[60]

In 1798 another Franciscan lodged a fervent protest against the mission system. Father Antonio de la Concepción Horra, who served briefly at Mission San Miguel before being removed by Lasuén, wrote a letter to the viceroy in which he portrayed neophytes as victims of a brutal disciplinary regime: "For any reason, however insignificant it may be, they are severely and cruelly whipped, placed in shackles, or put in the stocks for days on end without receiving even a drop of water."[61] He complained that he had been dismissed

---

60. Fernández in Beebe and Senkewicz, *Lands of Promise and Despair*, 262–65.
61. Concepción Horra in ibid., 272.

as a lunatic for denouncing such abuses. This prompted a lengthy investigation by Governor Borica, who considered the padres "very harsh" in their treatment of neophytes but concluded that Concepción Horra was not a sound and credible witness.

In 1801, while that investigation was underway, Lasuén refuted charges against the mission system in a lengthy statement. The crux of his argument was that his missionaries, with few exceptions, were laboring conscientiously to convert and civilize Indians whose nature and inclinations ran counter to a Christian or civilized way of life. They were so lazy and careless, he believed, that they would rather go hungry and naked than seek a secure existence requiring diligence and forethought. "They satiate themselves today, and give little thought to tomorrow," he maintained.[62] Such assertions were often made by one party or another in the contest for California to justify its claims to this country. Vancouver and later Anglo observers portrayed Hispanic colonists there in much the same way that Lasuén and other Spaniards pictured California Indians: as too thoughtless and indolent to improve their world and make the most of it.

Like many colonizers, Lasuén underestimated the cultural capacities of Native peoples, but he did not glorify his own role in subjecting them to a regimen that they often found confining and demoralizing. In contrast to Serra, who saw spiritual conquest as heroic, Lasuén felt that his task was necessary but thankless, for it involved destroying much that Indians cherished, including their freedom, in an effort to save them. "Here then we have the greatest problem of the missionary," he wrote in a memorable passage: "how to transform a savage race such as these into a society that is human, Christian, civil, and industrious. This can be accomplished only by 'denaturalizing' them. It is easy to see what an arduous task this is, for it requires them to act against nature." It took patience and persistence, Lasuén concluded, "to make them realize that they are men."[63]

---

62. Fermín Francisco de Lasuén, *Writings*, 1:202.
63. Ibid.

To be truly human was to act against nature, Lasuén believed, and he was not referring only to Indians. Franciscans lived close to nature but sought to harness and control it, much as they disciplined their own natural instincts. Lasuén had acted against nature in taking vows of poverty, chastity, and obedience and accepting one arduous task after another from his superiors. Many of those involved in the colonization of California had taken on similar duties against their natural inclinations. Spanish colonial society valued solidarity and security over freedom. From the Crown's point of view, free trade was not unlike free love—a promiscuous intercourse that would expose colonists to rapacious foreigners and spread greed, rebelliousness, and heresy. That stringent attitude hampered the economic development of Spanish California, but the colony would have suffered in other ways if self-serving free traders like Ebenezer Dorr had become models for enterprising Spanish colonists to emulate.

By the time Lasuén died in 1803, it was too late for Spain to reverse course and allow its colonists greater freedom and initiative. Having cast his lot with France, King Carlos IV was now at the mercy of Napoleon Bonaparte, whose schemes would do much to undermine the Spanish empire. Ignoring his treaty obligations to Spain, which had secretly returned Louisiana to France on condition that it not be transferred to a third party, Napoleon sold the Louisiana Territory to the United States in 1803. Promises, pretensions, and claims counted for nothing in this ruthless Napoleonic era. Wealth and power were everything, and the king of Spain had too little of either. The ties of patronage and dependence that bound colonists to their distant masters in Madrid and Mexico City were fraying, and California would soon have to fend for itself.

CHAPTER 6

The Smugglers' Coast

On March 17, 1803, the American merchant ship *Lelia Byrd* slipped past Point Loma and entered San Diego Bay, undeterred by a battery situated near the harbor's entrance to fend off pirates and smugglers. In charge of the vessel were two adventurers from Salem, Massachusetts, Richard Cleveland and William Shaler. They had determined by drawing lots that Shaler would serve as master and Cleveland as first mate and supercargo (business agent). Their main business was the sea-otter trade, and they had recently purchased 1,600 otter pelts while repairing the *Lelia Byrd* at San Blas. The price that Shaler and Cleveland paid for that "soft gold" was far less than they expected to receive in China, and they hoped to purchase more on similar terms in San Diego. This was smuggling, for trade between foreign merchants and Spanish colonists was forbidden, but they did not fear retribution. They knew of Vancouver's visit to San Diego in 1793, when he entered the harbor unchallenged. The battery installed there since then worried them so little that they passed it in broad daylight. As Cleveland related: "A brisk northerly wind prevented our gaining the anchorage till the afternoon, when, having passed near the battery without being hailed, we came to anchor about a mile within it."[1]

---

1. Richard Jeffry Cleveland, *Voyages and Commercial Enterprises of the Sons of New* (continued)

145

Shaler and Cleveland soon discovered that this harbor was not as hospitable to intruders as it appeared. Commandant Manuel Rodríguez of the San Diego presidio, who boarded the *Lelia Byrd* the next day, had confiscated nearly 500 sea-otter pelts two weeks earlier from Captain John Brown of the American ship *Alexander* after granting him permission to take on water and provisions for his ailing crew. Shaler and Cleveland claimed similar hardships and were allowed to purchase necessities, but Rodríguez left several soldiers on board as guards to see that they did not engage in any other trade. "We had been told at San Blas, that Don Manuel was an exceedingly vain and pompous man; and indeed, we found him so," remarked Cleveland. "He forbade our going to the town, which is distant about three miles, but gave us leave to go on shore in the neighborhood of the vessel."[2] Those were fair terms for foreigners with suspect intentions, but Cleveland dismissed Rodríguez in much the same terms used by Vancouver when he had described the vigilant José Arrillaga—back in California now as governor on a permanent basis—as rude and haughty. Few things riled enterprising visitors to Spanish California more than commanders who scrupulously enforced official restrictions on their activities.

Shortly after Rodríguez returned to the presidio, Cleveland related, "we made an excursion on shore; and, having rambled towards the battery . . . we availed ourselves of the opportunity to ascertain its strength and state." They were gathering intelligence on San Diego's defenses that they would share with other American traders seeking to circumvent Spanish laws, but they scoffed at authorities for keeping troublesome foreigners at bay. "As the examination of a battery belonging to a people the most jealous and suspicious on earth, was a delicate business," Cleveland concluded, "we did not remain long within its precincts, and, having had an agreeable excursion, returned on board at sunset."[3]

Cleveland could not imagine that Rodríguez was acting honorably in confiscating goods that Americans had obtained illegally.

England, 194; Bancroft, *History of California*, 2:10–16; Ogden, *California Sea Otter Trade*, 35–39; Batman, *Outer Coast*, 129–33.
2. Cleveland, *Voyages and Commercial Enterprises*, 195.
3. Ibid., 195.

He assumed that the commandant was out to feather his own nest and offered to buy pelts that Rodríguez had seized from Captain Brown and others. "He would have been as well pleased to sell, as we should have been to purchase them," Cleveland claimed. But colonists there "were all spies on each other," and Rodríguez could not connive with foreigners without being found out. In fact, Rodríguez had informed his superiors of the goods he confiscated and had no discernible motive in his dealings with fur traders other than enforcing the law. On March 21 he again visited the *Lelia Byrd* to see that the provisions had been delivered and, as Cleveland put it, "to receive his pay," implying that Rodríguez pocketed the proceeds.[4] He informed the Americans that they must leave the next day and posted guards on shore that night, suspecting that they were bargaining secretly with soldiers for pelts and would pick them up under cover of darkness. Such was the case, and three of the ship's crew were seized when they landed and were tied hand and foot.

When Cleveland learned of their fate, he concluded that Rodríguez had laid a trap for him by sending a soldier as a decoy to bargain for pelts. He wanted "an excuse to plunder us," asserted Cleveland, who feared that Rodríguez might now confiscate the otter pelts that he and Shaler had purchased illicitly at San Blas: "The choice presented us was that of submission, indignant treatment, and plunder; or resistance and hazarding the consequences. There was not the least hesitation with Mr. Shaler or myself in adopting the latter alternative." They seized and disarmed the guards left on board by Rodríguez. Then Cleveland went ashore with four sailors, "each with a brace of loaded pistols," and freed their captive shipmates.[5]

The *Lelia Byrd* did not get away unscathed. As it left the harbor, it came under fire from gunners at the battery, which was now well manned. Cleveland responded by using the captured guards as human shields and forcing them to stand "in the most exposed and conspicuous station." Rodríguez, in his official report of the

---
4. Ibid., 196.
5. Ibid., 197.

incident, stated that his gunners ceased fire when the sergeant of the guards shouted that their captors had promised to free them. Rodríguez was willing to spare the smugglers further pounding if they released their hostages, but they opened fire as they passed the fort, igniting a brief duel that damaged the ship but did no harm to the battery or its gunners. Cleveland conceded in his account that the *Lelia Byrd* took several shots to the hull that later required repair but claimed victory in what he grandly called this "battle of San Diego" because he supposedly silenced his opponents: "Our second broadside seemed to have caused the complete abandonment of their guns, as none were fired afterwards."[6]

Cleveland made no mention of promising to release the guards under duress, as Rodríguez claimed, but said that he freed them afterward to show that Americans were just and merciful: "The poor guards, who had been left on board, saw themselves completely in our power, without the chance of rescue, and probably calculated on such treatment as they knew would have been our lot, if equally in the power of their Commandant." They pleaded for their lives, he added, and gave thanks for their deliverance: "When landed, and their arms handed to them, they embraced each other, crossed themselves, and fell on their knees in prayer. As our boat was leaving them, they rose up and cried at the utmost stretch of their voices, *Vivan, vivan los Americanos* [Long live the Americans]."[7]

Cleveland's deceptive account, composed long after the event, was well crafted to appeal to American readers who believed that their own imperial designs were morally superior to those of Europeans. Much like Spanish colonists who portrayed actions that deprived Indians of their land and liberty as efforts to save them, Cleveland characterized his smuggling as righteous resistance to a rotten imperial system that left both Spaniards and foreigners at the mercy of venal commandants. His misrepresentations were not simply products of ignorance. He learned just enough about Spanish colonists in his brief encounters with them to sense what

---

6. Ibid., 197–98; Bancroft, *History of California*, 2:13 n. 17.
7. Cleveland, *Voyages and Commercial Enterprises*, 198.

their strengths and powers of resistance were and translate those virtues into vices, as he did in disparaging Rodríguez.

Such verbal assaults could have serious consequences in an age when imperialism was regarded by many of its practitioners as a noble cause. If this colony was morally bankrupt, as Cleveland implied, then Americans might feel entitled to redeem California and its inhabitants through conquest, much as Spaniards had considered it their duty to draw Indians there into "the sweet, soft, desirable vassalage of His Majesty," in the words of Viceroy Bucareli, and bathe them "in the light of the Gospel by means of spiritual conquest."[8] Among the incentives that drew imperialists of various nationalities to California was a yearning not just for profit or power but for the satisfaction of rescuing this presumably benighted country from misery or misrule and earning the respect and gratitude of its long-suffering populace ("Vivan los Americanos").

Despite charges of corruption leveled by disgruntled intruders like Cleveland, Spanish authorities in California generally adhered to the law. Foreigners intent on skirting the law often benefited as a result. Suspected smugglers sometimes had their ships seized and searched but were allowed to proceed with their cargo when inquiries produced no proof of illicit activity. No matter how scrupulous Spanish officials were in governing this colony, foreigners questioned their competence, if not their integrity, and argued that they were too weak and incompetent to hold so rich a prize as California. William Shaler, for one, echoed Vancouver when he wrote that California wanted "nothing but a good government to rise rapidly to wealth and importance. The conquest of this country would be absolutely nothing; it would fall without an effort to the most inconsiderable force."[9]

Spain could do little more to fend off such bothersome foreigners, for its empire was on the verge of breaking apart. In 1808 the discredited King Carlos IV would abdicate in favor of his son

---

8. Bucareli in Cook, *Flood Tide of Empire*, 58.
9. William Shaler, *Journal of a Voyage between China and the Northwestern Coast of America, Made in 1804*, 77.

Ferdinand VII, prompting Napoleon to intervene and place his brother Joseph on the Spanish throne. That in turn would undermine Spanish authority abroad and trigger tumultuous wars for independence in Mexico and South America. Colonists in California wanted no part of the bloody struggle that broke out in the Mexican heartland in 1810 when rebels defied Spanish royalists. Whatever resentments colonists native to California harbored toward the Spanish-born priests and officials who had dominated the colony since its founding, they still looked to Spain for aid and guidance.

Beginning in 1810, supply shipments from San Blas would be suspended for years by the turmoil in Mexico. Colonists in California would have little choice but to bargain with foreigners for the goods they lacked. Long before that, however, many were profiting by selling provisions legally to visiting ships or trading illicitly with foreigners. Dominican friars in Baja California and Franciscans in Alta California were among those who offered otter pelts gathered by mission Indians to Cleveland, Shaler, and other foreign traders. As Cleveland noted, the Dominicans he dealt with enjoyed trading as a sociable pastime: "Their object seemed to be principally recreation, though they brought a few sea otters' skins, which they bartered with us for European manufactures."[10]

Perhaps the greatest obstacle that Spanish authorities faced in enforcing trade restrictions was the irrepressible urge of people living in relative isolation to engage in rewarding exchanges with foreigners. In some Pacific ports, those exchanges were erotic; but in California most colonists contented themselves with commercial intercourse, which offered some of the excitement of an illicit affair with fewer attendant risks. Even padres gladly took part in such trysts, consoling themselves with the thought that they were acquiring articles of use to their missions and neophytes. As loyal Spaniards and Catholics, however, they may well have felt twinges of remorse. Those profane foreigners with their alluring offerings were like serpents in the garden. Though yielding to their

---

10. Cleveland, *Voyages and Commercial Enterprises*, 199.

temptations may have been necessary and inevitable, it foretold the fall of Spanish California and the loss of much that the missionaries and other defenders of the old imperial order cherished and hoped to preserve.

Russian Advances

The skirmish at San Diego that Cleveland described in triumphant terms was neither a battle nor a victory for Americans seeking to circumvent Spanish trade barriers. Captains of lightly armed merchant ships like the *Lelia Byrd* grew wary of the batteries guarding California's major ports and largely confined their smuggling activities to remote inlets or coves such as San Pedro (near Los Angeles) or Refugio (north of Santa Bárbara), where they were less likely to encounter armed resistance. Even those secluded areas became more hazardous for intruders as Governor Arrillaga stepped up military efforts to thwart illegal trade. Heightened vigilance prompted some American captains to enter into partnerships with Russians in Alaska, who sent Native hunters south in American ships to take sea otters and fur seals along the California coast. Some of those expeditions ran afoul of Spanish troops; but unlike merchant ships seeking goods from colonists they largely avoided populous areas and frequented desolate harbors or offshore islands like Catalina or the Farallones that had no Spanish forts or settlements.

Spanish authorities had long feared Russian intervention in California. Russian expansion in North America had been slowed by the same kind of internal problems faced by Spanish colonists, however, including reckoning with defiant Indians. Aleuts and Kodiaks—a distinct tribal group on Kodiak Island that became closely associated with peoples of the Aleutian Islands through colonization—had been ruthlessly subjugated in the 1700s by Russian traders. The Russians forced men to hunt for them by holding their wives and children hostage and inflicting deadly reprisals on those who rebelled. By the early 1800s the exploitation of Native labor had been systematized by the Russian American Company. This government-chartered monopoly required half the adult male population of the tribal communities under its control to hunt sea-otter pelts and other furs, for which those expert hunters received paltry compensation. Aleuts made up much of the population at colonial settlements such as New Archangel (Sitka), founded in 1799. They and the Russians became targets of tribes resisting these intrusions, notably the Tlingits, who acquired firearms from British and American traders in exchange for sea-otter pelts and devastated Sitka in 1802. The outpost was rebuilt but remained hemmed in by Tlingits and subject to famine. Russian supply ships were not very seaworthy, and many foundered in the stormy North Pacific, forcing colonists to bargain for food and other necessities with some of the same foreign traders who armed their Tlingit foes. Those commercial contacts led to joint ventures in the fur trade.

In October 1803 Captain Joseph O'Cain from Boston met on Kodiak Island with Aleksandr Baranov, director of the Russian American Company and governor of Russian Alaska. O'Cain proposed transporting Aleut hunters to California for the company in exchange for half of the pelts taken during the venture. Baranov, who was eager to expand Russian ventures southward as the company depleted the fur resources of coastal Alaska, accepted O'Cain's proposal. By year's end, Aleuts were paddling their kayaks in sultry breezes off Baja California. Spanish authorities learned of O'Cain's intrusion, but his ship was well armed. As Arrillaga reported ruefully, "There is no other way to prevent them except to tell them not to hunt and to this they pay no attention." Aleuts were so adept at harpooning sea otters that within a few months they had all but exhausted the supply around Bahía San Quintín, where O'Cain made his base. "There is not an otter left from Mission Rosario to Santo Domingo," Arrillaga lamented, perhaps overstating his case.[11]

---

11. Arrillaga in Odgen, *California Sea Otter Trade*, 46–47; Bancroft, *History of California*, 2:25–26; James R. Gibson, *Imperial Russia in Frontier America: The Changing Geography of Supply of Russian America, 1784–1867*, 3–15, 153–59; James R. Gibson, *Otter Skins, Boston Ships, and China Goods: The Maritime Fur Trade of the Northwest Coast, 1785–1841*, 12–21.

While Aleuts hunted, O'Cain traded furtively for sea-otter skins with Spanish colonists. He returned to Alaska in the spring of 1804 with 700 pelts secured through trade and 1,100 obtained through hunting, 550 of which went to Baranov and his company. O'Cain's half-share was worth more than the company's in the long run, because the Russians had higher operating costs. Barred from the port of Canton (Guangzhou) by the Chinese, who feared Russian expansionism, they shipped furs to the Siberian coast and then hauled them overland at great expense to trading posts on China's northern border. Baranov sometimes found it cheaper to pay American captains a commission to carry Russian furs to Canton. Americans exchanged pelts there for Chinese goods such as tea and porcelain that were highly valued along the Atlantic seaboard and brought them further profits when they returned home. While some Yankees involved in the China trade reaped gains of 500 percent or more over their investments, the Russian American Company never made enough from the fur trade to meet its expenses and had to be subsidized by the government.

O'Cain's profitable venture encouraged other Americans to contract with the Russians and exploit the fur resources of the California coast. Some American captains trespassed on Spanish territory by leaving hunters for months or years on coastal islands. The ease with which such parties operated on foreign ground encouraged the Russians first to defy Spanish trade barriers and later to establish a coastal settlement north of San Francisco. That process of expansion began inauspiciously in late 1805 when Nikolai Petrovich Rezanov, chamberlain to the tsar, arrived in Sitka to assess conditions in Alaska and seek ways of improving the colony's prospects. The situation in Sitka, just three years after Tlingits had wrecked the original settlement, could hardly have been worse. "We found upon our arrival at this new outpost of the Russian American Company a lack of all the necessities of life," wrote the German physician and naturalist Georg Heinrich von Langsdorff, who accompanied Rezanov. "I at times had to shoot ravens, hunt mussels or beg a piece of blubber or seal fat to still my hunger." Starvation was averted when the captain of the

American ship *Juno* agreed to sell that vessel and its provisions to the Russians, but Langsdorff noted that much of the food obtained through that purchase and through hunting expeditions went to the company's overseers and clerks, leaving their Aleut underlings malnourished and subject to scurvy. "If they lay exhausted and ill in bed," he remarked, "they were often thrashed out to work."[12]

Rezanov hoped to find a solution to the colony's chronic supply problems in California, which had progressed far beyond Russian Alaska in terms of food production because of advantages in climate and terrain. Indian labor was exploited in California largely for agricultural purposes that benefited many inhabitants rather than for a fur trade that profited few, as Langsdorff observed. In early 1806 Rezanov and company embarked in the *Juno* for San Francisco, where he hoped to persuade officials to sell him provisions as a prelude to regular trade. He was well aware that such trade violated Spanish restrictions but hoped to overcome those barriers through diplomacy.

Upon arriving at San Francisco in late March, the Russian delegation was received by "a Franciscan monk and various military people," Langsdorff related. "Since none of us spoke Spanish, the priest and I used Latin, the only language we had for communication." The commandant at San Francisco, José Darío Argüello, was away, leaving the presidio in charge of his son Luis Antonio Argüello, who would soon succeed his father there. Langsdorff evidently had never seen anyone wearing a serape, for he described young Argüello as a "well built man, disfigured only by his peculiar clothing ... a brightly striped wool wrap, similar to a bed coverlet, over his uniform." Spanish authorities hoped that Russia would reconsider its recent alliance with Britain and other European powers hostile to Napoleonic France and its ally Spain and had ordered that visiting Russian officials be treated hospitably. With the commandant away, his wife and son did the honors, hosting the foreigners at their residence. Like Vancouver during his earlier visit, the visitors were put off by the rude furnishings but charmed

---

12. Georg Heinrich von Langsdorff, *Remarks and Observations on a Voyage around the World from 1803 to 1807*, 1:52, 55–56.

by their gracious hosts, described by Langsdorff as "kind-hearted, good-natured people, who have almost no other diversion and amusement than family joys and domestic happiness."[13]

Señora Argüello, Langsdorff reported, "had had fifteen children, of whom thirteen were still alive." Several of her daughters were past puberty and thus of marriageable age, including fifteen-year-old Concepción, who stood out in Langsdorff's estimate "because of her liveliness, gaiety, love-inspiring, fiery eyes, very beautiful teeth, expressive, pleasing, facial features, beautiful stature and a thousand other charms."[14] Rezanov, in a letter describing his visit, referred to Concepción as a "Spanish beauty" whom he courted for diplomatic reasons. A widower in his early forties, he saw marriage to the commandant's daughter as a means of furthering Russia's interests: "My romance began not in hot passion, which has no place at my age, but from entirely different motives ... Should fate decree its completion, I shall be in a position to render new services to my country by personally examining the harbor of Vera Cruz, Mexico, and by a trip through the interior part of America."[15]

This courtship inspired a romantic legend that overlooked the worldly motives of Rezanov and Concepción, whom he described as driven less by passion than by a determination to broaden her horizons: "I perceived her active, venturesome disposition and character, her unlimited ambition, which at her age of fifteen, made her, alone among her family, dissatisfied with the land of her birth." Confiding in him, she summed up California as follows: "A beautiful land, a warm climate, an abundance of grain and cattle—and nothing else." This may be a rough translation of her words, at best, given the language barrier that the couple had to overcome. But Rezanov knew French, another Romance language, and picked up some Spanish during his visit. Concepción's parents were shocked

---

13. Ibid., 1:87–88; Bancroft, *History of California*, 2:64–78; Cook, *Flood Tide of Empire*, 495–99; C. Alan Hutchinson, *Frontier Settlement in Mexican California: The Híjar-Padrés Colony, and Its Origins, 1769–1835*, 22–26.
14. Langsdorff, *Remarks and Observations*, 1:89.
15. Nikolai Rezanov, *Rezanov Reconnoiters California, 1806*, 33; Richard A. Pierce, "The Nikolai Rezanov–Concepción Argüello Story," in Eve Iversen, *The Romance of Nikolai Rezanov and Concepción Argüello: A Literary Legend and Its Effect on California History*, 150–55.

when they learned she wished to marry Rezanov and live with him in Russia. The religious barrier between the couple could have been overcome quickly if the Russian Orthodox Rezanov had converted to Roman Catholicism, as other foreigners did who entered this society through marriage in years to come. But that was out of the question for an official as prominent as Rezanov. Her parents appealed to Franciscans, who "took poor Concepción to church, made her confess, and tried to make her refuse me, but her determination finally quieted everyone down."[16] She and Rezanov were secretly betrothed with the family's consent, he added, but could not marry until papal permission was granted.

While this private drama unfolded, Rezanov held talks with Governor Arrillaga. Langsdorff was impressed that this "upright old man" of about sixty had traveled there on horseback from Monterey "to pay us his respects, energetically support us and make our stay as pleasant as possible." Arrillaga eventually granted Rezanov's request to purchase "a complete shipload of grain and other foodstuffs," knowing that most of it was intended for hungry Russian colonists in Sitka. This deal did not go far beyond the established practice of allowing foreign vessels in distress to obtain supplies. But permission for regular trade between Russian and Spanish colonists could come only from Madrid, Arrillaga declared by Langsdorff's account, explaining that "even the Viceroy of Mexico could not act in such matters on his own accord."[17]

These negotiations took time and were often interrupted by dinners, dances, and exchanges of gifts, including a fine English musket that Rezanov presented to Luis Antonio Argüello, his would-be brother-in-law. He also sent gifts to Commandant Argüello and the missionaries to repay them for courtesies and "hide from them our poverty and need, of which the Boston vessels had told them to our disadvantage."[18] Among the festivities staged to honor the visiting Russians was a bullfight. Soldiers on foot and horseback "threw spears at a bull until it died after being

---

16. Rezanov, *Rezanov Reconnoiters California*, 16.
17. Langsdorff, *Remarks and Observations*, 1:105.
18. Rezanov, *Rezanov Reconnoiters California*, 4.

wounded many times," Langsdorff noted. He was surprised that padres, "who seem to display tender, humane emotions in all of their behavior and try to awaken these in their neophytes, have not opposed these basically cruel, national amusements." Having been exposed to such blood sports since childhood, the missionaries were "no more affected by the wanton, meaningless torture of animals than the people on Nukahiva when they are eating human flesh," Langsdorff concluded.[19] He need not have gone as far afield as cannibalism in the Marquesas to find analogies for the Spanish bullfight. Bear-baiting and fox hunts were common enough in his own country and other European lands.

As a doctor and naturalist, Langsdorff took a keen interest in the condition and customs of California Indians and visited Missions San Francisco and San José. It was a study in contrasts. San Francisco had struggled since its inception in 1776, whereas San José, founded in 1797 in fertile country, looked far more prosperous. Sandy soil and chill winds had reduced crop yields at San Francisco and stunted the fruit trees, and the neophytes themselves seemed underdeveloped. Echoing Vancouver's assessment, Langsdorff described them as short, poorly built, and displaying "such a miserable, dumb, dark, foolish, slovenly appearance that we all had to agree that we had never seen a race of human beings on a lower level."[20] Life at the aptly named Mission Dolores, recently plagued with sorrows in the form of hunger, disease, and unrest, evidently made these Indians look more inept than they were, for Langsdorff saw evidence of their ingenuity in their watertight baskets, intricate shell necklaces, majestic feather cloaks and headdresses, and the guessing games they played with sticks, demonstrating an agility and cunning that those who considered them foolish would be hard-pressed to match.

From San Francisco, Langsdorff headed south along the bay in a three-man kayak, accompanied by a Russian sailor and an Aleut hunter. Landing near Mission San José, he saw horses and cattle roaming free and foxes trotting amid the calves "in an incredible

---

19. Langsdorff, *Remarks and Observations*, 1:103, 107–108.
20. Ibid., 1:95–96.

intimacy, as if the cows were their mothers." The mission struck Langsdorff as highly promising, with rich soil, budding young fruit trees, and vineyards that yielded sweet wine like that from Málaga. Neophytes there were sturdier and livelier than those at San Francisco, Langsdorff noticed. The padres at San José did not simply tolerate tribal dances and other Native customs on holidays, as Franciscans elsewhere did, but actively encouraged those traditional activities. Father Pedro de la Cueva excused neophytes from work on the day Langsdorff arrived so that they could "dress themselves for the dance as perfectly as possible. For this purpose, he distributed some finery among the best dancers."[21] In doing so, Cueva usurped the role of tribal dance leaders. He evidently hoped that by sanctioning and supervising the dance he would reconcile neophytes to the padres and their mission regimen. Langsdorff watched the performers decorate themselves with cinders, clay, chalk, shells, and feathers and admired their dances and the mock battles and hunts that followed.

Langsdorff concluded that Cueva and the other missionaries he met in California were conscientious overseers who afforded neophytes "good treatment." But he noted that mission Indians still yearned for freedom and ran off, at the risk of being pursued and punished, and that some Indians in the area had actively resisted colonization and clashed with Spanish troops. He also observed that measles was reaching epidemic proportions in missions around San Francisco Bay, adding to the ravages of syphilis and other diseases. He suspected that stress caused by changes in diet and work habits made Indians who entered missions more susceptible to disease and found that many who fell ill rejected prescribed cures, which were largely ineffective, and gave up hope of recovery. As a physician Langsdorff could have done little to help them. He himself was part of a process that was transforming this bountiful environment with devastating impact. On his return from San José, he noticed that sea otters in the bay had not yet learned to fear humans. At one point, he and his companions

---

21. Ibid., 1:114–17; Milliken, *Time of Little Choice*, 195–200.

Dance of Indians at Mission San José, 1806.
*Courtesy The Bancroft Library, University of California,
Berkeley* (BANC PIC 1963.002:1023-FR).

encountered three of them, "sleeping without a care in the world as our baidarka glided past them. We shot them one after another in passing and took them along."[22]

The Russian delegation left San Francisco in May with plenty of provisions for the hungry colonists at Sitka. Rezanov departed with high expectations that included marriage to Concepción Argüello and a trade agreement with Spain. As Langsdorff related, Rezanov planned to travel from Sitka to St. Petersburg to report to the tsar before embarking "for Madrid, where he would settle any differences between the Courts. He would then sail from one of the Spanish ports to Vera Cruz and Mexico and come from there to San Francisco to claim his bride and to pursue active trade!"[23]

22. Langsdorff, *Remarks and Observations*, 1:118–19.
23. Ibid., 1:108, 128.

Traveling across Siberia that fall, Rezanov fell ill but pushed ahead in bitter weather. By the time he reached Irkutsk (a company outpost near the Mongolian border) in January 1807, he was near death. His thoughts were with his late wife, Anna, whose portrait he carried with him. "Today, my wedding anniversary, I gaze keenly at the picture of my former happiness," he wrote to a family friend shortly before he died. "I look at everything and weep bitterly. You too will shed a tear at this point... Shed that tear, pay her this pleasant tribute... I shall see her before you do and will tell her about it." His flirtation with Concepción and California seemed like an idle dream compared to his attachment to his wife and homeland. "Concepción is nice, like an angel, beautiful, good hearted, and she loves me," he confided. "I love her, too, and I shed tears that there is no room for her in my heart. Here, my friend, I am repentant like the sinner at confession, and you, like a pastor, will keep my secret."[24]

Earlier in San Francisco, when his vitality and hopes still ran high, Rezanov had described his courtship of Concepción as the first step in an elaborate diplomatic campaign that he entered into at some personal sacrifice to advance Russia's cause in North America. Concepción's attachment to him may indeed have been stronger than his calculated interest in her. She later exasperated her family by not marrying. She considered a proposal from another venturesome foreigner—Captain James Smith Wilcox from New England, who offered to convert to Catholicism—before deciding to remain single and devote herself to charity and the church, entering a convent in later years. The hidden love story behind this legendary courtship, however, was Rezanov's overriding attachment to the wife and the world he left behind in Russia. His odyssey from Sitka to San Francisco to Siberia, where death promised him a reunion with the one he cared most for, said much about the Russian adventure in North America. Russians built a formidable empire by expanding along their borders, but they never entirely succeeded in reproducing their society overseas

---

24. Rezanov in Iversen, *Romance of Nikolai Rezanov*, 153–54.

the way some other imperial powers did. Their North American colony depended on supplies shipped from Russia and the labor of Aleuts and Kodiaks. If the Russian American Company "should somehow lose the Aleuts," one officer conceded, then an enterprise based on taking sea otters and other fur-bearing species would collapse, "because not one Russian knows how to hunt the animals."[25]

Before he died, Rezanov proposed ways of making the Alaskan colony less dependent on Russian supply shipments, including trade with California. He hoped that option would be recognized by Spain as mutually advantageous but foresaw another possibility if Madrid rejected his overture—founding a settlement on the coast somewhere above San Francisco to raise crops and "supply our population to the north and on the Aleutian Islands with its output."[26] The settlement would also serve as a base for fur hunters, but Rezanov hoped that it would rely as much on Russian expertise in agriculture and other trades as on Native hunting skills. His recommendation would eventually bear fruit in the founding of Fort Ross. Like his private plans to gain entry to Spanish-American society, however, that project would require no small sacrifice in pursuit of an elusive goal. From beginning to end, the Russian courtship of California would remain a speculative affair, promising more than it delivered.

Yankee Adventurism

It took several years for Rezanov's proposal to become a reality. In the interim, Baranov continued sending hunters south from Alaska on American ships to pursue sea otters and fur seals along the California coast. He did so because the company still lacked the naval resources to mount its own ventures, but he did not want to "divide the profits of this business with anybody" and would soon launch the first fur-hunting expedition to California aboard a Russian ship, the *Kodiak*, which left Sitka in 1808.[27] That did not

---

25. Quoted in Gibson, *Imperial Russia in Frontier America*, 8.
26. Rezanov in ibid., 113.
27. Baranov in Odgen, *California Sea Otter Trade*, 58.

bring an end to Russian reliance on Americans, however. Baranov would continue to deal reluctantly with Yankee captains, whom he rightly regarded as rivals. Indeed, by contracting with Yankees the Russians were enlarging American territorial ambitions, which extended up the coast from California at least as far as the Columbia River, so named by a New Englander, Captain Robert Gray. His ship *Columbia* had entered the mouth of that river in 1792 on a fur-trading venture from Boston. Gray's exploit, and the arrival of the Meriwether Lewis and William Clark expedition at the mouth of the Columbia in late 1805, gave Americans some claim to the Pacific Coast along with Spain, Britain, and Russia, nations with larger and longer-standing claims that often conflicted. Amid the confusion and controversy, American expansionists came to regard the western rim of the continent as free for all and showed no more respect for Spain's solid claim to California from San Francisco Bay south than for its theoretical claim to the coast to the north.

That expansive outlook was evident in voyages undertaken in the early 1800s by members of the Winship family of Boston. They were actively involved in the sprawling Northwest fur trade, which reached from Baja California northward to the Aleutians and westward across the Pacific to Hawaii and Canton. The Winships had funded Joseph O'Cain's 1803 venture to Alaska, where he contracted with Baranov to carry hunters to California. In 1805 they sent the ship *O'Cain* out on another such mission, this time with Jonathan Winship, Jr., a veteran of that earlier voyage, as captain. After rounding Cape Horn at year's end, the *O'Cain* sailed northwestward on trade winds and stopped for provisions at Oahu, where Winship dealt with King Kamehameha I. According to William Dane Phelps, a merchant captain who took part in the American conquest of California in 1846 and chronicled earlier ventures there by the Winships using their logs and letters, Kamehameha insisted that the visiting Americans purchase hogs, fruit, and vegetables from him "at extravagant prices," preventing them from dealing with others who might have offered better terms. After laying in those costly supplies and enlarging the crew "by the addition by a few Kanakas," as Hawaiians were known in the trade, Winship headed for Sitka, where he contracted with Baranov to take on some fifty kayaks and one hundred Kodiak hunters as well as twelve Native women, "who were to do camp duty on shore, where gangs should be left to hunt."[28]

This expedition was described by its sponsors simply as a "hunt to the South." The Russians were deliberately vague about such matters and often referred to California north of San Francisco Bay as New Albion to signal that Spanish claims there were contested by the British, among others, and not to be taken seriously. The Russians at Sitka grew too convivial for Winship's liking, clambering aboard the *O'Cain* for a farewell drinking bout before the ship left port on May 22, 1806. "At 5 P.M. our visitors had the goodness to depart, doubtless not one sober man among them," he wrote. "I saluted them with five guns and three cheers, and heartily rejoiced at their departure."[29]

In mid-June the *O'Cain* entered Trinidad Bay, near the mouth of the Mad River. This was well north of the Spanish settlements, and sea otters and seals were plentiful. But Winship's Kodiaks met with resistance from Indians there, most likely Wiyots or Yuroks. The Indians sold sea-otter pelts for less than fifty cents' worth of beads apiece, a tiny fraction of their value in Canton, but did not want Kodiaks hunting in their territory and attacked them when they came ashore. Winship decided that it was better to abandon "the good hunting ground there," Phelps related, "than to remain and fight the natives, and probably occasion the loss of many lives. In such a conclusion Captain Winship manifested a regard for humanity and justice, not often exhibited by the N.W. traders."[30]

From Trinidad Bay, Winship made directly for Baja California, avoiding coastal inlets between San Francisco and San Diego, where Commandant Rodríguez and other officers remained

---

28. William Dane Phelps, "Solid Men of Boston in the Northwest," in Briton C. Busch and Barry M. Gough, eds., *Fur Traders from New England: The Boston Men in the North Pacific, 1787–1800*, 43–44.
29. Winship in ibid., 44–45.
30. Phelps in ibid., 46.

vigilant. Winship's Kanakas went ashore at Cedros Island off the Baja California coast to take fur seals while Kodiaks prowled for sea otters in the surrounding waters. Never one to stand idle when there was profit to be had, Winship left the hunters to their devices and traded along the coast with obliging Dominican friars, purchasing otter skins and provisions. Within three months, Phelps reported, Winship and his hunters had secured "furs worth about $60,000 in Canton." The expedition was so rewarding that the captain prolonged it, leaving the hunters well supplied on their island bases and returning to Sitka by way of Oahu to pick up more hunters and kayaks. Heading south with those reinforcements in 1807, Winship felt confident enough to try the Alta California coast. He landed an exploratory party on one of the Farallon Islands, where a vast number of fur seals were sighted, and stopped later to trade at San Pedro and Catalina Island, where enterprising Indians sold him "quite a quantity of wheat and vegetables."[31]

By the spring of 1807 more than 150 Kodiaks transported by Winship were hunting on islands off Baja California. They were poaching on foreign territory, but Winship cared no more for Spanish sovereignty there than Phelps did when he wrote later that "Spaniards, with a pretended jurisdiction, attempted to prohibit other nations from taking the fur-bearing animals on their coast." Had Spaniards landed on unoccupied islands in Massachusetts Bay and challenged the "pretended jurisdiction" of Americans there, Phelps might have considered it cause for war; but he hailed Winship for his intrusions, which did not go uncontested. "The Spaniards would sometimes capture and confiscate a stray canoe [kayak] with its contents," Phelps noted, "and the Indians of the missions would occasionally meet with the Kodiaks and have a scrimmage."[32] A few lives were lost in those clashes, but nearly all the Kodiaks who came south with Winship returned with him to Sitka that summer on a ship filled to the brim with furs and hunters. "We received on board one hundred and forty-nine Indian

---

31. Ibid., 47–48.
32. Ibid., 49.

men, twelve women, one infant, and three Russians," he wrote in his log.[33] At least two children were born during the voyage north, and Kodiaks passed the time with songs and dances that delighted the crew. After depositing the Kodiaks and Russians at Sitka, Winship gave the company its share of the furs and carried the rest to Canton, where his cargo was valued at $136,400, a handsome sum at a time when the expenses of such a voyage might amount to about $25,000.

Other American ships carrying hunters from Alaska were making inroads along the California coast around this time. In the spring of 1807 Captain Oliver Kimball of the *Peacock* anchored in Bodega Bay, where Aleuts built shelters on the beach. That base brought them within range of San Francisco Bay, which they entered safely by hugging the north shore, away from the presidio. The galling sight of Aleuts skimming across the bay in kayaks became all too common for troops there, who lacked boats of their own to pursue the hunters. Soldiers eventually learned to guard springs and other sources of fresh water visited by the hunters, capturing some of them and deterring others, who could not keep up their exertions for long without refilling the animal bladders that served them as canteens.

For the Winships, success in the Northwest trade nurtured hopes of moving beyond partnership with the Russians and establishing an American fur-trading base at the mouth of the Columbia that would also produce food for their crews. This was similar to Rezanov's proposal for a Russian settlement north of San Francisco, an idea approved in St. Petersburg in 1809. Captain Nathan Winship, who had served as mate under his brother Jonathan during the recent voyage of the *O'Cain*, left Boston in command of the *Albatross* in July 1809 and reached the Columbia the following May by way of Oahu. His efforts to establish a colony soon faltered, however, in the face of stiff opposition from Chinooks, who dominated the lower Columbia and feared that he would bypass them and trade directly with tribes upstream. It

---

33. Winship in ibid., 49–50; Gibson, *Otter Skins, Boston Ships, and China Goods*, 57.

was left to employees of fur magnate John Jacob Astor, arriving at the mouth of the Columbia overland and by sea, to establish the first American settlement on the Pacific Coast, Astoria, in 1811.

Rebuffed on the Columbia, Nathan Winship found compensation in California by depositing parties of seal hunters on the Farallones and other islands and teaming up to take sea otters with Jonathan Winship, who had returned in the *O'Cain* with hunters from Alaska. As Phelps related, "the two Captains Winship pursued their business of hunting and trading on joint account, in different directions, and with gangs on various Islands." Fur traders there gave no thought to conserving natural resources and took pride in depleting hunting grounds that Spaniards left exposed. Between 1809 and 1812 some 150,000 fur seals, valued at nearly two dollars a piece, were slaughtered for their skins along the California coast by parties from American ships, Phelps reckoned, "a fact which contrasts Spanish indolence and imbecility with the activity and enterprise of 'Boston men.'"[34] The Winships themselves might not have put it so bluntly, but they were forerunners of a relentless expansionist movement that recognized few limits on where Americans could venture or what they could take.

Not all Americans defied Spanish restrictions with impunity. In June 1813 Captain George Washington Eayrs lost his ship *Mercury* off Refugio Cove to a Peruvian privateer, Nicolás Noé, who claimed the vessel and its cargo as prizes because Eayrs was engaged in smuggling. At an inquiry conducted at the Santa Bárbara presidio by Commandant José Darío Argüello, formerly of San Francisco, Eayrs claimed that he was simply seeking supplies and provisions for his vessel as allowed by law. But that tired excuse was refuted by the captain's account book and letters he kept, which implicated him and several local missionaries and settlers in illicit deals consummated at the Rancho Refugio de Nuestra Señora, owned by a retired officer, José María Ortega. "I expect you to dine with me at the *casa del rancho*," wrote Father Luis Gil y Taboada of Mission Santa Bárbara to his "Friend Don Jorge," as

---

34. Phelps in Busch and Gough, *Fur Traders from New England*, 68, 74.

he addressed Eayrs; "we will talk of what is interesting in the news from Europe and the whole world. We will also trade, unless you bring things as dear as usual."[35] He evidently found the captain's terms acceptable, for he provided Eayrs with 300 otter skins in trade. A Spanish official who later reviewed the case found such conduct by padres reprehensible, but José Argüello pointed out that missionaries and the Indians they cared for were now so desperate for clothing and other essentials offered by foreign traders that they had little choice but to bow to necessity, which "makes legal what is illegal by law."[36]

The actions of Eayrs and his intrusive compatriots left Spanish authorities more fearful of American designs on California than of Russian encroachment. As early as 1805 Felipe de Goycoechea, former commandant at Santa Bárbara, had warned that Anglo-Americans through "arrogant boldness" were gaining such confidence there that their young nation, "constantly increasing its strength, may one day venture to measure it with Spain, and acquiring such knowledge of our seas and coasts may make California the object of its attack."[37] American fur traders suffered a setback during the War of 1812, however, when the British blockaded Canton and barred them from their prime market for pelts. Meanwhile, the Russians, who still had access to China overland, reduced their reliance on Americans by sending hunting parties to California aboard their own ships and putting their long-considered settlement plan into effect.

Founding Fort Ross

Before establishing that colony, the Russians tried to allay Spanish concerns by renewing their bid for trade relations in a proclamation wishing "Health, Happiness, and the Blessing of the All-Powerful to our friends and neighbors the noble and brave Spaniards, inhabitants of the Californias." The proclamation went on to state

---

35. Gil y Taboada in Robert Ryal Miller, *A Yankee Smuggler on the Spanish California Coast: George Washington Eayrs and the Ship Mercury*, 24.
36. Argüello in ibid., 58.
37. Goycoechea in ibid., 10–11.

View of Fort Ross, 1828, by Auguste Duhaut-Cilly.
Courtesy Library of Congress, Prints and Photographs Division (LC-USZ62-7919).

that Russia's formal request for trade with California had reached Madrid "at that unlucky time when the king, Carlos IV, renounced his crown and Spain's great misfortunes began."[38] The Russians were reminding colonists in California that they had no legitimate monarch in Madrid and would have to fend for themselves. (Carlos IV's designated successor, Ferdinand VII, remained a prisoner until December 1813, when Napoleon freed him to foil Spanish liberals who had rebelled against Joseph Bonaparte and set up a short-lived constitutional government, the Cortes of Cádiz.) Officials in California would not enter into any trade agreement with the Russians of their own accord, for they had no idea what had taken place in Spain recently and how the court there might respond to a deal made without its consent.

In the spring of 1812 Ivan Kuskov of the Russian American Company landed at Bodega Bay to oversee the building of Fort Ross (from Rus, meaning "Russian") at a site he had selected earlier, above Bodega Bay. Accompanying Kuskov were eighty Aleuts and ninety-five Russians. They built the fort on a promontory rising from the sea—a good defensive position should Spanish forces contest their right to settle there, with ample pasture for livestock

---

38. Quoted in Bancroft, *History of California*, 2:295 n. 2.

and plenty of timber and fresh water in the hills to the east. Pomo Indians living nearby welcomed the Russians as a buffer against Spanish troops and padres, who were making expeditions north of San Francisco Bay to retrieve fugitives from missions and seek fresh converts. Although Russian Orthodox priests converted Natives in Alaska, Fort Ross was not a base for mission work. Pomos labored seasonally there, harvesting crops for payment in food and clothing. "The inhabitants of Ross live in the greatest concord with the Indians," wrote Captain Otto von Kotzebue, a Russian navigator of German ancestry who first visited California in 1816. Some Indians there, he added, willingly gave "their daughters in marriage to Russians and Aleutians," fostering good relations that deteriorated when Russians began forcing Pomos to work for them.[39]

Russian expansionists like Kirill Khlebnikov, who visited Fort Ross in 1820 as assistant manager of the company, saw this outpost as a wedge that his countrymen could use to pry all or part of California loose from Spain. That nation was not gaining "any real profit" here, he argued. The missions were "maintained for their own enrichment," and foreign trade was conducted only with smugglers and brought no revenue to the government. Khlebnikov urged his superiors to strengthen their hold on northern California, which he saw as essential to maintaining the Russian presence in Alaska. "If we lose our place in New Albion, we will lose the entire northwest coast of America," he warned. "But how fortunate we would be if Russia could obtain the port of San Francisco! That would be enough to ensure that the Russian colonies remain strong and flourish."[40]

Khlebnikov's enthusiasm was not shared by his superiors, who lost interest in California, partly because Fort Ross did not produce enough food to meet the needs of Sitka and other bases in

---

39. Kotzebue in Gibson, *Imperial Russia in Frontier America*, 112–15; Bancroft, *History of California*, 2:297–308; E. O. Essig, Adele Ogden, and Clarence John DuFour, *Fort Ross: California Outpost of Russian Alaska, 1812–1841*, 5–10.
40. Kirill Khlebnikov, *The Khlebnikov Archive: Unpublished Journal (1800–1837) and Travel Notes (1820, 1822, and 1824)*, 85–86.

Alaska. Although grain yields were disappointing, root vegetables such as potatoes and turnips fared better; melons, peaches, and cherries helped vary the diet of settlers, who also raised livestock. In good years, Fort Ross fulfilled its own needs and part of Sitka's, but it never sustained Russian Alaska as a whole. "It is obvious that agriculture at Ross cannot supply the colonies with food," a company official concluded.[41] Authorities were also discouraged by a sharp decline in the number of sea otters taken by Aleuts as vigilant Spanish troops curbed poaching around San Francisco Bay and sea-otter colonies were depleted north of there. Aleuts were still taking thousands of fur seals each year at bases on the Farallones, but by 1819 their haul of precious sea-otter pelts was down to a paltry dozen or so. Russians compensated by offering Spaniards goods crafted by skilled artisans at Ross, including blacksmiths, carpenters, and shipwrights. The articles they produced were much in demand in California at a time when no Spanish supply ships were arriving there, and both colonists and officials defied trade barriers to obtain those goods.

Soon after the settlers began building the fort in 1812, Governor Arrillaga had sent Lieutenant Gabriel Moraga to investigate. According to the Russians, Moraga was receptive to their proposal for trade and returned a few months later with three horses and twenty cattle for the settlers as a goodwill gesture. Arrillaga himself permitted Russians in need to purchase provisions at San Francisco, as he had in 1806, a deal that helped Fort Ross survive infancy. At the insistence of the viceroy, he later demanded that the Russians abandon the settlement, but Kuskov replied that he could make no such move without orders from Baranov. Although no attempt was made to remove the settlers from Fort Ross, Spanish forces continued to contest Russian incursions from San Francisco Bay southward. In September 1815 troops captured a party of twenty so Aleut hunters led by Boris Tarasov of the Russian American Company when they went ashore at San Pedro to trade and obtain supplies. They and another party from the Russian

---

41. Quoted in Gibson, *Imperial Russia in Frontier America*, 125.

ship *Il'men*, seized when they landed at Refugio Cove several days later, were detained at length. At least one Aleut died in captivity before the prisoners were released.

Tensions between Russians and Spaniards were evident when Captain Kotzebue entered San Francisco Bay at the helm of the *Rurik* in October 1816. As commander of a Russian expedition sent to explore the California coast rather than exploit its resources, he expected to be welcomed there and saluted Spaniards at the presidio with seven shots. "This salutation was returned by the same number of shots, less two, according to the Spanish custom," related Adelbert von Chamisso, a naturalist who served as Kotzebue's interpreter. Kotzebue was not satisfied with that response, Chamisso added, and insisted that Commandant Luis Antonio Argüello "give us the two missing supplementary salutes." Argüello did so reluctantly and must have been deeply offended, but he and his officers were too polite, and too hungry for company and a decent meal, to refuse invitations to dine with Kotzebue. "We ate on shore, in the tent, and our friends from the Presidio were always promptly on hand," wrote Chamisso. "The misery in which they languished, forgotten and deserted for six or seven years by Mexico, their mother-land, did not permit them to be hosts; and the need felt to pour out their hearts to some one, drove them to us."[42]

After appeasing Argüello, Kotzebue managed to offend California's highest authority, Governor Pablo Vicente de Solá, who had succeeded Arrillaga after his death in 1814. Solá came all the way from Monterey to confer with Kotzebue, who had only to travel from his ship to the presidio to pay his respects to the governor. Instead he sent Chamisso ashore one morning to inform Solá that the captain awaited his visit aboard the *Rurik*. Chamisso was no great admirer of Spaniards or their colonizing efforts. The only argument Spain had for maintaining this backward colony, he stated, was "the pious intention of propagating the Christian religion," a task he felt the Franciscans were bungling. Yet he took

---

42. Chamisso in August C. Mahr, *The Visit of the "Rurik" to San Francisco in 1816*, 31–35; Bancroft, *History of California*, 2:309–11.

no pleasure in delivering Kotzebue's humiliating summons to Solá, whom he found in "full regimentals" but still wearing his "night cap," which may simply have been a cloth or handkerchief that men there often wore over their hair. "I delivered myself as well as I could, of my message," wrote Chamisso, "and saw that his face lengthened to three times its natural extent." Solá, who had not yet breakfasted, said that "he regretted he could not endure the sea before eating, and he was truly sorry that he must renounce the pleasure, for the present, of becoming acquainted with the Captain."[43]

That was a more diplomatic reply than Kotzebue deserved. The two might never have met had not the lookout at the presidio seen Kotzebue being rowed ashore to observe the midday sun and adjust his chronometer. When he heard that "the Captain was coming," Solá assumed that Kotzebue was coming to see him and "strode down the slope to meet him," related Chamisso. "The Captain, on his part, ascended the slope in order to receive the Governor; and so Spain and Russia, each going half-way, fell into one another's open arms!"[44]

For Solá, these preliminaries and the conference that followed were a sobering lesson in the limits of his authority as the representative of a fading imperial power that was fast losing control of California. He had entered office determined to take a hard line with intruding foreigners, only to be forced into the same sorts of concessions made by his predecessor, including trade deals that violated official restrictions but brought California desperately needed goods such as clothing for his ragged troops. In talks, Solá asked Kotzebue to order Fort Ross abandoned. In a familiar refrain, Kotzebue said such an order could only come from higher authorities. He promised to refer the matter to the tsar, and Solá pledged in return to refrain from hostilities until the issue had been resolved at court. This was no great concession, for he dared not attack the fort with his meager forces, but Kotzebue was offering even less. Russia, having withstood invasion by Napoleon in

---

43. Chamisso in Mahr, *Visit of the "Rurik" to San Francisco*, 39, 77–79.
44. Ibid., 39.

1812 and emerged triumphant, had little reason now to defer to Spain, a kingdom that the former French emperor had dominated and destabilized.

Colonists in California were not aware of the latest developments in Europe, but they could gauge the decline of Spanish power by the frequency with which foreigners defied imperial restrictions and infiltrated their shores. They were not fighting for independence, but it was being thrust upon them. In the process, they were coming to view themselves not as Spaniards but as Californios—settlers whose ties to this territory were stronger than their attachment to Spain or Mexico, an emerging nation that would soon claim them but would never entirely possess them.

CHAPTER 7

Imperial Sunset

Among those who came of age in California as Mexico was breaking free from Spain was Juan Bautista Alvarado, born in Monterey in 1809 and later governor of Mexican California. Alvarado was the product of two families with long ties to the colony. His paternal grandfather, whose name he bore, was among the troops who took part in the pioneering Spanish expedition to San Diego in 1769. His maternal grandfather, Ignacio Vallejo, came to Alta California as a soldier in 1774. Alvarado's father died shortly after he was born; he was raised by his maternal grandparents and took pride in his Vallejo ancestry, sometimes referring to himself as Alvarado y Vallejo. He was close to Mariano Guadalupe Vallejo, an uncle of his who was only a year or so older and also figured prominently in California's affairs as an adult. Both were creoles, born in America but similar in heritage and complexion to the Spanish-born *peninsulares* who governed California through much of the colonial era. Race-consciousness in California favored creoles but did not produce a caste system, and some mestizos would also do well there during the Mexican era. What distinguished Juan Alvarado and Mariano Vallejo was not their ancestry or breeding but their knack for seizing opportunities that came their way,

175

notably education, something few colonists there had access to in earlier times. Both were highly literate and left vivid historical memoirs that drew on their own recollections and the accounts of their elders to portray the sunset of the Spanish imperial age, when, as Alvarado put it, "bears were more numerous in California than Christians."[1]

The first event of political significance that left an impression on young Alvarado was the ceremony held in Monterey in 1815 to welcome Spanish-born Pablo Solá as governor. Californios might have preferred to see that appointment go to one of their own, José Darío Argüello, who served as acting governor between the time José Arrillaga died and Solá arrived. But they showed no violent resentment of the sort that set rebellious creoles, mestizos, and Indians against *peninsulares* elsewhere in Mexico. Instead colonists went to great lengths to honor Solá. "One missionary was present from each one of the Alta California missions," Alvarado related, "and each missionary was accompanied by a great number of neophytes in gala dress." The ceremony was held in the plaza of the Monterey presidio, which had been much improved since Father Font had arrived with Anza's colonists in 1776 and found the place dank and dismal. The buildings now had tile roofs, and the plaza was decorated for the occasion with boughs of pine and cypress and illuminated with clay lanterns fueled with beef tallow. "From a lofty flagpole in the center of the square waved the Spanish standard with the lion of Castile in its center," recalled Alvarado.[2] That flag had become an object of scorn elsewhere in Spanish America but still commanded respect in California.

Pro-Spanish sentiment was particularly strong among the missionaries, who celebrated Solá's safe arrival with a Mass of thanksgiving in the presidio chapel. Indian musicians and singers directed by a talented neophyte named José el Cantor took part in the service, as if to underscore the theme of the sermon delivered by

---

1. Juan Bautista Alvarado, "Historia de California," Bancroft Library, 1:39; Robert Ryal Miller, *Juan Alvarado: Governor of California, 1836–1842*, 3–20; Bancroft, *History of California*, 2:208–209 n. 19.
2. Alvarado, "Historia de California," 1:38, 40.

Father Vicente Francisco de Sarría, a Spanish-born Franciscan who oversaw the worldly affairs of the mission system as prefect (the role of president now being confined to spiritual matters). His message was that Indians were *gente de razón:* "rational beings capable of making progress in the arts and even in the sciences." Those were admirable sentiments, Alvarado commented in retrospect, but his own impression was that the padres made a point of "teaching the neophytes in such a way that they learned absolutely nothing at all." He conceded that there were cases "where a certain priest would take a liking to this or that Indian and teach him to read, write, play and sing," but most neophytes were "taught only the chanting of a few prayers."[3]

No such objections to the mission system were voiced during the ceremony that Alvarado described. This was a celebration of what the padres and other colonists there had accomplished under trying circumstances. After the service, Solá addressed the presidial troops, who "wore their hair very long," Alvarado recalled, "and on gala occasions allowed it to hang loosely down their backs." Solá saluted them as "Soldiers of Cortés!" and "Sons of Mars!" and assured them that their king would reward them for their services, a promise that drew hopeful cheers from men who had long gone unrewarded. Afterward, young women came forward to kiss Solá's hand and serve him at a banquet honoring him. Among them, Alvarado recalled, were three daughters of retired soldier Felipe García who embodied the creole ideal with their fair skin, "rosy cheeks and black hair reaching down to their well-shaped calves." They brought the bounty of California to Solá's table: "excellent olives from San Diego Mission, oranges and pomegranates from San Gabriel . . . exquisite wines from San Fernando Mission."[4]

Padres spared no expense to gratify the new governor. They hoped that he would return the favor by respecting their rights as overseers of the mission system, which was far more populous and productive than the secular California that Solá presided over. Mexican

3. Ibid., 1:41.
4. Ibid., 1:44–46.

chronicler Antonio María Osio, who arrived there a decade after Solá's inauguration, passed along a revealing tale he was told about the first meeting between the new governor and Prefect Sarría. Both men were Basques, and Sarría charmed Solá by conversing with him in Basque as well as Spanish (Castilian). "When they bade farewell to one another, they parted on such good terms that it seemed as if they had been friends for a long time," Osio wrote. Afterward, a friar who was speaking with some officers gestured to Sarría to inquire how he had fared with the governor: "The Superior understood and, in response, placed his right arm all the way up his large left sleeve to indicate he already had him in his pocket."[5]

It soon became clear to Sarría and other Franciscans, however, that Solá was not a representative of the pious old imperial order they favored but a patriotic reformer who supported recent efforts in Spain to form a constitutional government that would limit the powers of the Crown and the Catholic Church. He conveyed his cautious liberalism, which included support for an education system that involved more than religious instruction, to Juan Alvarado, Mariano Vallejo, José Castro, and other youngsters in Monterey. He thus had considerable impact on the future of California by fostering leaders who were not beholden to the clergy and favored secularizing the mission system, a measure long delayed by the padres' insistence that neophytes were not ready for it.

The first schools in California had sprouted up in the late 1700s at presidio communities and the pueblos of San José and Los Angeles. The teachers were mostly retired soldiers who charged for their services, but some literate women also taught girls at home or at missions. Governor Diego de Borica promoted schooling in the 1790s, but many parents felt that the results were not worth the expense. Youngsters who did receive formal education learned little more than how to read and copy religious texts. "There were no books at that time other than the spelling book, the reading charts, and the *Ripalda Catechism*," recalled José del Carmen Lugo, a relative of Mariano Vallejo born in Los Angeles in 1813.[6] Vallejo and Alvarado

---

5. Osio, *History of Alta California*, 32; Bancroft, *History of California*, 2:470–73.
6. Lugo, "Life of a Rancher," 187.

studied that same catechism—composed two centuries earlier by a Spanish Jesuit, Father Jerónimo Ripalda—at the school they attended with other boys in Monterey. (Girls attended a separate school there established by Solá.) The boys were taught by Corporal Miguel Archuleta, whose regimen differed little from the one imposed by other schoolmasters in California. As Vallejo recalled, the typical teacher in those days was "an old soldier, brutal, drunken, bigoted, and except that he could read and write, ignorant." Those who failed to learn their lessons, he added, were often scourged with a barbed whip that "drew blood, and if used with severity, left a scar for life. The only volumes used for reading were the books of religious formulae, which the pupils used cordially to hate all through their later life, for the torments of scourging were recalled."[7]

Solá offered Vallejo and Alvarado other texts to read, including the liberal constitution enacted in Spain in 1812 and the classic Miguel de Cervantes novel *Don Quixote*. (Vallejo would later be branded a "heretic" for purchasing a collection of books that included works by Rousseau and Voltaire and sharing them with Alvarado and Castro, an offense for which all three were briefly excommunicated by Father-President Narciso Durán.)[8] Solá also helped the boys out when they and their classmates rebelled against Corporal Archuleta, who punished them severely for leaving the schoolhouse without closing the *gatera* (cat's door), through which chickens entered in their absence and spoiled their handwritten copies of official documents. Archuleta was stingy in most things, Vallejo related, but "as liberal as Mycaenas when it came to dealing out drubbings," using "a ferule three feet long and weighing two pounds, with which he struck children of tender age across the palms."[9] This was more than his pupils could bear. They turned on their master, who reported them to the governor.

---

7. Vallejo in J. Andrew Ewing, "Education in California during the Pre-Statehood Period," 54–55; Hubert Howe Bancroft, *California Pastoral, 1769–1848*, 493–509.
8. José de la Guerra y Noriega in Louise Pubols, *The Father of All: The de la Guerra Family, Power, and Patriarchy in Mexican California*, 155.
9. Mariano Guadalupe Vallejo, "Recuerdos históricos y personales tocantes a la Alta California," Bancroft Library, 1:208; Alan Rosenus, *General Vallejo and the Advent of the Americans*, 3–9.

Solá handed their case to a sympathetic judge, Sergeant Ignacio Vallejo, Mariano's father and Juan's grandfather, who ruled that the boys must recopy the papers but deserved no further punishment because their hasty exit from school had been occasioned by a thrilling event—the arrival of the Spanish frigate *Princesa*, patrolling the coast against smugglers.

Such patrols did not stop one American captain, James Smith Wilcox (who would later propose to Concepción Argüello), from entering Monterey Bay in his ship *Traveller* in 1817. Ordered ashore to explain his presence, he made a forbidding impression on young Alvarado, who had never seen a Yankee up close: "He was dressed all in black, wearing a very tall black felt hat, trousers and a swallow-tailed coat." After admitting that he had come there to trade in violation of Spanish law, Wilcox was forced to wait in the plaza under guard while Solá and others held a "council of war" to determine his fate (some suspected him of spying). At noon, Alvarado recalled, the bells of the presidio chapel tolled the Ave Maria, "a prayer it was customary for all residents to repeat aloud at that hour, while they knelt with bared heads." When the soldiers gestured for Wilcox to kneel and remove his hat, he "suddenly grew pale, for he thought they were going to shoot him." He soon realized his mistake and did as asked. "When I saw him kneeling with his bald head uncovered," wrote Alvarado, "he seemed to me more like a Franciscan friar than a man of the sea."[10]

In his humbled state, without the full head of hair that denoted strength and virility there, Wilcox no longer frightened the boys: "We gathered courage and nerve, and went edging along on our knees and moving nearer to where the soldiers were." When Wilcox stood up, Alvarado noticed that "he had acquired two white spots on his fine black suit."[11] He was soon allowed to depart with his ship and cargo, but his brief detention served a useful purpose by demystifying this Yankee in the eyes of the townspeople. It was a lesson that Alvarado—who found much to admire in Americans

---

10. Alvarado, "Historia de California," 1:102–104; Bancroft, *History of California*, 2:285–87.
11. Alvarado, "Historia de California," 1:104–105.

and their democratic ideals but came to rue their presence in California—would never forget.

Californios learned a harder lesson in 1818 when French privateer Hipólito Bouchard, flying the flag of Argentina, which had declared independence from Spain, ransacked Monterey and other targets. Warned by an American trader, Captain Henry Gyzelaar, that Bouchard was fitting out two ships in Hawaii to prey on Spanish settlements, authorities in Santa Bárbara alerted Solá. He then had sacred objects removed from coastal missions and made other preparations. When the privateers targeted Monterey in November, Solá concluded that Bouchard, who had more than sixty cannons and some four hundred men at his disposal, could not be stopped by the eight-gun battery and forty or fifty soldiers defending the town. "What could I do, Your Excellency, in such a situation?" he wrote to the viceroy afterward. He ordered Monterey evacuated and retreated inland with his troops, leaving the capital to the mercy of marauders, who set fire to the presidio and "stole whatever they found useful in the midst of the poverty in which these inhabitants live."[12]

The damage done there and elsewhere along the coast was not great, but Californios lost what little confidence they had left in the power of Spain to protect them. Bouchard's raids, conducted largely by Argentineans in rebellion against the Crown, signaled that a revolution was coming to California whether colonists wanted it or not. For Alvarado, however, the Bouchard scare brought a welcome change in scene. He left Monterey and went to live with his mother and stepfather, widening the network of family ties that would serve him well in the future. Through his stepfather, for example, he got to know Ignacio María Ortega, whose family had been prominent in Santa Bárbara since its founding. Alvarado learned to ride at Ortega's ranch near Mission San Juan Bautista and helped him kill bears that preyed on his cattle. Through Ortega, he met a neighboring rancher, José Mariano

---

12. Solá in Beebe and Senkewicz, *Lands of Promise and Despair,* 302; Bancroft, *History of California,* 2:20–40.

Castro, whom he described as "the richest landowner in northern California."[13] Alvarado's father had helped Castro retain his land grant in full when its boundaries were challenged by the padres at San Juan Bautista. Castro now returned the favor by giving the boy two fine colts and a hundred pesos.

Part of that cash prize was expended when Alvarado served as godfather to the son of Joaquín José Soto, the *mayordomo* (civilian overseer) at San Juan Bautista. He accepted that responsibility only after consulting his mother, who assured him that the *mayordomo* was "one of the most important employees of the Mission and was considered a respectable person, along with his family." Alvarado had seen godparents tossing money about after baptisms and feared that he would lose his entire bequest from Castro if he did the same. His mother advised him to conserve his assets by changing twenty pesos into *cuartillas* (quarters), and giving one to each friend or relative attending the ceremony. After the baptism, in which he delivered a short speech wishing the infant well, Alvarado was handsomely compensated by Soto, who presented him with a saddle beautifully decorated with silver. "With this saddle and with my thoroughbreds," he wrote, "I expected to make my appearance in the capital, Monterey, as though I were the son of a rich landowner."[14] He was not yet wealthy in that sense, but at the age of ten he was already richly connected to several large and influential families. Those ties would earn him credit with hundreds of Californios in years to come.

Ceremonies that related one Californio to another, whether as godparent and godchild or husband and wife, were compacts between families. The marriage between Ignacio Vallejo (Juan Alvarado's grandfather) and María Antonia Lugo, for example, was contracted soon after she was born at Mission San Luis Obispo, where her father served with the guards. Vallejo, then a young soldier staying with the Lugos, decided on the spot that this was the family he wanted to join through marriage. By one

---

13. Juan Bautista Alvarado, *Vignettes of Early California: Childhood Reminiscences of Juan Bautista Alvarado*, 5, 15, 26–27.
14. Ibid., 28–30.

account, he assisted at the birth of his future wife before asking for her in wedlock. José Lugo, his wife's nephew, said nothing of Vallejo helping with the delivery (a function usually performed there by midwives) but confirmed the courtship story in essence: "Vallejo rocked the little girl in a hammock, and arranged that when she reached an age for marriage they should give her to him in matrimony."[15] They married when she was fourteen and went on to have thirteen children. Another link between prominent families was forged in 1815 when Governor Solá served as godfather to Angustias de la Guerra, whose father, José de la Guerra y Noriega, was then commandant at Santa Bárbara. That family tie did not prevent Solá from scolding the commandant when his timely and accurate warning about Bouchard's impending raid was not quickly fulfilled. As Angustias later remarked, shortly before the raid occurred the governor "wrote a very insulting letter to my father, accusing him of being influenced by cock-and-bull stories."[16]

The Dream of Independence

In January 1822 Solá received word that Mexico had won independence from Spain. As a proud Spaniard, he found that hard to believe. "Independence is a dream," he wrote, adding that "the immortal and incomparable Spanish nation has many and great resources with which to make herself respected."[17] It soon became clear, however, that Mexico was now its own empire and Solá would have to bow to it. The new regime of Emperor Agustín de Iturbide, a creole general who joined the struggle for independence belatedly, did not constitute a radical departure from Spanish traditions. As one sign that modest changes were now in order, however, Indian leaders at the missions, advised by their padres, were allowed to take part in elections for delegates who in turn selected a deputy to represent California in the newly established Congress in Mexico City. Solá was duly chosen and expected that Commandant de

---

15. Lugo, "Life of a Rancher," 187; Rosenus, *General Vallejo*, 5.
16. Angustias de la Guerra in Beebe and Senkewicz, *Testimonios*, 202.
17. Solá in Bancroft, *History of California*, 2:450.

la Guerra y Noriega, the senior officer in California, would take his place in Monterey. But the commandant's Spanish birth, long a prerequisite for the governorship, had become a liability. Later that year Canon Agustín Fernández de San Vicente arrived in Monterey as an envoy of the new regime and arranged for the popular commandant at San Francisco, Luis Argüello, to become California's first permanent native-born governor, his father having served in that position temporarily. Fernández gave Californios a say in the matter by allowing the delegates of their newly formed *diputación* (assembly) to cast ballots for governor, trusting that Argüello would prevail.

Some in California welcomed independence. "We younger people congratulated each other," recalled Alvarado, "but refrained from expressing our opinions in public."[18] They did so out of respect for Governor Solá, but others were freer with their feelings. Mariano Vallejo remembered the raising of the Mexican flag in Monterey as a festive occasion for mission Indians in particular: "When the neophytes saw that the Mexicans had lowered the flag upon which the lions were depicted and in its place had run up one in the middle of which was an eagle perched upon a cactus, they were greatly delighted, because before the arrival of Junípero Serra the eagle had been the emblem of their religious beliefs." There was some truth to this, for California Indians had long honored the spirits of eagles, condors, and other birds and used their feathers in ceremonies. But neophytes also hoped for freedom under the new flag. Most of the padres and more than a few soldiers, however, remained partial to Spain. Some officers in Monterey, Vallejo noted, were "out-and-out Spaniards . . . grieved by the change of flag."[19]

Juana Machado, born in 1814 at the San Diego presidio to Corporal José Manuel Machado and María Serafina Valdés, recalled the raising of the Mexican flag there in 1822 as a solemn occasion. "For a number of years the soldiers and their families had suffered many

---

18. Alvarado, "Historia de California," 1:168.
19. Vallejo, "Recuerdos históricos y personales," 1:222; Hackel, *Children of Coyote*, 374–75.

hardships due to a lack of clothing and other things," she related. "Supplies from the king were not arriving because of the war of independence in Mexico." The outcome of that struggle left them perplexed. As the commandant shouted, "Long live the Mexican Empire!" the Spanish flag was lowered in the plaza and the Mexican flag hauled aloft amid the booming of guns. Instead of reassuring the soldiers by offering them pay, the new regime took something precious away from them the next day by ordering them to "cut off their braids."[20] When Juana's father came home with shorn braid in hand, he was crestfallen and her mother was reduced to tears.

The pride these men had taken in their long hair was not unlike that of warriors among various Indian tribes. Many soldiers in California were partly of Indian ancestry, and even those who were not shared certain traits with their Indian foes. Juana Machado told of a battle in which a neophyte-turned-horse rustler named Agustín "grabbed hold of my father by his braided hair and pulled him down from his horse." Her father managed to draw his knife "and bury it in the Indian's belly. He ripped out all his guts and left him for dead. My father also cut off his ears and scalped him, which was what they used to do then."[21] Her father had taken his opponent's hair but was later deprived of his own cherished braid by order of Mexican officials, who were not much better than Spanish authorities at heeding the concerns of soldiers on this taxing Indian frontier.

Mexicans had long resented Spanish trade restrictions and were quick to open their ports to foreign merchants. In California, foreign trade was initially restricted to San Diego and Monterey, which was designated the port of entry; all ships were required to stop there and pay duties, which funded the local government. Merchants from various countries competed for California's trade, but the advantage went to two young British entrepreneurs, William Hartnell and Hugh McCulloch, who had operated legally in Chile and Peru in recent years and were fluent in Spanish. They

---
20. Machado in Beebe and Senkewicz, *Testimonios*, 126–28.
21. Machado in ibid., 125.

reached Monterey in 1822 and negotiated with Governor Solá before he stepped down and with Father Mariano Payeras, who had succeeded Sarría as prefect. The agreement they concluded gave Hartnell and McCulloch exclusive trading rights for three years with all missions whose padres chose to sign a contract with them. Armed with an endorsement from Payeras, who wrote that they would "do their best for the benefit of the missions," they soon had deals with most of them. Of particular interest to Hartnell and McCulloch were the vast herds of mission cattle, whose tallow (used to make soap and candles) had been exported to South America recently and whose hides could now be legally shipped to leather factories on either side of the Atlantic. The hide trade was a potential bonanza for padres, but Payeras trusted that they would never "increase their frugal fare and sad shroud however their missions issue forth with gold and silver from this proposed contract."[22]

That view was not shared by Hartnell, who proved better than McCulloch at dealing with the padres and remained in California after his partner left for South America to handle the company's business there. In a letter to his uncle written in 1823, Hartnell described the friars as "jolly, fat, good-natured fellows, who do nothing all day but pray and fill their bellies." This was sure to amuse his Anglican relatives in England, but even as he sketched this caricature of the jolly friar—a type that could indeed be found in California alongside padres who were lean, somber, and overburdened by their duties—Hartnell was drawing closer to the Franciscans and their faith. He soon converted to Catholicism, which served his interests in California but also reflected a genuine desire on his part to put an end to his ruinous drinking bouts and fruitless courtships in various ports and settle down under the supervision of missionaries. Those padres helped him become a father through marriage, which he could not do under Mexican law without converting. Like a true Californio, he approached

---

22. Payeras in Susanna Bryant Dakin, *The Lives of William Hartnell*, 35–36; Bancroft, *History of California*, 2:475–77.

marriage as a family affair and entered one of the territory's grandest households in 1825 by wedding Teresa de la Guerra, the elder sister of Angustias, in Santa Bárbara, where their enterprising father had used his leverage as commandant and *habilitado* (military supply agent and paymaster) to become a prosperous rancher and merchant as well. Like Hartnell, José de la Guerra y Noriega hoped to profit from this marriage alliance and welcomed the Englishman into his family, which grew to include more than one hundred direct descendants. That suited Hartnell, who hoped to have "many dependencies in the country."[23]

Other foreigners had taken up residence in California by this time, including Captain Henry Gyzelaar, whose good deed in warning of Bouchard's raid was not forgotten. But it took several years for such American merchants to break Hartnell and McCulloch's hold on the hide-and-tallow trade and overcome resentments among officials like Governor Argüello, who remembered the trouble that American smugglers had caused them before independence. The lowering of trade barriers did not end the worries of Argüello or the commandants under him, for they still had to contend with coastal traders who shirked paying duties. Their biggest concern, however, was a problem that had haunted California since its founding—resistance among Indians within the missions and beyond. Independence and the lowering of trade barriers did nothing to reduce reliance on Indian labor. Without the revenues earned on hides, tallow, and other trade goods that Indians produced or processed, the government there would collapse.

Traditions of Defiance

Resistance among California Indians took many forms. One was the time-honored defense of people who were forced to labor, which was to do as little work as they could without being punished. Hartnell was not alone in complaining of the apparent laziness of mission Indians. With these "enemies of work," he wrote, "there

---

23. Hartnell in Dakin, *Lives of William Hartnell*, 53, 72; Pubols, *Father of All*, 119–22.

is nothing else to do but have patience."[24] Some considered that laziness innate or the product of an overly generous environment that left Indians with little incentive to improve their condition. How hard neophytes worked depended on their circumstances and morale, which did not improve when they learned that Californios, often faulted by foreigners for their lack of industriousness, were now free of their Great Captain in Spain while they as neophytes remained under compulsion and restraint.

Other forms of resistance were cultural and involved clinging to tribal customs and beliefs abhorrent to those who had power over them. That neophytes were slow at their tasks bothered padres far less than that they adhered to practices deemed sinful or satanic. Some missionaries tactfully ignored the spiritual significance of dances and other tribal ceremonies performed by mission Indians. But most were painfully aware that neophytes were not exclusively Christian in their observances. A questionnaire filled out by California missionaries between 1813 and 1815 asked about the superstitions of neophytes. Among the many pagan practices cited in response were eagle sacrifices by those who believed that the bird's spirit if properly honored would "free them from their enemies and grant them whatever they ask," the ceremonial use of toloache (*Datura*) by neophytes in southern California who took the drug so that "darts and arrows may not pierce their bodies," and gifts made to old women who claimed the power to "cause fruits and seeds to grow." One padre wrote glumly: "Their superstitions are as numerous as they are ridiculous and are difficult to understand."[25]

Rituals that missionaries considered senseless were as important to these Indians, however, as rosaries and holy water were to their padres. As Father Gerónimo Boscana discovered when he investigated the ancestral customs and beliefs of neophytes at Mission San Juan Capistrano, such superstitions were part of a coherent religious worldview that saw the powers people exercised for good or ill as gifts from the spirits they honored. Boscana's informants—tribal

---

24. Hartnell in Dakin, *Lives of William Hartnell*, 72.
25. Quoted in Geiger and Meighan, *As the Padres Saw Them*, 47–51.

elders who "knew all the secrets," as he put it—referred to their creator or supreme being as Chinigchinich, meaning "all-powerful." To him they owed their existence and the skills and crafts that sustained their society. "I create all things," Chinigchinich proclaimed to their ancestors; "I will make you another people, and from this time, one of you shall be endowed with the power to cause it to rain, another to influence the dews, another to produce the acorn, another to create rabbits, another geese, another deer." Those who received such powers were honored as shamans by their fellow Indians, who offered them gifts to retain their blessings: "To offend them, would be to destroy all their productions of flesh and grain."[26] Boscana concluded that neophytes were deeply attached to their pagan beliefs and insincere in professing Christianity.

California Indians did not simply worship spirits; they became one with them through ceremonies and acquired their power. Those godlike powers were most heavily invested in shamans, but all Indians engaged in rituals designed to strengthen and renew them in spirit. The idea that worshipers could become one with their creator was central to the Christian sacrament of communion. Other parallels existed between Christian teachings and the traditional beliefs of Boscana's informants, who portrayed Chinigchinich as stern and demanding, much like the biblical God of judgment. "When I die, I shall ascend above, to the stars," said Chinigchinich; "and to those who have kept my commandments, I shall give all they ask of me; but those who obey not my teachings, nor believe them, I shall punish severely. I will send unto them bears to bite, and serpents to sting them; they shall be without food, and have diseases that they may die."[27] Christianity may have influenced these teachings, but Indians in California had long believed that the power of creation and renewal could be transformed into something punishing and destructive, as shown by their tribal customs. At Mission Santa Clara, for example, neophytes used herbs, feathers, and other "enchantments" both to

---

26. Boscana, *Chinigchinich*, vii, 6–7.
27. Ibid., 13.

"free themselves from their enemies and from illnesses" and to "injure others and obtain revenge."[28]

Such enchantments empowered many neophytes as Christian rites did not. Some found solace in Catholicism and contributed to its pageantry by singing in choirs or adorning churches with wall paintings that blended Spanish and Indian motifs. But others had to be prodded to attend Mass and seemed oblivious to what went on there. Louis Choris, an artist who accompanied Otto von Kotzebue to California in 1816, witnessed a Mass at Mission San Francisco at which the neophytes fell to the ground as if "half dead" and remained there "without making the slightest movement until the end of the service."[29] None of them received communion, which required that they first confess to a priest any mortal sins they had committed. Padres tried to confess all neophytes at least once a year, during Lent, so that they could take Easter communion, considered a duty for Catholics. For that purpose, missionaries composed elaborate *confesionarios* (confessional aids) in Native languages to probe for sins that neophytes had committed. Did you do "bad things for pleasure with a woman, with women, with a man, with men?" asked one *confesionario*. "Did you couple the right way?" Such inquisitions made the prospect of communing with Christ agonizing for Indians who found inspiration in various forms of sexuality. They regarded certain kinds of infidelity, such as sharing one's spouse with a sibling, as virtuous despite the insistence of padres that such intimacies were transgressions for which they deserved to be flogged or shackled. One path of resistance was to withhold their sins from the priest, but the *confesionario* spelled out the consequences of that in harrowing detail: "If you die in sin, your soul goes to Hell to suffer forever from every ill and every infirmity, much hunger, much thirst, much coldness, eternal darkness, and you will be there burning like a tile in the furnace, suffering such as I am unable to describe."[30]

---

28. Quoted in Geiger and Meighan, *As the Padres Saw Them*, 50–51.
29. Choris in Mahr, *Visit of the "Rurik" to San Francisco in 1816*, 97.
30. Quoted in Vecsey, *On the Padres' Trail*, 236–37; James A. Sandos, "Levantamiento!: The 1824 Chumash Uprising Reconsidered," 109–19; Sandos, *Converting California*, 96–98; Hackel, *Children of Coyote*, 199–215.

For neophytes who still harbored traditional beliefs of the sort described by Boscana, avoiding this Christian hell and following the padres' path to heaven meant offending their ancestral spirits and losing the powers and protections attributed to them. Some neophytes interpreted droughts, epidemics, and other disasters that befell them in missions as punishments for betraying those spirits. (In the words of Chinigchinich, "they shall be without food, and have diseases that they may die.") When epidemics ravaged Mission Santa Bárbara in 1801, a Chumash woman had a vision under the influence of *Datura* in which the earth goddess Chupu said that all neophytes would perish except those who purged themselves of baptism by washing in holy water called the "tears of the sun."[31] Her vision caused great excitement among the Chumash before padres suppressed the developing cult. Such spiritual protests by Indians were sometimes linked with armed rebellions, as happened in the late 1600s when the Pueblo visionary Popé led a revolt in which Spanish priests and colonists were driven from New Mexico and Christian Indians were immersed in rivers to cleanse them of the taint of baptism.

Mission efforts in California caused contests within tribal societies as neophytes wrestled with the conflicting demands of Christianity and their ancestral beliefs. This internal struggle was most pronounced among those who served as alcaldes or captains and were torn between loyalty to the padres, who put them forward for election, and a desire to command the respect of Indians at odds with the mission system. Pablo Tac, a literate neophyte born at Mission San Luis Rey in 1822, observed in an account he wrote as an adolescent that alcaldes served as intermediaries for their padres. "In the afternoon, the *alcaldes* gather at the house of the missionary," he related. "They bring the news of that day, and, if the missionary tells them something that all the people of the country ought to know, they return to the villages," passing along his message.[32]

---

31. Sandos, "Levantamiento!" 119.
32. Pablo Tac in Francis J. Weber, ed., *King of the Missions: A Documentary History of San Luis Rey de Francia*, 52.

Neophytes at San Luis Rey and other missions had their own villages, located near the mission compound, which housed those who were sick and being cared for in the infirmary, unmarried girls over seven years of age, and often unmarried boys of roughly the same age, who slept in a separate dormitory from the girls. Alcaldes thus performed an important function in overseeing the many neophytes living outside the compound. Some alcaldes commanded more respect than others because they had been leaders in tribal society before they entered the mission system. Yet, as Pablo Tac noted, they did not wield as much authority as captains did "of old, when they were still gentiles." The Spanish clothes they wore and the rods they carried as symbols of their office made it clear that they were products of the mission system and creatures of the mission fathers. Indeed, Pablo Tac portrayed Mission San Luis Rey (named for a king who was canonized) as an absolute monarchy, where everyone and everything belonged to the padre, who was "like a king. He has his pages, *alcaldes, mayordomos,* musicians, soldiers, gardens, *ranchos,* livestock, horses by the thousand."[33]

Pablo Tac was such a fine example of what the Franciscans hoped to achieve through conversion that they sent him to a seminary in Rome, where he composed his account. Yet he retained respect and affection for the ancestral traditions of his people, including their dances, which he described in fine detail. He wrote sympathetically of neophytes who could not resist the temptation to steal fruit from the mission garden, watched over by a stern Indian gardener. Those who wanted something from the garden had only to ask and the missionaries would provide, but the challenge of violating this protected space and tasting forbidden fruit was irresistible for some youngsters. As Pablo Tac related, one daredevil climbed a fig tree, grasped the object of his desire, and ate it whole, nearly choking on the fig, "until he cried out like a crow and swallowed it." The gardener heard his crowing and spotted the culprit. "I see you, a crow without wings," he said. "Now I will wound you with my arrows."[34] The intruder managed to escape before the gardener could make good

---

33. Ibid., 53.
34. Ibid., 50–51; Hackel, *Children of Coyote,* 240–52.

on his threat. Pablo Tac probably knew enough scripture to recognize that this young thief was like Adam, who could not resist the temptation to do the very thing his Father had forbidden him. But the literate young neophyte seemingly admired the trespasser for his daring—a trait prized in tribal society—and likened him to a deer leaping to freedom, while the Indian gardener remained trapped in the unenviable role of disciplinarian, enforcing the padres' rules.

Another forbidden enclosure that fascinated and tempted some neophytes was the girls' dormitory (*monjerío,* meaning convent or nunnery), a place watched over by an older neophyte who served as matron. At Mission San Gabriel, the girls called their matron "Madre Abadesa" (Mother Superior), recalled the woman who served as housekeeper there, Eulalia Pérez, born at Loreto in Baja California in the late 1700s and witness to the massive earthquake that shattered the church at Mission San Juan Capistrano in 1812 before she moved with her soldier husband to San Gabriel. Every night, she related, the *monjerío* there and the separate boys' dormitory "were locked and the keys were turned over to me. Then I would hand the keys over to the Fathers."[35]

Locks and bolts were not always enough to protect the sanctity of the convent or nunnery—terms indicative of the Franciscan practice of imposing the conventions of a religious order on Indians supposedly in training for life in civil society. Fernando Librado, a Chumash Indian raised at Mission San Buenaventura in the 1820s, recalled long afterward that girls in the convent helped boys scale an adobe wall and gain access to their quarters. "The young women would take their silk shawls and tie them together with a stone on one end and throw them over the wall," he related. "The boys would have bones from the slaughter house which were nicely cleaned, and they would tie them on the shawls so that they could climb these shawls using the bones for their toes."[36]

This could be fact or folklore, for Librado based parts of his narrative on stories told to him rather than his own experiences. He

---

35. Pérez in Beebe and Senkewicz, *Testimonios,* 107.
36. Fernando Librado, *Breath of the Sun: Life in Early California as Told by a Chumash Indian, Fernando Librado, to John P. Harrington,* 53.

was told, for example, that a certain padre at San Buenaventura had free access to the convent, where he could choose any girl he wanted and "carry out his desires." That too may be folklore, although one missionary among the Chumash in the 1820s, Father Blas Ordaz, was notorious for fathering illegitimate children. Even if read as tall tales, however, Librado's stories say much about the attitudes of neophytes. "The priest's will was law," he recalled. "Indians would lie right down if the priest said so." But when the priest was not looking, neophytes reasserted themselves. Librado told of a neophyte captain named Juan de Jesús who yearned after the matron of the convent and turned from being an enforcer of the law to a violator. Taking off his Spanish clothes and dressing like the other young men, he climbed the makeshift ladder of silk and bones and confronted the matron, who was complicit in the mischief. Threatened by him with punishment, she began to cry, and he offered her what comfort he could. "The only way to save yourself is to do what the others are doing," he told her. "Let's go into the other room."[37] In his own sly way, this philandering captain was rebelling against the mission system and trying to save himself, or preserve his cultural identity, by violating the padres' commandments. Other alcaldes would rebel in bolder fashion by taking up arms and defying the very priests who held them responsible for keeping neophytes in line.

Padres saw their pastoral enclosures as folds to keep the most vulnerable members of their flock from straying. For neophytes who clung to traditional beliefs, by contrast, salvation lay in defying limits placed on them and communing with powers that knew no bounds. Why huddle in missions like sheep, when they could roam free like their culture hero Coyote or cloak themselves in feathers and ascend to heaven in spirit with the birds they revered? Indians who kept faith with Chinigchinich, Boscana's informants told him, went to an idyllic place after death where there was "constant dancing and festivity . . . no one labored—no one was sorrowful . . . all were contented and happy—every one did as they

---

37. Ibid., 5, 53–54; Sandos, *Converting California*, 123.

pleased, and selected the number of wives they wished."[38] This was their Eden, without prohibitions or penalties.

Given such persistent beliefs, conflict between neophytes and their Franciscan guardians was inevitable. The mission system did not simply encounter resistance, however. It bred resistance and reinforced it in ways that Serra had not foreseen when he set the process in motion. He envisioned spiritual conquest as decisive and triumphant, but it became an interminable struggle, marked by countless acts of resistance, including a few cases in which neophytes killed padres considered unbearably strict or cruel. Missions brought groups such as the Chumash who had been divided into small tribes or chiefdoms together in larger congregations, where they preserved many of their traditions in modified form and gained a new sense of solidarity in response to challenges facing them. Some neophytes acquired skills such as horsemanship that could be turned against Spaniards in times of conflict. The horse had been a symbol of Spanish power in the New World since the days of the conquistadors. Thanks to the missions and their fast-growing herds, however, the skills of many Indian vaqueros (cowboys) in California rivaled those of Mexican horsemen. Mission San Gabriel had two classes of vaqueros, distinguished by dress. "Those who rode bareback received nothing more than their shirt, blanket, and loincloth," recalled Eulalia Pérez. "Those who rode with saddles received the same clothing as the *gente de razón*," including hat, boots, spurs, and "a large kerchief made of silk or cotton, and a sash of Chinese silk or red crepe cloth."[39]

This was one area where the mission system dressed Indians for success or prepared them handsomely for life beyond the cloister. But that success spelled trouble for Californios when vaqueros became fugitives and foes. By the 1820s large parts of the interior were infested—as Californios saw it—by runaway neophytes turned horse thieves, cattle rustlers, and potential insurgents, often acting in concert with Indians who had not been converted

---

38. Boscana, *Chinigchinich*, 58.
39. Pérez in Beebe and Senkewicz, *Testimonios*, 78–79.

and dreaded colonization like the plague it was for many Indians. Meanwhile, neophytes who remained at missions or worked at pueblos or presidios were acquiring other skills with military applications, including a knowledge of firearms and fortifications. During the Bouchard scare in 1818, Father Antonio Ripoll of Mission Santa Bárbara drilled a battalion of 180 Chumash neophytes, armed with lances, bows, and machetes. Before long, Chumash would turn such skills against their masters in the largest and most determined Indian uprising ever to occur in California.

Throwing Off the Cross

The Chumash Revolt of 1824 was planned by neophytes at Missions Santa Inés and La Purísima and spread to Mission Santa Bárbara, leaving only the Chumash at Mission San Buenaventura uninvolved. Hostilities were supposed to begin simultaneously at Santa Inés and La Purísima on Sunday, February 22, but fighting broke out prematurely on the twenty-first at Santa Inés after a neophyte visiting a relative held in detention there was flogged by order of the corporal of the guards. Missionaries later blamed the uprising on resentments among neophytes toward soldiers in general, noting that missions and their Indian laborers had been asked to contribute heavily in recent years to support presidios. As one padre put it, neophytes "bitterly complained that they had to work so that the soldiers might eat, and that nothing was paid them for their toil and their labor."[40] Yet Franciscans depended on those soldiers to protect them and retrieve neophytes who fled to avoid confessions, punishments, or the plagues of disease-ridden missions that might have collapsed without guards present to discourage fugitivism. The missionaries and the military were like the two planks of a cross, hammered together, and the rebellious Chumash were refusing to bear that cross any longer.

By one account, Father Francisco Xavier Uría of Mission Santa Inés responded militantly when the uprising began there by seizing

---

40. Quoted in Zephyrin Engelhardt, *The Missions and Missionaries of California*, 3:195; Sandos, "Levantamiento!" 120–21.

his musket and firing on the rebels along with soldiers of the guard. "The Father's shots were becoming accurate and deadly," wrote Antonio María Osio, who based his account of the uprising on stories he was told and added his own novelistic flourishes, noting that Uría was even faster with his hands when loading his gun than when "collecting alms." When Sergeant Anastasio Carrillo arrived with reinforcements on Sunday, the insurgents left the mission church in flames and withdrew to La Purísima, where the besieged guards ran out of ammunition. At the urging of Father José Antonio Rodríguez, who remained at La Purísima with the rebels, they agreed to let the soldiers and their families go with the other priest in residence, the notorious Blas Ordaz. Before they were released, Osio related, Ordaz offered confession to soldiers' wives, who "began to disclose things which their husbands, who were present, should not know." Perhaps fearing that his own misdeeds with them would be revealed, he told them to be quiet and "simply to recite the act of contrition instead of confessing, so that he could grant them absolution."[41]

The response of Father Antonio Ripoll at Mission Santa Bárbara when he learned of the uprising was far different from that attributed to Father Uría. "Father Ripoll loved his neophytes like a loving mother," remarked Angustias de la Guerra, whose father, Commandant de la Guerra y Noriega, and uncle, Sergeant Carrillo, helped put down the uprising. She recalled that when her father told Ripoll that he planned to send troops from the Santa Bárbara presidio to the mission to prevent the Chumash there from joining the revolt, the padre began to cry "like a woman" and pleaded: "My God! Do not kill my children."[42] He persuaded the commandant to keep his troops at a distance and withdraw the guards stationed at Mission Santa Bárbara, hoping that their departure would appease neophytes there. As those soldiers were leaving, Chumash snatched the guns from their hands, and two of the guards were slightly wounded with a machete. That was not much of an offense, in Ripoll's opinion. The commandant

---

41. Osio, *History of Alta California*, 58, 62, 270 n. 9.
42. Angustias de la Guerra in Beebe and Senkewicz, *Testimonios*, 205.

responded forcefully, however, and three neophytes were killed in the ensuing fighting. The troops then withdrew to the presidio, allowing many of the rebellious neophytes to flee. Some who remained behind were later attacked by soldiers, who killed five Indians with little or no provocation. "Consider, your Reverence," Ripoll wrote Father Sarría, "what my feelings were on hearing the soldiers relate these things to the commander as if they were heroic deeds."[43]

The Chumash who fled had been merciful to Ripoll and his fellow friar, Father Antonio Jayme, who was ailing and helped onto his horse by neophytes so that he could ride to safety at the presidio. This compounded Ripoll's grief and outrage. Yet he misread his neophytes when he blamed all the trouble at Santa Bárbara on the soldiers and their commandant. His trusted alcalde Andrés had encouraged neophytes at Mission Santa Bárbara to take up arms. Ripoll could not imagine that his "children" were rebelling against his own paternalistic regimen, supported by soldiers whose coercive measures he deplored. He persisted in his indignant opposition to the military and refused to serve as chaplain for an expedition sent to apprehend the fugitives, telling the commandant that only if "forced to go in chains would they take me along.... Was I to go out to see my sons killed?"[44] Like Junípero Serra, Ripoll would have preferred a spiritual conquest that involved no troops at all. In practice, Serra had found armed force indispensable to his efforts and had sent neophytes considered intractable to be punished at the Monterey presidio. But later Franciscan idealists like Ripoll shared his impossible dream of a perfect conquest for Christ, uncontaminated by the presence of soldiers, forever associated in Christian iconography with the crucifixion. (One neophyte artist at Mission San Fernando may have taken Spanish guards there as models for the Roman soldiers he portrayed in a haunting crucifixion scene on the walls of the church.)

---

43. Antonio Ripoll, "Fray Antonio Ripoll's Description of the Chumash Revolt at Santa Bárbara in 1824," 351; Engelhardt, *Missions and Missionaries of California*, 3:201.
44. Ripoll, "Fray Antonio Ripoll's Description of the Chumash Revolt," 356; Engelhardt, *Missions and Missionaries of California*, 3:205.

Imperial Sunset

Fearing retribution, the fugitives from Santa Bárbara fled inland to the Tulares (tule marshes) in the San Joaquín Valley, leaving the rebels at La Purísima to face a concerted assault by Lieutenant José María Estrada, dispatched from Monterey with more than one hundred troops. Before Estrada's force reached the mission, four travelers on their way to Los Angeles stopped there, unaware of the recent hostilities, and were killed by the insurgents. An estimated four hundred Indians, including some Yokuts allied with the Chumash, prepared for battle by fortifying their position and hauling into place two small ceremonial cannons. The adobe walls of La Purísima were no defense against the heavier gun that Estrada brought to bear on the morning of March 16. The battle lasted a little over two hours, by which time sixteen of the insurgents were dead—a steep toll in California, where the loss of more than a few men was a serious matter for Indians and settlers alike. Hemmed in by Estrada's cavalry and unable to inflict more than a few casualties on his forces, the survivors sent Father Rodríguez out to negotiate their surrender. Afterward, twelve rebel leaders were sentenced to long prison terms and seven Indians were condemned for killing the four civilians. "Some of the doomed men were about half dead," recalled one witness, Corporal Rafael González, "and had to be almost carried to the place of execution," where padres administered last rites before they were shot to death.[45]

In April soldiers sent to retrieve the fugitives from Mission Santa Bárbara turned back after clashing with them twice in the Tulares, where they found allies among local Indians. At the urging of Father Sarría, Governor Argüello then offered to pardon fugitives who submitted peacefully to a second party that he dispatched in June. Sarría and Ripoll agreed to join that expedition and helped induce most of the fugitives to return to the mission in June following an open-air Mass in the Tulares that symbolized their resubmission to Christianity and priestly authority. Before yielding, the fugitives had cast off restraints imposed on them by the padres and renounced their marriage vows. As one of them

---
45. González in Beebe and Senkewicz, *Lands of Promise and Despair*, 327.

later testified, "no one knew who was married and who was not for they were all mixed up."⁴⁶

Some fugitives from Santa Bárbara remained defiant and fled eastward to the foothills of the Sierra Nevada in what is now Kern County, where they joined with Yokuts and formed a society combining elements of Spanish and Indian culture. A decade later, a party of Americans including diarist Zenas Leonard encountered them at a village whose population Leonard estimated at seven or eight hundred. They could "talk the Spanish language," he noted, and had fled Mission Santa Bárbara after robbing "the church of all its golden images & candle-sticks." They were expert at bartering, Leonard added, and dealt shrewdly with traders on the coast in addition to raising crops and "making regular visits to the settlements for the purpose of stealing horses, which they kill and eat." The enterprising refugees retained "several of the images which they pilfered from the Church—the greater part of which is the property of the Chiefs."⁴⁷

Those Christian icons were still valued by the Chumash, and Christianity in some form may have been melded with their ancestral religious practices. According to Ripoll, neophytes at Santa Bárbara had urged the ailing Father Jayme to come with them when they fled, promising to "carry him and care for him." The respect that Chumash rebels demonstrated for Jayme, Ripoll, and other priests by sparing them and trusting in them as intermediaries indicates that this uprising was aimed not at the padres or their faith but at the coercive mission system, which they and the military perpetuated. Priests willing to minister to Indians without coercion, as some Franciscans did after the missions were secularized, retained influence among communities of former neophytes and helped make Christianity an enduring part of their culture. As the rebellious alcalde Andrés declared in a message to Ripoll: "Tell the padre that we think properly about God and what we have been taught in His name."⁴⁸

---

46. Quoted in Sandos, "Levantamiento!" 124.
47. Zenas Leonard, *Adventures of a Mountain Man: The Narrative of Zenas Leonard*, 200–201.
48. Andrés in Ripoll, "Fray Antonio Ripoll's Description of the Chumash Revolt," 354; Engelhardt, *Missions and Missionaries of California*, 3:200.

One factor that likely contributed to the Chumash Revolt was the appearance in the winter of 1823–24 of a comet, seen by many Indians as portending a great change. Such cosmic events held special significance for people who believed, as Boscana reported, that when honored chiefs and shamans died, "they went to dwell among the stars." Some neophytes saw the comet as a sign that they would soon be free to resume their traditional way of life, which may have encouraged the Chumash rebels. Others regarded it as a bad omen and issued a warning that proved grimly prophetic as Anglo-Americans infiltrated California in years to come. According to Boscana, elders at Mission San Juan Capistrano interpreted the comet as a signal from a revered chief in heaven "that another people would come, who would treat them as slaves, and abuse them—that they would suffer much hunger and misery, and that the chief thus appeared, to call them away from impending calamity."[49]

God and Liberty

Whether viewed as auspicious or ominous, the comet appeared at what was indeed a turning point in the history of California. All those born here under Spanish rule would find their world transformed in the new age that was dawning. As yet, Californios had been little affected by the revolutionary turmoil in the Mexican heartland. But in 1824, with the establishment of the Mexican Republic, they became part of an ambitious political experiment that would bring people in California fresh opportunities and expose them to new hazards. Mexico's struggle for independence had begun with a Native insurgency that dwarfed the Chumash uprising, triggered in 1810 by a rebellious creole priest, Father Miguel Hidalgo y Costilla, who called his Indian parishioners in the town of Dolores to action with his momentous *grito* (cry), during which he reportedly vowed "Death to the Spaniards!"[50] Not until that fiery revolt was snuffed out by royalists—and they in turn were defeated by forces led by Agustín de Iturbide, who

---

49. Boscana, *Chinigchinich*, 59, 71–72.
50. Quoted in Enrique Krauze, *Mexico, Biography of Power: A History of Modern Mexico, 1810–1996*, 96.

sought freedom from Spain without further social upheaval—did Mexico gain independence.

Deposed as Mexico's emperor in 1823, Iturbide attempted to return to power the following year and was executed. Thereafter, the young nation was governed first by federalists—liberals who supported the constitution of 1824 that promised Indians equal rights and granted Mexican states a measure of autonomy—and later by centralists, who favored a strong central government that would preserve order, unity, and the privileges of the military and the Catholic Church. Many Mexicans hoped to uphold their faith while achieving greater freedom, aspirations summed up by the motto with which officials concluded their letters and proclamations: "Dios y Libertad" (God and Liberty).[51] Yet it often seemed that those who stressed reverence and obedience were at odds with the proponents of liberty and equality.

That contest of principles reached California in 1825 when José María Echeandía arrived as governor. Appointed civil and military chief of both Baja and Alta California, he used that broad authority to advance his liberal agenda. One of his first official acts, while he was traveling with his aides from Loreto to San Diego, was to respond to the complaints of Indians at Mission San Vicente Ferrer in Baja California by removing a padre they accused of mistreating them. This "caused a great deal of surprise," wrote one Mexican chronicler, "especially because it was being done by the Governor, whose authority the Frontier people did not believe to be greater than that of a missionary."[52] Earlier governors had investigated charges against padres, but to take such action based solely on testimony from Indians was unprecedented and signaled the beginning of the end for the mission era in California.

Arriving in San Diego, where he resided for much of his term as governor, Echeandía met with skepticism and resistance from conservative Californios, who were unsettled by the recent Chumash uprising and worried that he would cause further trouble by

---

51. Quoted in George L. Harding, *Don Agustín V. Zamorano: Statesman, Soldier, Craftsman, and California's First Printer*, 7.
52. Manuel Clemente Rojo in Beebe and Senkewicz, *Lands of Promise and Despair*, 342.

promising neophytes freedom. He proceeded cautiously, issuing an emancipation decree that allowed only those neophytes who were considered good Christians and had "some means of gaining a livelihood" to leave the missions, subject to the approval of their padres and the local commandant.[53] But Echeandía's critics feared that his policies would encourage mission Indians to defy authorities and run rampant. He was "a man of advanced ideas and an enthusiast and lover of republican liberty," recalled Angustias de la Guerra. Like her father the commandant, she admired the governor's "fine manners" but considered his liberal notions naïve and dangerous. "Echeandía led the Indians to believe that they too were free men and citizens," she related. "This produced a harmful effect on the Indians' mind, for they began to demand that those rights be put in practice." Neophytes, she added, no longer obeyed their padres "like a child obeys his father—that is to say, the way children respected and obeyed their parents during that time." Looking back on Echeandía's tenure late in her life, after the American conquest and the loss of her daughter Manuela (who wed Alfred Sully without parental consent), Angustias saw the governor's arrival as the beginning of California's fateful exposure to liberty and the taking of liberties, which undermined the paternalism that governed not just the mission system but this society as a whole and bound one generation to the next. "Paternal authority had no limits," she remarked, "and it continued even after children married and had children of their own."[54]

Independence from Spain, however, encouraged liberal Californios such as Juan Alvarado and Mariano Vallejo to challenge the Franciscan fathers and secularize the missions. They were inclined to blame the padres rather than reformers like Echeandía for provoking rebellion by imposing a stifling regimen on neophytes. Those Indians might cause less trouble and be of more benefit to society, they reckoned, if their land and labor became available to enterprising citizens. The benefits of liberalization would

---

53. Quoted in Hackel, *Children of Coyote*, 376.
54. Angustias de la Guerra in Beebe and Senkewicz, *Testimonios*, 225.

go largely to ambitious Californios like Alvarado and Vallejo—who would manage secularization in their own interests—and to foreigners who profited when Mexico lowered the old imperial barriers that kept them from trading or settling there. Some former neophytes became self-sufficient landowners under this new regime, but for most mission Indians real freedom and opportunity remained elusive.

Alvarado, Vallejo, and other Californios who favored secularizing the missions were inclined to view foreigners who settled there legally as less of a threat to their interests than Mexican authorities, particularly those centralists who came to power in the 1830s and challenged the right of Californios to manage their own affairs. After ousting Governor Manuel Victoria, who succeeded Echeandía and blocked his secularization plan, defiant Californios would oppose the centralist regime of Antonio López de Santa Anna, who abandoned the federalist camp and clamped down on Mexico's states and territories, igniting rebellions along the nation's northern frontier. Alvarado, who proclaimed California independent as governor in 1836, would later reconcile with Mexico, but Californios felt little loyalty to Santa Anna or his successors. With no substantial aid from Mexico City, they had to rely on their own resources, notably revenues collected at Monterey from foreign merchants involved in the hide-and-tallow trade—a business that brought conspicuous wealth to some ranchers who obtained large land grants as the missions were carved up. Along with those rewards came new risks for Californios, whose alienation from the central government and internal political strife, often involving access to customs revenue, left them vulnerable to foreign infiltration and conquest, with the chief threat coming from the United States.

Unlike Mexico, which lost much blood and treasure during its prolonged struggle for independence and had no surplus population eager to emigrate to California and other remote territories, the United States broke free from Great Britain at less cost and maintained its expansive momentum in the early nineteenth century as millions of land-hungry settlers pressed west to the Mississippi River and beyond. Furthermore, white Americans maintained political cohesion during this period by putting off the divisive issues of emancipation and racial equality that convulsed Mexico and would later ignite the American Civil War. Until that conflict became irrepressible as a result of disputes between North and South over whether to allow slavery in western territories seized from Mexico and Indian tribes, Americans would direct their competitive energies outward, while Mexicans remained preoccupied with internal conflicts.

If the challenge from the United States had been limited to Yankee traders arriving by sea, Californios might have held their own, for they proved highly resourceful in dealing with foreign merchants and assimilating those who settled here. But soon after the Mexican Republic was founded and Californios began asserting themselves politically, their sovereignty was undermined by Americans intruding overland, following trails that within a few decades would become avenues of invasion. In that sense, the comet that blazed across the night sky in early 1824 signaled misfortune for Indians and Californios alike, heralding the end of one imperial order and the advent of another—a so-called empire for liberty that would make those native to this country aliens in their own land.

Part Three
TRADERS AND TRESPASSERS
(1826–1841)

CHAPTER 8

Paths of Subversion

In November 1826 a party of trappers led by Jedediah Smith, having made their way from the Great Salt Lake to the lower Colorado River, set out for the Mexican settlements of California across some of the bleakest terrain they had ever witnessed. It was not enough to call this a desert, for that term was applied loosely to any desolate expanse, including places that received more than a little rainfall. Smith, whose success as an explorer owed much to his powers of observation, was more precise in describing the wasteland known today as the Mojave. "The country since leaving the Colorado has been a dry rocky sandy Barren desert," he remarked comprehensively in his account of this first overland journey to California by an Anglo-American.[1]

Guided by two Serrano tribesmen native to the region, Smith and his men plodded westward on horseback, drinking at brackish springs before crossing the crusty bed of Soda Lake and following the occasional Mojave River, whose waters often vanished beneath the sand, up to its source in the San Bernardino range. Beyond

---

1. Jedediah Smith, *The Southwest Expedition of Jedediah S. Smith: His Personal Account of the Journal to California, 1826–1827*, 88. (Smith's journal was arranged and transcribed after the expedition by an assistant, Samuel Parkman. Some parts of it appear to reflect notes taken by Smith during the journey, while other parts are retrospective and indicate that he read the journal of his clerk, Harrison Rogers, before preparing his own account.)

209

those peaks lay the lush San Bernardino Valley, a prospect all the more inviting to Smith and company after two weeks of privation in the desert. Descending into that land of plenty, they found fresh grass nourished by autumn rains and something "still more pleasing" to famished men whose mounts were near exhaustion: "we began to see track of Horses and Cattle."[2]

That exhilarating moment inspired one of few lyrical flights in Smith's otherwise businesslike account. "The country through which we passed was strikingly contrasted with the Rocky and Sandy deserts through which we had so long been traveling," he related. "There for many days we had traveled weary hungry and thirsty drinking from springs that increased our thirst and looking in vain for a boundary of the interminable waste of sands. But now the scene was changed and whether it was its own real Beauty or the contrast with what we had seen it certainly seemed to us enchantment."[3]

Was this truly paradise, he wondered, or did it just look like heaven after the travelers went through hell to get there? Smith and later adventurers who pioneered overland trails to California offered westering Americans an arduous alternative to the harrowing ocean voyage around Cape Horn. But it would be many decades before travelers could embark for California by land or sea without praying for deliverance from the ordeals of passage. The journey was the gamble of a lifetime, undertaken in pursuit of profit, glory, or adventure—or sometimes out of sheer desperation. All of those motives may have impelled Smith, who said he crossed the Mojave because he needed supplies and fresh horses if he hoped to return to the Bear River in what is now Idaho and rendezvous at that "deposit" with his partners in the fur trade. That was his excuse for entering California, where foreigners required a Mexican passport to move about and a license to engage in trade. Smith had neither and could not admit to authorities that he had ulterior motives for going there, such as trapping beaver.

---
2. Ibid., 93.
3. Ibid., 96.

In a letter to William Clark of the Lewis and Clark expedition, now superintendent of Indian Affairs, Smith wrote that he had left the Bear River rendezvous with the aim of exploring a region "veiled in obscurity to the citizens of the United States. I allude to the country S.W. of the Great Salt lake west of the Rocky mountains."[4] Under terms agreed to by the United States and Spain in the Adams-Onís Treaty of 1819 and later confirmed by the United States and Mexico in 1832, Mexican territory beyond the Rockies extended northward to the forty-second parallel, including the Great Salt Lake. Such unmarked boundaries meant little to venturesome trappers like the 27-year-old Smith. He had been crossing frontiers with abandon ever since he enlisted in the fur trade under William Ashley in St. Louis in 1822 and headed up the Missouri River. Among the powers he had to reckon with on his journeys were not simply the rival British in the Northwest and Mexicans in the Southwest but various Indian nations that claimed the country he traversed by right of occupancy. In dealing with those tribal groups, Smith demonstrated courage, composure, and more diplomatic skill than most in his profession. By 1825 he was Ashley's partner, and a year later he bought him out and incorporated with two other resourceful mountain men, David Jackson and William Sublette.

As Smith remarked afterward in a letter to Joel Poinsett, U.S. minister to Mexico, he made the journey that brought him to California "for the purpose of prosecuting my Business."[5] In the fur trade, business often entailed exploration as trappers searched for beaver country whose riches had not yet been tapped. A further incentive for this Southwest Expedition was the possibility of finding the fabled Buenaventura River, which reportedly ran westward from the vicinity of the Great Salt Lake to the Pacific. If such a river existed, it might serve as a profitable avenue for trappers and their furs, rivaling the Columbia River to the north,

---

4. Smith in Harrison Clifford Dale, ed., *The Explorations of William H. Ashley and Jedediah Smith, 1822–1829*, 182.
5. Smith in David J. Weber, *The Californios versus Jedediah Smith, 1826–1827: A New Cache of Documents*, 58–59.

dominated by the Hudson's Bay Company, an imposing British firm. Apart from any material gain to be had, the glory of such discoveries enticed Smith. "I must confess that I had at that time a full share of that ambition (and perhaps foolish ambition) which is common in a greater or less degree to all the active world," he wrote. "I wa[nted] to be the first to view a country on which the eyes of a white man had never gazed and to follow the course of rivers that run through a new land."[6]

Given that ambition, Smith probably began the expedition with some thought of entering California and searching for beaver and the Buenaventura River before returning to the Bear River rendezvous, perhaps by way of the Columbia. Rumors of such an odyssey reached mountain man Daniel Potts at that rendezvous in July 1826, a month before Smith departed. Potts, who did not end up joining the expedition, wrote that he hoped to be among those leaving soon "to explore the country lying S.W. of the Great Lake where we shall probably winter. This country has never been visited by any white person—from thence to what place I cannot say, but expect the next letter will be dated mouth of Columbia River."[7] In fact, venturesome Spaniards and Mexicans had long been exploring southwest of the Great Salt Lake, but the terrain was virtually unknown to Americans.

Smith's party included American mountain men, recruits of British or French Canadian origin, a slave named John Peter Ransa (described by the expedition's clerk, Harrison Rogers, as a man of color), a Mexican called Manuel Eustevan, and two Indians from Canada who brought their wives and boys with them. Like Eustevan, those Indians left the company before Smith reached California, but he continued to receive aid and guidance from tribespeople encountered along the way. Like the Lewis and Clark expedition, this extension of American influence was made possible by the generosity of Indians who offered presents and assurances to outsiders rather than provocations. The Mohaves encountered along the

---

6. Smith, *Southwest Expedition*, 36–37.
7. Potts in Dale L. Morgan, *Jedediah Smith and the Opening of the West*, 193.

Colorado River, for example, supplied Smith's party with melons in such profusion that he had hundreds piled up outside his tent. Those Mohaves knew the way to the Mexican settlements, having long traded with tribes of coastal California. Some of them spoke Spanish, as did a member of Smith's party. "I therefore got the best instruction I could in regard to the route," he related.[8]

Smith and his men might well have perished, however, had they tried to cross the desert without the aid of their two young Serrano guides, whom he encountered among the Mohaves before setting out. They led the trappers to water and brought them to a village occupied by members of their Vanyume band, where the trappers feasted on acorn mush, pine-nut bread, and hares caught by their hosts. The two guides were later arrested when Smith's party reached Mission San Gabriel. They were charged with being fugitives from the mission, he reported, but he suspected that their real offense was conducting foreigners into California. One died in confinement, and the other "was kept in the guard house at night and at hard labor during the day."[9]

The rough treatment of his guides reinforced Smith's deep-seated distrust of Mexican authorities. "Spaniards," as he called them, possessed their "full share of that bigotry and disregard of the rights of a Protestant that has at times stained the Catholic Religion."[10] Smith's misgivings were reflections of the Black Legend, a myth dating back to Elizabethan times that portrayed Spaniards as ruthless inquisitors, bent on persecuting Protestants. In fact, Smith and his clerk Rogers, a self-described Calvinist, were treated with great courtesy by the padres at Mission San Gabriel. Governor Echeandía, who summoned Smith to San Diego to explain his presence in California, was a liberal who hoped to reduce the influence of the Catholic Church over civil affairs.

Like other Americans who entered Mexican California without permission in years to come, Smith saw himself as an innocent abroad and felt justified in evading and deceiving officials who

---

8. Smith, *Southwest Expedition*, 78, 83.
9. Ibid., 127
10. Ibid., 94.

might try to control or confine him. "They might perhaps consider me a spy imprison me persecute me for the sake of religion," he wrote. "Yet confiding in the rectitude of my intentions I endeavored to convince myself that I should be able to make it appear to them that I had come to their country as the only means by which I could extricate myself from my own embarrassing situation and that so far from being a spy my only [wish] was to procure such supplies as would enable me to proceed to my own country." In this convoluted passage, Smith all but admitted that the reason he gave for entering California was a pretense, meant to avert the governor's suspicions. Once resupplied, Smith had no intention of returning directly to his own country. As stated in his account, his objective after visiting the Mexican settlements was to "move on north. In that direction I expected to find beaver and in all probability some considerable river heading up in the vicinity of the Great Salt Lake."[11]

Smith stuck to that plan even after Echeandía, reassured by American ship captains and mates who had vouched for Smith, allowed him to purchase horses and supplies but insisted that when leaving he use the same route by which he had entered California, which meant traveling east back across the Mojave. Smith defied the order, claiming later in a letter to the governor that he could not follow the prescribed route because the snow-covered mountains "were impassable and I was obliged to go northwardly."[12] In fact, as revealed in his journal, Smith had no trouble making his way through the San Bernardino range when he left the valley in late January, and "there was no snow" once he came down on the far side of those mountains. He knew that the path he pursued was forbidden to him. Yet he nonetheless made his way north into the San Joaquín Valley, trapping beaver and moving with all the assurance of an expansive American who recognized no limit on his operations. Such "restless enterprise," he wrote, was "leading our countrymen to all parts of the world . . . until it can now be said there is not a breeze of heaven but spreads an american flag."[13]

---

11. Ibid., 77–78, 94.
12. Smith in Weber, *Californios versus Jedediah Smith*, 19, 45.
13. Smith, *Southwest Expedition*, 132; Weber, *Californios versus Jedediah Smith*, 20.

The Overland Challenge

Smith's intrusion did not bode well for Mexican authorities, who would face mounting challenges in years to come from overlanders following Smith's path and other trails. By demonstrating to Americans that formidable barriers like the Mojave Desert and the Sierra Nevada could be overcome, he opened a new chapter in the contest for California. The trails that he and other trappers and traders followed westward to the coast would become paths of subversion, undermining official Mexican restrictions on foreigners and inviting further intrusions by Americans in years to come. As a group, those who arrived overland were less willing to adapt to the customs of this country than were Yankees who came by sea and competed for commercial favors. Unlike the smugglers and poachers of the Spanish colonial era, those coastal traders were now welcomed by authorities if they paid the required duties. Many who settled there converted to Catholicism, married Mexican women, and became citizens of their adopted country.

Whether Americans arrived by sea or by land, however, they shared certain interests and loyalties that ran counter to those of their Mexican hosts. Captain William Cunningham, for example, was among the reputable Americans who vouched for Smith by certifying that the story he told Echeandía was "circumstantially correct" and that his reason for seeking to leave California by a different route—a request the governor denied—was "solely because he feels convinced that he and his companions run great risks of perishing if they return by the route they came."[14] Yet Cunningham knew that Smith had an ulterior motive, for he wrote after the explorer was released that "he intends to proceed northward in quest of beaver."[15] Thus the trust that Cunningham and others accrued through peaceful exchanges with Californios advanced the cause of an American pioneer who was less trustworthy and whose venture helped pave the way for later incursions by overlanders actively hostile to Mexican authorities.

---

14. Quoted in Dale, *Explorations of William H. Ashley and Jedediah Smith*, 209 n. 427.
15. Cunningham in ibid., 214 n. 429.

Echeandía's fear that Smith was spying on California was not entirely unfounded. Although Smith was not a government agent, he was gathering intelligence that would serve American interests as his nation expanded and challenged Great Britain in the Northwest and Mexico in the Southwest. He died in 1831 before fulfilling his ambition to transform his raw journal of the Southwest Expedition into a published narrative documenting his achievements and promoting American expansion. Like George Vancouver and other foreign critics of Spanish California, Smith felt that this country was in poor hands. He offered little indication in his journal that it was now part of the Mexican Republic and portrayed it instead as a vestige of the decrepit Spanish empire. For many years to come, American expansionists would continue to describe California and other northern Mexican territories as Spanish, implying that they remained under European imperial domination, culturally if not politically, and were in need of liberation.

Smith recognized, however, that Mexican independence had resulted in a new policy aimed at liberating neophytes. Mission Indians were "declared free and the fathers were ordered to inform them of the fact," he noted, "yet it does not appear that it has made any material change in their situation." Padres spoke to the Indians of freedom "in such a way that it appeared to them from their ignorance a change not to be desired." This had the effect of keeping them in "real slavery without the desire of freedom," Smith asserted.[16] He seemed unaware that Echeandía, in promising the neophytes liberty, was encountering resistance not just from Franciscans but from Californios who feared Indian uprisings if the missions collapsed. Many would conclude that secularizing the missions was indeed necessary, if only because it would give them greater access to Indian labor and land. But the culture that Americans encountered in California was cautious and conservative compared to the outlook of restless pioneers like Smith and the overlanders who followed in his wake. Many of them left their parents at an early age and never saw them again. They abhorred

---

16. Smith, *Southwest Expedition*, 129–30.

meddlesome officials and felt free to quarrel with their own leaders on the trail and part with them. Even those like Smith who harbored religious convictions might go years without setting foot in a church or heeding the words of a preacher.

Such men found far less to admire in Mexican California than did accommodating coastal traders like Alfred Robinson, who arrived in California in 1829 as a representative of Bryant and Sturgis, the firm that came to dominate the hide-and-tallow trade. Robinson learned at sea to regard prompt obedience to the captain's orders as a virtue and a necessity and admired Spanish traditions of dutifulness and deference that persisted in Mexican California. Furthermore, he profited by paying due respect to padres. He considered mission Indians far better off under Franciscan supervision than when left to their own devices, or at the mercy of Californios, and blamed the governor for turning neophytes against the padres and their rules. "Through the encouragement of Echeandía," Robinson wrote, "vice of all kinds had become prevalent, and the poor misguided Indians saw in the terms *libre* and *independente* a sort of license for the indulgence of every passion."[17]

The conflicting responses of Americans to the missions and their overseers amounted to an internal debate, a contest of principles in which the cherished frontier virtues of freedom and independence were weighed against the need for order and discipline as instilled by authorities. Even visitors wary of Catholicism like Smith and Rogers found redeeming qualities in the missionaries. They were charmed by the warmth and hospitality of Father José Bernardo Sánchez, who was hailed by Robinson as well: "Through his liberality, the needy wanderer, of whatever nation or creed, found a home and protection in the mission."[18] The other friar at Mission San Gabriel when Smith and Rogers arrived in November, Gerónimo Boscana, made less of an impression on them. But he was a remarkable figure in his own right, a pioneering ethnographer whose study of ancestral religious beliefs among neophytes

---

17. Alfred Robinson, *Life in California before the Conquest*, 129.
18. Ibid., 51; Maynard J. Geiger, *Franciscan Missionaries in Hispanic California, 1769–1848: A Biographical Dictionary*, 29–32, 217–22.

at his former mission, San Juan Capistrano, was later translated by Robinson.

Nothing in the Franciscan code prevented padres from enjoying a hearty meal in good company, and they treated Smith and Rogers to a veritable feast soon after they arrived. As Rogers reported in his journal: "I was introduced to the 2 Priests over a glass of good old whisky—and found them to be Joval friendly Gentlemen." Rogers was impressed with the fare and the prosperity of the mission as whole. He reckoned the workforce at "upwards of 1000 persons," who wove blankets; distilled whiskey; harvested wheat and ground it into flour at a water-powered mill; tended orchards laden with oranges, apples, peaches, and figs; and raised sheep, hogs, horses, and a huge herd of cattle, slaughtering thousands at a time for the hide-and-tallow trade. "The mission lives on the profits," Rogers concluded.[19]

In some ways, this mission enterprise resembled one of the larger plantations in the slave-holding South—a comparison often drawn by critics. Like Smith, Rogers took note of punishments meted out at San Gabriel, including one case in which two Indian "constables" sentenced five neophytes who had refused to work when ordered to a dozen lashes on their "Bare Posteriors." Americans were no strangers to bodily punishment of this sort. Earlier, Rogers noted, Smith had given James Reed, an unruly member of his party, "a little floggin . . . on account of some of his impertinence." That may have been one reason Reed later abandoned the company. In any case, Rogers did not liken the mission regimen to slavery, as Smith did. Remaining at San Gabriel while Smith was off dealing with the governor in San Diego, Rogers grew closer to his hosts and concluded that Sánchez, for one, was a true man of God, possessing "charity in the highest degree."[20]

On one occasion when speaking with "the Priest" (presumably Sánchez), Rogers remarked that he "did not believe that it was in the power of man to forgive sins. . . . and when I was under the

---

19. Rogers in Smith, *Southwest Expedition*, 216–18; Dale, *Explorations of William H. Ashley and Jedediah Smith*, 193–224.
20. Rogers in Smith, *Southwest Expedition*, 219–20, 223, 241.

necessity of confessing my sins, I confided them unto God." The priest responded that "when he was in church and his robe on he then believed that he was equal unto God, and had the power to forgive any sin . . . but when he was out of church and his common waring apparel on he was as other men, divested of all power of forgiveing sins." The idea that someone could be invested with the power of forgiveness was alien to Rogers, who believed that a man remained who he was regardless of the costume he wore or the title he held. In this he was fairly typical of the Americans who settled the West. Most rejected the notion that priests or high officials were sacrosanct and deserved more respect than ordinary people. And many resisted intermingling and intermarrying with those of other faiths or races. Rogers was approached one evening in his room at San Gabriel by an Indian woman who tried to seduce him by asking him to make her "a Blanco Pickaninia, which being interpreted, is to get here a white child—and I must say for the first time I was a shamed, and did not gratify her."[21] The very thought of yielding to her induced in him a feeling of remorse, much like that he might have experienced had he betrayed his faith by confessing to a priest.

Not all Americans who came to California shared these scruples. Rogers and Smith were prototypes of the settlers who arrived there overland in later years and kept their distance from Mexicans and Indians, forming a distinct Anglo colony. But some who came by land and many who arrived by sea fell gladly into the embrace of a culture that welcomed those who accepted its terms. More than a few sailors who reached California had already visited the Hawaiian Islands, where merchant ships enlisted the services of Polynesians. Life at sea amid racially diverse crews prepared Anglos landing in California to immerse themselves in this hospitable Hispanic society and take on new identities. Captains and traders received a particularly warm welcome, but common sailors who jumped ship and had skills to offer found harbor as well.

One such refugee, Joseph Chapman, worked as a handyman for the Franciscans and visited San Gabriel while Rogers was there.

---

21. Rogers in ibid., 226, 236.

By his own account, Chapman had been shanghaied in Hawaii by Hipólito Bouchard, the privateer who attacked Monterey in 1818. Chapman abandoned ship along the coast and became a ward of the Franciscans. Under their tutelage he converted to Catholicism, married a Mexican woman, and took the Christian name José. He was a favorite of Father Sánchez, who "declared it a marvel that one, so long 'in the darkness of the Baptist faith' could give such an example of true Catholic piety."[22] Yet conversion and assimilation did not eradicate his Anglo-American heritage. Journalist Edwin Bryant, who entered California in 1846 during the Mexican War, met Chapman's daughters and reported that they "called themselves Americans, although they did not speak our language, and seemed to be more proud of their American than their Spanish blood."[23] More than a few transplanted Yankees with family ties to Mexicans would side with American forces as they took possession of California.

While some Americans who assimilated remained potential enemies, others who stood apart from this culture proved susceptible to its appeal, among them Harrison Rogers. He was not converted by his stay at San Gabriel, but the experience left a deep impression on him. On New Year's Day, 1827, he composed an address for Sánchez that explored the common ground between their two faiths. "Standing on the threshold of a new year," he began, "I salute you with the most cordial congratulations and good wishes." The fact that "God has given us another year of probation," he went on, only served as a reminder that the summons to the next life could come at any time: "remember, Reverend Sir, that this world is not our home;—It is a world of trial—It is the dawn of an immortal existence." Preoccupation with the next life did not blind Rogers to the charms of his surroundings. "This country in many respects is the most desireable part of the world I was ever in," he wrote.[24] Sánchez took pleasure in nature and its blessings too, as did the

---

22. William Robinson quoted in Smith, *Southwest Expedition*, 101 n. 133; Dale, *Explorations of William H. Ashley and Jedediah Smith*, 213 n. 428.
23. Edwin Bryant, *What I Saw in California*, 421.
24. Rogers in Smith, *Southwest Expedition*, 229–30, 243.

founder of his order, Saint Francis. But that delight in the visible world was tempered by the conviction that life was fleeting and filled with temptations that could lead people to ruin. The very beauty and abundance that prompted some to liken California to Eden evoked somber thoughts in devout men like Sánchez and Rogers who believed that those who aimed too high and sought heaven on earth were sure to fall from grace.

Courting Disaster

For Smith and company, the remainder of this expedition would be a trial unlike any they had ever experienced. The same trait that brought them success—a determination to defy boundaries and press forward at all cost—would ultimately bring them to grief. Their illicit journey northward into the lush San Joaquín Valley yielded them plenty of beaver pelts, but Smith found no river that offered a corridor through the Sierra Nevada. He tried the American River in early May 1827; but it led him high into the mountains, where the snow was too deep for horses to plow through, and he had to turn back.

When several hundred neophytes fled Mission San José in mid-May, Father Narciso Durán blamed Smith's party for inciting them. Smith assured Durán in writing that he and his men had no hostile intent and were simply passing through. "We are Americans, on our journey to the River Columbia," he stated. "I went to San Diego and saw the General [Echeandía], and got a passport from him to pass on to that place." Smith did not in fact have Echeandía's permission to travel north through California to the Columbia. He further misled Durán by promising to depart as soon as he could "cross the mountains with my horses . . . I am a long ways from home, and am anxious to get there."[25] He neglected to tell Durán that he planned to leave most of his men and horses behind in the San Joaquín Valley with Rogers while he and two others crossed the Sierra, gathered supplies and fresh

---
25. Smith in Morgan, *Jedediah Smith and the Opening of the West*, 333.

recruits at the Bear River rendezvous in July, and returned by way of the Mohave villages to California, where he intended to resume the journey northward to the Columbia with his company later in the year. Smith's professed eagerness to return "home"—a veiled reference to the rendezvous—disguised his intention to continue his explorations in defiance of the governor.

Smith and his two companions barely survived their pioneering journey east across the Sierra and the searing Nevada desert. His return to California with eighteen trappers proved calamitous when Mohaves antagonized by a recent clash with another band of mountain men assailed them as they crossed the Colorado in August 1827. In that attack, Smith lost ten men, two Indian women, all of his horses, and most of his supplies. He and the other survivors then set out on foot across the desert. He had little choice at that point but "to again try the hospitality of the Californians," as he put it, by purchasing horses and supplies along the coast with furs obtained illegally in California.[26] His return did not go unnoticed by Echeandía, who nearly had him shipped to Mexico City for trial. Once again, however, an American involved in the coastal trade, Captain John Rogers Cooper, came to Smith's aid. After many years at sea, Cooper had settled in Monterey, converted to Catholicism under the name Juan Bautista, and married Encarnación Vallejo, a sister of Mariano Vallejo. At the suggestion of British trader William Hartnell, J. B. R. Cooper was given temporary consular status by Echeandía and took responsibility for Smith.

Echeandía allowed Smith to proceed to the Columbia River but insisted that his party travel under military escort to Mission San Francisco Solano, in what is now Sonoma. "From there the Americans may continue toward the north until leaving our territory," Echeandía allowed.[27] He did not want Smith to return to the Central Valley, where beaver were plentiful and the Indians were beyond Mexican control. Once again, Smith defied him and took the forbidden path, slipping away in late December and

---

26. Smith in ibid., 240.
27. Echeandía in Weber, *Californios versus Jedediah Smith*, 50.

heading up the Sacramento River. That infuriated Luis Antonio Argüello, Echeandía's predecessor as governor, now back in San Francisco as commandant. "As I see it," Argüello wrote Echeandía, "he mocks your excellency's high orders and even tramples upon sacred national laws . . . I have not the least doubt that these foreigners have illegal plans to upset the harmonious purposes of our nation." Argüello also questioned the motives of Smith's "fellow countrymen who live among us in the guise of mediators." In contrast to the insolence of Smith and his kind, he concluded the letter with words conveying his respect for the governor: "With the truest expressions of high solidarity, your loyal *compañero* who appreciates you, respects you, and kisses your hand."[28]

Argüello did not pursue Smith and company, in part because he considered the path they were following too dangerous for his troops, exposing them to tribes seen as wild and unpredictable. Indeed, Smith's party clashed with members of various tribes on their way north. Acts of theft by Indians prompted swift retaliation by these mountain men, although they too were often guilty of poaching. (As Argüello said of Smith, his aim was to remove as many furs as possible "from our territory.")[29] Sooner or later, men like Smith who recognized few limits on their operations were bound to come up against barriers, imposed on them legally as Echeandía did or forcefully as some Indians did. In July 1828, following an ominous incident in which Smith took a chief hostage and tied a rope around his neck to retrieve a stolen ax, Kelawatset Indians overran his camp along the Umpqua River in Oregon and killed Harrison Rogers and thirteen other men. Smith was away at the time and survived, along with three others. They found refuge in August at Fort Vancouver, a Hudson's Bay Company post on the Columbia from which that firm sent its own trapping brigades into California.

Smith's venture was so costly in lives and property that it hardly seemed likely to encourage similar forays. Yet American trappers

---
28. Argüello in ibid., 52–53, 55.
29. Argüello in ibid., 53.

and traders kept coming, driven by the same impulses that once led Spanish conquistadors to seek fortune in the New World after some of their predecessors met with disaster. In worldly pursuits as in spiritual conquests, misfortune and martyrdom could be incentives for those who knew that great risks brought great rewards. The legend of California as a paradise or promised land was enhanced by the hazards and prohibitions that surrounded this bountiful country and made its fruits harder to grasp. Many who overcame those obstacles and reached their goal as Smith did would feel redeemed and echo his memorable words: "But now the scene was changed and whether it was its own real Beauty or the contrast with what we had seen it certainly seemed to us enchantment."

Intruders from New Mexico

Although Smith's explorations demonstrated that California could be reached overland from the United States, it would be many years before a dependable emigrant trail was established. Since the early 1800s mountain men had followed the emerging Oregon Trail on horseback, but its potential as a wagon road had not yet been realized. The Santa Fe Trail was better defined, and wagon trains now moved regularly along that route, conveying American traders and their goods to New Mexico and returning to Missouri with Mexican silver, mules, and other assets. Trappers also followed the Santa Fe Trail to New Mexico. Some simply ignored the fact that foreigners were prohibited from taking beaver there; others obtained licenses through Mexicans who joined them. By 1826 parties made up of Americans, Mexicans, French-Canadians, and others were ranging far westward from Taos—favored as a rendezvous over Santa Fe, where authorities kept a closer eye on foreigners—and had California in their sights.

One American who told of those forays in writing was James Ohio Pattie, born on the Kentucky side of the Ohio River around 1803 and raised in Missouri. He and his father, Sylvester, ventured to New Mexico in 1825 and entered California with other

American trappers three years later. They may not have been the first from the United States to reach California by way of New Mexico. Mountain man Richard Campbell reportedly did so in 1827 and sold his furs to a ship captain in San Francisco Bay. But they were the first Americans traveling from New Mexico to come to the notice of authorities in California, where they were arrested. James Pattie's deceptive account of their ordeal gave this expedition notoriety and set the tone for an increasingly hostile relationship between American overlanders and Mexican officials in years to come.

Pattie and company approached California along the Gila River, flowing west from New Mexico to the lower Colorado River. Trappers found beaver in abundance along this corridor but also met with sharp opposition from Indians of various tribes. Pattie recalled one clash that occurred in 1827 after his trapping party, led by Ewing Young, passed down the Gila and turned north up the Colorado. A Mohave "captain" visited their camp and made signs indicating that this was his land, "and that we ought to pay him for what we had taken, by giving him a horse." That was a reasonable request to make of trappers poaching on Mohave territory, but Ewing saw it as extortion and refused. In the ensuing hostilities, his men killed the chief and gunned down other Mohaves when they retaliated. "We suspended those we had killed upon the trees," Pattie wrote, "and left their bodies to dangle in terror to the rest."[30]

Such assaults exposed others who came this way to deadly reprisals of the sort suffered by Jedediah Smith's party at the hands of Mohaves later that year. Mindful of those risks, shrewd leaders like Smith often appeased Indians by parleying with them and offering gifts, but they would not allow captains of other nations or tribes to restrict their movements. He and other American trappers acted as partisans in unlicensed campaigns of expansion. The U.S. Army had only a few thousand men in the 1820s, not nearly enough to patrol the nation's vast western holdings or enlarge that domain forcibly. But those regulars were supplemented by mountain men

---

30. James O. Pattie, *The Personal Narrative of James O. Pattie of Kentucky*, 144, 147.

like Smith and Pattie who advanced westward in armed companies or brigades and infiltrated foreign territory.

Pattie's western odyssey eventually carried him down the Colorado to the Gulf of California, where he and his father cached their furs and set out on foot with six other men across Baja California, nearly perishing of thirst before reaching Mission Santa Catalina near modern-day Ensenada in early 1828. Echeandía then had them conducted to San Diego, where they were interrogated and imprisoned. Their rations, Pattie complained, consisted of "dried beans and corn cooked with rancid tallow!" That was not such bad fare by local standards, but Sergeant José Antonio Pico (brother of future California governor Pío Pico) took pity on him and brought him food more to his liking. Pico's sister befriended Pattie and promised to intercede on his behalf with the governor. When Echeandía denied his request to visit his ailing father, who was confined separately and near death, the woman's eyes filled with tears, Pattie asserted, "and I had the consolation to know, that one person at least felt real sympathy for my distress."[31]

By contrasting this angel of mercy to the despotic governor, Pattie suggested that fair-minded Mexicans were ready to side with innocent Americans against oppressive authorities. This theme would be echoed by other American chroniclers and offered as a rationale for liberating Mexicans from misrule. Pattie, however, was too clumsy and biased a narrator to make American expansion appear so benign. Despite his professed gratitude to the Picos, he issued blanket denunciations of Mexicans, remarking at one point that death had set his father free "from the cruelty of this vile people."[32]

Pattie's account of his confinement was contradicted by Nathaniel Pryor, a member of his company, who remained in California after being released and told his story in later years to settler Stephen C. Foster. "Their detention was but for a few days," Foster

---

31. Ibid., 285, 295; Bancroft, *History of California*, 3:162–72; David J. Weber, *The Taos Trappers: The Fur Trade in the Far Southwest, 1540–1846*, 92–97, 134–41; Charles B. Churchill, *Adventurers and Prophets: American Autobiographers in Mexican California, 1827–1847*, 93–114; Richard Batman, *American Ecclesiastes: The Stories of James Pattie*, 224–38.

32. Pattie, *Personal Narrative*, 296–97, 304.

related, "and they fared sumptuously, for Mexican hospitality to strangers is great." Pryor attributed their prompt release to Father Antonio Peyri of Mission San Luis Rey, "who rode forty miles to tender his good services." The elder Pattie had been ill ever since his taxing journey across Baja California, Pryor added, and was so well cared for in San Diego that he agreed when the women nursing him urged him to be baptized a Catholic before he died. "The end soon came," Foster related, "and there was the grandest funeral San Diego had ever seen," led by Peyri and his acolytes, followed by James Pattie and his companions "and as many of the crew as could attend from a Boston vessel in port." Foster had no doubt that Pryor's story was closer to the truth than Pattie's account, "most of which is false," he insisted, "and has the same relation to the true narrative that Robinson Crusoe has to the journal of Alexander Selkirk."[33]

Although Pattie portrayed his detention as painful and prolonged, he admitted that Echeandía often allowed him to leave his cell to apply his knowledge of Spanish as a translator. Among those he served in that capacity was an American ship captain, John Bradshaw, charged with smuggling. Echeandía found him guilty and condemned his ship, the *Franklin*. Warned by Pattie that his arrest was imminent, Bradshaw escaped with the help of a French captain, Auguste Duhaut-Cilly, who had been trading with limited success along the California coast for two years and shared Bradshaw's disdain for Echeandía. "He enjoyed extensive power and often misused it," wrote Duhaut-Cilly, who claimed that the recently established assembly of delegates gathered only to applaud the governor's rulings, "most of which were not in the best interest of California." Yet Duhaut-Cilly acknowledged that Echeandía was in a difficult position, caught between the demands of his government, which imposed "excessive customs duties," and the need to accommodate foreign merchants, on whom California depended for revenue: "In order to provide for the expenses of his

---

33. Stephen C. Foster, "A Sketch of Some of the Earliest Kentucky Pioneers of Los Angeles," 32–33.

troops and his administration, he softened as much as he could the severity of the Mexican laws."[34]

Duhaut-Cilly delayed delivery of a boat that he sold to the governor to prevent soldiers from using it to board the *Franklin*, which then slipped away. In a scene reminiscent of the so-called battle of San Diego in 1803, when the American traders Cleveland and Shaler were targeted for smuggling, the *Franklin* exchanged shots with the battery at the entrance to the harbor. The damage done to the ship did not prevent Bradshaw and his crew from reaching Hawaii, where the vessel was repaired. Although Duhaut-Cilly observed that the Mexican gunners blasted away at the *Franklin* until it was out of range, Pattie claimed that they fled their post under fire. Echeandía "pretended great disgust" at their cowardice, he added, "but, I believe, had he been there, he would have run too. I have no faith in the courage of these people, except where they have greatly the advantage, or can kill in the dark."[35]

Not content simply to malign Mexicans, Pattie portrayed Americans as saviors of this misguided country. He claimed credit for suppressing an outbreak of smallpox during his stay, boasting that he and his companions introduced smallpox vaccine there, having carried it with them across the continent. In fact, a Russian ship brought vaccine to California during the outbreak, and inoculations were nothing new there. Pattie also claimed that he and other Americans put down a revolt against Echeandía in 1829 by a man they considered even worse—Joaquín Solís, an ex-convict supported by disgruntled troops who had not received their pay. "I knew him to be a bad man," Pattie asserted, "and destitute of all principle."[36] In truth, Americans and other foreigners in California cared little which contestant was the better man. They simply wanted to back the winner and protect their interests. As British merchant David Spence put it, they listened to Solís "from motives of courtesy," not wanting to offend him should he emerge

---

34. Auguste Duhaut-Cilly, *A Voyage to California, the Sandwich Islands, and around the World in the Years 1826–1829*, 83–84.
35. Pattie, *Personal Narrative*, 326–27; Duhaut-Cilly, *Voyage to California*, 196–99.
36. Pattie, *Personal Narrative*, 375; Batman, *American Ecclesiastes*, 258–61, 274–77.

victorious.³⁷ But when they realized that his cause was doomed, they fell in line behind Echeandía. Some helped secure the presidio in Monterey for the governor—a minor incident that Pattie portrayed as heroic. His ludicrous account of that revolt foreshadowed serious American interference in the affairs of Mexican California in years to come, when claims that Pattie and others made on this country in words were reinforced in action.

Conquest was not the inevitable outcome of the pioneering incursions of Americans in the 1820s, but their interactions with Mexicans gave them openings that they sometimes exploited to the detriment of their hosts. When an Anglo merchant married into a prominent Californio family, for example, he not only gained connections that were useful commercially but took priority over Mexicans aspiring to the same match. One such disappointed suitor may have been Governor Echeandía, who reportedly vied with American ship captain Henry Delano Fitch for the favors of Josefa Carrillo of San Diego. Her maternal grandmother was María Feliciana Arballo, who came to California with the Anza expedition and was disparaged by Father Pedro Font as a widow who sang naughty verses. She found a husband in San Diego, and her granddaughters Josefa and Francisca Carrillo (who wed Mariano Vallejo) drew attention from men of distinction. "It was well known to many of us that His Excellency himself aspired to the hand of Doña Josefa Carrillo," recalled Juan Alvarado, who as secretary of the assembly was acquainted with Echeandía. He could not marry her, for he had a wife elsewhere, but as Alvarado remarked he "was not indifferent to the call of beauty."³⁸ When Josefa Carrillo and Henry Fitch, who had converted to Catholicism, were about to wed, Echeandía forbade the union. His official reason was that Fitch was not yet a Mexican citizen, but Josefa believed that he was acting out of jealousy and could not abide her "preference for a rival whom he detested."³⁹ The couple then eloped by ship and took vows in Valparaíso.

---

37. Spence in Bancroft, *History of California*, 3:71.
38. Alvarado, "Historia de California," 2:40, 101; Bancroft, *History of California*, 3:140–44, 244 n. 8; Hurtado, *Intimate Frontiers*, 32–34.
39. Josefa Carrillo in Beebe and Senkewicz, *Testimonios*, 79.

Fitch later stood trial in California before an ecclesiastical court, presided over by Father Sánchez of Mission San Gabriel, who had to decide if the marriage was valid. Sánchez was not on good terms with Mexican officials. He and other padres had refused to pledge allegiance to Mexico except with the qualification: "So far as may be compatible with our religion and our profession."[40] Echeandía would not allow the oath to be qualified and left the matter hanging, neither expelling the friars, as directed by Mexico City, nor granting them passports to return to Spain, as Sánchez and others requested. Sánchez viewed American converts like Fitch as useful allies and trading partners at a time when the government seemed hostile to the mission system. After hearing evidence, he declared Fitch's marriage valid on condition that he do penance by providing "a bell of at least fifty pounds in weight for the church at Los Angeles, which barely has a borrowed one."[41]

Fitch may have been a thorn in Echeandía's side, but his willingness to embrace Californios and their culture was more typical of early American visitors there than the hostile response of Pattie. Nathaniel Pryor and two other Americans who reached California with Pattie settled in this country as Catholics and married Mexican women, as Fitch did. Yet their stories went all but unnoticed, while Pattie found a receptive audience for his provocative narrative with the help of editor Timothy Flint, whose heroic view of American expansion helped shape the tale. While others quietly came to terms with Mexican California, Pattie played to Anglo-American prejudices and condemned the "Spaniards" he dealt with there as corrupt and deceitful while proclaiming his own innocence and veracity. As he stated disingenuously at one point when cautioned by Echeandía to act in good faith and speak frankly: "I told him that my countrymen in that respect, had greatly the disadvantage of his people; for that it was our weakness, not to know how to say any thing but the truth."[42]

---

40. Quoted in Bancroft, *History of California*, 3:91, 96–97.
41. Sánchez in ibid., 3:144.
42. Pattie, *Personal Narrative*, 307.

The Spanish Trail

By 1830 trappers or traders of various nationalities were entering California from New Mexico with some regularity. On January 31 of that year Antonio Armijo reached Mission San Gabriel with a party of Hispanic New Mexicans after a journey of nearly three months that took the traders along what is now the Utah-Arizona border and across the Mojave Desert to the San Bernardino Valley. Armijo's pioneering venture set the stage for annual trade caravans between New Mexico and California. New Mexicans brought to the coast woolens and other goods loaded on pack mules and exchanged them mainly for mules and horses.

Typically, those caravans left New Mexico in the fall and returned in late winter, following a route through Utah that ran farther north than Armijo's path, thus reducing somewhat the hazards of desert crossings and dehydration. Known as the Spanish Trail, that path was first traversed in its entirety by a party led by Americans William Wolfskill and George Yount, who had come to New Mexico on the Santa Fe Trail. In September 1830 they left Taos for California with about twenty followers. According to Jonathan Warner, who reached California a year after Wolfskill and Yount, they were accompanied by "a number of New Mexicans, some of whom had taken *serapes* and *fresadas* (woolen blankets) with them for the purpose of trading them to the Indians in exchange for beaver skins. On their arrival in California, they advantageously disposed of their blankets to the rancheros in exchange for mules."[43]

Like most who ventured overland to California, Wolfskill and Yount had a rough time of it. The trail they followed had been traced in part by Spanish explorers in the 1700s, but they lost their way and nearly perished in a blizzard. "During several days, no one ventured out of camp," Yount recalled in an edited account based on his dictation. "There they lay embedded in snow, very deep, animals and men huddled thick as possible together." Like Smith's

---

43. Warner in Leroy R. Hafen and Ann W. Hafen, *Old Spanish Trail: Santa Fé to Los Angeles*, 171.

party and others who suffered ordeals by fire or ice on their way west, they found coastal California all the more inviting for the pains they took to get there. Yount's editor, the Reverend Orange Clark, portrayed Mission San Gabriel, which the party reached in early 1831, as heaven on earth, presided over by the saintly Sánchez. He reigned there as "Father, Patriarch, and Lord Supreme . . . His spirit was everywhere, & pervaded everything like that spirit, which of old 'moved upon the face of the waters' . . . Order, method, and regularity were perfectly maintained."[44] This was a nostalgic view, set down in the 1850s when the missions were crumbling and the problems that plagued them were largely forgotten. But Yount and Wolfskill were indeed charmed by what they encountered in California, for they settled there.

A number of Americans who arrived with trading or trapping parties chose to remain in California like Yount, Wolfskill, and Jonathan Warner, who set out from Missouri on the Santa Fe Trail in 1831 with a company led by Jedediah Smith, hoping to improve his health. He was not encouraged in that by Smith, who told him that "the chances were much greater in favor of meeting death than of finding a restoration to health."[45] As it turned out, Smith was the one who met death on that journey, in a confrontation with Comanches. Warner reached Santa Fe safely and continued on to California along the Gila River with David Jackson, Smith's partner. Jackson returned to New Mexico in 1832 with mules and horses, but Warner settled in California, converted to Catholicism, and emerged as Mexican citizen Juan José Warner, eligible for a land grant and destined to become a prominent rancher.

In the livestock trade, as in other businesses, newcomers to California sometimes skirted the law. Many horses, mules, and cattle roamed free and were rounded up only when it was time for them to be branded, sold, or slaughtered. There was little to

---

44. George C. Yount, *George C. Yount and His Chronicles of the West Comprising Excerpts from His "Memoirs" and the Orange Clark "Narrative,"* 90, 96–97. (This edition combines excerpts from narratives composed by Yount and by the Reverend Orange Clark, who based his account on stories that Yount told him.)

45. J. J. Warner, "Reminiscences of Early California from 1831 to 1861," 176–78.

stop thieves from making off with free-ranging livestock or traders from purchasing stolen animals. Among those accused of rustling in California were Indians of the interior, fugitives from the missions, Anglo-Americans, and New Mexicans, whom Californios often regarded with as much suspicion as they did Anglos arriving overland. In 1833 the alcalde in Los Angeles, José Antonio Carrillo, urged that all those arriving from New Mexico be required to present a passport and "evidence of good character" to discourage the influx of those who "without occupation or visible means of living, are gathering in Upper California to prey upon society."[46] Such measures did not stop the influx of undocumented aliens like American mountain man Thomas "Pegleg" Smith, who entered California about 1830 and left under a cloud, taking with him hundreds of stolen horses. Known as El Cojo (the cripple), he was later linked to a band of horse thieves haunting the San Joaquín Valley.

Some who purchased or stole horses in California were themselves targeted by Indian raiders and went to great lengths to recoup their losses. Such was the case with a trapping party led by Ewing Young that entered California from New Mexico around the same time as Pegleg Smith. With Young's company was Kit Carson—not yet twenty-one but already a trail-hardened veteran—who told of their strenuous journey across the Mojave Desert to Mission San Gabriel, which struck him as "paradise on earth." From there they moved north into the San Joaquín Valley, where they encountered a brigade of sixty trappers led by the accomplished Peter Skene Ogden of the Hudson's Bay Company. Such competition for furs was evidently taking its toll, for Carson and his companions found "but little beaver." They sold their pelts to a ship captain on the coast and used the proceeds to purchase horses at Mission San Rafael Arcángel. That night as they were returning to camp, Carson related, Indian raiders "frightened our animals, and ran off sixty head." He and several others pursued the thieves "upwards of one hundred miles into the Sierra Nevada" and surprised them as they were feasting on their take: "We charged

---

46. Carrillo in Hafen and Hafen, *Old Spanish Trail*, 178.

their camp, killed eight Indians, took three children prisoners and recovered all of our animals, with the exception of six that were eaten."[47]

Such mountain men were a law unto themselves. Young's party returned to New Mexico by way of Los Angeles, where authorities suspected them of foul play and demanded their passports. "We had none," Carson related. "They wished to arrest us, but fear deterred them."[48] After plying the suspects with liquor, they rode after them when they left town, hoping to apprehend them without a struggle. But intoxicated trappers were dangerous customers. As Young wrote afterward, two of his men "had a falling out about some very frivolous thing and one shot the other dead." With a posse trailing them, the trappers did not stop to bury the victim but left "him Lying in the rode where he was kild," in Young's words.[49] This casual murder, shrugged off by the company, appalled the pursuing Mexicans, Carson noted, "and they departed in all haste."[50]

Overlanders who settled in California had to be more circumspect. George Yount was called to appear before the authorities "and give bonds for his good behavior." Like Jedediah Smith, he was vouched for by an American trader, Captain William Goodwin Dana, a man of "some wealth and reputation" who became a Mexican citizen and acquired Rancho Nipomo near Mission San Luis Obispo.[51] Dana obtained a license to hunt sea otters along the coast and leased that license to Yount and others in return for part of the profits. In his hunting expeditions, Yount was aided by Kanakas who arrived from Hawaii as crewmen on merchant ships and performed various tasks along the coast, including paddling a boat that Yount made from elephant-seal skins stretched over a wooden frame, which he modeled after the buffalo-hide bull boats used by trappers on western rivers. Like Mexicans of means and

---

47. Kit Carson, *Kit Carson's Autobiography*, 13–17.
48. Ibid., 17–18.
49. Young in Edwin L. Sabin, *Kit Carson Days, 1809–1868: Adventures in the Path of Empire*, 1:59.
50. Carson, *Kit Carson's Autobiography*, 18–19.
51. Yount, *George C. Yount and His Chronicles of the West*, 100.

their Spanish predecessors, Yount and other American settlers profited by the cheap labor that abounded in California.

Among the Americans Yount befriended along the coast was Thomas Larkin, who arrived in Monterey by sea in 1832 with his future wife, Rachel Holmes, the first American woman to settle in California. Yount attended their wedding aboard the merchant ship *Volunteer* off Santa Bárbara in June 1833. The couple were Protestants, Yount noted, and "the laws of Mexican misrule" would not allow them to be married on Mexican soil.[52] Before he met Rachel Holmes, however, Larkin had been fully prepared to embrace Catholicism and wed a Mexican woman. "If I go to Monterey I shall do as the people do," he wrote. "And if I choose to marry there I should do it, providing that I had any (say a little) love for the Lady, and the Lady had enough loot for me."[53] Those plans were upset during his voyage to California when he fell for Rachel, who was due to join her husband, a ship captain. The ensuing affair between Larkin and Rachel produced an illegitimate child, born in January 1833 in Santa Bárbara, where Rachel spent her confinement with American settler Daniel Hill and his Mexican wife. She went there to avoid gossip in Monterey, where Larkin worked as a clerk for merchant J. B. R. Cooper, who had earlier aided Jedediah Smith. By the time her child was born, Rachel's husband had died at sea. But Larkin seemed in no hurry to marry her until he learned that she had inherited several thousand dollars—enough loot to satisfy him.

Larkin was later named U.S. consul in Monterey. He achieved that honor in part because he had not renounced his American citizenship like other assimilated Yankees there and was considered more loyal. Yet it was his good fortune in meeting Rachel Holmes and sharing in her inheritance that kept him officially in the American fold, which he might otherwise have abandoned to marry into a wealthy Mexican family. Yount's account reflects the heroic view of Larkin that prevailed after the American conquest:

---

52. Ibid., 116.
53. Larkin in Harlan Hague and David J. Langum, *Thomas O. Larkin: A Life of Patriotism and Profit in Old California*, 34.

"He does not accumulate wealth for the mere purpose of being rich—The influence of his fortune, and the power which he confers are felt for the benefit of the country where he dwells."[54] Much as Yount's editor idealized California's colonial past in his worshipful portrait of Father Sánchez, he idealized its capitalistic future in extolling Larkin, whose devotion to his country and flag was by no means selfless.

The focus of American colonization at this time was Monterey, where Larkin gained prominence as a merchant. Duhaut-Cilly, who visited the town in 1827, described it as consisting of the presidio and about forty houses, "roofed with tile and quite attractive with their whitewashed exteriors."[55] About a dozen foreign merchants lived there then, and more arrived in years to come. In 1832 some forty men, including Americans J. B. R. Cooper and Daniel Ferguson (who left Smith's party and settled there), enlisted in a company of foreigners in Monterey led by William Hartnell. They pledged support to Captain Agustín Zamorano, who challenged the right of Echeandía to govern the territory after rebels ousted the man sent to replace him, Manuel Victoria. Foreigners had never been fond of Echeandía, and those in Monterey feared that he might reject their town as California's port of entry in favor of San Diego, where he resided. Like most political uprisings in California, this one involved little bloodshed. None of the foreigners saw action before the dispute ended in 1833 with the arrival of the newly appointed governor, José Figueroa, to whom both sides deferred.

Walker's First Pass

In November 1833 a party of nearly sixty trappers led by mountain man Joseph Walker reached Monterey, having journeyed overland from the Great Salt Lake by way of the Humboldt River in Nevada. Walker's company was the first to enter California by

---

54. Yount, *George C. Yount and His Chronicles of the West*, 116.
55. Duhaut-Cilly, *Voyage to California*, 73; John Walton, *Storied Land: Community and Memory in Monterey*, 63–64; Bancroft, *History of California*, 3:221–22.

that promising path, which evolved into the California Trail and brought American settlers over the Sierra Nevada in wagons beginning in the early 1840s. The fullest account of Walker's pioneering venture was provided by Zenas Leonard, a young Pennsylvanian whose compelling narrative published in 1839 was significant both for what it revealed and for what it concealed. Although Leonard had "the advantages of a common English education," according to his publisher, he appeared ignorant of Mexico and regarded "Spaniards" in California as trespassers on American ground. He asserted at one point that most of the country on the western rim of the continent "belongs to the Republic of the United States" and urged Americans to protect their presumed property rights by fending off intruders along the Pacific: "The Spaniards are making inroads on the South . . . and further North-east the British are pushing their stations into the very heart of our territory."[56] Leonard seemed unaware that his government had recognized by treaty that California belonged to Mexico and that Oregon was free and open to British traders and settlers as well as Americans. Such geographic illiteracy, whether real or feigned, served the purpose of American expansion, which aimed at redrawing the map to produce a simpler picture of the West, cleansed of the inconvenient claims of rival nations.

Fortunately, Leonard was not a relentless propagandist and devoted much of the narrative to his honest impressions of a remarkable journey of some consequence for California. That venture grew out of an expedition by Captain Benjamin Bonneville, a French-born, West Point–trained officer. In 1831 he obtained leave to make a foray into the fur trade, during which he gathered intelligence of value to the army and the nation at large. After establishing Fort Bonneville on the Green River in 1833, he sent Joseph Walker, an enterprising mountain man from Tennessee in his mid-thirties, along with forty of the expedition's men and twenty independent trappers "to explore the Great Salt Lake," in the words of Washington Irving, who based his account on

---

56. Leonard, *Adventures of a Mountain Man*, xvii, 155.

Bonneville's unpublished narrative.[57] Privately, Bonneville may have given Walker leave to continue on to California, as implied by Zenas Leonard, who stated that Walker "was ordered to steer through an unknown country, towards the Pacific."[58] But if Bonneville approved so deep an intrusion into Mexican territory, neither he nor Irving cared to admit that publicly.

Setting out in July, Walker and his men moved quickly beyond the Great Salt Lake and picked up the Humboldt River, whose waters were vital both for travelers crossing the desert and for Paiutes native to this region, who were described by Leonard as "entirely naked and very filthy." He later noted more accurately that they wore a "shield of grass . . . around their loins" and robes of fur in cold weather. One Paiute gave the trappers "a large robe composed of beaver skins fastened together, in exchange for two awls and one fish-hook."[59] That was a steal for Walker's men, but other Paiutes then got the better of them by making off with their traps, which led to the killing of several Indians before Walker stopped the assaults.

Thereafter, Walker and his men assumed that any Indians who approached them were hostile. They rebuffed chiefs who wanted to enter camp "and smoke with us," Leonard noted, and opened fire with devastating effect on a large party of Paiutes who approached in a "saucy and bold" manner. That attack left thirty-nine Indians "dead on the field," he reckoned. Walker then told his men to put the wounded out of their misery. "The severity with which we dealt with these Indians may be revolting to the heart of the philanthropist," Leonard remarked, but "the country we were in was swarming with hostile savages, sufficiently numerous to devour us."[60]

Irving reported that Bonneville, no tender-hearted philanthropist, was disgusted when he learned of this incident. Walker's men,

---

57. Washington Irving, *The Adventures of Captain Bonneville*, 223; Robert Glass Cleland, *This Reckless Breed of Men: The Trappers and Fur Traders of the Southwest*, 276–84; William H. Goetzmann, *Exploration and Empire: The Explorer and the Scientist in the Winning of the American West*, 146–59.
58. Leonard, *Adventures of a Mountain Man*, 104.
59. Ibid., 110–12, 117.
60. Ibid., 114–17; George Nidever, *The Life and Adventures of George Nidever, 1802–1883*, 31–34; Churchill, *Adventurers and Prophets*, 177–87.

he added, suspected Paiutes of "crafty and daring conspiracies, which, it is probable, never entered into the heads of the poor savages. In fact, they are a simple, timid, inoffensive race, unpracticed in warfare."[61] Overlanders often described Paiutes and other Indians they encountered in Nevada and California as Diggers, meaning that they lived a hand-to-mouth existence, sometimes subsisting on roots or insects. They were not all as inoffensive as Irving claimed but posed little threat to well-armed parties like Walker's. Yet they repeatedly came under attack, first by mountain men and later by emigrants, who entered California with the same kind of siege mentality that Leonard revealed when he wrote of being hemmed in by voracious "savages."

By mid-October Walker and his men had come up against the Sierra Nevada and were seeking a way through. The path they followed may have taken them up a fork of the Walker River—one of several landmarks in the region bearing Walker's name—into mountains overlooking Yosemite Valley. At high elevations they encountered no game. Like the Diggers they derided, they found nothing more to eat than berries and insects. Soon their horses began to give way, Leonard related, and two of the animals were butchered by the famished men, who wolfed down that "black, tough, lean, horse flesh, as if it had been the choicest piece of beef steak."[62] Such grueling passages to California over burning deserts and frigid mountain passes could reduce white men to a state like that of the most wretched Indians they could imagine, capable of devouring anything at hand, including their fellow humans. The specter of starvation and cannibalism, the ultimate form of savagery, haunted a number of parties that crossed the Sierra Nevada in years to come, particularly in late autumn when snowstorms stranded travelers for months on end. Leonard and his companions were fortunate to make it through without facing that ordeal.

Walker and his party found their way down from the mountains by following an Indian trail, used by tribespeople who had been

---

61. Irving, *Adventures of Captain Bonneville*, 225, 233.
62. Leonard, *Adventures of a Mountain Man*, 126.

crossing the Sierra Nevada to trade long before Walker or Jedediah Smith made the trek. Pursuing that path, they beheld "a beautiful plain stretched out towards the west" and descended into the foothills bordering the San Joaquín Valley, where they found game plentiful and redwoods "16 to 18 fathoms round." Beyond lay lush grasslands, "swarming with wild Horses." Walker and company needed tame horses and obtained some "marked with a Spanish brand" through trade with Indians before proceeding down the Merced River and San Joaquín River toward San Francisco Bay, where the prospect of reaching "the *end* of the *Far West* inspired the heart of every member of our company with a patriotic feeling for his country's honor," Leonard wrote. Their national pride was heightened when they encountered the American merchant ship *Lagoda* on the coast. Its captain was John Bradshaw, who had fled San Diego under fire while Pattie was there and was back now, purchasing hide and tallow for Bryant and Sturgis. Bradshaw welcomed the trappers and "had a table spread with the choicest of liquors & best fare the ship would afford."[63]

In late November Walker and company reached Mission San Juan Bautista, near Monterey, and obtained permission from the padres to camp nearby. There they "erected a breast work," Leonard noted, "with which to defend ourselves in case we were attacked by Indians or anything else that chose to molest us." Perhaps they foresaw trouble with Mexican troops. Overlanders like Walker regarded unsettled areas of California as free for all—a presumption that Mexicans rejected, much as Americans did when foreigners trespassed on remote parts of their territories. Having reached the settlements, Walker acknowledged that he was on foreign ground by obtaining a passport from Governor Figueroa in Monterey and permission to spend the winter in the area and hunt for game. Figueroa's one condition was that the Americans not poach on tribal lands or trade with Indians (as they had done earlier and would do again on their way back east). "The Spaniards manifest a warm friendship for the Indians under their jurisdiction," Leonard

---

63. Ibid., 132–33, 136, 140–43, 146, 151.

explained, and "were constantly reminding us of the danger of wronging the Indians."[64] Figueroa himself was partly of Indian ancestry, and Native Californians fared better on balance under Mexican authority than they would later under American rule.

Relations between Walker and the governor remained cordial. The two men spent New Year's Day aboard the *Lagoda* with Captain Bradshaw, Leonard noted, and Figueroa later offered Walker "a tract of land seven miles square if he would bring 50 families, composed of different kinds of mechanicks, and settle on it." Walker was pleased with California, "but his love for the laws and free institutions of the United States, and his hatred for those of the Spanish Government, deterred him from accepting the Governor's benevolent offer." Why Walker should hate this government when the governor treated him so well was left unexplained by Leonard, who assumed that any self-respecting American would disdain Mexicans. In his view, Californios were unworthy rivals who stood between Americans and what supposedly belonged to them. When the trappers returned east in February 1834, he wrote, they left behind six men who chose to settle in California, all of whom had skills or trades, "which will no doubt be profitable to themselves, and of great advantage to the indolent and stupid Spaniard." Walker was eager to leave, Leonard claimed, because some of his horses had been stolen and a local magistrate declined to intervene, explaining that anyone there with a poor horse was free "to take a good one if he could find such, no matter who it belonged to."[65]

The taking of a stray animal or two was not of great concern to Californios, but Leonard had no basis for stating that stealing horses was "not recognized as a crime" or for asserting that Walker was so shocked to find rustlers operating freely that he thought it best "to pack up and leave the neighborhood, in order to avoid a difficulty with a people of a ferocious and wicked nature."[66] Walker, after all, had purchased horses bearing Spanish brands from Indians who might well have stolen them. Whether or not he

---

64. Ibid., 160, 165.
65. Ibid., 175–76.
66. Ibid., 185–86, 191, 195.

and his followers went a step further and stole horses themselves, as other mountain men later alleged, they clearly overstayed their welcome in California. According to Washington Irving, they "forgot all the purposes of their expedition; squandered away, freely, the property that did not belong to them; and, in a word, revelled in a perfect fool's paradise."[67] Thomas Larkin, whose general store in Monterey also served as a grog shop, may have profited by their presence; but, as George Yount recalled, most in town "were not made sorry at their departure."[68]

Although Leonard portrayed Walker as fed up with these "Spaniards" and their government, this would not be his last trip to California. He and his men left by way of Walker Pass, an inviting corridor through the southern end of the Sierra Nevada that he learned of from Indians and later disclosed to other Americans. In 1843 he would guide emigrants from the United States through that pass into the San Joaquín Valley, thus helping to loosen Mexico's grip on this country. Meanwhile, other American visitors would follow in the deceptive narrative tradition of Leonard and Pattie by further distorting the image of Californios and their culture in writing. Even as explorers like Smith and Walker charted paths of subversion, those literary surveyors would promote American expansion by portraying a postcolonial society seeking greater freedom and opportunity as a miserable vestige of Spanish imperialism—indolent, backward, and ripe for conquest.

---

67. Irving, *Adventures of Captain Bonneville*, 230; Cleland, *This Reckless Breed of Men*, 308.
68. Yount, *George C. Yount and His Chronicles of the West*, 119.

CHAPTER 9

Revolutionary California

Few settlers followed a more unlikely path to California than Victor Eugène August Janssens. Born in Brussels in 1817 to a French officer and his Belgian wife, he emigrated with them as a boy to Mexico and took the Spanish name Agustín. Apprenticed to businessmen in Mexico City, he grew restless and sought opportunity on the northern frontier. "In 1834 people began to talk of forming a colony in California," he recalled. "Flattering offers were made me to stay, but I began to want to see other lands and make my fortune without enslaving myself to anyone."[1] In April of that year he joined a party of some 240 men, women, and children who set out from Mexico City in wagons for the port of San Blas, where they would embark in two ships for Monterey.

No colonizing venture to California had been attempted on this scale since the Anza expedition some sixty years earlier, and its prospects looked bright. Among the colonists were printers, carpenters, blacksmiths, tailors, seamstresses, and shoemakers as well as twenty-two teachers, two doctors, a surgeon, and a midwife. Some in Mexico City found it hard to believe that they would freely

---

1. Agustín Janssens, *The Life and Adventures in California of Don Agustín Janssens, 1834–1856*, 6.

undertake this risky venture to a distant land still widely regarded as a desert. As Janssens recollected, "there was much opposition on the part of the public because some ill-intentioned and ignorant persons had noised it about that those who came with the colony had joined under duress." A mob nearly prevented them from leaving town, until it was made clear that they were going "voluntarily, in search of better fortune."[2] Indeed, the government had promised them free passage, free land, and financial assistance, hoping that the colony would pay dividends by bolstering California against foreign intruders. Without such incentives, few would have undertaken this arduous journey. Unlike the United States, Mexico had no glut of land-hungry settlers prepared to emigrate to remote territories at their own expense.

This colonizing expedition had strong support in Mexico City from Vice President Valentín Gómez Farías, who was holding forth in the capital while President Antonio López de Santa Anna remained in seclusion. A leader of the liberal faction known as federalists, Gómez Farías hoped to make a clean break with Mexico's colonial past by furthering democracy, reducing the power and privileges of the military and the Catholic Church, and allowing the nation's states to manage their own affairs in keeping with the Mexican constitution of 1824. Santa Anna would soon wreck those plans by shifting abruptly to centralism and asserting broad authority over the nation's newly designated departments (including states and territories such as California) with the backing of conservatives.

That did not bode well for the colonizing expedition and its liberal sponsors. Their plan was for colonists to settle on mission lands in California that were secularized, a long-delayed measure that federalists pushed through Congress in late 1833. The leader of the expedition, José María Híjar, was to succeed José Figueroa as governor or political chief of California while Híjar's top aide, José María Padrés, who had served as an officer in California under

---

2. Ibid., 11; Hutchinson, *Frontier Settlement in Mexican California*, 206–10, 265–67, 316–22, 347–51; Bancroft, *History of California*, 3:259–69.

Echeandía, would become military chief there if Figueroa chose to relinquish that role. Separating civil from military authority in this way had considerable support in California, particularly in Los Angeles and San Diego, where many felt that the governor in Monterey, by also serving as commandant general, wielded too much power and was thwarting their interests. Juan Bandini of San Diego, California's representative in Congress, helped promote this plan and returned to California with Híjar and Padrés to help implement it.

Soon after the colonists left Mexico City, Santa Anna emerged from seclusion, disbanded Congress, and forced Gómez Farías into exile. He then sent a message by express rider to Figueroa in Monterey, instructing him not to yield power as governor to Híjar. Figueroa already had orders to remain as commandant, so he would continue to exercise both civil and military authority in California, much as Santa Anna would in Mexico City as president and general in chief. Rafael Amador, the rider who carried his urgent message to Figueroa, reached Monterey in record time. He arrived a month earlier than Híjar, who made the last leg of his six-month trip to Monterey overland from San Diego after his storm-lashed ship *Natalia* put in there to spare the colonists further suffering. Janssens was one of the few passengers on that vessel not laid low by seasickness or disease. Several colonists died on board before the captain agreed to cut short the voyage, as Janssens related: "On seeing the harbor of San Diego, there was a joyful cry of thanksgiving to God."[3] Such ordeals at sea made the prospect of emigrating to California dreadful for people from the Mexican heartland, and the trek across the Sonoran Desert was no easier.

Híjar recuperated at the home of Juan Bandini while Janssens lodged at the presidio and other colonists slept in shacks where coastal traders stored hides. The family of Joaquín Carrillo, whose daughter Josefa had earlier eloped with the American ship captain Henry Fitch, "did everything possible for our comfort," Janssens

---

3. Janssens, *Life and Adventures*, 17–18.

recalled, "giving us milk, green vegetables, fruit, and whatever else we wished . . . without accepting a single centavo."[4] Following the Mission Trail up the coast, Híjar reached Monterey in mid-October, a few weeks after Padrés and other colonists traveling in the second ship had disembarked there.

Brandishing his recent order from Santa Anna, Governor Figueroa—who took pride in his Indian ancestry and saw himself as a defender of neophytes—refused to yield power to Híjar and opposed his plan to settle with his followers on mission lands. In response to the secularization law passed by Congress, which did not specify how mission property was to be distributed, Figueroa and the assembly in Monterey had recently instituted their own plan, which called for establishing Indian towns at the missions and limiting the padres to purely religious functions. In practice, this plan left former neophytes at the mercy of civil administrators, who would oversee mission lands not assigned to those Indians and could require them to labor on that property. But Figueroa dismissed Híjar's colonization scheme as an assault on the rights of Indians and a cynical attempt to appropriate the best land in California, a view shared by others.

Híjar's plan was not meant to benefit only those who accompanied him. His aim was to assign mission land in lots to Indians and to distribute the surplus to soldiers, civilians, and trustworthy immigrants such as his own colonists. Those provisions were not spelled out in law, however, and Híjar's word had to be taken on faith by Figueroa, who remained suspicious. Híjar clearly was not in favor with Santa Anna, and Padrés and Bandini had clashed with Figueroa's predecessor, Governor Manuel Victoria, and remained controversial figures in California. Padrés was "a man of extreme republican and liberal ideas which he imparted to the young men of the principal families of the territory," remarked colonist Antonio Coronel. "This aroused the antagonism of the old Spanish friars, who were monarchists and absolutists of the old school."[5] Bandini was director of the Cosmopolitan Company,

---
4. Ibid., 21.
5. Antonio Coronel, *Tales of Mexican California*, 12.

formed as part of the colonizing venture to win a share of the coastal trade, whose profits went largely to foreigners. Figueroa opposed the company as monopolistic, as did foreign traders and Californios allied with them. They were not sorry when the firm's chief asset, the *Natalia*, was wrecked in a storm in December while anchored off Monterey. "With this it seems to me that the great Cosmopolitan Company has come to its end," Figueroa wrote with satisfaction.[6]

After lengthy negotiations, Figueroa allowed the colonists to settle near Mission San Francisco Solano in the emerging town of Sonoma. That suited the purposes of the Mexican government, which wanted a settlement north of San Francisco Bay to serve as a buffer against the Russians at Fort Ross, a declining outpost that nonetheless remained worrisome to authorities. Híjar's colonists were not to occupy mission lands, but Figueroa agreed to furnish supplies from various missions to support the venture, which he considered unlikely to succeed. "A people who are going to be founders need to be hard-working and to have strong arms," he wrote. "They must be men accustomed to work in the fields and used to a frugal and simple life." These "delicate" colonists would be better off settling in existing towns, Figueroa argued, but Híjar was intent on establishing a colony in the north as planned.[7]

Settling in distant Sonoma did not free the colonists from oversight. Figueroa was kept informed of their activities by Lieutenant Mariano Vallejo, commandant at San Francisco, whose domain had expanded northward to include Sonoma, where he served as administrator of the mission and built a fort. Vallejo was indebted to Figueroa—who granted him Rancho Petaluma, which would grow to embrace 66,000 acres around Sonoma—and shared the governor's disdain for Híjar and Padrés, engaged in a project that Vallejo felt he could better manage himself. The colonists, for their part, regarded Vallejo as "something of a tyrant," in the words of Janssens, and thought he was conspiring with Figueroa against them.[8]

---

6. Figueroa in Hutchinson, *Frontier Settlement in Mexican California*, 334.
7. Figueroa in ibid., 343.
8. Janssens, *Life and Adventures*, 33–35; Rosenus, *General Vallejo*, 13–15.

Figueroa, meanwhile, was beginning to suspect the leaders of the expedition of plotting against him. In March 1835 colonist Francisco Torres, who had been sent south by Híjar with dispatches, was implicated in an abortive revolt against Figueroa in Los Angeles. Although he had no proof that Torres was acting on orders from Híjar or Padrés, Figueroa had the two leaders arrested and deported to San Blas along with other prominent colonists. Figueroa was in poor health and awaiting retirement. He did not want his last days in office tarnished by an uprising like the one mounted against his predecessor, Victoria, who had exiled Padrés from California in 1831 on charges that included plotting to carve up the missions and divide the spoils with his confederates. (Padrés was also accused by Father-President Narciso Durán of denying the existence of hell and undermining the fear of God on which "obedience and fidelity" to church and state depended.)[9] Banishing Padrés had not stopped like-minded Californios from ousting Victoria when he refused to convene the assembly and scrubbed a secularization plan drawn up by Padrés for Echeandía, who regained power in southern California after Victoria departed. That coup was opposed by Captain Agustín Zamorano, who served as rival governor to Echeandía in Monterey until Figueroa arrived in 1833 and ended the rift between north and south. Figueroa commended Zamorano for opposing the revolt against Victoria and upholding "the honor and dignity of the central government."[10] When faced with what he saw as a similar threat to his own authority in 1835, he promptly deported Padrés, Híjar, and others he suspected of sedition.

The remaining settlers at Sonoma were disarmed and dispersed. Many stayed in California and served as artisans or teachers. "The young men who today occupy public offices," remarked California's deputy in Congress a decade later, "were taught by these unhappy colonists."[11] Not all of them lamented their fate. Janssens, for one, became a successful rancher and found that California was

---

9. Durán in Hutchinson, *Frontier Settlement in Mexican California*, 145.
10. Figueroa in Harding, *Don Agustín V. Zamorano*, 152.
11. Manuel Castañares in Hutchinson, *Frontier Settlement in Mexican California*, 324.

"Scene on an Old Californian Cattle Ranch, in Early Spring, on the Eve of a General Rodeo," ca. 1870, by Edward Vischer. *Courtesy Library of Congress, Prints and Photographs Division* (LC-USZ62-48139).

indeed a "true Land of Promise," as Padrés had assured him.[12] He benefited from a dramatic change in land policy, which had long favored the missions but now fostered private ownership. Many former neophytes left the secularized missions because they were unable to make a living on the land assigned them or were mistreated by the administrators. As the resident Indian population dwindled, large tracts of mission property were declared vacant and granted to ranchers, some of whom acquired vast spreads roamed by immense herds. Even Commandant José de la Guerra y Noriega, a conservative who opposed secularization and did not seek mission lands, profited from the largesse of liberal Governor Juan Alvarado, who in 1837 granted him the government-owned Rancho San Julián, bringing his holdings around Santa Bárbara to more than 200,000 acres. His daughter Teresa, who wed William Hartnell, recalled that her father amassed more than 58,000 head of cattle. Their value lay largely in the hides and tallow, for the meat far surpassed the needs of the population and could not profitably be preserved and exported. Travelers "were allowed to kill steers

---

12. Janssens, *Life and Adventures*, 15.

in the fields whenever they needed them for food," she related. "The only thing required was that they leave the hide staked so the owner could pick it up when he passed through his property."[13]

Some ranchers supplemented what they earned in the hide-and-tallow trade by pursuing other ventures. Juan Francisco Dana, the son of American merchant William Goodwin Dana and María Carrillo of Santa Bárbara, recalled that Rancho Nipomo, which his father obtained after becoming a Mexican citizen, had a blacksmith shop, a soap factory, and rooms where clothing was woven and furniture was crafted. "Additions to the Casa seemed to be made all the time and the Indians who did the work, although slow, were constantly being trained," he remarked. "Most of them had learned some trade at La Purísima and Santa Inés missions and were willing and sometimes, skilled workers."[14] Although faulted by critics for not preparing Indians for life in civil society, Franciscans bequeathed a capable workforce to such ranches, which replaced the missions as centers of production. Shrewd ranchers like Agustín Janssens, who obtained a land grant near Mission Santa Inés, sought the services of former neophytes as artisans or vaqueros. He had "many people employed in handling the cattle" on his ranch, which left him free to engage in other business, including a store he operated in Santa Bárbara.[15]

Janssens and other resourceful colonists who had come under suspicion in California were ultimately rewarded for their pains. For the colony's leaders, however, banishment and censure were poor recompense for their efforts to bolster Mexico's vulnerable northern frontier. Figueroa proved relentless in denouncing them. "The genius of evil has appeared among you, scattering the deadly poison of discord," he proclaimed after ordering them deported.[16] Shortly before he died in September 1835, he elaborated on that theme in his fiery *Manifesto to the Mexican Republic*. Printed on a

---
13. Teresa de la Guerra in Beebe and Senkewicz, *Testimonios*, 62–63; Robinson, *Land in California*, 65–71.
14. Juan Francisco Dana, *The Blond Ranchero: Memories of Juan Francisco Dana as Told to Rocky Dana and Marie Harrington*, 19–20.
15. Janssens, *Life and Adventures*, 118.
16. Figueroa in Bancroft, *History of California*, 3:287.

press imported by ship from Boston by the enterprising Captain Zamorano, who set up shop in Monterey and employed one of the colonists from Mexico City as a typesetter, this was the first book of any length published in California. "I restrained their pretensions," Figueroa wrote of Híjar and Padrés, "drew aside the curtain from their aims, revealed their imprudence, resisted their doctrines, confounded their presumptions, thwarted their projects, humbled their arrogance, destroyed their plans, curbed their audacity, extinguished the revolutionary torch they had lit, saved the properties of the Indians and the wealth of the missions, and rescued the unfortunate colonists from the precipice to which they were being led."[17]

As implemented, the secularization plan approved by Figueroa dispossessed many mission Indians, but he insisted that his intentions were good and those of his opponents evil. Such moral certainty came readily to California's contentious pioneers. Righteous disdain for the presumed failings of Híjar and Padrés helped Figueroa and his supporters fend off a supposed threat from intruding Mexicans, but such internal struggles left California susceptible to greater challenges from Anglo-Americans, who would exploit the growing rift between Californios and their mother country. As yet, few prominent Californios were openly hostile to Mexico, but leaders like Vallejo with close ties to foreigners often found it easier to deal with them than with Mexicans from outside the territory. After Híjar and Padrés were banished, Vallejo colonized Sonoma on his own terms, welcoming American settlers. Within a decade, however, the area would become a hotbed of Yankee resistance to Mexican rule, and Vallejo would see his authority as overseer of California's northern frontier scorned and subverted.

Dana's Liberties

While the last concerted Mexican colonizing effort was unraveling, a young American visitor was gathering material for one of the most influential accounts of California published in the United

---
17. José Figueroa, *Manifesto to the Mexican Republic*, 94–95.

Richard H. Dana, Jr., 1842.
*Courtesy The Bancroft Library,
University of California, Berkeley
(California Faces: Selections from
The Bancroft Library Portrait Collection).*

States before it annexed the territory. Richard Henry Dana, Jr., who arrived on the coast in January 1835 aboard the *Pilgrim*, a ship engaged in the hide-and-tallow trade for Bryant and Sturgis, did not set out to chronicle California. His original purpose was to improve his poor health and weak eyesight through a rigorous apprenticeship at sea. That in turn led him to compose a compelling and seemingly unvarnished account of his experiences as a common sailor at a time when most naval literature was romanticized. Dana's celebrated memoir, *Two Years before the Mast*, was not free of imaginative flourishes. Within its realistic framework, he drew artful contrasts between the discipline and constraints of life at sea and the seemingly idle pleasures and pastimes of the Californios. His impressions were fleeting, gained from stops he made along the coast over sixteen months, on duty or at liberty. Yet he came away believing that he knew California intimately and took liberties with it in writing, contributing to the emerging Anglo-American legend of Hispanic California that served as a pretext for conquest.

The grandson of Francis Dana, chief justice of Massachusetts, Dana saw his family's fortunes decline under his father, a lawyer with literary aspirations who described himself as "a lazy, luxurious dreamer" and published an unsuccessful journal entitled *The Idle Man*.[18] Perhaps it was partly in reaction to his father's laziness that Dana shipped out after three uninspiring years at Harvard and a debilitating bout with measles. Except at night and on Sundays, he wrote, "you will never see a man, on board a well-ordered vessel, standing idle on deck, sitting down, or leaning over the side. It is the officers' duty to keep everyone at work. . . . In no state prison are the convicts more regularly set to work, and more closely watched."[19] He took pride in his ability to withstand this regimen and disdained those in California who stood idle.

Harder for Dana to bear during the voyage was the verbal hazing that he and his mates were subjected to by their captain, Frank Thompson. Romantics might imagine an ocean voyage as a passage to paradise, but Thompson had something quite different in mind for his men if they resisted his demands. "If we get along well together, we shall have a comfortable time," he told them soon after they left port; "if we don't we shall have hell afloat." After a harrowing circuit around Cape Horn in November 1834, they lost a man overboard and could only pray that God would go easier on that poor sailor than their captain had. As Dana summed up their thoughts: "*To work hard, live hard, die hard, and go to hell after all would be hard indeed!*" When they dared suggest that Thompson might be short-changing them in their bread allowances, he denied them any right to appeal his summary judgments: "Away with you! . . . I'll haze you! I'll work you up! If you a'n't careful I'll make a hell of heaven!"[20]

Thompson proceeded to do just that when they reached California and glimpsed what looked much like heaven after five months at sea. Coming ashore in San Diego for a day's leave, Dana felt like a condemned man reprieved: "This day, for the first time, I may truly say in my whole life, I felt the meaning of a term which I had often heard—the sweets of liberty." Yet such idylls only made life aboard the *Pilgrim* harder to bear as Thompson tightened the

---

18. Richard Henry Dana, Sr., in Samuel Shapiro, *Richard Henry Dana, Jr., 1815–1882*, 4; Churchill, *Adventurers and Prophets*, 93–114.
19. Richard Henry Dana, Jr., *Two Years before the Mast: A Personal Narrative of Life at Sea*, 12.
20. Ibid., 3, 32, 46.

screws, knowing that proximity to land and liberty made the crew restless and defiant. Soon after their arrival, he flogged a man for impertinence. The sailor protested, "I'm no Negro slave," to which Thompson replied, "Then I'll make you one." When another man asked what his mate had done to deserve such punishment, he too received a whipping, delivered with such fury that he begged Christ for mercy. "Jesus Christ can't help you now," the captain told him. "'You've got a driver over you! Yes, a *slave driver—a nigger driver!*'"[21]

Many travelers went through hell in one form or another on their way to California, but for Dana the ordeal had a moral intensity that distinguished his narrative. Unlike other visitors from the United States who saw their country stereotypically as the land of the free and the home of the brave and found Mexican California deficient in both respects, Dana acknowledged that Americans too were often denied freedom and justice by their masters. He was chiefly concerned with the plight of common sailors and hoped that his book would help promote reforms and improve their lot. But his frequent references to sailors as little better than slaves served as a reminder that degrading labor conditions were all too common in the United States, both on southern plantations and in northern cities where whites toiled in such wretched conditions that some called them wage slaves.

As an ordinary seaman, Dana was closer in status to Indian servants in California than to the wealthy ranchers who employed them and purchased fancy clothes and other luxuries from coastal traders like Thompson. "Among the Mexicans there is no working class (the Indians being practically serfs, and doing all the hard work)," he asserted; "every rich man looks like a grandee, and every poor scamp like a broken-down gentleman." Dana and his mates, after spending hard days ashore hauling hides like "West India Negros," got even with well-to-do Californios, whose dread of the ocean he likened to "hydrophobia," by seeing that they got soaked as they were rowed out to the ship to make purchases. As he put it, "we liked to have a Mexican wet with salt water."[22]

---

21. Ibid., 89–92, 102.
22. Ibid., 66, 78, 195–97.

Revolutionary California

Envy and resentment may have warped his view of the society he encountered briefly in California. He claimed, for example, that "each person's caste is determined by the quality of the blood," with whites of pure Spanish ancestry at the top of the heap: "From this upper class, they go down by regular shades, growing more and more dark and muddy, until you come to the pure Indian."[23] Dana evidently never met Governor Figueroa, a dark-skinned man who commanded respect from light-skinned creoles like Vallejo. Here as in other racially diverse societies of colonial origins, to be white was socially advantageous; but those who were not white had better prospects for advancement in Mexico at this time than in the United States.

Dana also overstated the case when he branded Californios an "idle, thriftless people" who could "make nothing for themselves."[24] To be sure, many observers shared this opinion, and they were not all Anglos. Missionaries had long portrayed settlers in California as wastrels who exploited Indians mercilessly and lived off their labor—an indictment summed up by Father Narciso Durán: "If there is anything to do, the Indian has to do it; if he fails to do it, nothing will be done."[25] Such critiques were echoed by other Hispanic observers, including José Bandini, a Spanish-born trader who settled in Peru, where his son Juan was born, before moving to San Diego in the 1820s. "Some are occupied in breeding cattle and planting wheat, maize, and beans," he wrote of Californios. "Others devote themselves to military service.... But most of them live in idleness; it is a rare person who is dedicated to increasing his fortune. They exert themselves only in dancing, horsemanship, and gambling, with which they fill their days."[26]

This would seem to confirm the stereotype of the idle Californio, but Bandini prefaced his critique by citing two main occupations there: soldiering and ranching or farming (ranchers often raised crops where possible). Most of those described as idle by Bandini

---

23. Ibid., 69; Hutchinson, *Frontier Settlement in Mexican California*, 154.
24. Dana, *Two Years before the Mast*, 67.
25. Durán in Hutchinson, *Frontier Settlement in Mexican California*, 133–34.
26. José Bandini, *A Description of California in 1828*, 9; David J. Langum, "Californios and the Image of Indolence."

and other witnesses were probably involved in one occupation or the other. The ready availability of cheap Indian labor left many time to dance, gamble, and ride about, but ranching or soldiering still involved work and could sometimes be strenuous. "My life from the age of sixteen years was purely that of a rancher, devoted almost entirely to work in the field," recalled José del Carmen Lugo, whose ranch was a day's journey from Los Angeles. "I went to the town only occasionally, and then it was on some urgent business." He and his family were in bed by eight and up at three for prayers, he noted: "After this, the women betook themselves to the kitchen and other domestic tasks. . . . The men went to their labor in the field—some to herd cattle, others to look after the horses. The milking of the cows was done by the men or the Indian servants."[27]

Not all Californios were as diligent as Lugo. Generous land grants and handsome profits from the hide-and-tallow trade brought some ranchers greater ease, allowing them to hire *mayordomos* to supervise their Indian laborers. It was those leisurely Californios that Dana and others involved in the trade often encountered. He faulted them for paying dearly for items that they could have produced themselves for less. "The country abounds in grapes," he wrote, "yet they buy, at a great price, bad wine made in Boston and brought round by us . . . and buy shoes (like as not made from their own hides, which have been carried twice round Cape Horn) at three and four dollars."[28] Shoemakers and vintners did exist in California, but goods imported from Boston, even when sold at a premium, found a ready market in a country with no factories and few stores other than those foreign traders set up aboard ship or in ports. This was partly the legacy of mercantilism, which drew raw materials from colonies and discouraged manufacturing there. But the dependence of Californios on imports, which Dana saw as backward, was in fact the wave of the future, dictated by relentless economic forces that broke down trade barriers there and elsewhere over time and would one day

---

27. Lugo, "Life of a Rancher," 215, 236; Beebe and Senkewicz, *Lands of Promise and Despair*, 434–42.
28. Dana, *Two Years before the Mast*, 67–68.

make American California the conduit for a flood of manufactured goods from Asia.

The irony for Dana was that the grim efficiency of "slave-drivers" like Captain Thompson and his counterparts back East who oversaw factories and sweatshops allowed Americans to dominate this distant market. Dana was proud that ten men on his vessel seemingly accomplished as much as thirty men on a rival Italian merchant ship. Yet he also noticed that those Italians had a better time of it than he did. "They often joined in a song," he recalled, and their Easter liberty lasted three full days, for which Dana and his mates greatly envied them. "So much for being Protestants," he lamented. "American shipmasters get nearly three weeks' more labor out of their crews, in the course of a year, than the masters of vessels from Catholic countries."[29]

As Dana recognized, California was not the most congenial setting for the Protestant work ethic. He himself, when sent ashore to cure hides in San Diego for a few months, followed a routine that was more like that of Californios by working hard for the first part of the day before dining and relaxing: "Immediately after dinner we usually took a short siesta, to make up for our early rising, and spent the rest of the afternoon according to our own fancies." Many of his free hours were spent at the "Kanaka Hotel," an abandoned "oven" (bakery) on the beach occupied by Hawaiians, who impressed him with their dignity and self-possession. Unlike other sailors, who signed their souls away for the duration of the voyage, he observed, "they for the most part sign no articles, leave whenever they choose, and let themselves out to cure hides at San Diego." They were energetic at work but prized their liberty and shared their earnings freely with their mates. "So long as they had money, they would not work for fifty dollars a month," Dana remarked, "and when their money was gone, they would work for ten."[30]

Dana's knowledge of California did not extend far beyond the beach, but he caught glimpses of Hispanic society and tried to

---
29. Ibid., 121–22, 144.
30. Ibid., 128, 130, 138.

make sense of it. In early 1836 Juan Bandini traveled aboard the *Pilgrim* from San Francisco to Monterey as a guest of the company's agent in California, Alfred Robinson. Knowing little of Bandini's history, Dana portrayed him as the feckless son of a Spanish aristocrat (José Bandini) who had "settled at San Diego, where he built a large house with a courtyard in front, kept a retinue of Indians, and set up for the grandee of that part of the country." Sent to Mexico City for an education, Juan returned to find his family's estate diminished by misfortune and overexpenditure, leaving him "accomplished, poor, and proud, and without any office or occupation, to lead the life of most young men of the better families—dissipated and extravagant when the means are at hand; ambitious at heart and impotent in act."[31]

This fable trivialized the eventful career of Juan Bandini, who was no mere student in Mexico City but a deputy in Congress there before he returned to California with the colonizing expedition of 1834. The collapse of that venture was a setback for him, but he remained a force to be reckoned with, serving later as administrator of secularized Mission San Gabriel. Dana portrayed him as the dupe of a scheming Yankee trader, who was "eating out the vitals of the Bandinis, fattening upon their extravagance," perhaps referring to Abel Stearns, a merchant from Massachusetts who married Juan Bandini's daughter Arcadia. Bandini welcomed the opportunities that arose when Mexico lowered trade barriers and looked forward rather than backward, but Dana pictured him as a sorry creature of the past, a decadent hidalgo outmatched by purposeful Anglos. "In the hands of an enterprising people, what a country this might be," concluded Dana, echoing a theme sounded by Vancouver forty years earlier. Yet Dana wondered how long Americans, who were "fast filling up the principal towns, and getting the trade into their hands," would remain industrious in a land inimical to their work ethic. The children of those who wed Californios "are brought up Mexicans in most respects," he noted, "and if the 'California fever' (laziness) spares the first generation, it is likely to attack the second."[32]

---

31. Ibid., 216–17.
32. Ibid., 157, 217; Bancroft, *History of California*, 2:709–10.

Revolutionary California

The truth Dana hinted at but never quite acknowledged in his ruminations on California was that intervals of laziness or leisure were life's saving grace. God himself rested after the labor of creation, it was written, and contemplated his work at leisure. Toil was God's curse on Adam and his descendants, but he allowed them to rest and reflect on the Sabbath, a time for them to commune with their creator and renew their own creative powers. In precious moments of leisure, Dana's gained insights into his experience and began transforming his journey into a journal or coherent narrative. His sweet liberties on shore allowed him to become briefly a "lazy, luxurious dreamer" like his father, whose literary ambitions he shared and later fulfilled. His most revealing encounter with Californios came when he was at liberty, attending a fandango in Santa Bárbara to celebrate the wedding of Alfred Robinson, who joined the leading family there through his marriage to Ana María de la Guerra, sister of Angustias and Teresa. (Teresa's husband, William Hartnell, had disappointed her father by faltering as a merchant, but Robinson helped fill that void.) Unlike society weddings in Boston, Dana noted, this ceremony involved the entire community: "We found nearly all the people of the town—men, women, and children—collected and crowded together ... for on these occasions no invitations are given, but everyone is expected to come, though there is always a private entertainment within the house for particular friends."[33]

In this hospitable setting, Dana and his mates found themselves "great objects of attention.... Our sailor dresses—and we took great pains to have them neat and shipshape—were much admired, and we were invited, from every quarter, to give them an American dance." They could not compete with Juan Bandini, who gained stature in Dana's eyes when "he gave us the most graceful dancing I had ever seen ... dressed in white pantaloons, neatly made, a short jacket of dark silk gaily figured, and thin morocco slippers upon his very small feet." He was followed on the dance floor by the awkward bridegroom, Robinson, wearing a "tight black swallow-tailed coat just imported from Boston, a high stiff cravat, looking as

---

33. Dana, *Two Years before the Mast*, 220.

if he had been pinned and skewered, with only his feet and hands left free." After that sad spectacle, Dana and his mates refrained from dancing, for "we thought they had had enough of Yankee grace."[34] It would have been gracious of them to honor their hosts with a lively jig. But Dana later paid them a rare compliment by describing their celebration fondly and without condescension, testifying to the allure of a society that was more enterprising than its critics acknowledged and managed to pursue profit and distinction without forfeiting leisure and conviviality.

A Pastoral Interlude

Anglos like Robinson who settled in California often wrote appreciatively of the country and its customs while suggesting as Dana did that this quaint existence was destined to give way before a more advanced and industrious culture. They portrayed social life with its fandangos, flirtations, and other diversions as a pastoral idyll—a carefree interlude of ease and indulgence before California reached maturity. Like adults looking back on their lost youth, they expressed nostalgic affection for those simpler, happier times while picturing Californios as naïve rustics, unequal to the challenges of the modern world. Influenced by the accounts of Anglo settlers that he and his staff compiled, historian Hubert Howe Bancroft later summed up that patronizing view in a volume entitled *California Pastoral*: "And indeed, life here was almost like a returning of the world to its infancy; a returning of mankind to artless, thoughtless boyhood, when science held little sway, and men lived simple lives, and excess of piety and excess of culture had not sobered the mind and made serious the art of living."[35]

Some Anglo observers were so intent on portraying life in early California as an age of innocence that they reduced its inhabitants to caricatures of wholesomeness. One such nostalgic chronicler was American trader William Heath Davis. Known as "Kanaka Davis"

---

34. Ibid., 221–23.
35. Bancroft, *California Pastoral*, 266.

because his maternal grandmother was Hawaiian, he settled in 1838 in Yerba Buena—the town later known as San Francisco—and later married María Estudillo, the daughter of a wealthy rancher and customs officer. "The native Californians were about the happiest and most contented people I ever saw," he recalled in an account written several decades later, "as also were the early foreigners who settled among them and intermarried with them, adopted their habits and customs, and became, as it were, a part of themselves." Californios always "kept their business engagements," Davis avowed, and "paid their bills promptly at the proper time in hides and tallow, which were the currency of the country, and sometimes, though seldom, in money."[36] In fact, some Californios fell deeply into debt and failed to meet their obligations.

In the same nostalgic vein, Davis stated that it was hard to find "an intoxicated Californian" or an unfaithful one. "The California women, married or unmarried, of all classes, were the most virtuous I have ever seen," he asserted.[37] Other evidence, however, suggests that intoxication and infidelity were more common than he recollected. Juan Alvarado, for instance, was given to debilitating drinking bouts and embarrassing absences. He failed to appear for his inauguration as governor and missed his own wedding, where his half-brother stood in for him. Soon after his wife gave birth, he had an illegitimate child by a mistress. Dana was not the only witness who implied that wives here could sometimes be as wayward as their mates. "If their husbands do not dress them well enough," he claimed, "they will soon receive presents from others."[38]

Anglo perceptions of Californios were contradictory in other respects as well. Admiring observers like Davis viewed the men as chivalrous not only for their skill on horseback—seemingly at one with their mounts like centaurs—but also for their courtesy and charity. Critics, however, denounced them for abusing Indians

---
36. Davis, *Seventy-five Years in California*, 49–50, 61; Churchill, *Adventurers and Prophets*, 37–69.
37. Davis, *Seventy-five Years in California*, 45.
38. Dana, *Two Years before the Mast*, 69; Miller, *Juan Alvarado*, 51, 69–71, 94–95; David J. Langum, "Californio Women and the Image of Virtue."

and subjecting some to what amounted to slavery (a practice officially prohibited in Mexico), spurring their horses mercilessly and riding them to exhaustion, and reveling in bullfights and other blood sports. Such was the view of Lieutenant Charles Wilkes of the U.S. Navy, who visited California in 1841 as commander of an expedition intended like earlier ventures by Vancouver and other foreign explorers to gather scientific information and project the power of an expansive nation far beyond its borders. In a scathing passage diametrically opposed to Davis's assessment, Wilkes declared: "The Californians, as a people, must be termed cruel in their treatment to their wives, as well as to the Indians; and in a still greater degree to their slaves and cattle. They are exceedingly ignorant of every thing but extortion, riding horses, and catching bullocks."[39] Like Dana's Captain Thompson, Wilkes seemed intent on making "a hell of heaven" or puncturing any romantic notion that this country was paradise on the Pacific.

Some Anglo witnesses encompassed such contradictory responses by offering a mixed assessment of California and its inhabitants. Faxon Dean Atherton, a New Englander who served for two years as a clerk in the California hide trade, was dismayed by Monterey when he arrived there by ship from Hawaii in April 1836. "Found it to be far different from what I expected," he wrote in his journal. The ground was littered with the bones of slaughtered cattle, he observed, "and the air almost filled with carrion crows and vultures which are said to be a great benefit to the country by eating up the carcasses of the cattle which are killed for their hides and tallow and thereby preventing a pestilence which would otherwise arise from such an immense amount of putrid flesh."[40] Other visitors were similarly dismayed by the grisly after-effects of the *matanzas* (slaughters), during which ranchers claimed only as much meat as they could use from the carcass and left the rest to scavengers. Yet in promoting the hide trade, Atherton and other foreigners contributed to such carnage and the relentless

---

39. Charles Wilkes, *Narrative of the United States Exploring Expedition*, 5:176.
40. Faxon Dean Atherton, *The California Diary of Faxon Dean Atherton*, 3–4.

Yerba Buena (San Francisco), 1837,
based on a watercolor by Captain Jean Jacques Vioget,
who completed the first survey and map of Yerba Buena in 1839.
*Courtesy Library of Congress, Prints and Photographs Division
(LC-USZ62-34704).*

proliferation of cattle that was altering and in some places despoiling this environment.

The picture was not all bleak. When Atherton sailed along the coast from Yerba Buena to Monterey, he was charmed by vistas that combined the wild beauty of redwood forests and surf-swept coves with the domestic tranquillity of pastures and fields. "It appears to me that I have never seen anything so pleasant as it now is in sailing along in a beautiful sunshiney day with a fair wind in a fine fast sailing vessel within a few hundred yards of the land," he exulted. "Here a hill covered with wood, there a deep gulch with a small stream of water at the bottom gamboling among the stones; then a deep valley covered with cattle, horses, sheep, next a large field with corn, wheat, potatoes, beans, etc., all growing luxuriantly, and almost without the care of the husbandman."[41]

In truth, cultivating this land required considerable effort, but Anglos gave most of the credit to foreign settlers or Indians conditioned to such labor by their Franciscan overseers. Some observers complimented Mexican women for tending gardens and selling

---

41. Ibid., 15.

their produce, but the men were portrayed as energetic only when riding, dancing, gambling, or scheming. Atherton characterized the Californios he encountered in Los Angeles as "a rascally set of vicious cut throat villains among whom, however, are some very good men though of small abilities. The best houses and stores are without exception the property of foreigners, principally American hunters." Similarly, he dismissed the *pobladores* of San José at first glance as "a most villainous set of scoundrels, their chief pride being to see who can cheat a foreigner the most." After getting to know Californios better, he likened them more charitably to French settlers in Louisiana, "simple in their manners, honest and hospitable."[42] Few Anglos offered a more generous assessment, and none felt that Hispanic California could long withstand foreign competition. Whether seen as a welcome redemption for a neglected land or the sad end of a bucolic golden age, its conquest by a stronger power was viewed as inevitable.

Alfred Robinson paid due tribute in his account to the hospitality and goodwill of the society he joined by taking vows to his Mexican wife, her church, and her country. But he remained a foreigner at heart, whose criticisms were more subversive of Mexican rule, or misrule, than Dana's complaints. Having dealt cordially with Franciscans, Robinson considered them the only competent authorities in California and saw secularization as a calamity. He recalled the retirement of Father Peyri of Mission San Luis Rey, "who, disgusted with the political changes in the country, had resigned his laborious duties." Tears of regret coursed down Peyri's cheek as he recalled "the once happy state of California," Robinson wrote. "His great penetration of mind led him to foresee the result of the new theory of liberty and equality among a people where anarchy and confusion so generally prevailed, and who, at the time, were totally unprepared for and incapable of self-government." Robinson was not blind to the problems of the missions, remarking elsewhere that neophytes at San Luis Rey were "miserable indeed, and it is not to be wondered at that many attempt to escape from

---

42. Ibid., xix, 24, 36.

the severity of the religious discipline." Yet such constraint seemed to him preferable to the illusory freedom promised mission Indians by Mexico. "Rapine, murder, and drunkenness were the result," he concluded, "and in the midst reveled the Mexican chieftain."[43]

It was not just Indians in California who were "incapable of self-government," Robinson emphasized. Following the death of Governor Figueroa in 1835, he noted, Californios rebelled against his successors Mariano Chico and Nicolás Gutiérrez—who were loyal to Santa Anna's centralist regime—and proclaimed independence, with Juan Alvarado emerging as governor and Mariano Vallejo as commandant general. Higher authorities considered sending troops to quell the uprising, Robinson remarked sarcastically, but "the Californians were permitted to govern themselves, this being, in the opinion of the Mexicans, the best method of chastisement." In fact, the defeat of Santa Anna by Texas rebels in 1836 left Mexico hard-pressed to subdue defiant Californios. Alvarado would eventually reconcile with higher authorities and pledge allegiance to the central government. But like other foreigners who witnessed this upheaval, Robinson concluded that California was slipping from Mexico's grasp and that, lacking the capacity for self-rule, its inhabitants would look for support and leadership to a major power such as Great Britain or the United States. "Whatever may be its fate," he remarked of California, "it can never be in worse hands than the present."[44]

The Graham Affair

Among the foreigners who helped Alvarado take power was a Kentuckian named Isaac Graham, who arrived in California overland around 1833. "He had grown up in the forest and had received no formal education," wrote Antonio María Osio, who witnessed Graham's evolution from a staunch supporter of Alvarado to a subversive charged with attempting to overthrow him. "He did

---

43. Robinson, *Life in California*, 45, 155–56; Churchill, *Adventurers and Prophets*, 17–35.
44. Robinson, *Life in California*, 215, 240.

Juan Bautista Alvarado. Courtesy The Bancroft Library, University of California, Berkeley (*California Faces: Selections from The Bancroft Library Portrait Collection*).

not even know one letter of the alphabet. However, he had learned how to use a rifle."[45] Indeed, Graham personified the Kentucky rifleman, a figure legendary in California by this time. Dana, who shipped out shortly before Alvarado recruited Graham and became governor, passed along a rumor that reached him while he was hauling hides at San Pedro. Reportedly, a Yankee in nearby Los Angeles was sitting quietly at home with his Mexican wife and children "when a Mexican with whom he had had a difficulty entered the house and stabbed him to the heart before them all." Authorities failed to punish the culprit, so a posse including some "forty Kentucky hunters, with their rifles" took the law into their own hands and executed the offending Mexican. Those Kentuckians went on to avenge the murder of another victim, it was said, a Mexican slain in the road by "his own wife and the man with whom she ran off."[46]

In fact, the vigilance committee that punished those guilty lovers included Hispanic as well as Anglo residents of Los Angeles. But Dana's tale testified to the fabled ferocity of "Kentuckians," a term

---

45. Osio, *History of Alta California*, 199.
46. Dana, *Two Years before the Mast*, 154–55; Bancroft, *History of California*, 3:417–19, 637–38 n. 5.

applied generically to mountain men from throughout the Appalachian region who arrived overland with rifles in hand. (Graham was described variously as a Kentuckian and a Tennessean and had ties to both states.) It was not just Anglos who subscribed to the legend of those indomitable riflemen. José María Híjar claimed that during his dispute with Governor Figueroa an unnamed conspirator offered him the services of "as many as seven hundred of these men, armed with rifles and provided with ammunition," so that he could oust Figueroa. Híjar took this outlandish offer seriously and claimed credit for rejecting it: "I, who had come seeking peace and avoiding war, did not want to use any violent measures."[47] The rifles carried by such "Kentuckians" made them formidable even in small numbers. Most firearms in California were pistols or cumbersome flintlock muskets, which were not very reliable. Soldiers there preferred to fight on horseback with lances as their colonial predecessors had. Isaac Graham's company consisted of no more than thirty riflemen, recruited at a distillery and grogshop he operated near Monterey. Some were sailors who had jumped ship and may not have been very good shots, but their mere presence gave Alvarado a psychological edge over his foes.

Other foreigners in Monterey, including American trader William Hinckley, joined Graham and company in supporting Alvarado and opposing the central government. They did so not because they were scandalized by the behavior of the Mexican loyalists who preceded Alvarado as governor—Chico arrived in Monterey with a "niece" who turned out be his mistress and Gutiérrez reportedly kept a harem of Indian women—but because the policies of those officials ran counter to their interests. Chico tried to bring foreigners under stricter control and forbade coastal traders to sell goods aboard their vessels. Gutiérrez threatened action against customs administrator Angel Ramírez, notoriously obliging to merchants who paid him favors. "When he assumed his post," Osio wrote of Ramírez, "duties paid to the public treasury became negotiable, provided that he received sufficient advances to

---

47. Híjar in Hutchinson, *Frontier Settlement in Mexican California*, 283.

defray the very high costs of his continual dances, gambling tables, and picnics in the countryside."[48] Some foreigners in Monterey who backed the ouster of Chico and Gutiérrez went so far as to design a lone-star flag like that flown by Anglo-Americans who rebelled against Santa Anna in Texas, to be raised aloft when Alvarado proclaimed California independent.

Like most political upheavals in California, this one was virtually bloodless. Chico sailed away with his mistress in mid-1836 after being invited to leave by Alvarado, acting as head of the assembly in Monterey. The exiled governor promised to return with troops but never made good on that threat, leaving his office to Gutiérrez, who served only a few months before Alvarado raised forces against him. While plotting with Isaac Graham in Monterey, Alvarado was nearly seized by soldiers loyal to Gutiérrez but managed to escape on horseback. "Bullets whistled all around," he recalled, "but not a single one reached me."[49] That was as close as he or his antagonists came to martyrdom. In early November 1836 the rebels besieged Gutiérrez and his men in the presidio and fired a single cannonball, which hit the roof and showered the governor with debris. Fearing further bombardment, Gutiérrez agreed to a truce and left Monterey to the rebels. "It is wonderful, uncle, with what order our expedition has been conducted," Alvarado wrote his kinsman and confederate Mariano Vallejo. "Everybody shouts *vivas*, for California is free!"[50]

Foreigners often disparaged Californios for settling such heated disputes with little or no bloodshed. Alfred Robinson referred to Alvarado and his men sarcastically as "daring rebels."[51] And Faxon Dean Atherton, who witnessed the uprising in Monterey, felt that Gutiérrez had yielded too readily. "Thus after a siege of one day was this famous place, the capital of Upper California, taken by 15 riflemen and about 100 rancheros of which very few had any

---

48. Osio, *History of Alta California*, 152; Bancroft, *History of California*, 3:420–28, 445–48, 452.
49. Alvarado in Miller, *Juan Alvarado*, 47.
50. Alvarado in Bancroft, *History of California*, 3:464.
51. Robinson, *Life in California*, 215.

guns but pikes," he wrote. "It surprised most every one that there was no greater defence made by a place capable of so great a one. However, they could not place much dependence on their soldiers who were all frightened at the idea of a rifleman."[52] He might have added that in a territory with such a small non-Indian population, a prolonged struggle claiming many lives would have been calamitous. Furthermore, men on opposing sides in these quarrels were often linked by family ties. Alvarado's bloodless victory and readiness to pardon his foes earned him credit among Californios, as did his willingness to reward allies and pacify potential enemies by granting them land and other favors.

Alvarado stopped short of making a complete break with Mexico, and no lone-star flag flew over Monterey. His quarrel was with the overbearing centralists, he insisted. He remained faithful to Mexico's original constitution as opposed to its new one, enacted by centralists in 1836, and declared California independent "until the federal system of 1824 shall be reestablished." Alvarado also pledged that Catholicism would remain the state religion but that no resident would be molested "for his private religious opinions," a promise reassuring to foreigners of other faiths who backed him.[53]

Graham and his riflemen continued to support Alvarado as he campaigned against political opponents in southern California. Among his antagonists there was Osio, a native of Baja California who had settled in Los Angeles and served on its *ayuntamiento* (town council). He blamed Alvarado's declaration of independence on the "connivance of foreigners," particularly Americans who hoped to annex California, and portrayed the governor's pledge of religious tolerance as an invitation to Protestants to settle in California and wed Catholic women without parental consent. Mothers alarmed by his warnings assured Osio that their husbands and sons "would take up arms for the sake of their family honor."[54] Others opposed Alvarado for their nation's honor, among them veterans of

---

52. Atherton, *California Diary*, 33.
53. Proclamation of Alvarado and the assembly (*diputación*) in Bancroft, *History of California*, 3:470–71 n. 28; Miller, *Juan Alvarado*, 50.
54. Osio, *History of Alta California*, 158–60.

the Híjar-Padrés expedition such as Antonio Coronel and Agustín Janssens, who carried a certificate confirming his allegiance "to the supreme government of the republic, as was proper for a good Mexican citizen." He was shocked to hear drunken revelers celebrating California's newfound freedom with shouts of "Death to Mexico! Kill the Mexicans!"[55] Most of those who opposed Alvarado and independence did so out of loyalty to their hometown, however, rather than devotion to Mexico or Catholicism. Under Alvarado, Monterey remained California's capital (a distinction coveted by Los Angeles, whose residents felt that a governor situated there would better serve their interests) and its port of entry (an honor with financial rewards sought by San Diego).

Southerners hostile to Alvarado received aid from an unexpected quarter when a French-Canadian adventurer named Jean Baptiste Chalifoux (or Charlevoix) joined their cause with some forty Shawnee Indians. Like Graham, he was a suspect figure who hoped to gain favor here by backing the winning side. He and his Shawnees made frequent forays from New Mexico to California as horse traders, Janssens reported, "though usually they stole more horses than they bought." Schooled by decades of contact and conflict with whites, Shawnees were good shots. Two of them gave Janssens and Coronel a scare one night as they sought Chalifoux's help. "They had their firearms aimed at us and seemed disposed to shoot," Janssens recalled. "I spoke to them in French, and when I mentioned Chalifoux, they lowered their guns and took us to camp."[56]

Those Shawnees might have proved a match for Graham and his riflemen, but the two forces never came to blows. The southerners had no leader to rival the politically cunning and well-connected Alvarado, who descended from Monterey with his forces and won over Santa Bárbara—a swing district in the struggle between north and south—while his foes in Los Angeles and San Diego were debating how to respond. Outmaneuvered, they conceded to Alvarado without a fight in early 1837. Fresh challenges to his

---

55. Janssens, *Life and Adventures*, 57–59.
56. Ibid., 74–75.

authority soon arose from ambitious southerners such as Juan Bandini and José Antonio Carrillo, California's delegate to Congress, who had his brother Carlos, a prominent figure in Santa Bárbara, appointed governor. Alvarado, who was related to the Carrillos, responded with a show of force that induced them to yield. Before reaching that settlement, he reconciled with the central government, which revoked Carlos Carrillo's appointment and confirmed Alvarado as governor when he abandoned the nation's old constitution in favor of the new. "*Viva la Constitución del año de '36!*" he proclaimed. "*Viva la Unión!*"[57]

Alvarado was never entirely secure in his position, for he faced lingering resistance from domestic rivals and growing opposition from foreigners, including some of the same men who had helped him achieve power. He continued to trust in naturalized citizens of foreign birth such as William Hartnell, who served under him as inspector of the secularized missions, some of which had been woefully neglected or plundered by their administrators in recent years, depriving Indians there of the benefits they had been promised. "They ask to be rid of the administrator," Hartnell wrote after meeting with Indians at Mission San Miguel, where a Franciscan continued to serve as their priest; "they want to be alone with the padre."[58] Their complaints were echoed by Julio César, an Indian born at Mission San Luis Rey in 1824, who accused the administrators of seizing mission property and exploiting Indians. "They didn't pay us anything," he declared. "They only gave us food, a loincloth, and a blanket which they replaced each year. They did, however, give us plenty of whippings for any wrongdoing, however slight."[59] Hartnell resigned in frustration in 1840 after clashing with powerful figures such as Pío Pico, an administrator at Mission San Luis Rey, and Mariano Vallejo, who evicted Hartnell when he tried to inspect Mission San Rafael.

---

57. Alvarado in Miller, *Juan Alvarado*, 55.
58. Hartnell in Dakin, *Lives of William Hartnell*, 232.
59. César in Beebe and Senkewicz, *Lands of Promise and Despair*, 470–71; Weber, *King of the Missions*, 88–93; Carlos Manuel Salomon, *Pío Pico: The Last Governor of Mexican California*, 45–67.

Alvarado and his aides met with similar resistance from merchants who evaded customs duties on which his administration depended. Osio, who reconciled with Alvarado and served as his customs administrator, noted that while merchants with large financial interests such as Alfred Robinson "acted in good faith," many traders of limited means often tried to deceive him. "Such people smuggled for the enjoyment of it," Osio surmised, "for the insignificant items they were hiding were hardly worth the risk."[60] More significant were the cargos that merchants unloaded furtively on the Channel Islands or elsewhere along the coast before paying duties on the remainder at Monterey. Among the offenders was William Heath Davis, who told of arriving in San Francisco Bay aboard the ship *Don Quixote* with a precious cargo of silk and other goods without first stopping in Monterey as required. An official in Yerba Buena tried to prevent Davis and his mates from bringing the goods ashore by placing a guard on the vessel, but that evening they took the guard prisoner and assured him that he had nothing to fear: "He was told that he could have his supper and could take his smoke, and then go into the stateroom, where he would find a nice bed, a bottle of Madeira, a bottle of *aguardiente*, cigars, and everything to make him comfortable . . . and in the morning he would be let out and given $20 in gold." While he slept, they unloaded "all the more valuable goods" for sale at a store owned by American Nathan Spear, who was Davis's uncle, before freeing their compliant prisoner and embarking for Monterey. There they paid duties "to the satisfaction of the customhouse, having saved a handsome sum by our night's operations."[61]

Davis claimed that that he and others who evaded customs in this way were not considered lawbreakers and were "benefiting the people and doing a service to the country" by selling imported goods at lower prices than would have prevailed had they paid full duties.[62] The financial impact on Alvarado's administration, however, was debilitating. He quarreled with his uncle Vallejo over

---

60. Osio, *History of Alta California*, 198.
61. Davis, *Seventy-five Years in California*, 78–79.
62. Ibid., 80.

the distribution of scarce funds to presidial companies and other matters. "The forts were neglected," Alfred Robinson asserted, "and Alvarado cared little for the safety of any other place but the one where he was located."[63] Charges that Alvarado and his aides in Monterey were serving local interests and neglecting California at large may have been warranted, but no governor could have done much more there without boosting revenue through customs enforcement, for which he lacked resources. The pressures of office taxed his health—he was sometimes too ill, or intoxicated, to perform his duties—and made him increasingly suspicious and defensive. When reports surfaced in April 1840 that Isaac Graham was plotting to overthrow him, Alvarado cracked down on all foreigners he considered disloyal or disreputable.

According to Alfred Robinson, this Graham Affair, which had international repercussions, stemmed from the governor's desire to distance himself from Graham and others who felt that they had not been properly rewarded for services rendered. Once "firmly established in power, the Gobernador felt more sensibly the dignity of his situation," Robinson observed, "and wished to put an end to the freedom with which his rude foreign friends were wont to treat him ... He was ever 'not at home' to their calls."[64] Alvarado was "known to fly into a rage" when drunk, as Osio remarked, which may have led to some heated exchanges when those foreigners overindulged at Graham's grogshop and descended on the governor, known respectfully to acquaintances as Don Juan Bautista, to press their case.[65] "I was insulted at every turn by the drunken followers of Graham," Alvarado complained to Robinson; "and when walking in the garden they would come to its wall and call upon me in terms of the greatest familiarity, 'Ho, Bautista, come here; I want to speak to you.' 'Bautista' here, 'Bautista' there, and 'Bautista' everywhere."[66]

Among those with a claim against Alvarado was George Nidever, a native of Tennessee who had arrived in California in 1833

---

63. Robinson, *Life in California*, 220.
64. Ibid., 220–21.
65. Osio, *History of Alta California*, 189.
66. Alvarado in Robinson, *Life in California*, 225.

with Joseph Walker's party. Like George Yount, his friend and fellow settler, Nidever hunted sea otters for a while on the Channel Islands under a license obtained by Captain William Dana, whose marriage to María Carrillo (daughter of Carlos Carrillo, Alvarado's rival for the governorship) lent him prominence in Santa Bárbara. While hunting along the shores of Santa Rosa Island in early 1836, Nidever recalled, he and a band of a dozen men working for Dana (including three Kanakas) clashed with a party of "N.W. Indians" employed by a rival captain, killing several of them. Those Indians, most likely recruited around Vancouver Island, had for some time "been the terror of the Coast," Nidever claimed. He and his fellow hunters boasted of their success in battle and were enlisted by Alvarado when he entered Santa Bárbara with his forces. "Alvarado and Graham came to see us," Niedever declared. "Alvarado offered us $2 per day and the privilege of taking up vacant lands if we would join him. I accepted the offer."[67]

Two dollars a day was good pay then, but the land that Nidever hoped for was not forthcoming. "I went to see Alvarado but was put off with some excuses," he recalled, "and so a second, third, and fourth time." Alvarado finally told him that he could not obtain a land grant under Mexican law unless he "married a Californian" or became a Catholic and a Mexican citizen. Foreigners who backed Alvarado hoped that he would free them from such legal restraints, but after renewing ties with the central government he showed little sympathy for those who tried to skirt the law. Isaac Graham received no clemency from Alvarado when he was convicted of stealing cattle from a neighbor in January 1838 and sentenced to eight months' hard labor. Afterward, Graham considered "raising a company to go back across the plains to the States," Nidever related, but the few recruits Graham mustered were not equal to the task.[68] So he continued to operate his distillery near Monterey, where he entertained malcontents and plotted against the governor—or so Alvarado believed. Day by day, the governor's

---

67. Nidever, *Life and Adventures*, 44–47.
68. Ibid., 48–49, 55.

"disgust increased for '*los malditos extranjeros* [damned foreigners],'" wrote Alfred Robinson, "and an opportunity to rid himself of their importunities and threats soon offered."⁶⁹

Alvarado took action against those foreigners after learning that an acquaintance of Graham's had spoken vaguely of a plot against the government while confessing to a priest. Alvarado's suspicions were seemingly confirmed when Englishman William Garner informed on Graham, whose offense may have amounted to little more than making idle threats against the governor. In any case, Alvarado sent troops led by José Castro—who served as his top military aide while Commandant General Vallejo remained ensconced at Sonoma—to arrest Graham and those with him. Graham accused Castro's men of trying to kill him and claimed that they failed to do so only because their pistols misfired. They had him in their power and could have done away with him if they wished but instead hauled him and his fellow suspects to Monterey as instructed. Meanwhile, authorities elsewhere were rounding up other foreigners "who were illegally introduced into the country," in Alvarado's words, "and who had no other object here but the increase of public disorder." He described those undesirables as "deserters from merchant vessels and vessels of war, who were secretly hidden in the ranchos and woods."⁷⁰ Some of them had useful skills and worked as blacksmiths or as sawyers in forests that were now being exploited commercially. As a group, however, they were viewed as dangerous, and not just by Alvarado. Captain Edward Belcher of the Royal Navy, who visited California in the late 1830s, told of a "band of deserters from American and English whalers" who threatened to "set all law at defiance."⁷¹

Well-established Anglos such as Alfred Robinson and Thomas Larkin of Monterey, who remained an American citizen, were not arrested. Others with commercial interests such as Nathan Spear of Yerba Buena were confined briefly and then released. According to William Heath Davis, Spear was let go by order

---

69. Robinson, *Life in California*, 221.
70. Alvarado in ibid., 223; Bancroft, *History of California*, 4:1–15.
71. Belcher in Bancroft, *History of California*, 4:144.

of "the governor, who had been a clerk for Spear in former years at Monterey and had a high esteem for him." Alvarado may have suspected Spear of smuggling, but this crackdown was not aimed at foreigners with close financial ties to Californios. Davis himself went free after being detained hospitably in Yerba Buena by a local official, who honored him with a fandango. "The affair was so very enjoyable that I hardly realized that I was a prisoner of the state," he recalled. Much like the Mexican guard he confined to a well-supplied stateroom while smuggling goods to Spear's store, Davis was held comfortably for the night and released the next day. He bore no grudge against his captors and admitted that he and others from the United States, while not conspiring against the government, hoped one day to call California their own and "would never permit any other nation to be the possessors of this territory."[72]

The subtleties of Anglo-Hispanic relations were lost on author Thomas Jefferson Farnham, who reached Monterey from Oregon by way of Honolulu as the Graham Affair unfolded and protested the captives' plight. A lawyer from New England, Farnham had traveled overland to the Columbia River in 1839 with a party that quarreled and split up. That ended any hope he had of settling in the Northwest and helping to wrest control of contested Oregon from the British. So he turned to California, arriving there with a warped view of Mexicans as heirs to the grim legacy of the Spanish Inquisition and ruthless Spanish-American conquests. To sustain that fable of Hispanic iniquity, he idolized Graham, portraying him as "sturdy backwoodsman, of a stamp which exists only on the frontiers of the American States—men with the blood of the ancient Normans and Saxons in their veins—with hearts as large as their bodies can hold, beating nothing but kindness till injustice shows its fangs, and then, lion-like, striking for vengeance." Alvarado owed his position to the intrepid Graham and his riflemen, Farnham claimed, but refused to honor his debt to them: "Like Spaniards of all ages and countries, after having

---

72. Davis, *Seventy-five Years in California*, 37.

been well served by his friends, he rewarded them with heartless ingratitude."⁷³

Farnham's feverish account of the Graham Affair amounted to a literary inquisition—a highly prejudicial proceeding in which Alvarado and his "right hand villain, Captain José Castro," were presumed guilty as "Spaniards" of persecuting innocent Anglos. Before being arrested, Graham confronted the governor, Farnham asserted, and demanded in vain that he live up to his promises: "A Spaniard tell the truth! A Spaniard ever grateful for services rendered him! He should have knocked at the tombs of Columbus and Cortés, and every other man who ever served that contemptible race."⁷⁴

Farnham's flagrant bias undermined his case, which was not entirely without foundation. By his own admission, Alvarado was unable to establish a "competent tribunal" in Monterey for the one hundred or so foreigners arrested and imprisoned there for up to two weeks in squalid conditions.⁷⁵ Farnham's scathing description of their jail, whose unpaved floor was so muddy that prisoners sank into it up to their ankles, was later confirmed by Mexican inspectors, who called the place a "sink-hole of filth."⁷⁶ Many Americans accustomed to trial by jury found fault with the administration of justice in California, where defendants were sometimes held at length without bail until an alcalde or justice of the peace with no legal training passed judgment. The Mexican government was seeking to create a national court system that would deal uniformly with serious criminal charges like those leveled against Graham and others. But no such court had been established in California when Alvarado hauled in those foreigners.

After cursory hearings in Monterey to determine whether there was reason to continue holding the suspects, roughly half were released. Graham and the rest were shipped south in shackles to

---

73. Thomas J. Farnham, *The Early Days of California: Embracing What I Saw and Heard There, with Scenes in the Pacific*, 61, 65–66; Churchill, *Adventurers and Prophets*, 219–42.
74. Farnham, *Early Days of California*, 64, 66.
75. Alvarado in Robinson, *Life in California*, 223.
76. Quoted in David J. Langum, *Law and Community on the Mexican California Frontier: Anglo-American Expatriates and the Clash of Legal Traditions, 1821–1846*, 83–84.

San Blas and jailed in nearby Tepic, where they were aided by the British vice consul and also received some help from Farnham, who stopped by on his way back to New England and touted his role in obtaining justice for them. Around thirty of them were deported from Mexico as illegal aliens. The rest were allowed to return to California, although Graham and three others were not freed until they had been tried and acquitted. Warships from Britain, France, and the United States visited Monterey afterward to warn Alvarado not to harass their citizens, and Castro was court-martialed on charges that he mistreated the prisoners. He too was acquitted, but the incident brought little credit to him or to Alvarado, who was commended for keeping a sharp eye on foreigners but faulted for expelling suspects without proof of wrongdoing.

In sum, the Graham Affair was not the great outrage that Farnham claimed it was. Those detained without due cause were offered a few hundred dollars in compensation, no small sum in those days. Graham sued for damages and was ultimately awarded more than $38,000. When he and others returned to Monterey in July 1841, Alfred Robinson observed, they "came on shore dressed neatly, armed with rifles and swords, and looking in infinitely better condition than when they departed."[77] They owed their redemption in part to foreign pressure but also to the fact that Mexico inherited from Spain a legal system affording all the country's inhabitants, including Indians and foreigners, certain rights. In Mexico as in the United States, laws were not always scrupulously enforced on the frontier, but Farnham and others ignored the legal constraints under which officials like Alvarado operated by portraying them as petty tyrants who made up the rules as they went along.

That was a convenient rationale for conquest, as underscored by a statement that Farnham attributed to Graham as he left Monterey in chains: "I reckon these villains will see me die like a man. And if I do die, I wish you to go to Tennessee and Kentucky, and tell the boys of our sufferings. Two hundred Tennessee riflemen could

---

77. Robinson, *Life in California*, 228; Miller, *Juan Alvarado*, 81–83; Bancroft, *History of California*, 4:29–41; Doyce B. Nunis, Jr., *The Trials of Isaac Graham*, 22–45.

take the country; and it's a mighty pity it should be held by a set of vagabonds who don't regard the honor of God or the rights of men."[78] From the Mexican point of view, intruders like Graham were the vagabonds, who showed little regard for God's laws or the rights of those they considered their inferiors. Indeed, Alvarado's transgressions in the Graham Affair were minor compared to the wrongs done in years to come to Californios, Indians, Asians, and others by Anglo-Americans who promised liberty and justice for all.

78. Graham in Farnham, *Early Days of California*, 115.

John A. Sutter.
*Courtesy The Bancroft Library, University of California, Berkeley
(California Faces: Selections from The Bancroft Library Portrait Collection).*

CHAPTER 10

The Emigrant Tide

One prominent foreigner left undisturbed while Isaac Graham and others were rounded up was a man who would do much to loosen Mexico's grip on California— John Sutter. He arrived there in July 1839 and received permission from Alvarado to settle in the Sacramento Valley, beyond the supervision of Mexican authorities. That was an extraordinary concession to one who was not yet a Mexican citizen, but Sutter was a man of many countries who used charm and finesse to cross frontiers and create his own domain. Born Johann August Sutter in the German state of Baden in 1803, he moved to Switzerland as a youth, emigrated to the United States in 1834 to escape debt and disgrace, settled briefly on the Missouri frontier as a trader, ventured to New Mexico on the Santa Fe Trail, and later made his way to Oregon before voyaging to California by way of Honolulu and Sitka. His travels exposed him to most of the cultures that went into the making of California and brought him letters of recommendation from businessmen in various ports and the services of ten Kanakas, obtained in Hawaii from King Kamehameha III. Adept at gaining the trust of influential men while leaving behind him a long trail of disappointed creditors, Sutter was something of a confidence man. But an air of confidence and command was a great asset for a frontier adventurer. It took confidence to settle "on the banks of the river Sacramento," in Sutter's words, because Indians there "would not allow white Men and particularly of the Spanish Origin to come near them, and was very hostile."[1] If he had not impressed Alvarado as bold and enterprising in taking on that challenge, Sutter would not have won his confidence.

By claiming to have served France as an officer, Sutter associated himself with a Catholic nation respected in California and considered less of a threat to Mexican sovereignty than the United States or Great Britain. It helped that Sutter was not one of those intrusive and sometimes unruly Anglos who were causing Alvarado so much concern. Had Sutter assimilated like Jean Louis Vignes, a Frenchman who established a commercial vineyard near Los Angeles, Alvarado's trust in him might have been well placed. But when Sutter became a Mexican citizen in 1840, it was a mere formality. Pledging that he was a Catholic when he was in fact raised as a Protestant, he received title to the land and an appointment as justice of the peace. Among his responsibilities was to guard against "adventurers from the United States."[2] In truth, Sutter was no more a Mexican than he was a Frenchman or a Catholic, and his interests as a landholder led him to aid and employ unauthorized American settlers. In retrospect, Alvarado would characterize Sutter's foreign cohorts much as he did Graham and company, describing them as deserters, horse thieves, and other "depraved creatures," whose one virtue was that they were good at fighting Indians.[3]

Alvarado gambled on Sutter because he could see no other way of colonizing or controlling the interior, which remained the haunt of unruly foreigners of the sort employed by Sutter as well as defiant Indians, including fugitives from the missions who raided ranches and stole livestock. Sutter's efforts could make things no worse there, Alvarado reckoned, and might improve matters if he fulfilled his duties as a Mexican official. Furthermore, Alvarado

---

1. Sutter in Kenneth N. Owens, ed., *John Sutter and a Wider West*, 4; Albert L. Hurtado, *John Sutter: A Life on the North American Frontier*, 1–56.
2. Quoted in Bancroft, *History of California*, 4:137.
3. Alvarado in Hurtado, *John Sutter*, 77.

was increasingly at odds with Mariano Vallejo and saw Sutter's ambitions as countering those of his powerful uncle in Sonoma.

Sutter visited Vallejo before venturing up the Sacramento River in 1839 and found much in Sonoma to emulate as he planned his own fiefdom. A few dozen families had settled there in recent years under the protection of Vallejo's troops, bolstered by Indian forces loyal to his ally, Chief Solano of the Suisun tribe. William Heath Davis, who dealt with Solano when he came to Yerba Buena to purchase goods for a ranch he obtained with Vallejo's help, recalled that the chief stood well over six feet and "could read and write and keep accounts, having been educated by the old missionaries." He and Chief Camilo of the Coast Miwoks, Davis added, were treated by Vallejo "with high consideration," because through them he subdued and controlled other tribes and commanded the Indian laborers needed for the "vast improvements he introduced at Sonoma and Petaluma."[4] Sir George Simpson of the Hudson's Bay Company, who visited Sonoma a few years after Sutter did, noted that Vallejo's holdings included thousands of cattle, a vineyard he assumed as administrator of Mission San Francisco Solano that had yielded more than five hundred gallons of wine, and a farm of some six hundred acres, worked by Indians who were "badly clothed, badly lodged, and badly fed."[5]

Sutter hoped to establish a similar colony by exploiting Indian labor in the Sacramento Valley. When Vallejo suggested that he settle instead near Sonoma, Sutter replied that he wished to be on a navigable river. "This was my excuse," he admitted later, "though in reality my real object was to get farther away from the Spaniards." He did not want to defer to higher authority like those in Sonoma who doffed their hats to Commandant General Vallejo: "I preferred a country where I could keep mine on, in other words where I should be absolute master."[6] So in early August 1839 Sutter

---

4. Davis, *Seventy-five Years in California*, 103; Beebe and Senkewicz, *Testimonios*, 3–15.
5. Sir George Simpson, *Narrative of a Voyage to California Ports in 1841–1842*, 65–66; Rosenus, *General Vallejo*, 43–45.
6. John Sutter, "Personal Reminiscences of General John A. Sutter," Bancroft Library, 22–23; Hurtado, *John Sutter*, 58.

headed upriver in sailboats with his Kanakas (two of whom were women), several white men with mechanical skills, and sailors hired to man the vessels. Among those recruits was young Davis, who recalled that Sutter brought with him arms and artillery and said he planned to "build a fort as a means of defense against the Indians, and also against the government of the department of California in case any hostility should be manifested in that quarter."[7]

It took Sutter and company several days to navigate Carquínez Strait and Suisun Bay and locate the mouth of the Sacramento, which was not easily distinguished from the mouth of the San Joaquín River nearby. Their journey up the Sacramento took them through marshy country that had changed little since Spaniards first colonized California sixty years earlier. Game abounded, as did mosquitoes, "exceeding anything we ever experienced before," Davis noted.[8] Malaria, a mosquito-borne disease introduced by foreign trappers, was taking a steep toll among Indians there, as was smallpox. Like earlier settlers, Sutter encountered Indians whose susceptibility to such diseases and exposure to trade goods altered their subsistence patterns and made them less resistant to colonization.

Approaching what is now the city of Sacramento, Sutter's party encountered a party of two hundred or so Indians. They were "armed & painted & looked very hostile," he wrote. But some of them spoke Spanish, and he was able to make a treaty of sorts with them.[9] The presents and trade goods that he offered to such parties did as much to appease them as the implied threat of his weapons. Sutter landed with his colonists where the American River enters the Sacramento. A few of his mechanics grew fearful, he recalled, and left him, returning with the sailors to Yerba Buena. According to Davis, "Captain Sutter gave us a parting salute of nine guns—the first ever fired at that place—which produced a most remarkable effect. . . . the camp of the little party was surrounded by Indians, who were excited and astonished at the unusual sound." Deer and

---

7. Davis, *Seventy-five Years in California*, 15–16.
8. Ibid., 15; Hurtado, *John Sutter*, 59–61, 70–71.
9. Sutter in Owens, *John Sutter and a Wider West*, 5.

elk were startled as well, "running to and fro . . . while from the interior of the adjacent wood the howls of wolves and coyotes filled the air, and immense flocks of waterfowl flew wildly over the camp." As viewed in retrospect by Davis after the Gold Rush transformed this area, Sutter's alarming salute "was the first echo of civilization in the primitive wilderness so soon to become populated and developed into a great agricultural and commercial center."[10]

Like Vallejo, Sutter pacified Indians near his settlement, including Miwoks and Nisenans, by rewarding those who cooperated with him and punishing those who defied him. "The Indians was first troublesome," he related, "and would it not have been for the Cannons they would have Killed us for the sake of my property . . . I had a large Bull Dog which saved my life 3 times, when they came slyly near the house in the Night: he got hold of and marked them most severely." Until he succeeded in recruiting Indian laborers, Sutter relied largely on the efforts of his original colonists and others he hired as vaqueros to tend livestock that he purchased on credit from landholders such as Ignacio Martínez, owner of Rancho Pinole near what is now the town of Martínez. The presence of livestock led to further raids on his budding colony, Sutter recalled. Informed in 1840 that a few hundred warriors had gathered along the Consumnes River, he launched a preemptive strike. "The fighting was a little hard," he stated, "but after having lost about 30 men, they was willing to make a treaty with me." After this punishing lesson, "they behaved very well, and became my best friends and Soldiers," he added. "They became likewise tolerable good laborers and the boys had to learn mechanical trades."[11]

This was not the last time Sutter would use deadly force against Indians, but he achieved more through incentives than through intimidation. Indians toiling at the colony, which was dubbed New Helvetia in honor of his Swiss homeland, were paid with metal disks that could be redeemed for goods at his store, thus binding them to him economically much as sharecroppers were later bound to plantation owners in the American South. By July 1841, when

---

10. Davis, *Seventy-five Years in California*, 15–16; Hurtado, *John Sutter*, 62–65.
11. Sutter in Owens, *John Sutter and a Wider West*, 5–7.

American merchant William Dane Phelps visited New Helvetia, it had grown substantially. "Capt Sutter now has about 20 white men with him of difft. nations," Phelps noted. "He has also at his beck 4 or 5 Indian tribes, whom he has won by acts of kindness, and also intimidated by punishments, but by preserving and ruling them with an even hand and being just to all, they now seem devoted to him." Many of them, Phelps observed, wore clothing obtained from Sutter in exchange for their labors, which included raising wheat and other crops and building an adobe fort. Phelps, who traded with Californios but remained apart from them and disdained Catholicism, considered Sutter's regime benign compared with the old mission system, asserting that padres sent soldiers to "hunt the poor native, even with the lasso, and having caught him, branded him with the mark of Holy Mother church and then employed him to entrap his fellow."[12]

In fact, both Sutter and the missionaries relied primarily on inducements such as food and clothing to entice Indians. Unlike the padres, however, Sutter took little responsibility for the Indians beyond observing legal formalities. "I had no clergy or church," he recalled. "At burials and marriages I officiated myself."[13] Although Sutter told Phelps that he was planning a hospital and a school for Indians at his fort, nothing came of those plans. He boasted that an Indian such as Homobono, who served in his uniformed army of some two hundred men, could read and write while many Mexican soldiers could not. But Homobono became literate as a mission Indian before joining Sutter. When a measles epidemic swept through the Sacramento Valley, Sutter hired a physician to treat his laborers, but the doctor could do little to save the Indians afflicted or protect Sutter's economic interests, which were paramount. "I am sorry to say that I will loose at least about 3000 fanegas of Wheat in the fields," Sutter wrote, "on account [of] the prevailing decease among the Indians."[14] He routinely hired out his laborers to other ranchers in California and sometimes sold

---

12. William Dane Phelps, *Alta California, 1840–1842: The Journal and Observations of William Dane Phelps, Master of the Ship "Alert,"* 197–98.
13. Sutter, "Personal Reminiscences," 46.
14. Sutter in Hurtado, *John Sutter*, 210.

The Emigrant Tide

"Sutter's Fort—New Helvetia," ca. 1846,
by Joseph Warren Revere, from *A Tour of Duty in California* (1849).
Courtesy Library of Congress, Prints and Photographs
Division (LC-USZ62-8112).

Indians captured by his forces as slaves. Having left his wife and children behind in Switzerland, Sutter took Indian women or girls as mistresses and provided others as companions to employees and business partners—favors that left those men indebted to him.

Just two years after arriving in California, Sutter was one of its leading men. William Dunlop Brackenridge, who accompanied the American expedition led by Charles Wilkes that visited New Helvetia in 1841, reckoned that "in a few years there will be nothing in California to compete with him in point of strength, wealth, & influence."[15] Sutter exercised "supreme power in his own district," Wilkes observed, "condemning, acquitting, and punishing, as well as marrying and burying those who are under him." He hoped to dominate the fur trade in the Sacramento Valley, Wilkes added, by serving as employer or purchaser for "a large party of hunters and trappers, mostly American, who enter here into competition with those of the Hudson Bay Company."[16]

---

15. Brackenridge in ibid., 95.
16. Wilkes, *Narrative of the United States Exploring Expedition*, 5:178–79; Hurtado, *John Sutter*, 89–101.

Sutter went so far as to ban that powerful British outfit from California, an edict that exceeded his authority and was overturned by Alvarado, who like Vallejo grew increasingly wary of Sutter. Both men were alarmed when Sutter purchased Fort Ross from the Russian American Company in late 1841, a deal that Vallejo had hoped to make, if not on behalf of Mexico then on his own. But Mexico would not pay for a post maintained illegally on its own soil, and Vallejo found the $30,000 asking price too steep. Sutter did not flinch at offering that much because, as usual, he was buying on credit and considered such deals renegotiable. Technically, he was purchasing only the livestock, equipment, and buildings at Fort Ross and a smaller company outpost nearby at Bodega Bay. Mexico owned the land, having never ceded it to the Russians. But Sutter obtained a spurious deed from them and hoped that it would be recognized as legitimate if Mexico lost or sold California to the United States. The Russians, for their part, claimed the right to seize New Helvetia as security if Sutter defaulted—a nightmarish prospect for Alvarado and Vallejo, who would be damned in Mexico City if foreigners gained control of the interior.

That was bound to happen anyway, in the opinion of Sir George Simpson, who as governor of the Hudson's Bay Company considered Sutter a rogue, partial to intruding Americans. "If he really has the talent and the courage to make the most of his position," Simpson wrote, "he is not unlikely to make California a second Texas," which had broken with Mexico and was inviting annexation by the United States. The Americans harbored by Sutter in the Sacramento Valley were much like those Texas rebels, Simpson asserted, "ready for all sorts of mischief." And once they were "masters of the interior," they would seek a maritime outlet and occupy San Francisco Bay, if not the entire coast, subjecting California to domination by a society that allowed slavery and exported it to places such as Texas. California would be far better off, Simpson argued, if acquired by the British, whose supposed virtues as colonizers (they had in fact recently abolished slavery in their empire) he contrasted to the vices of American expansionists.

"Either Great Britain will introduce her well-regulated freedom of all classes and colors," he concluded, "or the people of the United States will inundate the country with their own peculiar mixture of helpless bondage and lawless insubordination."[17]

Prophet of Preemption

John Marsh seemed ill suited to play the part of Moses, urging Americans across the Western wilderness to their promised land on the Pacific. Solitary and self-absorbed, he attracted no followers and never served as a trailblazer like Jedediah Smith or Joseph Walker. Yet he had a vision that proved prophetic, and he helped inspire the first party of American settlers to set out for California by wagon. Such pioneers were aptly described as emigrants because they continued to be governed in their thoughts and deeds by the country they had left behind, not by the country they entered as immigrants. Like Marsh, they remained American to the core and thought that California belonged to them in spirit and would soon be theirs in title. Expansionists like Marsh saw that influx as preempting any competing claims to this country made by Europeans. Among those urging a British takeover of California through colonization or other means were George Simpson and Alexander Forbes, a Scottish merchant and author residing in Tepic, Mexico, who wrote that he could think of no place better calculated than California "for receiving and cherishing the superfluous population of Great Britain."[18] French envoy Eugène Duflot de Mofras, who visited California in 1841 and assessed its prospects in writing, harbored similar hopes for his nation and left his suspicious host, Mariano Vallejo, with the impression that France was "intriguing to become mistress of California."[19] But Duflot de Mofras's dream of a "New French America" on the Pacific went unfulfilled.[20] European designs on California were remote and speculative compared

---

17. Simpson, *Narrative of a Voyage to California Ports*, 73–74.
18. Alexander Forbes, *California: A History of Upper and Lower California*, 321.
19. Vallejo in Rosenus, *General Vallejo*, 25.
20. Eugène Duflot de Mofras, *Travels on the Pacific Coast*, 21.

with the urgent migration of land-hungry Americans set in motion by Marsh.

Marsh left the United States under a cloud, but that did not discredit him as an American pioneer, more than a few of whom went west to escape financial or legal troubles. A native of Massachusetts, he ran afoul of the law in the early 1830s while serving as an Indian agent in Wisconsin, where he lived with the daughter of a French trapper and a Sioux woman. Accused of selling guns to Indians during the Black Hawk War, Marsh left his companion, Marguerite, and their son. He sought refuge first on the Missouri frontier, where he crossed paths with Sutter, and later in Santa Fe, where he picked up some Spanish before continuing on to Los Angeles. As a foreigner, he had to appear before the town council there and justify his presence. Presenting his bachelor's degree from Harvard, he claimed to be a doctor. (He had in fact dispensed medicine and treated wounds.) The council judged his diploma authentic and concluded that he would be useful to the community. Marsh earned enough as a doctor to purchase land in northern California from José Noriega, a veteran of the Híjar-Padrés expedition who was eager to sell Rancho Los Meganos because it lay in a remote and dangerous area, east of San Francisco Bay, between Mount Diablo and the mouth of the San Joaquín.

Marsh did mind not settling in what was essentially Indian country, for he had experience dealing with Indians and could serve them as a medicine man by dispensing quinine to those suffering from the fever and chills of malaria. Nor did he mind professing Catholicism and taking on Mexican citizenship to gain title to Los Meganos. Such formalities meant no more to him than they did to Sutter. The ceremony that truly bound foreigners to this country was marriage to a Mexican woman. Sutter avoided that commitment by explaining that he was already married, but Marsh's union with Marguerite, who died before he reached California, had never been solemnized. Marriage to a Mexican was not a requirement for citizenship, but foreigners who remained single or took Indian mistresses, as Marsh did, were regarded with suspicion. His reputation as a doctor, however, made him sought after by Mexicans who might otherwise have avoided him. "My wife is very ill," wrote Antonio Suñol, an official in San José, situated some forty miles from Marsh's ranch. "I wish you would be so kind as to come and make her a visit. . . . Bring some remedies with you, if you can, as none can be found here."[21] For such lengthy house calls, Marsh charged a fee of a few hundred cattle or cowhides, it was said, a steep sum that did not endear him to his clients. In a society noted for its generosity and hospitality, his cupidity and reclusiveness set him apart.

Marsh's sense of alienation increased during the Graham Affair when he was hauled to Monterey and held there briefly. Although he was not among the suspects expelled, he complained afterward that American diplomats had done less than British officials to help free those captives. "Our government thinks we are better able to take care of ourselves than the people of any other nation, and I am disposed to think there is some truth in the opinion," he wrote. "Be this as it may, in a year or two more we shall at least be able to protect ourselves in California."[22] He planned to enhance the American presence there by promoting overland emigration by men who brought wives and children with them and thus would not be assimilated through intermarriage with Californios. Settling beyond the scrutiny of Mexican authorities in the Central Valley, they would form distinct colonies and make Americans "masters of the interior," in Simpson's words, much as families following the Oregon Trail would help secure American claims to that territory.

Through conversations and correspondence with other overlanders, Marsh concluded that the best path to California for those traveling in wagons would be to take the Oregon Trail as far as Fort Hall in present-day Idaho before heading south to the Humboldt River and following its winding course westward to a pass through the Sierra Nevada. Marsh's instructions were vague, for he had never traveled that route and no party had ever crossed the Sierra by wagon. Yet such was the enthusiasm among prospective

---

21. Suñol in George D. Lyman, *John Marsh, Pioneer: The Life Story of a Trail-Blazer on Six Frontiers*, 226.
22. Marsh in ibid., 236.

emigrants that his letters to acquaintances in Missouri touting the virtues of California and urging settlers to follow his proposed route and "come direct to his rancho" struck a responsive chord. As Joseph Chiles, one of those who heeded that summons, recalled, they "learned through Dr. Marsh's letters the latitude for San Francisco Bay, and they thought the sun was sufficient to guide them."[23]

Further encouragement came from men who had been to California and returned. John Bidwell, who helped organize the first emigrant party from Missouri to California in early 1841, was inspired to do so when Marsh's "glowing account" was confirmed by meetings with Antoine Robidoux, a Missourian of French Canadian heritage recently returned from California. "He said it was a perfect paradise, a perpetual spring," Bidwell recalled. Addressing the newly formed Western Emigration Society, Robidoux assured Bidwell and others that moving to California would make them all wealthier and healthier. "There never was but one man in California who had the chills," Robidoux replied blithely when asked about malaria. "He was from Missouri and carried the disease in his system. It was such a curiosity to see a man shake with the chills that the people of Monterey went eighteen miles into the country to see him."[24]

Robidoux and Marsh were telling people what they wanted to hear, but discouraging words from others dampened their enthusiasm. Thomas Farnham, after returning from his western travels, wrote letters to the press disparaging Mexican officials and making California sound inhospitable to foreigners. Merchants who feared losing clients through emigration made sure that Farnham's warnings received ample coverage in newspapers there. Of the five hundred or so enthusiasts who joined the Western Emigration Society over the winter, only about seventy assembled in May 1841 at Sapling Grove, their appointed rendezvous just west of the Missouri-Kansas border. Among them were five women and

---

23. Chiles in Doyce B. Nunis, Jr., ed., *The Bidwell-Bartleson Party: 1841 California Emigrant Adventure, the Documents and Memoirs of the Overland Pioneers*, 143; George R. Stewart, *The California Trail*, 7–8; Bancroft, *History of California*, 4:265–74.
24. Robidoux quoted by Bidwell in Nunis, *Bidwell-Bartleson Party*, 77–78.

ten children. Nancy Kelsey, a 17-year-old who embarked on the journey with her infant Ann and husband Benjamin, remarked afterward that she could "better endure the hardships of the journey, than the anxieties for an absent husband."[25] Among the worries of wives who remained at home was that their husbands would forsake them for new companions. Such was the case with another member of this company, Paul Geddes, who left his wife and children in Pennsylvania after embezzling $8,000, assumed the name Talbot Green, found a second wife in California, and had a son by her. His fellow emigrant Nicholas Dawson recalled that Green was "a young man of evident culture and very pleasing address," who carried a mysterious parcel, supposedly containing lead, to which he clung "most solicitously."[26] (Not until Green ran for mayor of San Francisco in 1851 was his past exposed.)

Before setting out in mid-May, the company elected as captain John Bartleson of Missouri. "He was not the best man for the position," remarked Bidwell, who might have welcomed the honor but was only twenty-one years old and did not bring any followers or family members to the company. Bartleson, who was in his fifties and had several men with him, indicated that if not elected captain "he would not go," Bidwell related, and was chosen because the emigrants did not want their numbers diminished.[27] Bidwell would later gain recognition for promoting this venture, known to posterity as the Bidwell-Bartleson party. "It was a very mixed crowd," wrote Dawson. "There were heads of families going out first to find a spot to bring their families to, and heads of families taking the families along to share whatever fortune might bring."[28] Rounding out the company were young men without family ties such as Dawson, Bidwell, and Josiah Belden, who had reveled in the tales of James Fenimore Cooper as a boy and hoped to "see something of a wild country, of buffalo hunting, and to have some

---

25. Nancy Kelsey in Stewart, *California Trail*, 20.
26. Nicholas Dawson, *Narrative of Nicholas "Cheyenne" Dawson (Overland to California in '41 and '49, and Texas in '51)*, 9, 25; Nunis, *Bidwell-Bartleson Party*, 146, 154, 247–48, 260–61.
27. Bidwell in Nunis, *Bidwell-Bartleson Party*, 104.
28. Dawson, *Narrative*, 9; Nunis, *Bidwell-Bartleson Party*, 146.

adventures among the Indians."[29] Fortunately for those greenhorns, they soon linked up with a consummate veteran, mountain man Thomas Fitzpatrick, who was guiding Father Pierre Jean De Smet and other Jesuit missionaries to the Northwest and would serve as the true leader of the Bidwell-Bartleson party for as long as it remained on the Oregon Trail. Without him, Bidwell reckoned, none of them would have reached California.

Thanks to Fitzpatrick, who like Jedediah Smith defied the stereotype of the mountain man as truculent and trigger-happy, the emigrants avoided clashes with Indians. Along the Platte River in early June, Dawson carelessly went off on his own to hunt antelope and was cornered by a band of Cheyennes, who relieved him of his mule, his weapons, and his outer clothing, leaving him to suffer the taunts of his companions, who dubbed him Cheyenne Dawson. Some in the party panicked when the same band approached their camp a short time later, but Fitzpatrick purchased peace by bargaining with the Cheyennes for Dawson's lost goods. "He and I and the Indians sat around in a circle," Dawson recalled, "and for every article to be returned, gifts of blankets, clothes, etc., had to be thrown down, a peace pipe smoked by all, and much haranguing done."[30] It was a useful lesson in diplomacy for settlers bound for interior California, which was still very much Indian country, but few overlanders had Fitzpatrick's capacity for converting potentially violent exchanges into peaceful ones.

Fitzpatrick advised the emigrants against trying for California with their cumbersome wagons—and without an experienced guide. A number of them heeded his advice. After crossing the Great Divide and reaching Soda Springs (not far from Fort Hall), all but one family decided to continue with Fitzpatrick to Oregon, the exception being Benjamin and Nancy Kelsey and their baby. They were among thirty-four pioneers who headed south from Soda Springs down the Bear River in August. Their plan was to turn west near the Great Salt Lake and seek the Humboldt River.

---

29. Belden in Nunis, *Bidwell-Bartleson Party*, 128.
30. Dawson, *Narrative*, 12; Nunis, *Bidwell-Bartleson Party*, 80, 130, 147–48, 184.

The Emigrant Tide

"A Parley: Prepared for an Emergency," ca. 1866,
by John Cameron, Currier & Ives. *Courtesy Library of Congress,
Prints and Photographs Division* (LC-USZ62-636).

In years to come, wagon trains bound for California would follow paths from the Oregon Trail to the Humboldt that avoided the treacherous salt flats around the Great Salt Lake. But Bartleson and Bidwell knew no better and descended into country that was abysmal for wagons and the animals hauling them. "We traveled all day without water," Bidwell related, "and at midnight found ourselves in a plain, level as a floor, incrusted with salt, and as white as snow . . . This plain became softer and softer until our poor, almost famished, animals could not pull our wagons."[31]

They managed to free their vehicles from the salt flats but made only fitful progress in the days ahead amid bleak country that offered little sustenance for humans or beasts. At the rate they were going, they stood little chance of reaching California before winter descended and snowstorms trapped them in the Sierra. Abandoning their ponderous wagons, they packed their possessions inexpertly on horses, mules, and oxen and dispensed with some of their goods to lighten the load. As they did so, Bidwell

---

31. Bidwell in Nunis, *Bidwell-Bartleson Party*, 112.

wrote, they were approached by a solitary Indian "well advanced in years," who "told us by signs that the Great Spirit had spoken to him to go down upon the plains in the morning," where he would receive gifts from strangers. "We gave him all such things as we had intended to throw away; whenever he received anything which he thought useful to him, he paused and looked steadfastly at the sun, addressed him in a loud voice, marking out his course in the sky, as he advanced in his invocation."[32]

This haunting incident left an indelible impression on Dawson, who recalled many years later: "We signed to our aged host that the wagons and everything abandoned were his, all his, and left him circumscribing the heavens—the happiest, richest, most religious man I ever saw. Why was he in that valley alone? What was his faith?"[33] This Indian was evidently engaged in some sort of pilgrimage or vision quest and valued the gifts all the more because he saw them as proof that the powers above had heeded his prayers and blessed him. Perhaps in honoring this lonely supplicant, the emigrants too were blessed. They were truly fortunate to weather the ordeals that lay ahead and fulfill their own quest, which tried their souls and stripped them of pride and possessions before they reached the land beyond.

Not until early October did they glimpse the Sierra in the distance as they traveled along the Humboldt River. Bartleson set a hectic pace and grew impatient with those who lagged behind. When Bidwell took him to task, the company split. Bartleson declared that "all who could keep up might go with him and the rest could go to H[ell]." Most stayed with Bidwell and ascended into the mountains along the Walker River, which they reached from the Humboldt Sink with the help of an Indian guide. Bartleson's group, meanwhile, went astray and fell far behind. As Bidwell noted on October 14: "This morning we saw at a distance Captain B. with his 7 men, coming in a direction towards us, but we made no halt." Two days later, Bidwell paused and sent out

---
32. Ibid., 44.
33. Dawson, *Narrative*, 18; Nunis, *Bidwell-Bartleson Party*, 151.

scouts to seek a pass through the Sierra, allowing the trailing group to catch up. "I well remember Captain Bartleson's exclamation as he sat eating what we had cooked for him," Bidwell related: "Boys! If I ever get back to Missouri, I will never leave there again. Why I would be glad to eat from the same trough with my dogs there."[34] Resentment toward his captain and rival may have colored Bidwell's account, but Bartleson was not in fact much of a pioneer and returned to Missouri for good in 1842. As the tensions within this party demonstrated, Americans bound for California were no less quarrelsome than their Hispanic predecessors and were quicker to part company in times of stress.

Like the Walker party in 1833, the Bidwell-Bartleson party crossed the Sierra perilously late in the year and came close to starvation. Unlike the Rocky Mountains, the high Sierra had few "parks" or meadows that harbored game in the colder months. The emigrants had only a few oxen left when they entered the mountains and were later reduced to eating mules raw or "half roasted, dripping with blood," in Bidwell's words. Although they found a pass through the Sierra, their descent along the Stanislaus River into the San Joaquín Valley was brutal and prolonged, "with no prospect of a termination to the mts., mts., mountains!"[35] They held off butchering their horses and mules for as long as they could and often had to dismount and lead the animals along treacherously narrow paths. While Dawson was struggling to keep his mule from tumbling into a precipice, he looked back "and saw Mrs. Kelsey a little way behind me, with her child in her arms, barefooted, I think, and leading her horse—a sight I shall never forget."[36] As she herself declared in later years: "I walked barefooted until my feet were blistered." By the time they reached the valley, she added, they were so hungry that they "lived on roasted acorns for two days."[37] Because they did not leach the acorns first to remove the acidic tannin as Indians did, they fell ill, as Bidwell

---

34. Bidwell in Nunis, *Bidwell-Bartleson Party*, 48, 89–90.
35. Ibid., 50, 52.
36. Dawson, *Narrative*, 23–24; Nunis, *Bidwell-Bartleson Party*, 153–54.
37. Nancy Kelsey in Nunis, *Bidwell-Bartleson Party*, 198.

recalled: "So much so we could not bear to see an acorn, and weak as we were, as far as possible avoided passing under oak trees."[38]

Remarkably, this inexperienced party that went west with no better guidance than Marsh's invitation to "come direct to his rancho" did just that, arriving there intact in early November. Bidwell was unimpressed with Marsh's home, built like most houses in Mexican California of adobe bricks, with no internal fireplace and a dirt floor matted with bulrushes. The reclusive Marsh soon tired of playing host to his hungry compatriots and remarked to Bidwell after they had consumed a hog and bullock that they "had already been more than $100 expense to him—God knew whether he would ever get a rial [real] of it or not." Bidwell concluded that he was "perhaps the meanest man in California."[39] Although faulted by Bidwell for charging three dollars apiece to obtain passports for the newcomers from Mariano Vallejo, Marsh joined Sutter in offering bond to keep the Americans from being detained as illegal aliens. Vallejo accepted those assurances, hoping that the newcomers would acknowledge his authority and help develop California. But he worried that he and his few Mexican soldiers might be swamped by the incoming tide of emigrants and lose control of the frontier. "We find ourselves forced to accept them," he informed the Ministry of War in Mexico City, "as we cannot prevent them from entering, and all because we lack troops."[40]

Settlement without Assimilation

Vallejo had reason to be alarmed by the arrival of the Bidwell-Bartleson party. Although a company that included young Nancy Kelsey and baby Ann might appear harmless, the presence of women in emigrant parties undermined the best defense that Californios had against foreign domination—the custom of intermarriage, which drew outsiders into the heart of their culture

---

38. Bidwell in ibid., 93.
39. Ibid., 69.
40. Vallejo in Beebe and Senkewicz, *Lands of Promise and Despair*, 426; Rosenus, *General Vallejo*, 39–43; Bancroft, *History of California*, 4:274–76.

and hastened assimilation. Thus far, few foreigners had achieved prominence or notoriety there without intermarrying: men such as Marsh, Sutter, and Thomas Larkin, all of whom posed a challenge to Mexican authority. (Larkin as U.S. consul in Monterey would try to induce Californios to invite American annexation.) Soon the ranks of unassimilated and potentially subversive Americans would increase substantially as emigrant parties including wives and children forged a viable wagon trail across northern Nevada and over the Sierra.

That route would serve as the main avenue of invasion for American settlers, more than a thousand of whom would enter California by late 1846—roughly one American for every six Californios in the territory. But several other paths were also followed by such emigrants, including some who reached California around the same time as the Bidwell-Bartleson party. In October 1841 three families arrived at Sutter's Fort from Oregon with a party led by Lieutenant George Emmons of the Wilkes expedition. Among them were Joel and Mary Walker and their children, who had reached Oregon by wagon the year before. Nancy Kelsey recalled meeting them at Sutter's Fort in December, taking care to assert priority as the first American woman to enter California overland: "We arrived at the fort on Christmas Day, where I met Joel Walker, who had just arrived with his wife and children—I had been in California five months."[41] In fact, she had been there only a few months, entering the Sacramento Valley a bit later than Mary Walker, whose journey was no small undertaking but could not compare with the Kelseys' trek over the Sierra Nevada. Joel Walker, brother to Joseph Walker, claimed that his wife was "the first white American woman in Sacramento," neglecting to mention that two other wives arrived at Sutter's Fort with them.[42] They were all pioneers, and all found refuge at New Helvetia,

---

41. Nancy Kelsey in Nunis, *Bidwell-Bartleson Party*, 199; David J. Weber, *The Mexican Frontier, 1821–1846: The American Southwest under Mexico*, 195–202; Bancroft, *History of California*, 5:524–26;

42. Joel P. Walker, *A Pioneer of Pioneers: Narrative of Adventures thro' Alabama, Florida, New Mexico, Oregon, California, & c.*, 13; Bancroft, *History of California*, 4:278–79.

where Sutter welcomed Americans as helpmates in his ongoing campaign to achieve virtual independence from Mexico and mastery of interior California.

Like John Bidwell, Joel Walker was employed by Sutter, receiving by his own account "a salary of Five Hundred Dollars a year as superintendent of his farm," where Indians toiled for a pittance.[43] As Bidwell observed in recommending California to prospective emigrants: "You can employ any number of Indians by giving them a lump of beef every week, and paying them about one dollar for same time." Such was Sutter's renown among Indians of the region that incoming emigrants would have no trouble finding the way to his place, Bidwell added, by asking them in broken Spanish: "*Por donda esta el rancho de Capitan Sutter?*"[44] Sutter was gambling that the American influx he encouraged would not undermine his authority. Like Vallejo and Alvarado, he hoped to use foreigners to enhance his domain but risked losing control of them in the long run.

Among those bothersome newcomers were John Rowland and William Workman, who led a party consisting largely of Americans from New Mexico to California along the Spanish Trail in late 1841. Arguably, no emigrants who settled legally in California during this period were less worthy of being welcomed here by authorities than Rowland and Workman. They were naturalized Mexicans with Mexican wives, but that concession to local culture meant less in their home town of Taos than it did in California. Among their associates in Taos was the powerful American trader Charles Bent, who also had a Mexican wife but remained deeply at odds with his adopted land, declaring in writing on one occasion that Mexicans were "not fit to be free" and "should be ruled by others than themselves."[45] Bent later sided with American troops who seized New Mexico in 1846 and served as governor of the occupied territory until insurgents assassinated him. In 1841 Rowland, Workman, and others close to Bent were suspected of aiding Texans who

---

43. Walker, *Pioneer of Pioneers*, 14.
44. Bidwell in Nunis, *Bidwell-Bartleson Party*, 61, 68.
45. Bent in Stephen G. Hyslop, *Bound for Santa Fe: The Road to New Mexico and the American Conquest, 1806–1848*, 294, 300.

infiltrated New Mexico, part of which was claimed by the breakaway Republic of Texas. That threat was stamped out by Governor Manuel Armijo of New Mexico, who accused Workman of plotting to kill him. Rowland, Workman, and other suspects concluded that "it was not safe for us to remain longer in New Mexico," in the words of Benjamin Wilson, and left for California shortly before the intruding Texans were captured.[46] In a letter to the Ministry of War, Armijo described the fugitives as "traitors who have gone to the Californias to seduce and confuse its inhabitants."[47]

Traveling on horseback with pack mules, Rowland and Workman entered California with a few dozen followers, including some Hispanic New Mexicans. Workman brought along his wife, Encarnación Martínez, and their children, while Rowland left his family behind and returned for them later when the furor over the Texans had subsided. Joining Rowland and Workman were four Missourians who had set out too late to join the Bidwell-Bartleson party and ventured instead to Santa Fe. As Benjamin Wilson recalled, the Rowland-Workman company departed New Mexico in September 1841, "met with no accidents, drove sheep with us, which served us as food, and arrived in Los Angeles early in November of the same year."[48]

Reports that Rowland, Workman, and others had plotted against the government in New Mexico reached Alvarado, who requested aid from his superiors to cope with the threat posed by these and other intruders. Yet after the persuasive Rowland met with Alvarado, he allowed members of this suspect party to settle in California and granted Rowland one of the choicest parcels of land in southern California, the 20,000-acre Rancho La Puente, attached to Mission San Gabriel. Father Narciso Durán, who presided over California's dwindling missions, argued that this land belonged to Indians who remained at San Gabriel and protested

---

46. Benjamin D. Wilson, "Benjamin David Wilson's Observations on Early Days in California and New Mexico," 86; Donald E. Rowland, *John Rowland and William Workman: Southern California Pioneers of 1841*, 41–48; Hafen and Hafen, *Old Spanish Trail*, 199–214.
47. Armijo in Rowland, *John Rowland and William Workman*, 48.
48. Wilson, "Benjamin David Wilson's Observations," 86; Bancroft, *History of California*, 4:276–78.

"against the sale or alienation of said Rancho of la Puente, as well as against the transfers of many other pieces of land which this territorial government has effected with flagrant wrong and prejudice to the poor neophytes."[49] This land grant appeared so irregular that Alvarado was suspected of yielding to bribery. Rowland himself later claimed that he offered the governor "a thousand dollars in gold" to approve the deal.[50] Whatever his motives, the grant was consistent with Alvarado's earlier actions, including his generous concession to Sutter. As a liberal committed to the economic development of California, Alvarado gambled that naturalized foreigners of means who received land would play a constructive rather than a subversive role. He hoped to exploit them, while raising suspicions that they were exploiting and corrupting him.

Whether Alvarado tried to stem the foreign tide, as he did during the Graham Affair—or went with that flow, as in his dealings with Sutter and Rowland—he and his successors had little chance of holding California for Mexico much longer. By now, Alvarado was weary of the task and relieved to hear that a new governor, Manuel Micheltorena, was due to replace him. Vallejo, for his part, warned the Ministry of War that California was under siege by foreigners, with Americans posing the greatest threat. "And if the invasion which is taking place from all sides is carried out," he wrote, "all I can guarantee is that Californians will die; I cannot dare to assure you that California will be saved."[51]

49. Durán in Rowland, *John Rowland and William Workman*, 69.
50. Rowland in ibid., 62–63.
51. Vallejo in Beebe and Senkewicz, *Lands of Promise and Despair*, 426.

Part Four
THE AMERICAN CONQUEST (1842–1848)

CHAPTER 11

Intervention at Monterey

"We are now approaching the shores of California, the territory of Mexico, the enemy of our country, whose flag it is our duty to strike, and hoist in its place our own." With those words, issued aboard the frigate *United States* on October 18, 1842, Commodore Thomas ap Catesby Jones ordered men of his Pacific Squadron to seize Monterey. "It is not only our duty to take California," he added, "but we must keep it afterwards, at all hazards."[1] Jones was acting on the mistaken assumption that his country was at war with Mexico. His occupation of Monterey would last barely a day before he learned otherwise, lowered the Stars and Stripes, and withdrew his forces. Yet his seemingly errant and abortive act was not out of line with his nation's policies and objectives in this era of insistent American expansion. Although Jones was recalled, he would later be restored to command and praised at the highest level. President James Polk, elected in 1844 on an expansionist platform, assured Jones through the secretary of the navy that his peremptory seizure of Monterey demonstrated "an ardent zeal in

---

1. Jones in Charles Roberts Anderson, ed., *Journal of a Cruise to the Pacific Ocean, 1842–1844, in the Frigate United States*, 83–84; Neal Harlow, *California Conquered: War and Peace on the Pacific, 1846–1850*, 3–13; Bancroft, *History of California*, 4:298–329; Gene A. Smith, "The War That Wasn't: Thomas ap Catesby Jones's Seizure of Monterey."

the service of your Country, and a devotion to what you deemed to be your duty, regardless of personal consequences, which entitle you to anything but censure from your Government."[2]

The circumstances that led Jones to commit an act of war without a declaration of war were much like those that later impelled Captain John Charles Frémont to risk battle with Mexican forces in California before hostilities with Mexico began in May 1846. Like Jedediah Smith and other American adventurers in earlier days, Jones and Frémont defied Mexico on their own authority, confident that they were upholding their nation's interests in a country they regarded as ripe for the taking. Their interventions had special significance, however, because they were officers representing the United States. One might say they misrepresented the nation by acting rashly and exceeding orders, but Americans were known to honor bold and impetuous officers like Andrew Jackson, who in 1818 launched an unauthorized invasion of Spanish Florida and was rewarded for that and other exploits with two terms in the White House. Expansionists like President John Tyler, who annexed Texas shortly before he left office in 1845, and his successor Polk, a political disciple of Jackson, needed officers with Jacksonian daring and gall like Frémont and Jones if they hoped to extend Jefferson's "empire for liberty" across the continent.

Born in Virginia, Jones had served in the U.S. Navy for thirty-seven of his fifty-two years when rumor and conjecture led him to conclude he was duty-bound to take Monterey. He was patrolling the Pacific coast of South America and keeping a sharp eye on French and British warships when he entered the port of Callao, Peru, in September 1842 and received a letter sent in June by John Parrott, U.S. consul at Mazatlán, Mexico. Mexican-American relations were quickly deteriorating, Parrot warned, and "it is highly probable there will be a war between the two countries."[3] At issue was Texas, involved in a bitter border dispute with Mexico that threatened to embroil the United States if it aided the defiant

---

2. Quoted in Anderson, *Journal of a Cruise to the Pacific Ocean*, 101.
3. Parrott in ibid., 80.

Texans or annexed their country. This crisis, aggravated by long-standing American financial claims against Mexico, was not as grave as Parrott suggested when he wrote that war was highly probable. Jones had no way of knowing that, however, and felt he could not afford to wait months for official confirmation from Washington if war was in the offing. He was further alarmed by reports that Mexico had ceded California to Great Britain to settle old debts and prevent Americans from claiming that prize. The sudden departure of three British warships from Callao seemingly confirmed those rumors and spurred Jones into action on September 7, when he left Callao aboard the *United States* and proceeded to Monterey with the sloop-of-war *Cyane*. He now had a solemn national principle to defend—the Monroe Doctrine, which stated that lands and peoples of the Americas were not to be subject to future colonization by European powers.

The Monroe Doctrine would long serve as a pretext for U.S. military intervention in Latin American countries, raising angry cries of Yankee imperialism. Proud American expansionists like Commodore Jones, however, drew a sharp distinction between what they saw as the selfish and cynical imperial designs of European powers like Britain and France and the generous desire of Americans to widen the scope of their democratic empire and share its blessings with others. As his flagship neared Monterey, Jones drew up a proclamation conveying his idealized view of America's high imperial mission. "Inhabitants of California," he declared, "you have only to remain at your homes, in pursuit of peaceful vocations, to ensure security of life, persons, and property, from the consequences of an unjust war, into which Mexico has suddenly plunged you."[4]

Jones had little basis for asserting that war had commenced—and none whatsoever for portraying Mexico as the aggressor—but it was an article of faith among American expansionists that war and conquest were forced upon them by foreign despots whose oppressed subjects were yearning for liberation. By placing

---
4. Jones in ibid., 88.

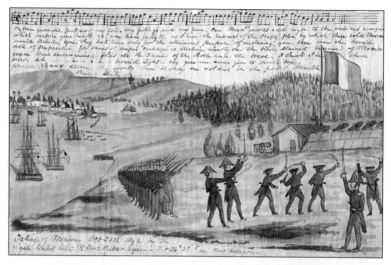

"Taking of Monterey," 1842, by William H. Meyers.
Courtesy The Bancroft Library, University of California,
Berkeley (BANC MSS C-F 92).

Californios under the American flag, Jones proclaimed, he was translating their defeat into victory and granting them newfound freedoms: "Those stars and stripes, infallible emblems of civil liberty, of liberty of speech, freedom of the press, and above all the freedom of conscience, with constitutional right and lawful security to worship the Great Deity in the way most congenial to each one's sense of duty to his Creator, now float triumphantly before you, and, henceforth and forever, will give protection and security to you, to your children, and to unborn countless thousands."[5] For Jones, this Jeffersonian promise of civil and religious liberty—conceived in a pluralistic society quite different from Hispanic California, where one faith prevailed—was enough in itself to justify his Jacksonian show of force. Like Spanish colonizers in earlier times, he tried to portray conquest and coercion as righteous and redeeming, but the full benefits he promised would

---

5. Ibid., 88–89.

be realized by few Californios of this or future generations, many of whom would find that they were not secure in their property as he had pledged.

Jones's lofty view of American intervention was not shared by William Henry Meyers, a gunner on the *Cyane* who saw this as a rousing mercenary adventure. "So it appears we are going to have a fight," he noted in his diary on October 19 after Jones announced his intention to take California. "Bueno!" Meyers hoped for glory and plunder but wondered if this fight would be his last. "At 8 turned in for a nap," he wrote, "before I am popped out of this world."[6] He had little need to worry, for the occupation of Monterey went unopposed. Governor Alvarado, awaiting the arrival of his successor, Manuel Micheltorena, was in no position to reject the ultimatum that he received from Jones, which called on him "to avoid the sacrifice of human life and the horrors of war" by surrendering "the fort, military posts, and stations, under your command, together with all troops, arms, and munitions of war."[7] Alvarado was "in shock as he read the note, which was written in Spanish," recalled Antonio María Osio, serving then as customs agent at Monterey. "After a period of silence his face suddenly became pale and then immediately turned red, as if blood were about to burst from his eyes. In a voice choked with emotion he told the commodore's secretary, who was a Spaniard, that if he had only half the number of men in the commodore's force he would consider their forces equal."[8]

In fact, Alvarado could muster only about fifty soldiers to contend with several hundred fighting men aboard the *United States* and *Cyane*, who between them could bring eighty big guns to bear against the dozen or so cannons guarding the harbor. Micheltorena had recently arrived in Los Angeles from Mexico with additional troops. But many of them were convicts (*cholos*), who did more to frighten Californios than reassure them. In any case, they were

---

6. William H. Meyers, *Journal of a Cruise to California and the Sandwich Islands in the United States Sloop-of-War Cyane, 1841–1844*, 6.
7. Jones in Anderson, *Journal of a Cruise to the Pacific Ocean*, 85.
8. Osio, *History of Alta California*, 208.

too far from Monterey to be of help. Reluctantly, Alvarado signed articles of capitulation, stating that Mexican troops who surrendered would be paroled and that the governor had been induced to sign "from motives of humanity; the small force at his disposal affording no hope of successful resistance against the powerful force brought against him."[9] On October 20 "the Mexican flag was hauled down," Meyers noted in his diary, and the U.S. flag was "raised with 3 cheers."[10] But no cheers were heard from those Osio called true Californios, "people who loved their country and were proud of their nationality." They watched in pained silence as the Mexican banner was replaced by the Stars and Stripes. "This flag was alleged to be the symbol of liberty," Osio commented, "but that was actually a lie. It belonged to an oppressor who displayed arrogance against the weak."[11]

Belatedly, Jones took the trouble to investigate a report from the well-informed Thomas Larkin, soon to be named U.S. consul in Monterey, who had visited the commodore's flagship the night before Jones took possession of the town and informed him that the latest news from Mexico made no mention of war. Not until October 21 did Jones send his secretary to look into the matter. That search, he reported, turned up newspapers and letters showing that "Mexico had not commenced hostilities against the United States up to the 22nd of August," two months later than the alarming message that Jones had received from John Parrot suggesting that war was imminent. Jones concluded that "the late difficulties between the United States and Mexico have been amicably adjusted" and ordered his forces withdrawn from Monterey and the Mexican flag rehoisted.[12] The commodore's abrupt decision to "resurrender the place," as William Meyers put it, left him and his mates nothing to brag about. "So perish all my greatness," Meyers wrote, "adieu my visions of prise money, I am dumb henceforth."[13]

---

9. Quoted in Anderson, *Journal of a Cruise to the Pacific Ocean*, 87–88.
10. Meyers, *Journal of a Cruise to California*, 7.
11. Osio, *History of Alta California*, 209.
12. Jones in Anderson, *Journal of a Cruise to the Pacific Ocean*, 90, 95–97; Harlow, *California Conquered*, 9.
13. Meyers, *Journal of a Cruise to California*, 8.

Hosting the Intruders

Far from retreating in the wake of this unwarranted intrusion, U.S. forces remained along the coast of California for some time to come. Jones arranged to meet with Micheltorena, who assumed the governorship on December 31 and conferred with Jones in Los Angeles a few weeks later. In the interim, sailors coming ashore in Monterey were treated well by Californios, who appreciated that they had heeded Jones's order to "avoid insult or offense to any unoffending inhabitant" during their brief occupation.[14] Serenaded by the flagship's "splendid band," Larkin reported, the visitors and their hosts "had as many Balls as there was Sundays in the month. . . . Some who never danced before danced here."[15] Yet the continued presence of foreign troops who had violated Mexican sovereignty made it clear that Californios were powerless to resist such incursions and had little choice but to extend to these Americans the conventions of hospitality that had long served to disarm potentially threatening intruders.

Richard Maxwell, assistant surgeon aboard the *United States*, detected an undercurrent of resentment beneath the genial surface of Mexican-American relations. "We soon became intimate with many of the families in town, and used to spend our time pleasantly there," he recalled. "But the Californians were very bitter, Castro especially." Formerly commandant in Monterey, José Castro had served as Governor Alvarado's enforcer during the crackdown on Isaac Graham and other suspect foreigners in 1840. He did not like Americans who meddled in California's affairs and gave Maxwell a scare at a feast held at Mission San Carlos in late 1842. The padre there "cautioned me not to leave his side while we were there," Maxwell related, "as Castro, who was a very brutal man, and half drunk, was inciting the Indians to kill us." That evening, as Maxwell and others rode home to their ship, they looked back and saw "Indians chasing along, as we supposed in pursuit of us, Castro at their head." He was probably just trying to frighten

---

14. Jones in Anderson, *Journal of a Cruise to the Pacific Ocean*, 84.
15. Thomas O. Larkin, *The Larkin Papers: Personal, Business, and Official Correspondence of Thomas Oliver Larkin, Merchant and United States Consul in California*, 2:6.

the Americans and repay them for intimidating Californios by seizing Monterey. According to Maxwell, Castro was "called to account" for this stunt: "He made many apologies, and attributed his conduct to his having been drunk at the time." At a ball in Monterey on New Year's Eve, Maxwell added, Castro "made what he considered ample amends to me by embracing me and kissing me on each cheek."[16]

This gesture did not mean that Castro had reconciled with intruding Americans, for he later opposed their occupation of California in 1846. The willingness of Castro and other Californios to engage in peaceful exchanges with foreigners was conditional on their good behavior and respect for the customs of the country. Americans like Maxwell, who disparaged the locals and their habits, might be tolerated for a while, but they were not welcome—and they knew it. Maxwell faulted women from town who visited his ship and made free with the food offered there. "Every woman would spread her handkerchief on her lap," he recalled, "and whatever we had on the table they would eat a part of, and carry off a part in their handkerchiefs,—nuts, figs, everything. Their manners were exceedingly primitive." The women evidently did not consider it bad manners to take such treats home to share with others. Nor would they have been faulted for doing so by accommodating foreign merchants in earlier years. As a further example of "primitive" behavior, Maxwell related an incident that a more polite and obliging visitor would not have mentioned. As he was escorting a niece of American merchant J. B. R. Cooper and his wife, Encarnación Vallejo, to a ball in town, he recalled, "she said 'Excuse me for a moment,' and sat down by the fence, and discharged the contents of her bladder. There were a couple of midshipmen behind us at the time. These women were as unsophisticated as so many cats."[17]

Such disdain for women who bore the presence of intrusive foreigners with grace and fortitude—and surely saw them relieving

---

16. Richard T. Maxwell, *Visit to Monterey in 1842*, 28–29, 31–32.
17. Ibid., 33.

themselves in public on occasion without drawing attention to it—may help explain why the women of Mexican California in particular feared an American takeover and resented the occupation when it took place. As trader William Heath Davis remarked, they would not countenance an invasion of their country by the United States or any other foreign power. One prominent woman in Monterey who found the American occupation in 1842 hard to bear was Angustias de la Guerra. Her brother Pablo was acting as customs administrator there and took refuge with her father in Santa Bárbara. When the commodore's secretary came to her home and demanded the key to the customs house, she refused to hand it over. Maxwell evidently had her in mind when he told of a relative of Pablo de la Guerra who hated Americans so much that "she promised to marry anybody who would bring her a necklace made of their ears."[18] This anecdote was somewhat misleading: Angustias de la Guerra was already married in 1842 and would later welcome Americans to her home. But as Davis confirmed, she deeply resented Yankees who abused the courtesy shown them and imposed on Californios.

One such obstreperous American was merchant-ship captain William Dane Phelps, who was preparing to take on hides in San Diego when he learned that Jones had occupied Monterey. He had been trading in California for two years, but he had no family ties there and no sympathy for Mexico in its dispute with his homeland. Assuming that war had indeed broken out, Phelps resolved to defend his flag and cargo against assault. "At all events I shall do my best to protect both ship & property," he wrote in his diary. Fearing that Micheltorena and his "vagabond troops" would descend on San Diego and seize his vessel, Phelps and his crew spiked the guns at the fort guarding the entrance to the harbor. "Out of a pile of shot we also picked out all that would fit our own guns & returned on board," he wrote. Joining him aboard the *Alert* that evening were American otter hunters, armed with rifles and anticipating

---

18. Ibid., 36; Beebe and Senkewicz, *Testimonios*, 257–58, 265; Davis, *Seventy-five Years in California*, 37.

a fight. They "appear extremely anxious for a brush," Phelps noted, "most of them being men who have travelled through New Mexico and over the Rocky Mountains and all having a mortal hatred to Mexicans." Yet aside from the defiant words of the alcalde in San Diego, who urged "all citizens to take arms in defence of the country, or they would be considered traitors," Americans there went unchallenged. Phelps was sorry to learn that Jones had backed out: "I hope this is not true, but that the American Govt. will hold on to this country and will take ample satisfaction of Mexico for her oft repeated insults & aggressions on our flag."[19]

Reparations Denied

Governor Micheltorena, for his part, wanted satisfaction for insults done to the Mexican flag by Commodore Jones and presented him with articles of reparation to sign when the two met in Los Angeles in January 1843. In his account of that conference, Jones dismissed Micheltorena as a typical posturing "*Mexican*, a descendant of the once proud and haughty Castillians, so celebrated for bombast in diplomacy, demanding everything and *insisting* on nothing but the privilege of using high toned and unmeaning words." Jones gave the governor and his aides credit for receiving him courteously and putting on a fine show. "I must confess that I have never seen more splendid or better fitting uniforms than graced this group," he wrote. But all that glittered was not gold, and Jones deemed Micheltorena a counterfeit. He ridiculed the governor's claims against American forces for occupying Monterey as attempts to make up for his own failings and those of his disorderly troops, who "could not be trusted with arms in their hands." All Micheltorena could do under the circumstances, Jones asserted, was to "issue high toned, inflated proclamations, breathing destruction to every foreigner and claiming honors and rewards for battles never to be fought and for victories never to be won."[20]

---

19. Phelps, *Alta California*, 330–36.
20. Thomas ap Catesby Jones, *Visit to Los Angeles in 1843: Unpublished Narrative of Commodore Thomas ap Catesby Jones*, 20, 23.

Jones, who was himself given to high-toned, inflated proclamations, capped his indictment of Micheltorena by citing his seemingly frivolous demands for reparations, including 1,500 infantry uniforms to replace those lost or spoiled in the "violent march and the continued rains" as Mexican forces supposedly hurried to defend Monterey and "a complete set of military musical instruments, in place of those ruined on this occasion." Other articles that Micheltorena presented to Jones were more serious and substantive, including demands that Jones admit seizing Monterey in error and join Micheltorena in promising not to engage in acts of war without an express declaration of war and that he pay the Mexican government $15,000 to compensate for the "expense incurred from the general alarm created in this department by the invasion and occupation of the port of Monterey." Jones refused to sign the articles, explaining that he lacked authority to do so and considered them *"objectionable."*[21]

With that the two men parted. Micheltorena expressed the hope that if war should bring them "into conflict in their country's cause," they would nonetheless meet again as friends when "strife was ended." This was probably meant as a polite warning to Jones not to risk war with another provocative show of force, but the commodore came away convinced that he had lulled Micheltorena into affectionate submission and transformed his petty resentments into respect for Jones and the nation he represented. "I can but feel highly gratified," he concluded, "tho' however severely my acts may be criticised by our respective Governments, that all good people in California, even those who had a right to consider me their country's foe, have done me the justice to judge me fairly, and to duly appreciate my *motives.*"[22] How far from the truth this was may be judged by the reaction of Mariano Vallejo, who was by no means hostile to Americans but denounced Jones's intervention as a "violation of the rights of hospitality, of the law of nations, and the trust with which he had been received by the authorities at

---

21. Ibid., 24; Bancroft, *History of California*, 4:318–19 n. 39.
22. Jones, *Visit to Los Angeles*, 26.

Monterey."[23] Like Micheltorena, Vallejo met with Jones after he withdrew his forces from Monterey, greeting him courteously at Sonoma in keeping with his obligations as host. But his younger brother Salvador Vallejo, who was growing increasingly exasperated with intruding Americans, was not so polite to their visitor. At one point, while observing a war party of Suisun Indians led by the Vallejos' ally, Chief Solano, Jones noticed that women were present and asked if they took part in the fighting. They did not fight against rival Indians, Salvador replied, "but if it were a matter of fighting the Yankees, they would take part in the battle and would know how to give a good account of themselves."[24]

The intervention of Commodore Jones riled some Anglo-Americans as well, including merchant John Coffin Jones, a native of Boston who served as U.S. consul in Honolulu before settling in Santa Bárbara. As he wrote to Thomas Larkin shortly after the incident: "I can only say that the taking of Monterey by Comd. Jones, without any orders, on the mere supposition, that a war existed between the U States and Mexico, is a proceeding, so strange & so unaccountable, that the more I think of it, the more I am puzzled to reconsile it with the act of any one but that of a mad man." He felt ashamed as a Yankee—"I have drawn my head within my shell," he declared, "and sneak about like a condemned criminal"—and feared dire consequences for Mexican-American relations.[25] Indeed, the incident hampered efforts by the administration of President Tyler to purchase California and resolve the deepening dispute with Mexico. Jones was not seeking to provoke war. And his motives were, as he insisted, patriotic. Yet patriotism in this era was heavily laden with jingoism. Some expansionists believed, as journalist John O'Sullivan wrote in 1845, that it was America's "manifest destiny to overspread the continent allotted by Providence for the free development of our yearly multiplying millions."[26] For eager officers like Jones, the Monroe Doctrine

---

23. Vallejo in Bancroft, *History of California*, 4:312.
24. Salvador Vallejo as quoted by Mariano Vallejo in Rosenus, *General Vallejo*, 53.
25. Jones in Larkin, *Larkin Papers*, 1:310–11.
26. O'Sullivan in Hyslop, *Bound for Santa Fe*, 323.

and the traditional right of belligerents to seize enemy ground in wartime were all the authority they needed to fulfill America's imperial ambitions.

Jones may have recognized before he took action that seizing Monterey, however briefly, would send a signal to Mexico and the world at large that was stronger and more emphatic than any official disclaimers that might follow if he proved wrong in his assumptions and had to withdraw. As indicated by his disdainful account of his meeting with Micheltorena, he viewed Mexicans as blusterers who would yield to superior force when challenged and thus considered it unlikely that his intervention would lead to hostilities if the two nations were not already at war. He took a calculated gamble and succeeded in demonstrating what many informed observers already suspected: Mexico was unable to defend California. This demonstration further damaged Micheltorena in the eyes of Californios, who were already dismayed by the arrival of his *cholos*. Before long, Micheltorena would be toppled in a rebellion, with resident Americans figuring prominently on both sides of the conflict, indicating that Mexico was fast losing control of this country.

Jones could not have foreseen all those consequences when he barged into Monterey and raised the Stars and Stripes. Yet undermining Mexican sovereignty there was surely not an unwelcome outcome for an officer so enamored of his country and its cause that he saw no reason why anyone would oppose an American takeover. Fully half of California's inhabitants, "including all property holders," would rather live under the American flag than under Mexico's standard, Jones claimed. And "with the other half," he contended, "it is a matter of perfect indifference under what government they live."[27]

---

27. Jones, *Visit to Los Angeles*, 23.

John C. Frémont, by T. Knight,
from a daguerreotype by Mathew Brady.
*Courtesy Library of Congress, Prints and Photographs
Division* (LC-USZ62-57631).

CHAPTER 12

Frémont's Forays

Lieutenant John Charles Frémont was exceeding his orders and overstepping America's boundaries, but he felt compelled to enter California. By crossing the snowbound Sierra Nevada at great peril with his exploring party in early 1844, he staked an unofficial claim to that territory for his expanding nation. This was the second expedition led by Frémont as an officer with the U.S. Topographical Corps. Like the first, carried out in 1842, it was largely concerned with surveying the Oregon Trail and encouraging American emigration to the Pacific Northwest, where the United States and Great Britain were competing peacefully for preeminence under a treaty of joint occupation. After reaching the Columbia River Gorge in late 1843, however, Frémont moved southward into Mexican territory along what is now the California-Nevada border. Among his objectives, he said afterward, was to probe for the "reputed *Buenaventura* River," which supposedly cut through the Sierra Nevada to the Pacific.[1] Jedediah Smith had searched in vain for the Buenaventura in the 1820s, and he and other astute mountain men had concluded that

---

1. John Charles Frémont, *Memoirs of My Life*, 285; John Charles Frémont, *The Expeditions of John Charles Frémont*, 1:574–611; Tom Chaffin, *Pathfinder: John Charles Frémont and the Course of American Empire*, 194–208; Goetzmann, *Exploration and Empire*, 240–52.

319

no such river existed. Yet the myth persisted, offering Frémont a rationale for trespassing on foreign ground.

Frémont's stated intention if he discovered the Buenaventura was not to follow it to the California coast, thus risking a confrontation with Mexican authorities, but to camp with his party until spring along its upper reaches, "where, in the softer climate of a more southern latitude, our horses might find grass to sustain them, and ourselves be sheltered from the rigors of winter and from the inhospitable desert."[2] Then he would return east to American territory, having advanced geographical knowledge without causing offense to Mexico. Foreign officers since Vancouver's time had been intruding on Spanish or Mexican territory with similar professions of innocence and goodwill, but Frémont's case was unusual because he was acting without authority from his superiors.

Frémont and his men were well south of the forty-second parallel, the northern boundary of Mexican territory in the Far West, when they came within sight of Pyramid Lake on January 10, 1844. "For a long time we sat enjoying the view," he related. "It was set like a gem in the mountains, which, from our position, seemed to enclose it almost entirely." In days to come, Frémont and company followed the swift-flowing Truckee River, which fed Pyramid Lake, up into the foothills of the Sierra, encountering Indians who offered them delectable "salmon-trout" (cutthroat). Frémont and his men might have wintered there along the Truckee, feasting on cutthroat and grazing their horses on what he called "tolerably good grass." But he worried that those animals were too footsore to survive the long journey back across the Great Basin and Rockies, and he did not have enough iron to reshoe them. "I therefore determined to abandon my eastern course," he declared, "and to cross the Sierra Nevada into the Valley of the Sacramento," where horses abounded.[3]

The run-down condition of his horses was convenient for Frémont, as it had been for Jedediah Smith when he entered Mexican California without authorization in 1826 to obtain fresh mounts

---

2. Frémont, *Memoirs*, 298.
3. Ibid., 313–17.

and supplies. Similarly, Frémont found it convenient to resuscitate the fading Buenaventura legend—a quest that lent significance to Smith's intrusion—before dispensing with the myth. "No river from the interior does, or can, cross the Sierra Nevada," he stated afterward in an account dictated to his wife, Jessie Benton Frémont, daughter of Missouri senator Thomas Hart Benton. Frémont's conclusion that California had no passageway comparable to the Columbia River Gorge seemingly confirmed the importance of Oregon over California as a target for American expansion. Yet the imposing obstacles that had to be overcome to reach California made it all the more precious to Frémont and other adventurous Americans. It was so alluring that Frémont's men welcomed the news that they would be crossing the forbidding Sierra in midwinter to get there. "My decision was heard with joy by the people," he related, "and diffused new life throughout the camp."[4]

Frémont's party was well suited for the trial that lay ahead, consisting largely of mountain men used to such hardships. Serving as guides were two of the most gifted members of their profession, Thomas Fitzpatrick and Kit Carson, who had journeyed to California as a youngster not long after Smith arrived there. Frémont himself—a 30-year-old prodigy without military schooling who had entered service as a mathematics instructor—was more of a trail leader or caravan captain than a conventional officer, and his penchant for pursuing his own path sometimes caused friction with superiors. Colonel John J. Abert, chief of the Topographical Corps, had reacted angrily when he learned that Frémont had armed his explorers like a war party with pistols, carbines, and a howitzer. This was supposed to be "a peaceable expedition," he wrote Frémont in May 1843, "similar to the one of last year, an expedition to gather scientific knowledge. If there is reason to believe that the condition of the country will not admit of the safe management of such an expedition ... you will immediately desist in its further prosecution and report to this office."[5] Abert's letter reached the Frémont residence in St. Louis after he had departed

---

4. Ibid., 317, 364.
5. Abert in Frémont, *Expeditions*, 1:344–45; Chaffin, *Pathfinder*, 148–50.

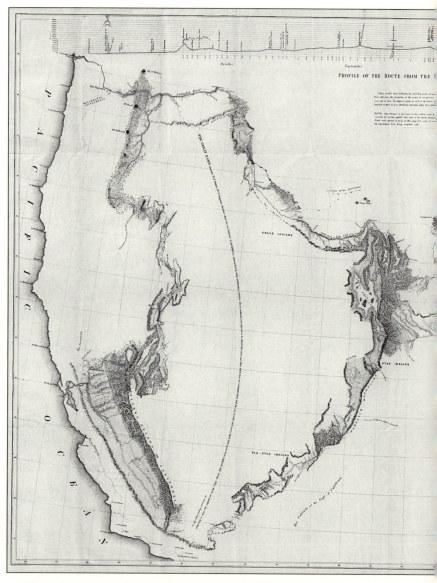

Frémont's map of his explorations in 1842 and 1843–44.
Courtesy David Rumsey Map Collection (www.davidrumsey.com).

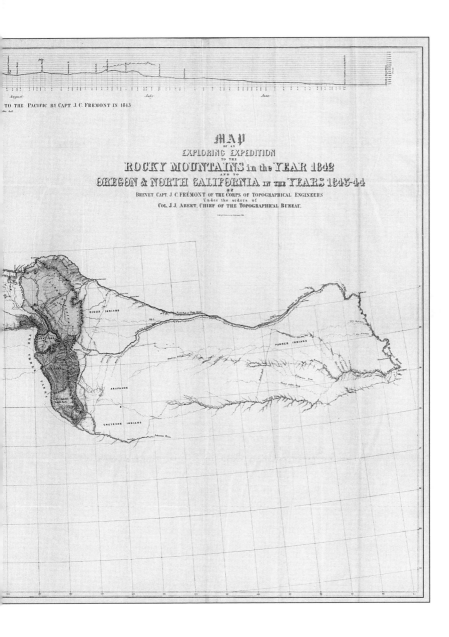

for Westport Landing, on Missouri's western frontier, to launch his expedition. Jessie Frémont later claimed credit for suppressing the letter and urging her husband to get underway promptly, before anyone in Washington could interfere with his plans.

Frémont's rationale for bringing along a howitzer was to fend off attacks by Indians. But as his plans expanded to include a deep incursion into Mexico, he may also have viewed the cannon as a reassuring deterrent against Mexican forces. Hauling the howitzer and its ammunition was no small burden for the expedition and sometimes impeded progress. "If we had only left that ridiculous thing at home," wrote the German-born artist and cartographer Charles Preuss in his diary.[6] Not until late January when Frémont's party encountered deep snowdrifts at higher elevations did he reluctantly abandon the weapon. He was seemingly unaware that Preuss, for one, was glad to be rid of the gun. "We left it," Frémont declared, "to the great sorrow of the whole party, who were grieved to part with a companion which had made the whole distance from St. Louis, and commanded respect for us on some critical occasions, and which might be needed for the same purpose again."[7]

Such was young Frémont's air of authority that mountain men older and wiser than he was in gauging the risks they took followed him on this treacherous errand without flinching. As Kit Carson recalled in later years, "we had to cross the mountains, let the consequences be what they may."[8] Preuss had often sniped at Frémont in his diary earlier in the expedition, but once they entered the Sierra he accepted the grim necessity of pushing forward and could only pray that his leader's gamble would pay off. "We are getting deeper and deeper into mountains and snow," he wrote on February 3. "We pay one roving Indian after the other to guide us across. They march with us a few miles and leave us as soon as they have a chance."[9] Indeed, Indians with whom Frémont

---

6. Charles Preuss, *Exploring with Frémont: The Private Diaries of Charles Preuss, Cartographer for John C. Frémont on His First, Second, and Fourth Expeditions to the Far West*, 83.
7. Frémont, *Memoirs*, 326.
8. Carson, *Kit Carson's Autobiography*, 79.
9. Preuss, *Exploring with Frémont*, 105.

"Pass in the Sierra Nevada of California," 1844, based on a sketch by Charles Preuss, from Frémont's *Report of the Exploring Expeditions to the Rocky Mountains in the Year 1842 and to Oregon and Northern California in the Years 1843–44* (1846). Courtesy Library of Congress, Prints and Photographs Division (LC-USZ62-32177).

communicated warned him repeatedly in words or gestures not to persist in what they considered a mad pursuit. As he paraphrased one such doomsayer: "Rock upon rock . . . snow upon snow . . . even if you get over the snow you will not be able to get down from the mountains." Hearing this, a young Chinook Indian who had been with Frémont's party since they left the Columbia River "covered his head with his blanket, and began to weep and lament."[10]

As the explorers ascended the eastern slope of the Sierra, the snow proved too deep and soft to support the weight of their horses, so they had to pack down the surface using snowshoes and sledges. They could not afford to abandon the animals, which hauled supplies until they were too weak to bear loads and were slaughtered to feed the hungry men. Among the sacrificial victims consumed on this arduous trek were numerous horses, a few dogs,

---

10. Frémont, *Memoirs*, 332; Chaffin, *Pathfinder*, 211–14.

and Preuss's trusty mule Jack. "Last night we received a sledful of his meat," he noted on February 13, "but I did not eat any of it and do not intend to . . . On the fire are two pots and a tea kettle. In one pot are peas and pieces of the meat of my Jack; in the smaller pot is half of the dog."[11] However unsavory, such offerings gave men strength to carry on. On February 20 Frémont reported that "we encamped with the animals and all the *materiel* of the camp, on the summit of the pass in the dividing ridge."[12] This may have been Carson Pass, south of Lake Tahoe. Earlier in the month, before the men had packed down a path for the animals, an advance party including Frémont, Fitzpatrick, and Carson had reached this pass on foot and glimpsed the promised land to their west. "We could see the green valley of the Sacramento," Carson recalled, "and in the distance the Coast Range. . . . Our feelings can best be imagined when we obtained a view of such a beautiful country."[13]

Reaching the pass did not mean deliverance for Frémont's weary party, for they still had to make a harrowing descent along icy, rock-strewn slopes to the valley below. "Finally we are out of the snow," Preuss wrote on February 24. "Yesterday was still a bad day: snow, rocks, brush. Terrible march. In nine hours we made three miles." Not long afterward, Preuss became separated from his companions and spent days searching for them. "Since yesterday morning I have not eaten a thing except a few sweet onions which I just scratched out of the ground," he noted on March 3. "At the same time, I found an ants' nest, a portion of which I bit off and swallowed . . . How will this end?" Reduced to the condition of the lowly Diggers, scorned by emigrants for subsisting on roots and insects, he could only hope that he would soon encounter Indians who might share with him the food they gathered. He was not afraid of them, he wrote: "Unlike Kit [Carson], I don't see a murderer in every miserable human being." Sure enough, Preuss came upon Indians the next day "and gave them to understand that I was hungry. They immediately served me acorns, some of

---

11. Preuss, *Exploring with Frémont*, 108–109.
12. Frémont, *Memoirs*, 338; Frémont, *Expeditions*, 1:638; Chaffin, *Pathfinder*, 215–17.
13. Carson, *Kit Carson's Autobiography*, 79.

which I ate, and others I put in my pocket." Thus replenished, he continued his search for his mates and found a fire that they had recently abandoned: "I collected my last ounce of strength, and before sunset I saw the lodge before me. Friends—beautiful grass—magnificent country."[14]

This meeting on the evening of March 5 reunited Preuss with Frémont and his advance party, who hoped to reach Sutter's Fort and purchase supplies for those still making their way down from mountains. On the following day, Frémont reported, they met with a well-dressed Indian who introduced himself in Spanish as a vaquero employed by Sutter and told the explorers that they were on the "Rio de los Americanos, (the river of the Americans), and that it joined the Sacramento river some 10 miles below. Never did a name sound more sweetly!"[15] It pleased Frémont to hear the term "American" applied to one of the principal rivers flowing down from the Sierra Nevada, which no longer shielded the Central Valley from intrusions by his compatriots.

Officially, Sutter was a representative of Mexico, authorized to dispense justice in California under Mexican law. But he relied increasingly on incoming Americans as customers and employees. John Bidwell of the pioneering Bidwell-Bartleson party, for example, now served as Sutter's chief clerk at the fort and described it as "a place of protection and general rendezvous" for incoming Americans.[16] Sutter later recalled that his fort was sometimes so full of emigrants "that I could scarcely find a place to sleep myself."[17] Among the Americans who had found refuge there recently were Joseph Chiles, who arrived with Bidwell in late 1841 before returning to the Missouri frontier and organizing an emigrant wagon train to California, and Lansford Hastings, who led a party of more than thirty settlers down from Oregon in 1843. Hastings soon returned east and wrote an ill-informed but influential book, *The Emigrants' Guide to Oregon and California*. Posing as an expert

---

14. Preuss, *Exploring with Frémont*, 112–13, 117–19.
15. Frémont, *Memoirs*, 350.
16. John Bidwell, *In California before the Gold Rush*, 62.
17. Sutter, "Personal Reminiscences," 72.

on the subject, he portrayed California as uniquely calculated to "promote the unbounded happiness and prosperity of civilized and enlightened man," by which he meant Anglo-Americans, whose task it was to redeem the territory from oppressive Mexican rulers and their lowly subjects.[18] Such chauvinistic assumptions that Americans deserved this country and foreigners would have to yield to them did not bode well for Sutter. But given his close ties with American settlers, he could be counted on to aid Frémont's party.

On March 6, Sutter related, Frémont arrived at the fort with Kit Carson and "told me that he was an officer of the U.S. and left a party behind in Distress and on foot.... I received him politely and his Company likewise as if an old acquaintance." This was, in fact, his first meeting with Frémont, but it was in his interest to make the explorer feel at home and cater to his needs. "I sold him about 60 Mules and about 25 horses," Sutter reckoned.[19] By the time troops sent by Governor Micheltorena to investigate Frémont's intrusion reached Sutter's Fort in late March, Frémont and his men had obtained all they needed from their obliging host and departed southward, returning to the United States by way of the Mojave Desert and the Spanish Trail.

One consequence of Frémont's visit was to draw Sutter deeper into the American web. Shortly after Frémont departed, Sutter received a letter from Thomas Larkin, U.S. consul in Monterey, asking him to keep Larkin informed on American emigrant parties that reached Sutter's Fort and other matters "of consequence in which my countrymen are concerned."[20] The request appeared innocent enough; but by providing Larkin with reports Sutter was aiding a foreign nation increasingly at odds with Mexico, to which he owed allegiance. He may well have been nudged in that direction by the arrival of Frémont, whose foray suggested that his government was prepared to back the claim to this region asserted unofficially by emigrants like Bidwell and Chiles. By overcoming the Sierra Nevada in the depths of winter, Frémont made an

---

18. Hastings in Bancroft, *History of California*, 4:397–98.
19. Sutter in Owens, *John Sutter and a Wider West*, 9–10.
20. Larkin in Hurtado, *John Sutter*, 129.

American takeover of the Sacramento Valley, a region over which Mexico never had firm control, appear almost inevitable. Wisely, he made no move toward the coast after leaving Sutter's Fort, for that might have brought him up against Mexican troops and infuriated his superiors in Washington, who were not yet prepared to fight for California. In any case, the conquest of the coast was a task best left to the U.S. Navy, which had sufficient resources to seize California's lightly defended ports, as Commodore Jones had demonstrated at Monterey in October 1842. Frémont's contribution to the cause of American expansion on this journey was to expose the corresponding weakness of California's interior defenses. Neither Sutter nor any other Mexican authority there stopped this intruding officer and his armed men from gathering intelligence on the country and the paths leading into it.

In sum, Frémont's foray demonstrated that California could be taken overland and should be taken—if, as American expansionists believed, the purpose of claiming a country was to settle and organize it and subdue or sweep aside its native inhabitants. None of those objectives had been accomplished by Mexico in the Central Valley except at Sutter's Fort, which was more an American or international outpost than a Mexican one. Elsewhere in the interior, with the exception of Mariano Vallejo's outpost at Sonoma, unassimilated Indians and fugitives from the missions remained in control. The path that Frémont followed after he left Sutter's Fort, down through Oak Creek Pass and across the Mojave, had no Mexican settlers or forts. The area was unsafe for Mexican travelers, as shown by an incident that occurred in late April at a desert campsite called Archilette. Six people traveling ahead of a caravan bound for New Mexico were ambushed there by Indians, who killed four of them and stole most of their horses and mules. The survivors, Andreas Fuentes and Pablo Hernández, reached Frémont's camp. Kit Carson and another mountain man, Alexander Godey, volunteered to track down the Indian culprits.

Late the next day, Frémont related, "a war-whoop was heard . . . and soon Carson and Godey appeared, driving before them a band of horses, recognized by Fuentes to be part of those they had lost. Two bloody scalps, dangling from the end of Godey's gun, announced that they had overtaken the Indians as well as the horses."[21] Carson offered no apology for scalping Indians who had "horribly mutilated" their Mexican victims.[22] But Preuss took exception to the deed and the praise that Frémont heaped on the avengers. "To me, such butchery is disgusting," he wrote, "but Frémont is in high spirits. I believe he would exchange all observations for a scalp taken by his own hand."[23]

Frémont's account of this incident helped make Kit Carson legendary. In the process, he idealized not just the man but the larger enterprise in which he was engaged—a task that would be called the winning of the West. As Frémont put it: "Two men, in a savage desert, pursue day and night an unknown body of Indians into the defiles of an unknown mountain—attack them on sight, without counting numbers—and defeat them in an instant—and for what? To punish the robbers of the desert, and to avenge the wrongs of Mexicans whom they did not know."[24] Frémont's account implied that Mexicans sorely needed such help, having failed to prevent marauding Indians from wreaking havoc. In fact, Californios had mounted many reprisals against Indian raiders or rebels over the years, among them Estanislao, a defiant fugitive from Mission San José whose uprising was brutally suppressed in 1829 by troops led by Mariano Vallejo. But there were not enough Mexican forces in California to quell hostilities by Indians, who still greatly outnumbered Hispanic settlers. The Americanization of the territory would ultimately bring an end to Indian raids, but that would not be accomplished by the feats of a few brave enforcers like Carson and Godey, advancing against superior numbers to impose rough justice on evildoers. Instead it would be achieved by a vast influx of settlers and fortune-hunters, bringing with them apocalyptic changes for California Indians in the form of disease, displacement, starvation, and murderous vigilante attacks that made what Preuss called butchery look tame by comparison.

---

21. Frémont, *Memoirs*, 372–73.
22. Carson, *Kit Carson's Autobiography*, 85.
23. Preuss, *Exploring with Frémont*, 127–28.
24. Frémont, *Memoirs*, 374.

Frémont's compelling narrative (to which Jessie, his eloquent wife and amanuensis, added literary flourishes) contributed to that fateful influx by drawing attention to California at a time when most emigrants were setting their sights on Oregon. Published in 1845 as Frémont was organizing another western expedition with far-reaching consequences, his report caused a sensation and helped increase the flow of pioneers to California from a trickle to a stream. Before long, that fast-rising river of emigrants to which he lent impetus would reach flood stage and prove irresistible, sweeping westward to the Pacific like the fabled Buenaventura.

Forerunner of Conquest

This time Frémont made no secret of his intention to enter Mexican territory. He implied as much in correspondence by stating that he intended to revisit "the region west of the Rocky Mts," much of which belonged to Mexico.[25] And those who joined his third expedition knew from the start where they were headed. "As far as I have learned we will winter in California," wrote 20-year-old Theodore Talbot, a family friend who had earned Frémont's trust during the second expedition and helped organize the sequel. Frémont's renown was so great that hundreds of adventurers flocked to St. Louis in May 1845, hoping to accompany him. "His house is absolutely besieged," wrote Talbot in early June. The recently promoted Captain Frémont selected around sixty men, most of them "fine looking fellows and still more of them superb riflemen," Talbot observed. That would not make them welcome in California, where sharpshooting "Kentuckians" were dreaded by authorities. In August Frémont's party reached Bent's Fort, within sight of the Rockies, where they were joined by several seasoned mountain men, including Kit Carson and Joseph Walker, who knew the trails to California as well as anyone and was hailed by Talbot as "the best man in the Country."[26]

---

25. Frémont, *Expeditions*, 1:415.
26. Theodore Talbot, *Soldier in the West: Letters of Theodore Talbot during His Services in California, Mexico, and Oregon, 1845–53*, 12–14, 25–26, 32; Chaffin, *Pathfinder*, 249–60.

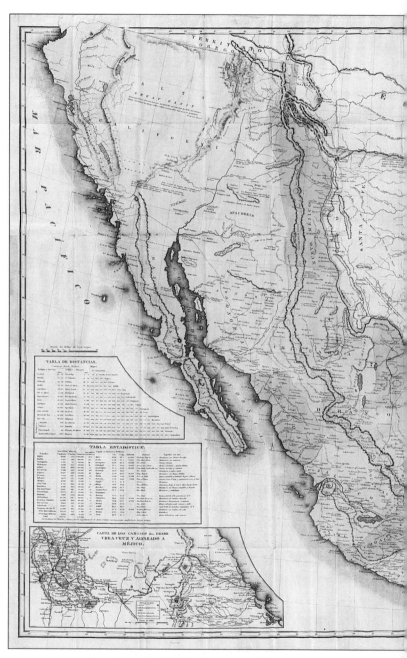

Map of Mexico, 1846, published by John Disturnell.
Courtesy David Rumsey Map Collection (www.davidrumsey.com).

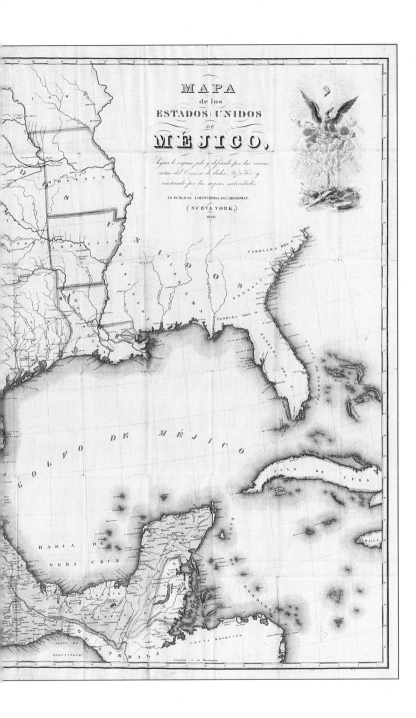

Frémont's written orders from his chief, Colonel Abert, instructed him to detach a party led by the colonel's son, Lieutenant James Abert, from his company at Bent's Fort to reconnoiter Mexican territory south of the Arkansas River but said nothing about Frémont venturing west of the Rockies. Yet Frémont evidently had permission to conduct such an expedition, for Colonel Abert later urged him to conserve funds "to meet the events of your own efforts for more distant discoveries, which will probably keep you sometime longer in the field than he [Lieutenant Abert] will be."[27] Frémont stated in his memoirs that he was authorized to return to California by his father-in-law, Senator Benton, "and other governing men in Washington," who were eager to take possession of California in the event of war with Mexico, which appeared increasingly likely after the United States annexed Texas in early 1845. Frémont did not specify that recently elected President James Polk—intent on acquiring both Oregon and California—was among those governing men who gave him "discretion to act."[28] But in October 1845, as Frémont and his men crossed the Great Basin, Benton met with Polk at the White House and broached the subject. "Some conversation occurred concerning Capt. Frémont's expedition, and his intention to visit California before his return," wrote Polk in his diary. "Col. Benton expressed the opinion that Americans would settle on the Sacramento River and ultimately hold the country."[29]

Benton and Polk had their differences, but they shared the conviction that California would soon slip from Mexico's grasp and wanted to make sure that the United States rather than Great Britain came away with that prize. Polk was not prepared to wage war on Mexico, however, for negotiations with Britain over Oregon had yet to produce a settlement on that front. It still appeared possible that California might be acquired peacefully through purchase. Frémont thus had to tread carefully when he entered

---

27. Abert in Frémont, *Expeditions*, 1:395–97, 422.
28. Frémont, *Memoirs*, 423.
29. James K. Polk, *Polk: The Diary of a President, 1845–1849, Covering the Mexican War, the Acquisition of Oregon, and the Conquest of California and the Southwest*, 19.

California until he knew whether his nation and Mexico were at war. "For me," he wrote, "no distinct course or definite instruction could be laid down, but the probabilities were made known to me as well as what to do when they became facts."[30]

In early December Frémont crossed the Sierra through Donner Pass with fifteen men, having sent the remainder with Talbot and Joseph Walker on a southward loop through Walker Pass. Frémont and his party moved quickly through the mountains, which were not yet clogged by snow, and reached Sutter's Fort on December 10. Sutter was away at the time, leaving Bidwell in charge. As Bidwell recalled, Frémont "at once made known to me his wants," including sixteen mules to haul provisions to the larger party that he had sent off with Talbot and Walker. When Bidwell replied that he had no mules to sell, only horses, which would not serve as well as pack animals, Frémont "became reticent, and, saying something in a low tone to Kit Carson, rose and left without saying good-day." Hoping to make clear that "we were always glad of the arrival of Americans, and especially of one in authority," Bidwell visited Frémont's camp and was told by him "in a very formal manner, that he was the officer of one government, and Sutter the officer of another; that difficulties existed between those governments; and hence his inference that I, representing Sutter, was not willing to accommodate him."[31]

If Frémont thought that Sutter and Bidwell were holding out on him, he soon learned otherwise. "A few days sufficed to purchase some animals and a small drove of cattle, with other needed supplies," he related. Yet this simmering rivalry between two empire-builders—one seeking to preserve his own domain here and the other intent on expanding America's turf—would soon boil over. Sutter later traced their dispute to Frémont's first visit to the fort in 1844, when the explorer accused several men in his party of theft. As magistrate there, Sutter tried the accused and found them not guilty. He later hired one of those men, Samuel Neal,

---

30. Frémont, *Memoirs*, 423; Frémont, *Expeditions*, 2:4.
31. Bidwell, *In California before the Gold Rush*, 93–94.

after Frémont dismissed them. Frémont claimed that they were "discharged with their own consent" and said nothing of their being accused or tried.[32] That may have been a courtesy to Neal, who aided him when he returned to California. Or perhaps Frémont did not care to admit that Sutter as a Mexican official had asserted legal authority over him and his men.

Since Frémont's first visit, Sutter's stature in California had declined as a result of his botched attempt in early 1845 to secure victory for embattled Governor Micheltorena against rebels opposing him, led by former Governor Alvarado and Commandant José Castro. That uprising ousted the last man sent by Mexico to rule Californios and left them isolated from their motherland as Frémont and other expansive Americans descended on their country. Micheltorena's career in California had gotten off to a dismal start in late 1842 when he failed to respond forcefully to the seizure of Monterey by Commodore Jones. But that did not rankle Californios as much as the presence in their homeland of Micheltorena's three hundred or so *cholos*: unruly soldiers who received little or no pay and supported themselves by stealing chickens, among other offenses. Micheltorena's opponents may have exaggerated the misdeeds of those troops and overlooked the governor's efforts to restrain them. Antonio Coronel, a veteran of the 1834 Híjar-Padrés expedition who served as a judge in cases involving the *cholos*, recalled that Micheltorena punished severely those convicted of crimes and "lamented his precarious situation: abandoned by the central government, struggling with the depravity of the troops given him."[33]

However serious their offenses, those *cholos* were poor soldiers, impoverished and ill-trained. Their presence served as a painful reminder to Californios that they could expect little help from authorities in Mexico City, who sent Micheltorena to protect and defend them without giving him the means to do so. As *hijos del país* (sons of the country, meaning natives of California), Alvarado

---

32. Frémont, *Memoirs*, 353, 442; Hurtado, *John Sutter*, 128–29, 164–68.
33. Coronel, *Tales of Mexican California*, 27.

and Castro attracted more support from its disgruntled inhabitants than the outsider Micheltorena did and agreed to recognize his authority only after he promised in late 1844 to exile his *cholos*.

If Micheltorena ever intended to honor that pact, he abandoned his pledge after receiving assurances from Sutter, who was recruiting settlers and Indians in the vicinity of his fort to fight for the governor. In return, Sutter sought concessions from Micheltorena that would help him escape debt and act as an *empresario* like Stephen Austin of Texas, luring more settlers to his domain with promises of land. Some Americans enlisted to fight for Micheltorena hoping to obtain land grants from Sutter without becoming Mexican citizens. Others, like Isaac Graham, joined up because they resented Alvarado and Castro for arresting them as suspect foreigners in 1840. When Charles Weber, a German-born settler who arrived with the Bidwell-Bartleson party and settled among Californios in San José, tried to dissuade foreigners from enlisting at Sutter's Fort to fight for Micheltorena, he was seized and placed in irons there.

By January 1845 Sutter had mustered about one hundred foreign riflemen, many of them Americans, along with a comparable force of Indian warriors and an artillery battalion. Among the American recruits were Dr. John Townsend and twenty other members of an emigrant party led by Elisha Stevens. They had arrived at Sutter's Fort in December after hauling wagons through Donner Pass and leaving those vehicles, the first ever to cross the mountains, in a snowbound camp on the western slope of the Sierra along with the rest of their company, including women, children, and two men. Now those stragglers had to fend for themselves while Townsend and others went off campaigning with Sutter. He persuaded them that they would not be secure in California if Alvarado and Castro prevailed over Micheltorena and that a relief expedition to the Sierra in midwinter would be impractical. James Clyman, a mountain man from Virginia who had arrived there by way of Oregon, described Townsend in his journal as a man "much attached to his own oppinions as likiwise to the climate and country of California."³⁴ Townsend's wife and others stranded at the camp were in no position to enjoy California's climate. Not until late that winter would they be sought out by men of their party and brought down safely. Like other early emigrant companies, this was a fragile association of self-reliant pioneers whose own concerns or convictions sometimes took precedence over their obligations to one another.

Alvarado and Castro responded to Sutter's impressive recruitment effort by accusing Micheltorena of making common cause with marauding Indians and mercenary "adventurers from the United States . . . a most infamous proceeding for a Mexican general."³⁵ Those charges hit home when Alvarado and Castro sought support in Los Angeles, where fear of Indian attacks ran high and both Californios and foreign settlers looked askance at malcontents like Isaac Graham, who seemed unwilling to adapt to their adopted country. Several prominent Anglos in the Los Angeles area with Mexican wives and Mexican citizenship—including John Rowland, who had recently obtained a hefty land grant from Alvarado—joined Pío Pico and other Angeleños in siding with Alvarado and Castro and worked to dissuade foreigners in Micheltorena's camp from continuing their campaign.

Like many civil disputes in Mexican California, where men were reluctant to shed the blood of opponents, who were often relations or acquaintances, this one was resolved without carnage. As Agustín Janssens noted, Castro honored Alvarado as his *compadre* (close friend and confidant) but also recognized Micheltorena, who had helped advance Castro's military career, as his *padrino* (patron or godfather). He told Janssens that "he owed many favors to the general [Micheltorena] and that he would do everything possible to avoid having any conflict with his forces."³⁶ When the two sides converged in February at Cahuenga Pass, they exchanged cannonfire, killing a few horses, and engaged in maneuvers. Micheltorena's

---

34. James Clyman, *Journal of a Mountain Man*, 204; Bancroft, *History of California*, 5:751; Stewart, *California Trail*, 73–80.
35. Alvarado and Castro in Bancroft, *History of California*, 4:489.
36. Janssens, *Life and Adventures*, 120–21.

forces, depleted as foreign riflemen drifted away, were incapable of pressing forward and taking Los Angeles. Raising a white flag, Micheltorena parleyed with his foes and agreed to step down, leaving Pico as governor in Los Angeles, which emerged briefly as capital of California. Castro remained the military chief in Monterey, which retained the customs house, giving Castro and his compadre Alvarado a financial advantage over Pico.

The collapse of Micheltorena's campaign was mortifying for Sutter—who feared for his life but was pardoned by his foes—and for foreigners who enlisted with him. It was now clear to Americans who wished to remain in California without bowing to Mexico that they could not achieve that end by backing Sutter or any other representative of a government they disdained. They could do so only by defying that government. Frémont's return to California with riflemen in late 1845 gave those inclined to rebel against Mexico hope that the United States might support them in that enterprise. Frémont was aware of the "probabilities" or prospects for war between his nation and Mexico. His actions in the months ahead encouraged American resistance to Mexican authority in California in advance of a formal declaration of war.

Edging toward Conflict

Frémont's overriding concern when he left Sutter's Fort in mid-December of 1845 was to link up with Talbot and Walker's party in the San Joaquín Valley and reunite his company. Their appointed rendezvous was the Kings River, but Talbot and Walker were waiting mistakenly on what Frémont dubbed the Kern River in honor of expedition artist and cartographer Edward Kern. So Frémont returned to Sutter's Fort in mid-January of 1846, trusting that they would eventually show up. He then requested a passport from Sutter to visit Monterey. His purpose, he stated in his memoirs, was to seek permission to "bring my party into the settlements in order to refit and obtain the supplies that had now become necessary. All the camp equipment, the clothes of the men and their saddles and horse gear, were either used up or badly in want of repair." Supplies were somewhat limited at Sutter's Fort that winter, according to Bidwell. But visiting Monterey had another advantage for Frémont, allowing him to confer with U.S. consul Larkin, who had the latest reports from Washington and Mexico City and might be able to clarify Frémont's ambiguous position in California as an explorer engaged in a supposedly peaceful survey with an armed party that he later described as well suited for frontier warfare. After traveling by boat down the Sacramento River to San Francisco Bay and spending a few days at Yerba Buena, Frémont reached Monterey on January 27 "and went directly to the house of our consul, Mr. Larkin."[37]

Larkin would soon receive a letter from Secretary of State James Buchanan appointing him "confidential agent" for President Polk and instructing him to assure leading Californios that if they declared independence from Mexico and desired "to unite their destiny with ours, they would be received as brethren."[38] Larkin believed that California might indeed secede from Mexico of its own accord and seek union with the United States, as Texas had. When Frémont arrived, Larkin had no indication that war with Mexico was imminent or inevitable and tried to allay concerns raised in Monterey by the appearance of an American officer seeking supplies for sixty men. He accompanied Frémont when he called on Commandant General José Castro, former governor Alvarado, and other officials there. Frémont told them that he was "engaged in surveying the nearest route from the United States to the Pacific Ocean," that the objectives of his survey were scientific and commercial, and that his men were "citizens and not soldiers." He claimed in his memoirs that the permission he sought—to bring his men "into the settlements" to obtain supplies—was "readily granted."[39] But that assertion, made long after the event, contradicted earlier testimony in which he stated that he came to Monterey to purchase supplies and was granted leave

---

37. Frémont, *Memoirs*, 454; Frémont, *Expeditions*, 2:63–64, 111.
38. Buchanan in Hague and Langum, *Thomas O. Larkin*, 114.
39. Frémont, *Memoirs*, 454.

there by authorities to winter with his men in the San Joaquín Valley, where there were "no inhabitants to be molested by our presence."[40] That statement was largely consistent with a message Castro sent to the minister of war in Mexico City in early March, in which he stated that Frémont asked only for "permission to procure provisions for his men, whom he had left in the mountains, which was given him."[41]

After leaving Monterey, Frémont set up camp near San José, where Talbot and Walker's party, having learned of his whereabouts, joined him and the rest of his men in mid-February. Later that month a local resident complained to the alcalde in San José that he had been rudely treated by Frémont while trying to retrieve animals from the American camp that he claimed had been stolen from him. Frémont responded in writing that it could be proven "on oath by thirty men here present" that the animals in question had been with them since they left the United States. The man who claimed that they were stolen from him was ordered to leave the camp at once and "should have been well satisfied to escape without a severe horse-whipping," Frémont added. "You will readily understand that my duties will not permit me to appear before the magistrates of your towns on the complaint of every straggling vagabond who may chance to visit my camp."[42]

Master of all he surveyed, Frémont felt free to do as he wished and go where he pleased in California, regardless of any restrictions that officials there might place on him or any assurances that he may have given them. Larkin told officials in Monterey that Frémont would depart for Oregon as soon as he obtained supplies for his party. Yet when Frémont broke camp in late February, he headed instead toward Monterey. He claimed that he was "resuming the work of the expedition," but was that venture strictly scientific or was it now governed largely by military concerns?[43] The most likely explanation for Frémont's provocative

---
40. Frémont in Bancroft, *History of California*, 5:5 n. 4.
41. Castro in ibid., 5:11.
42. Frémont, *Expeditions*, 2:68–70.
43. Ibid., 70; Frémont, *Memoirs*, 456.

move is that he wanted to be close to the capital, where news of war might soon arrive by ship, giving him an important part to play in the conquest. That he aspired to such a role was obvious to one acquaintance, William Leidesdorff, U.S. vice-consul in Yerba Buena. When informed later that hostilities were imminent, he wrote that it was "Glorious news for Capt Freemont."[44]

In early March Frémont camped in the Salinas Valley at the ranch of William Hartnell, less than twenty-five miles from Monterey, and sent a message to Larkin, asking for "any intelligence you may have received from the States" and indicating that he would be not be heading north any time soon. "The spring promises to be a glorious one," he wrote, "and a month or two will pass quickly and usefully among the flowers while we are waiting on the season for our operations in the north."[45] As a naturalist, Frémont welcomed the opportunity to collect spring flowers, but why an intrepid explorer who had recently crossed the Sierra with his men in midwinter had to wait until April or May to begin a trek to Oregon was left unexplained. When José Castro learned of Frémont's presence nearby, he informed him by letter on March 5 that he and his men had violated Mexican law by entering the settlements and must "immediately retire beyond the limits of this same Department such being the orders of the supreme Government."[46] Castro's view was that Frémont and his men were acting not as citizens but as soldiers with hostile intent. As if to confirm that conclusion, Frémont spurned Castro's order and took up a defensive position with his men atop Gavilán Peak, overlooking the Salinas Valley, where he built a log fort and raised the American flag. Warned by Larkin on March 8 that Castro might soon challenge him with two hundred or more troops, Frémont wrote back the next day, pledging defiance: "I am making myself as strong as possible, in the intention that if we are unjustly attacked we will fight to extremity and refuse quarter . . . if we are hemmed in and assaulted here we will die every man of us under the Flag of our country."[47]

---

44. Leidesdorff in Harlow, *California Conquered*, 80.
45. Frémont, *Expeditions*, 2:73.
46. Castro in ibid., 2:75.
47. Frémont in ibid., 81–82; Frémont, *Memoirs*, 463.

Frémont's words echoed those of Texas revolutionary William Barret Travis, who as Mexican troops surrounded the Alamo in 1836 wrote memorably: "*I shall never surrender or retreat* . . . I am determined to sustain myself as long as possible & die like a soldier who never forgets what is due to his own honor & that of his country—*Victory or Death.*"[48] In the end, however, Frémont chose not to stage a sacrificial Texas-style uprising and acted instead in the cautious tradition of California revolutionaries, whose deeds were seldom as drastic as their words. During their rebellion against Micheltorena, for example, Alvarado and Castro had vowed that "we will shed our blood rather than permit our country to endure this infamous oppression."[49] Yet when challenged by Micheltorena's troops, they had avoided confrontation until they gained enough strength to overawe their opponent and win a bloodless victory. Men vying for power in Mexican California typically hesitated to take costly actions that might further reduce the small number of troops at their command and cause them to be censured by higher authorities with whom they were out of touch. Frémont operated under similar constraints, and Larkin's warning that armed conflict between his men and Castro's forces "may cause trouble hereafter to Resident Americans" served to remind the ambitious young captain of the political risks of waging unauthorized war.[50]

On the evening of March 9 Frémont retreated with his men, citing as an "indication for us to move" an ominous accident in camp, where the flagpole had fallen to the ground.[51] It was a poor excuse for backing down, and Joseph Walker abandoned Frémont's party in disgust. Others remained with their leader, however, and found various ways of rationalizing the withdrawal in later years. Thomas Martin recalled that he and the others "were getting ready to go down in the night and surprise Castro at the San Juan Mission" when Frémont supposedly received a dispatch from Larkin

---

48. Travis in William C. Davis, *Three Roads to the Alamo: The Lives and Fortunes of David Crockett, James Bowie, and William Barret Travis*, 541.
49. Alvarado and Castro in Bancroft, *History of California*, 4:489–90.
50. Larkin in Frémont, *Expeditions of John Charles Frémont*, 2:79.
51. Frémont, *Memoirs*, 460; Chaffin, *Pathfinder*, 287.

instructing him to withdraw, which was not the case.[52] Kit Carson insisted that Castro not Frémont was the one who lost heart: "We remained in our position on the mountain for three days, and became tired of waiting for the attack of the valiant Mexican General."[53] Frémont himself presented a brave front in a letter to his wife. "The Spaniards were somewhat rude and inhospitable below, and ordered us out of the country, after having given me permission to winter there," he wrote from the vicinity of Sutter's Fort on April 1. "My sense of duty did not permit me to fight them, but we retired slowly and growlingly before a force of three or four hundred men, and three pieces of artillery."[54]

Settlers in the Sacramento Valley evidently agreed that Frémont had given Castro a good scare before pulling back "slowly and growlingly" like a grizzly, the notoriously combative creature that would soon serve as a totem for American rebels there. As Frémont headed north up the valley toward Oregon—"disgusted with everything belonging to the Mexicans," he assured Jessie, and eager to leave this country behind—settlers appealed to him to lead an uprising that would bring California into the American camp.[55] This request he "peremptorily refused," according to settler William Hargrave.[56] But Frémont was more obliging to another group of settlers who reached him at the ranch of the Danish-born pioneer Peter Lassen in April and sought his support against Indians who were reportedly gathering to attack them. He declined, saying that he had no right to fight Indians, according to Martin, but agreed to discharge those in his company who wished to aid the settlers "and take us again afterwards."[57] Many of Frémont's men volunteered for this expedition, which targeted a nearby encampment of Indians who may or may not have had hostile intentions. "We found them to be in great force," Carson

---

52. Thomas S. Martin, *With Frémont to California and the Southwest, 1845–1849*, 6–7.
53. Carson, *Kit Carson's Autobiography*, 94.
54. Frémont, *Memoirs*, 460–61.
55. Frémont, *Expeditions*, 2:129–30.
56. William Hargrave in Chaffin, *Pathfinder*, 294.
57. Martin, *With Frémont to California*, 7.

related. "We attacked them, and although I do not know how many we killed, it was a perfect butchery."[58]

Frémont claimed credit for this punitive expedition in his memoirs, calling it a "rude but necessary measure to prevent injury to the whites."[59] In what may have been a deliberate distortion, he placed the attack later in 1846, after the inception of the Bear Flag Revolt, and referred to alleged efforts by Castro and other Mexican authorities to incite Indians against foreign settlers. That accusation was often leveled by Bear Flag rebels to justify their insurrection, but their troubles with Indians in the Sacramento Valley had begun earlier and stemmed from the growing presence of Americans in the region. Many of them had been at odds with Indians before reaching California and made little distinction between peaceful bands and those who subsisted by raiding ranches and stealing horses. Frémont thought that the attack his men took part in helped suppress Indian hostilities, but such punitive assaults often had the opposite effect by increasing tribal resistance and prolonging conflict. The American conquest of California that he helped instigate meant war on Indians as well as Mexicans, and that brutal Indian war would continue long after annexation in 1848.

By early May Frémont had crossed into Oregon and reached Upper Klamath Lake. By his own account, he was glad to be done with Mexican California and back in familiar country, which he had explored before and helped attach to the United States. (In June Congress would ratify a treaty with Great Britain, recognizing Oregon as American territory below the forty-ninth parallel.) Frémont looked forward to entering the Cascade Range and surveying its snow-capped peaks. "No one had penetrated their recesses to know what they contained, and no one had climbed to their summits," he wrote; "and there remained the great attraction of mystery in going into unknown places—the unknown lands of which I had dreamed when I began this life of frontier travel." He

---

58. Carson, *Kit Carson's Autobiography*, 95.
59. Frémont, *Memoirs*, 502–503, 516–17; Chaffin, *Pathfinder*, 291.

was deflected from that inviting prospect by the arrival of messages from Washington, delivered to him on May 9 by Lieutenant Archibald Gillespie of the U.S. Marines. "How fate pursues a man!" wrote Frémont, who felt compelled after conferring with Gillespie to abandon his preferred role as an explorer and fulfill "my duty as an officer of the American Army," supplied with "authoritative knowledge that the Government intended to take California."[60]

Here as elsewhere in his memoirs, Frémont shaded the truth to counter accusations that he was a reckless adventurer, who exceeded his orders and invited hostilities. In fact, he had been in no hurry to leave California, where he appeared eager to play a military role. What Gillespie conveyed to him were not clear-cut orders to that effect but messages indicating that war with Mexico was imminent and giving him cause to resume what he had been doing for several months—asserting America's proprietary interest in California by his presence there with armed men. Gillespie had sailed to Monterey by way of Veracruz, carrying letters for Frémont from Senator Benton and Secretary Buchanan. Before reaching Frémont, Gillespie was informed that the U.S. Navy was preparing for hostile action along the Mexican coast. Word that Mexico and the United States had commenced hostilities would not reach California until July, but Frémont grasped the import of Gillespie's messages. "I saw the way opening clear before me," he wrote. "War with Mexico was inevitable; and a grand opportunity now presented itself to realize in their fullest extent the far-sighted views of Senator Benton, and make the Pacific Ocean the western boundary of the United States."[61]

These were not the words of a man who turned to conquest reluctantly when fate caught up with him in the person of Lieutenant Gillespie, carrying orders from superiors. Frémont had long been charting a path for conquest by infiltrating Mexican territory and defying Mexican officials. Like Jedediah Smith and other Americans who overcame the geographical barriers shielding Mexican

---

60. Frémont, *Memoirs*, 486–88.
61. Ibid., 490.

California from invasion, he harbored ambitions as an explorer that were inextricably linked to his national pride and his determination to further American expansion. Although political leaders in Washington like Polk and Benton encouraged and abetted this movement, it was instigated on the frontier by traders, trappers, sailors, smugglers, and impulsive officers like Commodore Jones and Captain Frémont who did not require explicit instructions to cross boundaries and raise their flag on foreign ground. Frémont's venturesome band of citizen soldiers epitomized the spontaneous nature of American expansion, spearheaded by companies who learned to fight not by drilling in military camps but by clashing with Indians on trade routes and emigrant trails. As Frémont wrote in tribute to Kit Carson and others in his party who would join him now as conquistadors in California, they "constituted a formidable nucleus for frontier warfare, and many of them commanded the confidence of the emigration."[62] Indeed, Frémont and his men emboldened emigrants to follow in their subversive path and pursue a takeover scheme led not by distant politicians but by defiant frontiersmen who refused to remain within limits set by authorities at home or abroad.

---

62. Ibid.

CHAPTER 13

The Bear Flag Revolt

Like other settlers who took part in the American conquest of California, William Ide saw himself not as an aggressor but as an aggrieved victim. The fears and resentments that led him and his confederates to rise up against Mexican authorities had deep historical roots among frontier Americans, who had long dreaded conspiracies between hostile Indians and rival powers such as France, Britain, or Spain. For Ide, born in 1796 in Massachusetts, where memories of the French and Indian War and other colonial struggles remained fresh, that defensive frontier mentality was reinforced as he and others journeyed westward to California. They were quick to credit rumors that Mexican officials there were inciting Indians to drive them from their homes. Viewing themselves as innocent victims of "injustice, tyranny and theft," in Ide's words, they defied authorities who had in fact done much to accommodate incoming Americans over the years and joined Frémont in a rebellion that some of their own compatriots considered unwise, unwarranted, and unjust.[1]

Ide maintained that he and others who reached California overland on the eve of the Mexican War had purely peaceful intentions

---

1. William Ide in Simeon Ide, *A Biographical Sketch of the Life of William B. Ide*, 104. (This edition includes William Ide's account of the Bear Flag Revolt.)

and were "unstained even by the blood of the untaught savage."[2] In truth, the party of emigrants to which Ide and his family belonged had spilled blood on several occasions as they ventured to California in 1845. They were guided by mountain man Caleb Greenwood, who served as an agent for Sutter and encouraged emigrants bound for Oregon to try instead for California. As one member of the party, Benjamin Bonney, recalled, Greenwood met them at Fort Hall, where the emerging California Trail diverged from the Oregon Trail, and promised that Sutter would help them "over the mountains with their wagons" and grant them land near his fort.[3] (In fact, those who were not Mexican citizens were now prohibited from settling in California.) Greenwood also claimed that there was no danger from Indians along the California Trail, although Paiutes and other tribal groups often targeted the livestock of emigrant parties and sometimes responded forcefully when threatened.

Ide's party included several men of violent disposition, including Caleb Greenwood's son John, who was half-Sioux. Ide's daughter Sarah recalled how John Greenwood "shot down an Indian by the road-side, and afterwards boasted of it."[4] No less provocative was a Texan named Sam Kinney, who captured an Indian during the journey and took him as a slave. After being collared and whipped, that captive escaped, carrying news of the white man's affront to others of his tribe. A third member of this troublesome company later poisoned a steer that had been killed near camp by Indian raiders, "so that should they eat the meat, it would be the cause of their death." Afterward, noted emigrant Jacob Snyder in his diary, an Indian approached the spot, "walked cautiously around the steer that lay dead," and was in the act of retreating when he was shot by men of the company waiting in ambush. "When the ball struck him he wheeled & ran for the bushes," Snyder related. "He must have been severely wounded judging from the traces of blood."[5] All this was done by pioneers who according to Ide were unstained by blood.

---

2. Ibid., 106.
3. Bonney in Stewart, *The California Trail*, 91.
4. Sarah Ide in Ide, *Biographical Sketch*, 35; Stewart, *The California Trail*, 94–97.
5. Jacob R. Snyder, "Diary," 252; Stewart, *The California Trail*, 97–98.

Few emigrants sought trouble with Indians, but once trouble arose through the reckless deeds of men like Sam Kinney and John Greenwood or raids by warriors who targeted their animals, companies united against their tribal foes in fear and loathing. The effect of such encounters on emigrants was to reinforce feelings of vulnerability and victimization that persisted even when they were in little danger from Indians or substantially stronger than them. That siege mentality carried over into California and left rebels like Ide convinced of the righteousness of their cause as they acted in presumed self-defense against Mexican authorities who were not nearly as powerful or pernicious as they were made out to be. In the opinion of mountain man James Clyman, who reached California in 1845, the government here was too "weak imbecile and poorly organized" to exercise much control over its own citizens or police the incoming foreigners, whom he described as a "poor discontented set of inhabitants" with little cause for complaint. Clyman thought they were fortunate to live under such a "free and easy" government, one that exacted from them no taxes, labor, or service: "In every respect the people live free."[6]

Most Americans who arrived overland resented Mexican officials, however, and refused to bow to them. This stance posed a dilemma for Sutter, whose allegiance to Mexico conflicted with his commercial interest in promoting foreign settlement. He sold supplies to Ide's company and other parties arriving from the United States. And though he could not legally grant land to American citizens, he did nothing to stop them from building cabins and raising crops in the area, hoping that their efforts would improve his trade and raise the value of his property, thus bailing him out of his financial difficulties. As his chief clerk John Bidwell recalled, Sutter "found himself immensely—almost hopelessly—involved in debt" and struggled to satisfy his creditors, notably the Russian American Company, to which he owed payment in the form of large shipments of wheat after purchasing Fort Ross.[7] In late 1845 Sutter proposed selling his entire estate of New Helvetia to

---

6. Clyman, *Journal of a Mountain Man*, 215.
7. Bidwell, *In California before the Gold Rush*, 64.

the Mexican government for $100,000, but nothing came of that. By early 1846 the increasing presence of self-reliant and sometimes unruly settlers near his fort was beginning to worry him. "Some of the foreigners in the Valley are committing depredations," he wrote John Marsh, "and I have no force to prevent them from so doing."[8] Sutter heard that two thousand Mexican troops would soon arrive in California and hoped that they would help restore order. In fact, several hundred additional troops had been assigned to California, but before they embarked they were caught up in a revolution that brought Mariano Paredes to power. He took a defiant stand against the United States as war loomed but failed to secure California against subversion and invasion.

Sutter may have regretted luring to this country Americans who now seemed beyond his control, but he only encouraged American resistance by claiming in May 1846 that José Castro was inciting Indians to attack him and settlers living near his fort. As Sutter put it, Castro's aim was to "revolutionize all the Indians against me" and induce them "to Kill all the foreigners, burn their houses and Wheat fields etc."[9] Word of this plot came from a Miwok Indian chief, who told Sutter that he had learned of Castro's intentions while visiting San José. A short time later, Sutter and Indians loyal to him were menaced by warriors of a rival tribe. He took that as confirmation that Castro—whom he had opposed during the rebellion that ousted Governor Micheltorena in 1845—was indeed out to destroy him and the foreigners he harbored. Sutter's charges ran counter to Castro's recent actions, however. Despite receiving orders from Mexico City to prevent Americans who arrived overland from settling in California, Castro had "deemed it best, to permit them to remain, provisionally, in the department." To most Californios, raids by Indians of the interior were more to be feared than intrusions by land-hungry Americans, whose parties were often "composed of families and industrious people," as Castro acknowledged.[10] To incite a bloody uprising that might

---

8. Sutter in Hurtado, *John Sutter*, 168; Bancroft, *History of California*, 4:448–49, 527–29, 608–16.
9. Sutter in Owens, *John Sutter and a Wider West*, 16; Hurtado, *John Sutter*, 191–93.
10. Castro in Bancroft, *History of California*, 4:606.

embolden those Indians would have been playing with fire and out of character for a calculating officer like Castro, who seldom took unnecessary risks.

By the time Frémont reversed course in late May and returned to California with his riflemen, many Americans living near Sutter's Fort or Mariano Vallejo's outpost at Sonoma feared that Castro intended to drive them from the country. His grim reputation among Americans went back to 1840, when he and his troops had arrested Isaac Graham and other suspect foreigners. More recently, Castro had foiled Americans recruited by Sutter to fight for Governor Micheltorena and forced Frémont to retreat from Gavilán Peak near Monterey. Americans who mistakenly believed that Castro had earlier invited Frémont and his company to go where they pleased considered this an act of treachery. Sutter's accusations against Castro heightened the anxieties of newcomers who lived on isolated homesteads. A few provocateurs may have spread alarming stories about Castro that they knew to be false, but other Americans truly believed that they would soon be targets of a Mexican and Indian war. As Richard Owens of Frémont's company testified: "When we returned to the valley we found the people expecting an attack from the Californians, and in fear of an outbreak among Indians, which they expected every hour. The report was, and it was generally believed, that Castro had instigated the Indians to rise and burn the crops of the settlers."[11]

American traders residing in Monterey and other coastal settlements had a better understanding of Castro's situation and intentions. But they had little contact or influence with settlers in the interior such as William Ide, who distrusted those assimilated Yankees and accused them of conspiring with the corrupt Mexican elite. "They had, in many instances, intermarried and become associated with the native citizens, and enjoyed their common advantages," he wrote. "Indeed, a portion of them had become the merchants and financiers of the country; and thus failed not, in the genuine spirit of Yankeedom, to direct and profit by those political impositions . . . by which, during ten years of increasing

---

11. Owens in U.S. Senate, *California Claims*, 38.

Monterey, California, ca. 1846, by Joseph Warren Revere, from *A Tour of Duty in California* (1849). *Courtesy Library of Congress, Prints and Photographs Division* (LC-USZ62-63153).

distress and ruin, the main body of the people were made *miserably poor.*"[12] This facile judgment by a newcomer who knew little of California's history overlooked the fact that this country had grown less impoverished since Spanish colonial times as families of modest origins acquired land and profited from their dealings with foreign merchants who sojourned or settled there. One well-informed foreigner, U.S. consul Thomas Larkin, believed that intermarriage and trade between Californios and Anglos had created an opportunistic new society whose leaders might soon seek further advancement by severing ties with troubled Mexico and inviting annexation by the United States or another foreign power.

Leading figures were contemplating that option, as indicated by reports of a meeting held in Monterey in late March or early April involving José Castro, Mariano Vallejo, and other prominent Californios and foreign residents. By one account, Castro startled those in attendance by blasting his mother country for failing to provide for California's defense. "How greatly to be pitied is the

---

12. William Ide in Ide, *Biographical Sketch*, 107.

condition to which Mexico has reduced us!" he declared, suggesting in conclusion that California would be better off under the protection of Catholic France.[13] Others in attendance reportedly favored Britain, while Vallejo argued that annexation by the United States was not just inevitable but desirable. "In contemplating this consummation of our destiny, I feel nothing but pleasure, and ask you to share it," he remarked according to an account written by Lieutenant Joseph Warren Revere of the U.S. Navy. Revere arrived in Monterey that spring aboard the sloop *Cyane* and learned of the meeting from a participant. "Why should we shrink from incorporating ourselves with the happiest and freest nation in the world, destined soon to be the most wealthy and powerful?" Vallejo declared, according to Revere. "Why should we go abroad for protection when this great nation is our adjoining neighbor?"[14]

Those were not Vallejo's exact words, but he himself later used similar terms when recounting this speech in his memoirs and may have served as Revere's informant. What Revere did not tell his American readers—who were no doubt flattered by the speech—is that Vallejo reached this conclusion only after determining that the American influx could not be stopped. He had warned his superiors that settlers were streaming in from the United States at a "frightful" rate and urged them to send troops and take other measures to regulate immigration.[15] When Mexico failed to act, Vallejo evidently concluded that it could not hold California much longer and that as a neighboring republic the United States had more to offer California than the distant British or French monarchies. He and Castro, his successor as commandant general, speculated on California's future under another flag, but they did not subvert Mexico or aid its enemies. Castro sought to deter armed incursions by foreigners like Frémont's company. Yet his limited military resources and reliance on trade with foreigners for revenue were strong incentives for him not to provoke American settlers and drive them into an alliance with Frémont.

---

13. Castro in Miller, *Juan Alvarado*, 115–16.
14. Joseph Revere, *Naval Duty in California*, 23; Bancroft, *History of California*, 5:59–63.
15. Vallejo in Rosenus, *General Vallejo*, 78.

All this was lost on isolated newcomers like Ide, who harked back to the Black Legend of Elizabethan times by portraying Castro and others in authority as sinister Spaniards. Ide asserted that a proclamation issued by the "Spaniards" on April 30 threatened him and others "with extermination."[16] In fact, this decree simply affirmed the existing policy that foreigners who were "not naturalized and legally introduced" to the country could not acquire land there and that squatters could be expelled "whenever the Government may find it convenient."[17] Settlers' fears of deportation or "extermination" were heightened in early June when Castro called for volunteers to join him in camp at Santa Clara, near San José. His ostensible purpose was to repel Frémont, whose return to California "appeared equivalent to a declaration of war," in the words of Frémont's aide Edward Kern.[18] But this show of force may also have been intended to overawe Castro's political rival in Los Angeles, Governor Pío Pico.

Settlers in the interior, however, assumed that Castro was preparing to attack them. As Ide recalled, greatly exaggerating the number of troops at Castro's disposal: "Six hundred armed men were known to be foaming out vengeance against a few foreigners."[19] Thomas Knight, who arrived with Ide's party and settled in the Napa Valley, heard reports that "the Spaniards were going to rise, and were coming over from the south side of the bay to kill us all. That was the common rumor. The Spaniards who were living about us denied this; they were friendly."[20] Such assurances failed to calm Americans who had no legal right to settle there and feared retribution. When Castro went to Sonoma with a dozen or so men to obtain horses from Vallejo for his troops, rumor transformed that party into a horde of Mexican cossacks, bent on terrorizing settlers, who looked to Frémont for protection. On

---

16. William Ide in Ide, *Biographical Sketch*, 139.
17. Proclamation by Manuel Castro, prefect of Monterey, in Frémont, *Memoirs*, 503.
18. Kern in Oscar Lewis, ed., *California in 1846, Described in Letters from Thomas O. Larkin, "The Farthest West," E. M. Kern, and "Justice,"* 45; Bancroft, *History of California*, 5:51–53.
19. William Ide in Ide, *Biographical Sketch*, 111.
20. Thomas Knight, "Statement of Early Events in California," Bancroft Library, 7.

June 8, Ide related, he and others received this unsigned message: "Notice is hereby given, that a large party of armed Spaniards on horseback, amounting to 250 men, have been seen on their way to the Sacramento valley, destroying the crops, burning the houses, and driving off the cattle. Capt Freemont invites every freeman in the valley to come to his camp... and he hopes to stay the enemy."[21]

If Ide reproduced this note exactly—and elsewhere in his account Frémont's name is spelled correctly—then this summons probably did not come directly from Frémont, as Ide suspected. William Hensley, who arrived in California overland in 1843, later testified before Congress that he and Samuel Neal, who left Frémont's company at Sutter's Fort early in 1844, gave notice to all Americans in the Sacramento Valley in June 1846 "to meet together and take measures for our common safety. Captain Frémont's camp was appointed the place of meeting."[22] Ide believed that Frémont withheld his signature from the message summoning "freemen" to his camp because he did not want to take legal responsibility for the ensuing conflict. But Hensley and Neal may well have issued the notice without consulting Frémont, hoping that he would yield to pressure from distraught settlers as they flocked to his camp and be drawn into a fight with Castro.

Not all American settlers in the area answered that summons or sympathized with the incipient Bear Flag Revolt. Among those who held back was Charles Brown, a New Yorker who came to California aboard a whaler in 1833 and "took French leave," as he put it, when his ship anchored in San Francisco Bay. After serving as a handyman at Mission San Rafael, he converted to Catholicism, married a Mexican woman, and pursued various trades around the Napa Valley, where he gained a grudging respect for the power of Mariano Vallejo. "His will was law, and no one dared gainsay it," Brown recalled. He campaigned against hostile Indians with Vallejo and his ally Chief Solano, who appalled Brown by slaying a pregnant woman and her child during an attack on a tribal village

---

21. Quoted in Ide, *Biographical Sketch*, 112–13.
22. Hensley in U.S. Senate, *California Claims*, 34.

but earned his lasting gratitude in that same fight by rescuing him after he was pierced by several arrows and healing his wounds with herbal medicine. Such ordeals—and the soothing rituals of baptism and marriage—initiated Brown into this frontier society and gave him closer ties to Californios than to incoming Americans who refused to assimilate. Not even the shock of being arrested as a suspect foreigner during the Graham Affair in 1840 and held in shackles in Monterey for two weeks before being released severed his attachment to his adopted country and kin. "That was the only time the Californians failed to treat me kindly," he recalled.[23] When the Bear Flag Revolt loomed and disgruntled American settlers invited Brown to join their cause, he refused to take sides, incurring their hostility and the scorn of Frémont's men in the ensuing contest.

Frémont was reluctant to start that fight, for he did not yet know whether the United States and Mexico were at war. But he told Ide and others who reached his camp near Sutter's Fort that he would back the rebels if Castro initiated hostilities or was provoked by settlers into striking the first blow. Ide dismissed this as a "plan for neutral conquest" and criticized Frémont for refusing to allow Kit Carson and others to resign from his company so that "they might be at liberty to join us."[24] Carson, for his part, stated that he and others in that company joined the fight against Castro only after Frémont learned "positively that war had been declared."[25]

Frémont claimed credit for the Bear Flag Revolt afterward and implied that he was calling the shots from the start. He may not have instigated the uprising, which began on June 10 with a dawn raid on soldiers driving horses from Sonoma to Castro's camp at Santa Clara. But he took charge of the rebellion less than a week after it began—long before he knew that war had been declared—and overshadowed Ide, who saw himself as champion of the cause and resented the renown that Frémont gained as the conqueror of California. Among Frémont's motives for backing the revolt was

---

23. Charles Brown, "Early Events in California," Bancroft Library, 8–17.
24. William Ide in Ide, *Biographical Sketch*, 114, 117.
25. Carson, *Kit Carson's Autobiography*, 105.

one that he shared with the disgruntled settlers: antipathy toward Castro, who had embarrassed him by forcing him to retreat from Gavilán Peak. "I cannot, consistently with my own feelings and respect for the national character of the duty in which I am engaged, permit a repetition of the recent insults we have received from Genl. Castro," he wrote in June. "If therefore, any hostile movements are made in this direction, I will most assuredly meet or anticipate them."[26] Castro's actions were insulting only if one accepts Fremont's premise that his own actions earlier in the year were in no way provocative. Like Ide, Frémont acted as if he and other Americans had every right to intrude on California, violate its laws, and defy those who tried to bring them under Mexican authority.

Seizing Sonoma

The rebels with whom Frémont cast his lot were a varied bunch. "Some were good men," recalled John Bidwell, "and some about as rough specimens of humanity as it would be possible to find anywhere." Among the roughest of those customers was Ezekiel Merritt, who led the horse raid on June 10. "He was an old mountaineer and trapper," Bidwell observed, "lived with an Indian squaw, and went clad in buckskin." Merritt was inordinately fond of liquor, Bidwell added, "chewed tobacco to a disgusting excess, and stammered badly. He had a reputation for bravery because of his continual boasting of his prowess in killing Indians."[27] A member of the overland party that entered California with Joseph Walker in 1833, Merritt later settled in the Napa Valley. In 1844 he and other future Bear Flaggers, including Granville Swift and Benjamin Kelsey (who arrived with the Bidwell-Bartleson party in 1841 along with his brother Andrew and was known to be hot-tempered), were accused of aiding Dr. Edward Bale, a British physician at Sonoma who fired shots at Mariano Vallejo's brother Salvador. Bale later reconciled with Salvador Vallejo, to whom he was related by marriage. But Merritt continued to bear a grudge

---

26. Frémont, *Expeditions*, 2:152, 182; Chaffin, *Pathfinder*, 315–23.
27. Bidwell, *In California before the Gold Rush*, 107.

against the Vallejos and blamed them for the 1846 decree stating that settlers who were not Mexican citizens were subject to expulsion. Emigrant Patrick McChristian claimed that he and Merritt were among some twenty Americans summoned to Sonoma after that order was issued and advised by Mariano Vallejo to "leave the country immediately, without horses, arms or cattle." Afterward, McChristian added, "we talked the matter over with 'stuttering' Merritt . . . and concluded we might as well die in California as to go to the mountains without arms, horses and cattle."[28]

McChristian may have erred in his recollections. Vallejo had been generous to American settlers, giving them "much work and employment," as Thomas Larkin reported, and "always speaking in their favour."[29] In portraying him as a callous enforcer of a cruel order, McChristian was likely influenced by Merritt, who emerged as the leader of an extreme faction within the Bear Flag party that tarred Mariano Vallejo with the same brush as Castro and viewed the gracious Vallejo residence at Sonoma as an enemy stronghold. Soon after conducting the horse raid—and reportedly sending word to Castro, if he wanted the horses back, "to come and get them if he was a man"—Merritt led a larger party to Sonoma on his own authority, arriving there around dawn on June 14.[30] Sonoma, a frontier garrison once closely guarded by Mexican troops and Indian auxiliaries loyal to Mariano Vallejo and Chief Solano, was now undefended. Although Vallejo was still honored as a general, he had disbanded his forces, entrusting the defense of the region to Castro. He had little fear that Americans would turn against him. His sister Rosalía was married to American-born trader Jacob Leese, a naturalized Mexican citizen who lived with his wife and children in an adobe building on the plaza not far from Vallejo's imposing two-story Casa Grande.

Roused at dawn by a neighbor who told her that "ragged desperados had surrounded General Vallejo's house," Rosalía Vallejo

---

28. Patrick McChristian, "Statement of Patrick McChristian," Bancroft Library, 114; Rosenus, *General Vallejo*, 76, 249 n. 22.
29. Larkin, *Larkin Papers*, 4:331; Rosenus, *General Vallejo*, 99.
30. Kern in Lewis, *California in 1846*, 46.

emerged from her adobe to see the general's French-born secretary, Víctor Prudón, rushing to the aid of Salvador Vallejo, who was being threatened by a "ruffian named Benjamin Kelsey." Only Prudón's intervention, she reckoned, saved Salvador from being murdered. His situation may not have been as desperate as that, but he exchanged harsh words with his captors. He might indeed have come to harm had hotheads like Merritt and Kelsey not been restrained by cooler confederates, including Robert Semple, a towering figure from Kentucky who struck Rosalía as "more humane than the rest of that godforsaken bunch."[31] The wild appearance of the raiders, many of them wearing buckskin and some without shirts or shoes, made them dreadful to her and others in town and caused Mariano Vallejo to refer to them afterward as "White Indians."[32] Patrick McChristian, who took part in this raid, recalled that "the Californian women residing in Sonoma were very much frightened at our untidy appearance" and feared that they would be murdered or mistreated.[33] Rosalía Vallejo never forgave the raiders or their countrymen, declaring to an interviewer in 1874: "Those hateful men instilled so much hate in me for the people of their race that, even though twenty-eight years have gone by since then, I still cannot forget the insults they heaped upon me." She would have nothing to do with those who seized her home and country and "refused to learn their language."[34]

Mariano Vallejo, who had avoided direct involvement in earlier disputes involving Californios and foreigners such as the Graham Affair and the ouster of Micheltorena, did his best to calm the excitable rebels and prevent violence. "To what happy circumstances shall I attribute the visit of so many exalted personages?" he inquired magisterially as Merritt and others barged into his parlor.[35] Californios had long used hospitality to appease potentially troublesome foreigners, and Vallejo did the same by offering these

---

31. Rosalía Vallejo in Beebe and Senkewicz, *Testimonios*, 25–26.
32. Mariano Vallejo in Rosenus, *General Vallejo*, 110; Bancroft, *History of California*, 5:109–19.
33. McChristian, "Statement," 116.
34. Rosalía Vallejo in Beebe and Senkewicz, *Testimonios*, 29.
35. Mariano Vallejo in Rosenus, *General Vallejo*, 110.

intruders brandy and engaging them in talks, with Leese serving as mediator. Waiting outside with other rebels as the talks dragged on, Ide grew impatient and entered the parlor, only to find that Vallejo's antagonists had become his "merry companions . . . The bottles had well nigh vanquished the captors."[36] By humoring the intruders, Vallejo had secured favorable terms. In exchange for agreeing not to take up arms against the rebels, he and his associates in Sonoma were to remain safely at home.

This deal dismayed those rebels who were not party to the talks and expected to seize captives and booty. They had earlier elected John Grigsby, a more respectable figure than Merritt, to serve as their chief negotiator; but he was under the false impression that Frémont had ordered this raid and resigned when he learned otherwise. That left the rebels in chaos, and some were inclined to back out. Into the breach stepped Ide, who vowed to continue the fight alone, if necessary, and liberate California single-handedly. "*I can go to the Spaniards, and make* FREEMEN *of them,*" he declared by his own account, ignoring the fact that Mexicans had won freedom from Spain a quarter-century earlier. Elected captain, Ide composed a declaration of independence as bombastic as any proclamation ever issued by Spanish or Mexican propagandists, pledging defiance to the "military despotism" of Castro and his confederates, who had "shamefully oppressed and ruined the laboring and producing inhabitants of California."[37] He and his followers then raised a rebel flag produced by William Todd (a nephew of Mary Todd Lincoln) and others, featuring a rough likeness of a grizzly bear beneath a lone star reminiscent of the revolt in Texas.

Ide claimed credit for preventing his Bears from plundering Sonoma in keeping with the agreement negotiated with Vallejo. But he did not stop his men from nullifying that deal by taking as captives Mariano and Salvador Vallejo as well as Víctor Prudón and Jacob Leese, who offered to serve as interpreter for the others and ended up in jail along with them. Leese's assurances that

---

36. William Ide in Ide, *Biographical Sketch*, 124–25.
37. Ibid., 127, 138–39.

General Mariano Vallejo.
Courtesy The Bancroft Library, University of California, Berkeley (California Faces: Selections from The Bancroft Library Portrait Collection).

Mariano Vallejo sympathized with Americans were unavailing, as was his plea that the rebels not make off with two fine horses belonging to his children. One raider replied bluntly: "We go in for good horses."[38]

Frémont Takes Charge

Ide would soon be eclipsed as leader of the uprising by Frémont, who took charge of the prisoners and confined them at Sutter's Fort. He arrived there on June 19 and promptly asserted his authority. According to Bidwell, Frémont addressed Sutter as a "Mexican" and said that if he did not like what they were doing, "he would set him across the San Joaquín River and he could go and join the Mexicans." Tearful and agitated, Sutter swallowed his pride and deferred to Frémont, "because he thought him to be acting in accordance with instructions from Washington." Frémont soon

---
38. Quoted in Rosenus, *General Vallejo*, 116.

removed Vallejo and the other prisoners from the care of Sutter's employee Bidwell, who tried to make the captives "as comfortable as possible" in return for past favors that Mariano Vallejo had done him and other settlers.[39] Henceforth they would be guarded by the brash young American Edward Kern, whom Frémont placed in charge of Sutter's Fort. Kern considered Mexicans trustworthy only when in the presence of someone they feared. "Beat them and they will love you," he wrote in response to an assault by Mexicans in June that left two Americans dead, "treat them well and they'll kill you."[40] Kern did not in fact beat Vallejo and the other captives, but he brought their tolerable confinement under Bidwell and Sutter to an abrupt and demeaning end. The hardest thing to bear, Salvador Vallejo recalled, was to hear his jailer refer to them repeatedly as "damned greasers."[41] Jacob Leese sent a message to Frémont offering the captain his services as an American by birth who did not want it said that he opposed his native country. But Frémont disdained those like Sutter and Leese who had pledged allegiance to Mexico, and Leese remained in jail with the others.

Frémont wrote in his memoirs that he lent his full weight to the insurgency because he felt it would be "unsafe to leave events to mature under unfriendly, or mistaken, direction. I decided that it was for me rather to govern events than to be governed by them."[42] Yet some of his own men proved more provocative and unruly than the Bears in the days ahead. While Frémont camped near Sutter's Fort, gathering recruits for an anticipated showdown with Castro, Ide remained in charge of the rebels at Sonoma and sent out parties that clashed with Mexican forces. The sharpest fighting occurred on June 24, when Bears led by Henry Ford—who had trained as a dragoon (mounted infantryman) at Carlisle Barracks in Pennsylvania before deserting in 1842 and starting life anew in California—surprised troops commanded by Lieutenant Joaquín de la Torre. Ford's party killed one man, wounded two others, and made off

---

39. Bidwell, *In California before the Gold Rush*, 100–102.
40. Kern in Lewis, *California in 1846*, 48.
41. Salvador Vallejo in Bancroft, *History of California*, 5:125 n. 3; Rosenus, *General Vallejo*, 142.
42. Frémont, *Memoirs*, 520.

with several captives. "We have whipped them," he told Ide, "and that without receiving a scratch."[43] Ford and his men felt that they had settled a score with their opponents, who had captured several Americans in recent days. Two of them were later found dead in the incident referred to by Kern, with their bodies reportedly mutilated. While Ford fought conventionally, men under Frémont avenged the deaths of those Americans in brutal frontier fashion.

On June 25 Frémont reached Sonoma with his forces and joined the campaign against Castro. Three days later his scouts spotted three Mexicans disembarking from a small boat on the north shore of San Pablo Bay. "Captain, shall I take those men prisoners?" Kit Carson asked Frémont, according to Jasper O'Farrell, an Irish-born settler residing in the area. "I have got no room for prisoners," Frémont reportedly replied. A short time later the three men were shot dead. O'Farrell said that Carson regretted shooting them and told him that this "was not the only brutal act he was compelled to commit" under Frémont's command.[44] Another member of the company, Alexander Godey, claimed that Carson and others shot the men when they resisted arrest. Frémont, for his part, attributed the deed to his scouts, "mainly Delawares," acting impulsively in retaliation for the killing of the Americans.[45] Two of the victims, Francisco and Ramón de Haro, were carrying a message from Castro to Lieutenant Torre. The third man, José de los Reyes Berreyesa, had accompanied them in the hope of securing the release of his son, held captive by the Bears.

Charles Brown, who later married Rosalía de Haro, sister of the ill-fated Francisco and Ramón, declared that their father "never ceased brooding over the sad fate of his beloved sons" until 1848, when death "put an end to his suffering." Brown cursed their assailants as "fiends of hell," who richly deserved "punishment at the hands of man, instead of which, I dare say, some have received honors."[46] Whether or not Frémont ordered the killings, he bore

---

43. Ford quoted by William Ide in Ide, *Biographical Sketch*, 173.
44. O'Farrell in Sabin, *Kit Carson Days*, 1:480.
45. Frémont, *Memoirs*, 525; Sabin, *Kit Carson Days*, 1:478–84; Chaffin, *Pathfinder*, 330–32.
46. Brown, "Early Events in California," 25–26.

responsibility for them by committing to this uprising men who were accustomed to taking such reprisals. His irregulars were more dangerous and disruptive than the Bears, in this instance, and made this unlicensed conquest of California even more of a frontier war, subject to the harsh conventions of Indian fighting.

Frémont began to govern events in California only when the rebellion he furthered was subsumed within a conventional military occupation, launched by American naval forces in July. Critics of Frémont and the Bears would later argue that their insurgency contributed nothing to the American takeover and only complicated that task by alienating Californios, who might otherwise have been more receptive to annexation. By subordinating Sutter, however, and subduing Mariano Vallejo—who remained in jail with his fellow captives until August—Frémont and his confederates neutralized those two guardians of the California interior and left Mexico powerless there. Together, Frémont's recruits and the Bears at Sonoma formed a larger and better-armed force than the 160 or so men under Castro, who in late June withdrew the contingents that he had sent out under Torre and other officers and conceded the country north and east of San Francisco Bay to the rebellious Americans. Those insurgents indeed offended Californios, but so did regular American officers like Commodore Robert Stockton and Lieutenant Archibald Gillespie, who later seized Los Angeles, triggering violent opposition to American rule in southern California while the north remained relatively quiet.

Both the Bear Flag rebellion in June and the official American occupation that began in July were products of the same expansionist impulse. The Mexican War stemmed from an American-led settlers' rebellion in Texas that was not unlike the uprising in California a decade later. From that rebellion came an independent Texas whose annexation by the United States in 1845 inflamed Mexican-American relations and set the stage for conflict. Opponents of the Mexican War such as Illinois congressman Abraham Lincoln did not deny that settlers in Texas had real grievances against Mexican authorities. Indeed, Lincoln argued that "any people anywhere, being inclined and having the power, have the *right* to rise up, and shake off the existing government, and form a new one that suits them better." But that did not give Polk or others in power the right to join with rebels like those who took Texas in defying Mexico and seizing its territory, which Lincoln feared would be used to extend slavery westward from Texas. "I more than suspect," he said of Polk, "that he is deeply conscious of being in the wrong,—that he feels the blood of this war, like the blood of Abel, is crying to Heaven against him."[47] Critics like Lincoln came to view the annexation of Texas and other Mexican territories—which heightened tensions between North and South and led ultimately to disunion—not as a triumph but as a tragedy visited on a nation haunted by its original sin of slavery, which the founders embedded in the Constitution, dividing future generations of Americans as bitterly as Cain and Abel.

Whether praised or damned for leading the nation to war, Polk and his aides did not deserve all the credit or blame. They did not succeed in expanding their country dramatically at Mexico's expense simply by issuing orders. The task required men of action on distant frontiers who shared the administration's goals and were prepared to act on their own initiative to achieve those objectives—officers such as Frémont and Captain John Montgomery of the sloop-of-war *Portsmouth*, who sailed into San Francisco Bay and offered Frémont unquestioning support by letter on June 3, more than a month before news of the Mexican War reached California. Without asking him to define his mission there, Montgomery promised to do what he could "to aid & facilitate your operations."[48] Despite contrary assurances to Mexican authorities, Montgomery sent arms and ammunition to Frémont, further enhancing the prospects for an uprising that was not prompted by the American government but was in keeping with its aims as hopes for peaceful annexation were dashed and war loomed. Frémont's defiant return to California and Montgomery's presence

---

47. Lincoln in Carl Sandburg, *Abraham Lincoln: The Prairie Years and the War Years*, 95–96.
48. Montgomery in Frémont, *Expeditions*, 2:143.

suggested to the Bear Flag rebels that their government would countenance hostile action against Mexico. Since revolutionary times, the impetus for expansion had come from restless pioneers on the frontier, whose cause was embraced by higher authorities and translated into policy. That policy was then implemented and augmented by officers raised on the frontier, like Andrew Jackson, or imbued with the self-reliant spirit of the frontier, like Frémont and Montgomery.

Fittingly, the Bears raised their last hurrah on the Fourth of July, which they celebrated at Sonoma with dancing and feasting. On the following day Ide stepped down as their leader in deference to Frémont, who took command of the rebels and became *Oso Número Uno* (Bear No. 1), an ironic designation for a man who did as much as anyone to impose American rule and anglicize California. Having not been present at the creation of the Sonoma republic, he chose "to annul and wipe out all that had been done up to the 5th of July," in Ide's words, by launching the movement anew.[49] "California was declared independent," Frémont wrote, "the country put under martial law, the force organized and officers elected."[50] On July 10 he learned from Montgomery that hostilities had commenced between the United States and Mexico and that Commodore John Sloat, commanding the Pacific Squadron, had seized Monterey. With that, Frémont's volunteers ceased to be rebels and became occupiers, licensed to steal California from Mexico under the rules of war.

---

49. William Ide in Ide, *Biographical Sketch*, 205.
50. Frémont, *Memoirs*, 546.

CHAPTER 14

Occupation and Resistance

Commodore John Sloat was a reluctant conqueror. Unlike Frémont, who intervened militarily in California on his own authority, Sloat had orders as commander of the Pacific Squadron from navy secretary George Bancroft to blockade or occupy California's ports "in the event of actual hostilities."[1] When he left Mazatlán for Monterey in early June 1846, Sloat knew of the recent clashes between American and Mexican forces along the disputed Texas border and did not have to await confirmation that war had been declared before taking action. Yet after anchoring in Monterey harbor on July 2, he sent an officer ashore to tender the usual civilities to Mexican authorities by offering to salute their flag. They replied that they would be unable to return the salute for lack of ammunition, suggesting that they were in no position to resist if Sloat chose to occupy the town. Officers of the squadron were surprised "that the commodore should have tendered these civilities," remarked John Wilson, a midshipman on Sloat's flagship, *Savannah*, for they knew that the U.S. Navy was "blockading the coast of Mexico on the Gulf."[2] That night Sloat sent a note to U.S. consul Thomas

---
1. George Bancroft in Harlow, *California Conquered*, 117; Bancroft, *History of California*, 5:195.
2. Wilson in U.S. Senate, *California Claims*, 40–41.

Larkin in Monterey offering no hint that this was anything other than a friendly visit. His men had not been ashore for months, and he wanted to give them twenty-four hours of liberty in town: "They may (as you know sailors will) make some noise in the place but they will not do any harm."[3]

Sloat's reluctance to act forcefully may have been due in part to fear of repeating the gaffe committed in 1842 by Commodore Jones when he seized Monterey on the mistaken assumption that the United States and Mexico were at war. Sloat was sixty-eight and had recently asked to be relieved of command because of ill health. He did not want to end his career on a sour note and did not anticipate that proceeding cautiously would earn him a reprimand from Secretary Bancroft, who wrote that Sloat's "anxiety not to do wrong" had lulled him into "a most unfortunate and unwarranted inactivity."[4] Yet that inactivity also stemmed from contradictions in the policy and professions of President Polk and his aides, who portrayed their militant, expansionist agenda as benign and protective. Sloat found himself in an ambiguous position: while his orders freed him to take offensive action in California he was still expected "to preserve if possible the most friendly relations with the inhabitants" and encourage them "to adopt a course of neutrality."[5] Larkin was acting under instructions to encourage Californios to declare independence and invite annexation by the United States. His efforts were undermined by the Bear Flag Revolt, but as late as July 4 he was still "dreaming of trying to persuade the Californians to call on the Commodore for protection, hoist his Flag & be his Countryman, or the Bear may destroy them."[6] The dream that California would fall freely and fairly into America's lap died hard, and Sloat might be excused for holding fire while Larkin and his superiors continued to tout this as a friendly takeover.

When Sloat learned of the Bear Flag Revolt and of the involvement in that uprising of Captain Frémont of the Topographical

---

3. Sloat in Larkin, *Larkin Papers*, 5:96.
4. George Bancroft in Bancroft, *History of California*, 5:205.
5. George Bancroft in ibid., 5:195; Harlow, *California Conquered*, 117–21.
6. Larkin, *Larkin Papers*, 5:102.

Corps, Captain Montgomery of the Navy, and Lieutenant Gillespie of the Marine Corps, he realized that Americans were engaged in actual hostilities in California and felt compelled to occupy Monterey. "We must take the place!" he told Larkin on July 6. "I shall be blamed for doing too little or too much—I prefer the latter."[7] The next day he issued a proclamation to the people of California, assuring them that he was about to "hoist the standard of the United States" at Monterey and "carry it throughout California" not as their enemy but as "their best friend, as henceforward California will be a portion of the United States, and its peaceable inhabitants will enjoy the same rights and privileges as the Citizens of any other portion of that Nation."[8] This assertion that raising the flag transformed Mexicans into Americans was presumptuous and premature while the war was ongoing and the fate of California and other occupied territory remained unresolved. But Sloat was simply echoing the official line in Washington, where the administration hoped to sustain the illusion that this act of war was amicable and to pacify the inhabitants without committing large numbers of troops, who were needed elsewhere to defeat Mexico and force it to accept vast territorial losses.

Sloat tried to conciliate Californios by ordering his men to refrain from plunder and "avoid that eternal disgrace which would be attached to our names and our Country's name by indignity offered to a single female."[9] His men evidently heeded those orders and made a better impression on townspeople than did Frémont's rowdy recruits when they entered Monterey on Sunday, July 19. "The soldiers who came ashore behaved very well," recalled Dorotea Valdez of Monterey. "But the riffraff who came later with Captain Frémont acted more like thieves than soldiers ... his men stole horses, saddles, *aguardiente*, and anything else they could lay their hands on."[10]

---

7. Sloat quoted by Larkin in Bancroft, *History of California*, 5:228 n. 6; Harlow, *California Conquered*, 122.
8. Sloat in Larkin, *Larkin Papers*, 5:105–106.
9. Sloat in ibid., 5:108.
10. Valdez in Beebe and Senkewicz, *Testimonios*, 40–41.

Californios viewed Frémont as an intruder and provocateur, and the menacing aspect of his men as they rode into town did nothing to alter that assessment. "A vast cloud of dust appeared first, and thence in long file emerged this wildest wild party," recalled a British observer, Lieutenant Frederick Walpole. Frémont led the way, followed by "five Delaware Indians, who were his bodyguard," Walpole added. "The rest, many of them blacker than the Indians, rode two and two, the rifle held by one hand across the pommel of the saddle." Frémont allowed his men no liquor in camp, but they took liberties in Monterey and passed a few days there in "drunkenness and debauchery."[11] Many in Monterey may have felt as Mariano Vallejo did when the Bear Flag rebels he called "White Indians" raided Sonoma. Frémont's intent was not hostile, but his unwelcome presence undermined Sloat's efforts to reassure the inhabitants and reminded them that this occupation was indeed an act of war, placing them at the mercy of Americans who brought to California not only democratic ideals conceived when they threw off British imperial rule but also a defiant frontier mentality acquired as they extended their own empire westward at the expense of Indians, Spaniards, Mexicans, and others.

Frémont's free-wheeling frontier ways were not to the liking of the cautious Sloat, who was shocked when the captain declared that in backing the Bear Flag Revolt he had acted on his own responsibility "and without any expressed authority from the Government to justify hostilities."[12] Sloat had invited Commandant General José Castro and Governor Pío Pico to come in for talks, but Frémont's hostile actions left little room for them to adopt a "course of neutrality." In mid-July Sloat prepared to relinquish command of the Pacific Squadron to the recently arrived Commodore Robert Stockton, whose view of California was shaped by Frémont, Gillespie, and the Bear Flag rebels, whose cause those two officers embraced. In a letter to Secretary Bancroft, Gillespie portrayed Castro as a fiend bent on "horrible bloodshed and rapine" who set

---

11. Walpole in Bancroft, *History of California*, 5:248–49 n. 39.
12. Frémont in Chaffin, *Pathfinder*, 342.

Indians against American settlers and promised his "miserable soldiery the ravishing of the women, and the destruction of the children." After a tense interview with a skeptical Sloat, Gillespie conferred with Stockton and found him anxiously awaiting the opportunity to take command and bring "to an early conclusion, the operations, which he was pleased to say, had been so happily commenced in the North by Cap't Frémont and myself."[13] Their influence on Stockton was evident in an abrasive proclamation that he issued on July 29 after succeeding Sloat, in which he accused Castro of pursuing Frémont and his men "with wicked intent" and promised to put an end to the "lawless depredations daily committed by Gen. Castro's men." He ordered the people of California "to remain quiet at their respective homes and stations." Those who dared "abandon their dwellings" or caused injury in defiance of his authority would be "treated as enemies, and suffer accordingly."[14]

The hard line taken by Stockton and adopted later by Gillespie, whom he placed in charge of occupied Los Angeles, contributed to a rebellion that began there in October and led to several deadly clashes between American and Mexican forces in California before the uprising ended in early 1847. But this was not a matter of a few overbearing American officers acting contrary to the interests or designs of their government. It was no accident that such men were on the scene in 1846 as President Polk sought to acquire California and war loomed as the means to that end. Much like Spanish authorities who sent soldiers as well as priests to colonize California as part of the so-called Sacred Expedition, officials in Washington anticipated that conversion would not be achieved there without some coercion. While continuing to portray their expansive mission as generous and redemptive, they put officers in place who would not wait idly for war orders from Washington to take California by force.

---

13. Archibald Gillespie, "Gillespie and the Conquest of California," 275–77; Harlow, *California Conquered*, 137–43.
14. Stockton in Bancroft, *History of California*, 5:255–56 n. 1.

The Roots of Resistance

The American occupation initially faced little opposition, leading some observers to conclude that Californios would soon be reconciled to their conquerors. Walter Colton, who arrived as chaplain aboard the U.S.S. *Congress* in Sloat's squadron, found them "more astounded than indignant, and quite as intent over problems of preservation as measures of resistance." Some in Monterey, recalling the abortive occupation of 1842, clung to the hope that "the American government would repudiate our possession of California, and order the squadron withdrawn." But when news arrived in August that war had been declared, Colton added, Mexican loyalists appeared "resigned to their fate," while others seemed ready to accept "almost any government that promises stability."[15]

Colton tried to provide stability by dispensing justice in an even-handed manner as alcalde of occupied Monterey, a position to which he was appointed by Stockton. As a Protestant clergyman new to California, however, he found himself at odds with long-established customs of the country. "Another bright and beautiful Sabbath has dawned; but there is little here to remind one of its sacredness," he noted in his journal on Sunday, October 11. "More liquors are retailed on this day than any other three. I have the power to close these shops, and shall do it."[16] In one case involving an Indian who lassoed a horse that did not belong to him and rode it to Monterey after his own mount gave out, Colton sentenced the accused to three months' labor—a draconian penalty in a country where travelers often borrowed loose horses in that manner. Colton's tendency to impose his own exacting standards did not bode well for those whose traditions and values conflicted with the precepts of their newly installed Anglo-American rulers.

Unlike the Bear Flag rebels and officers such as Gillespie who demonized Castro, Colton did not regard the commandant general as a serious threat. Castro was "an officer of high pretensions, but utterly deficient in strength and steadiness of purpose," Colton wrote. "His followers had gathered to him with as little discipline,

---

15. Walter Colton, *Three Years in California*, 13, 29.
16. Ibid., 71.

sobriety, and order, as would characterize a bear-hunt . . . It was the same thing to them whether their weapon was a rifle or a guitar,—whether they were going to a skirmish or a fandango." This dismissive view of Californios as men of action was similar to that of Richard Henry Dana, Jr., who portrayed their way of life as a pastoral idyll, given over to fiestas and siestas and devoid of any serious purpose or strenuous effort. California was so bountiful that even those who did not bother to plough and sow could reap wild oats in abundance, Colton claimed. "But where are the reapers? On horseback, galloping about and carousing at this rancho and that." He doubted that Castro and his "waltzing warriors" would hold out long against determined Yankees who understood that the struggle for California was no fandango. "The American engaged in this war puts his life on the die," Colton asserted. "He must prevail or perish."[17]

Not all Anglos disparaged Californios as warriors. Benjamin Wilson—known as Don Benito after he acquired Mexican citizenship and a Mexican wife and settled in the San Bernardino Valley, an area subject to Indian raids—rode with mixed parties of Americans and Californios in campaigns against their tribal foes and prized the services of his Hispanic allies. On one occasion, Wilson related, he wrote to his "old friend and companion Don Enrique Avila, to ask him if he would join me with ten picked men, and renew our campaign down the River Mojave. He answered that he would do so, *con mucho gusto.*" Overlanders like Wilson, who arrived in 1841 with the Rowland-Workman company, were renowned as riflemen, but few could match Californios at fighting from horseback, with the lance as their preferred weapon. Together, they formed a powerful combination against their Indian opponents, including refugees from the secularized missions. During his campaign with Avila, Wilson recalled, they surrounded a hostile village and kept up the attack "until every Indian man was slain."[18] The women and children were captured,

---
17. Ibid., 14–15, 93, 99.
18. Wilson, "Benjamin David Wilson's Observations," 94; Hafen and Hafen, *Old Spanish Trail*, 217–18.

he added, and taken to Mission San Gabriel. Other Indians seized in such raids ended up laboring for their captors in exchange for food, shelter, and clothing—an enduring form of servitude that some Americans in California readily adopted.

American observers often acknowledged the remarkable equestrian skills of Californios but slighted that expertise by implying as Colton did that they were at a loss when not in the saddle. The Californio's home is on horseback, wrote Colton: "Leave him this home, and you may have the rest of the world." In truth, horsemanship was the means by which Californios secured their world and defended it against challengers. The determined struggle they waged against American occupiers showed how attached they were to their home ground, but glib detractors like Colton dismissed the insurgents as rootless adventurers with no more stability or staying power than desert nomads. "They drift about like Arabs, stealing the horses on which they ride, and the cattle on which they subsist," he claimed. "Men of substance will regret their loss about as much as the Egyptians the disappearance of the locusts."[19]

A more discerning view of the Californios and their motives for resisting occupation came from an American resident of longer tenure there, Thomas Larkin. The sudden seizure of Monterey, Yerba Buena, and other settlements by U.S. forces, based "only on conjecture of War," left the inhabitants "highly exasperated," wrote Larkin to Secretary Buchanan, but their real hatred was reserved for the "adventurers who took Sonoma." The provocative actions of that Bear Party, "supposed to be put in motion by Messrs Frémont and Gillespie," had so alarmed Californios that their leaders would not come to terms. Larkin was baffled by the defiant proclamation issued by Stockton on July 29 and had no idea where the commodore "obtained the statements it contains."[20] But Larkin still hoped to resolve matters peacefully with Pico and Castro. To that end, he accompanied Stockton when he embarked from Monterey on August 1 with 360 men, destined for San Pedro,

---

19. Colton, *Three Years in California*, 38, 86.
20. Larkin, *Larkin Papers*, 5:146, 180–81.

from which he planned to march on Los Angeles. Stockton hoped to coordinate that advance with Frémont, whose battalion, now officially enlisted as U.S. troops, had sailed south in late July to occupy San Diego.

Pico and Castro, who had been at odds since overthrowing Governor Micheltorena a year earlier, failed to form an effective alliance against the Americans. Before he learned of the occupation, Pico as governor in Los Angeles was preparing to challenge Castro as commandant in Monterey, which remained the chief source of revenue for Mexican California through its customs house. "Things had come to such a point that I was convinced that Castro and I could not exist at the same time in the department and that one or the other had to go," Pico recalled. Informed by Castro that Monterey had fallen, Pico met with his rival on July 12 at Santa Margarita, near San Luis Obispo, where they "embraced in token of reconciliation" and vowed to defend their country. Pico's men "feared Castro was playing one of his intrigues," however, and the two parties marched separately to Los Angeles to defend the capital.[21] Although Pico called on all men from fifteen to sixty to take up arms and "defend the just cause," few heeded that summons.[22] Between them, Castro and Pico had only about two hundred poorly supplied troops to hold off the forces of Frémont and Stockton.

Larkin's hope of arranging an accord between Stockton and the leaders of Mexican California rested on two premises. One was that Stockton, who landed at San Pedro on August 6, would allow Pico and Castro to avoid the shame of surrendering California outright by declaring it independent before placing it under the protection of the United States. The other was that Abel Stearns, who had lived in Los Angeles for many years and was now a Mexican citizen, could use his influence with prominent Californios to induce them to come to terms with an officer whose forces had invaded their country. Stearns was in a precarious position, for he was serving both as

---
21. Pío Pico, *Don Pío Pico's Historical Narrative*, 130–31.
22. Proclamation of Pico in Bancroft, *History of California*, 5:263 n. 9.

an American agent in Los Angeles, having recently accepted Larkin's invitation to act as his "confidential correspondent" and further the interests of the United States, and as a Mexican official there.[23] Pico had such trust in Stearns that he left him in charge of Los Angeles as subprefect when he headed north to confront Castro.

By acting confidentially for Larkin, Stearns was behaving in a manner that some Mexicans might consider traitorous. But such divided loyalties were not uncommon among the elite in California, where trade and intermarriage had blurred the lines separating one nationality from another. Stearns was married to Arcadia Bandini, the daughter of Juan Bandini, a man who grew closer to Americans as California slipped from Mexico's grasp. When Pico invited Bandini to join the California assembly and help organize resistance to the American invaders, Bandini pleaded ill health and held back while assuring the governor that he remained loyal to Mexico. Yet when Frémont occupied San Diego a few weeks later, Bandini was there to welcome him with a fine horse as a gift. Like Stearns, Bandini saw nothing traitorous in easing the seemingly inevitable transition of his California homeland from Mexican to American rule.

Stearns's assignment from Larkin was to persuade Pico and others in authority that "the time for declaring California free and independent has come—and that under Com Stockton they proceed without delay to so declare the country."[24] That was no easy task, for a declaration of independence issued "under" Stockton and the threat of armed force would reduce California to an American dependency and expose its leaders to charges that they were colluding with Mexico's enemy. Pico would make no such deal and said that any truce would have to be negotiated with Castro as commandant. Whether at the urging of Stearns or of his own accord, Castro then wrote to Stockton asking for a suspension of hostilities as a prelude to talks. Stockton's blunt response left no room for negotiations. "I do not wish to war against California

---

23. Larkin in Doris Marion Wright, *A Yankee in Mexican California: Abel Stearns, 1798–1848*, 130–31; Harlow, *California Conquered*, 143–47.
24. Larkin, *Larkin Papers*, 5:185.

or her people," he wrote Castro; "but as she is a department of Mexico, I must war against her until she ceases to be a part of the Mexican territory." He would not recognize a declaration of independence by California unless Castro first agreed "to hoist the American flag in California."[25] Only then would Stockton halt his forces and negotiate a treaty. He would be faulted for precluding talks by handing Castro an ultimatum that he could not meet without dishonoring himself. But American forces were there to seize California, not liberate it; there was no point in pretending otherwise. Once force was applied and the occupation was underway, independence could not be freely declared or credibly maintained. A bogus treaty that spared Castro the shame of raising the Stars and Stripes while leaving a supposedly free California under American duress would have dishonored both sides.

Stockton reckoned that he could take Los Angeles without offering Castro any concessions, and events proved him right. Lacking the strength to withstand the American challenge, Castro disbanded his forces and fled California. Pico followed suit, leaving the path to Los Angeles open. Before departing, Pico gave Benjamin Wilson a message for the commodore, which Wilson recalled as follows: "You go to-morrow, meet Stockton, wherever he may be, *Y dele muchas saludes de mi parte* [and give him my best wishes], tell him of my intention to abandon the country, and that I hope he will not ill treat my people."[26] Wilson and John Rowland met Stockton as he advanced on Los Angeles and told him that Castro and Pico had cleared out. Stockton's march took on the air of a triumphal procession, with a military band leading the way. On August 13 he linked up at the outskirts of Los Angeles with Frémont, who described their entry into the capital as "having more the effect of a parade of home guards than of an enemy taking possession of a conquered town."[27]

A few days later Stockton received confirmation that the United States and Mexico were indeed at war and made plans to return to

---

25. Stockton in Bancroft, *History of California*, 5:269 n. 16.
26. Wilson, "Benjamin David Wilson's Observations," 103–104.
27. Frémont, *Memoirs*, 566; Chaffin, *Pathfinder*, 348.

naval duty with his squadron as soon as possible. Confident that California was secure, he aimed to move south along the coast and blockade Mexican ports. He also hoped that Frémont might muster enough troops among American settlers there to provide an expeditionary force that could land at Mazatlán or Acapulco and advance inland toward Mexico City. That was not to be, for few Americans recruited in California were willing to campaign beyond its bounds. Nonetheless, Stockton was intent on wrapping up his business soon and joining the fight for the Mexican heartland. In early September he placed Frémont in charge of California as commandant, with the promise that he would become governor there when military rule ended. Los Angeles fell under the jurisdiction of Lieutenant Gillespie, who was left to hold the town with forty-eight men detached from Frémont's battalion. By Gillespie's account, those men made a dismal impression on the townspeople, who viewed them in much the same light as the despised *cholos* who had been brought there as soldiers by Governor Micheltorena, ousted by rebellious Californios in 1845. "They were men unaccustomed to control," Gillespie said of his troops, "perfect drunkards whilst in this Ciudad of wine & Aguadiente, but serviceable Riflemen in the field. They were men for whom the Californians could have no respect, & whom, from the spirit of insubordination they constantly evinced, the Californians thought they could overcome."[28]

Gillespie made things worse by bearing down on the populace while his unruly soldiers did much as they pleased. Like Colton in Monterey, he served as magistrate and handed out stiff penalties for offenses that Californios considered minor, such as making off with stray animals. He "passed sentence according to his own whim," recalled Antonio Coronel, a liberal who had arrived with the Híjar-Padrés expedition in 1834 and felt that a military ruler had no business dispensing justice to civilians. Gillespie's "oppressive rules made him as popular as a toothache with the Angeleños," he added.[29] American settlers there with close ties

---

28. Gillespie, "Gillespie and the Conquest of California," 325.
29. Coronel, *Tales of Mexican California*, 34; Werner H. Marti, *Messenger of Destiny: The California Adventures, 1846–1847, of Archibald H. Gillespie, U.S. Marine Corps*, 84; Bancroft, *History of California*, 5:306–307 n. 19.

to Mexicans agreed that Gillespie's regime was "despotic and in every way unjustifiable," in Benjamin Wilson's words. "He had established very obnoxious regulations to annoy the people, and upon frivolous pretexts had the most respectable men in the community arrested and brought before him."[30]

Gillespie's actions and those of his ill-mannered troops made an uprising all but inevitable. But even well-led and well-disciplined soldiers would have been hard-pressed to maintain control, given the naïve assumption that underlay this campaign and some later interventions by U.S. troops abroad—the belief that American occupiers would be welcomed as friends and liberators, enabling a small force to secure a large area without facing serious resistance. Gillespie and his paltry contingent were responsible for maintaining order from Los Angeles south to the Baja California border. In mid-September he received a warning from American merchant Henry Delano Fitch that trouble was brewing in San Diego and sent a detachment there led by the former Bear Flag rebel Ezekiel Merritt. That left Gillespie with barely two dozen soldiers to control a town of more than a thousand people ill-disposed toward the occupiers.

The revolt began on September 23 with a predawn attack on Gillespie's quarters, repulsed by his riflemen. Foreigners in town then "rallied to my assistance," he wrote, giving him a "respectable force of 59 men."[31] Those gains were more than offset when hundreds of Angeleños joined the insurgency, which came under the leadership of José María Flores. Formerly Micheltorena's secretary, he remained loyal to Mexico—a sentiment shared by many Californios now that hopes for independence had been nullified by American occupation. Resistance was strongest around Los Angeles, home to a number of people like Flores and Coronel who came from elsewhere in Mexico and felt attached not just to California but to their nation at large. When Gillespie cracked down on those loyalists, many reacted as Coronel did when he heard that an order for his arrest had been issued: "I got out a pair

---
30. Wilson, "Benjamin David Wilson's Observations," 106.
31. Gillespie, "Gillespie and the Conquest of California," 326.

of pistols and a sword I had hidden and immediately mounted my horse."[32] He was ready to fight the invaders.

This uprising spelled trouble not just for Gillespie but for Benjamin Wilson and other American settlers in the San Bernardino Valley who had enlisted under Stockton to guard against incursions from the east by hostile Mexicans or Indians. Anticipating attack by the insurgents, those Americans gathered on September 26 at Rancho Chino, mistakenly believing that its owner, Isaac Williams, had plenty of ammunition. When they learned otherwise, Wilson urged that they flee to the mountains. But many of them were newcomers to this country who had a low opinion of the Californios' "courage and fighting qualities," Wilson recalled, "and seemed to be of the unanimous opinion that a few shots would suffice to scare away any number of them that should come to attack us."[33] For Williams, a naturalized Mexican citizen who had arrived with mountain man Ewing Young in the early 1830s, the clash that ensued was a family affair, pitting him against his brother-in-law, José del Carmen Lugo, who joined in a blistering attack on the ranch at dawn the next day. A few shots were not in fact enough to fend off the attackers, who hurdled fences on horseback and suffered casualties before setting fire to the ranch house and forcing the Americans holed up there to surrender. Lugo claimed credit for rescuing his nephew and two nieces from the flames and delivering them to their father, Williams. "I told him that he should thank me for saving his children," Lugo declared, "but neither he nor they gave me any signs of thanks afterward."[34]

On September 29 the outnumbered Gillespie agreed to abandon Los Angeles to the insurgents on condition that he and his men be allowed safe passage to San Pedro, where they were supposed to remain "only long enough to prepare for embarkation for Monterey."[35] Gillespie and other Americans heaped scorn on insurgents like Flores who had been captured earlier and paroled

---

32. Coronel, *Tales of Mexican California*, 35.
33. Wilson, "Benjamin David Wilson's Observations," 106.
34. Lugo, "Life of a Rancher," 204; Bancroft, *History of California*, 5:311–14; Harlow, *California Conquered*, 164–65.
35. Terms of capitulation in Marti, *Messenger of Destiny*, 82.

after pledging to refrain from further hostilities—vows they proceeded to break. Yet Gillespie was none too scrupulous in observing his own terms of surrender, to which he gave his word of honor. After reaching San Pedro, where he could have embarked on the merchant ship *Vandalia* within a few days, he stalled for nearly a week and fortified his position against attack until Sloat's former flagship, the *Savannah,* arrived from the north. The warship had been dispatched by Stockton when he learned of the uprising—news that caused him to postpone his planned departure with his squadron until he and Frémont could quell the uprising. Upon boarding the *Savannah* on October 6, Gillespie found Captain William Mervine determined to land his sailors and marines the next day and join Gillespie's men in retaking Los Angeles. Gillespie had learned not to underestimate his opponents, but Mervine expected an easy victory. He made "no preparations for carrying wounded," wrote Gillespie, "and scorned the idea of the necessity of taking a piece of artillery; indeed! he was without reason."[36]

On October 8 some two hundred Mexicans armed with a small cannon used for ceremonial purposes encountered more than three hundred Americans advancing under Mervine and Gillespie along the road from San Pedro. Led by José Antonio Carrillo, whose father had arrived there as a soldier with the first Spanish colonists in 1769, the insurgents used tactics well calculated to confound an overconfident and overeager foe. After each cannon shot fired, they pulled back, daring the impetuous Americans to follow. "Shot after shot told upon the Marines and Sailors with dreadful havoc," wrote Gillespie; "but on they charged, not one order was given to bring them into line, or get them from the road or save the loss of life." Instead, Mervine berated Gillespie's men for "taking advantage of obstacles and falling upon the ground to avoid the fire."[37]

Americans on embattled frontiers liked to think that they were braver than their Indian or Mexican foes and disparaged them for shrinking from cannonfire. "Nothing alarms the Californians so much as a piece of flying-artillery," wrote Walter Colton. "They

---

36. Gillespie, "Gillespie and the Conquest of California," 335.
37. Ibid., 337.

had rather see the very Evil One come scraggling over the hills."[38] As shown in this battle, however, a single antiquated four-pounder could wreak havoc among Americans when they did not have any artillery of their own to counter the threat. Gillespie faulted the bull-headed Mervine for exposing his men to those blasts, which left at least a dozen Americans dead or wounded and forced the invaders back to San Pedro, where they took refuge aboard the *Savannah*. Gillespie called it "one of the most disgraceful defeats our arms have ever sustained," which overstated the case but showed how deeply the pride of Americans had been wounded by this spirited challenge to their moral authority.[39]

Having prematurely declared his mission accomplished in California, Stockton now had to reconquer much of the territory. Defiant Californios chased a small detachment of American recruits from Santa Bárbara in early October, and Monterey too was considered vulnerable. "The success of the insurgents at the south has emboldened the reckless here," wrote Walter Colton, who slept with a rifle at his side and two pistols under his pillow, dreading an attack like that made on Americans during the Bear Flag Revolt in June: "I will not be taken, tortured, and hacked to pieces, as two of our countrymen were a few months since."[40] Those fears receded in late October when Frémont returned to Monterey with his men after a recruiting expedition in the Sacramento Valley. His plan now was to descend overland on Los Angeles while Stockton—who reached San Pedro aboard the *Congress* on October 25 and proceeded with the *Savannah* to San Diego on the October 30—approached the capital from the south.

Among the newcomers who enlisted to serve under Frémont was Edwin Bryant, a journalist from Kentucky who arrived with a company of overlanders at Sutter's Fort in late August and kept an informative journal that he later published. A day or two before reaching the fort, Bryant and company stopped at the ranch of

---

38. Colton, *Three Years in California*, 98.
39. Gillespie, "Gillespie and the Conquest of California," 339; Bancroft, *History of California*, 5:318–20; Harlow, *California Conquered*, 167–68.
40. Colton, *Three Years in California*, 73–74.

New Englander William Johnson and saw there a copy of the *Californian*, the territory's first newspaper, put out in Monterey by Colton and Robert Semple. The leading paragraph, Bryant noted, called on Californians to organize a "territorial government, with a view to immediate annexation to the United States," even as Mexican troops and insurgents were fighting to retain this country. Such bold assertions of American authority on embattled frontiers, commented Bryant, were "well calculated to excite the pride and vanity, if they do not always tally with the reason and judgment, of American citizens and republicans."[41]

At Sutter's Fort, Bryant and his companions found the former master of that place reduced to the status of a tenant. Sutter "came to the gate, and saluted us with much gentlemanly courtesy," Bryant observed. "He said that events had transpired in the country, which, to his deep regret, had so far deprived him of the control of his own property, that he did not feel authorized to invite us inside of the walls to remain."[42] Mariano Vallejo and others captured at Sonoma by the Bears and transferred there by Frémont in June had since been released; but the fort remained in the hands of American troops, commanded by 23-year-old Edward Kern. In a letter to his brother back in Philadelphia, Kern boasted that he was now a real "Commandante of a Fort, with power to do as I pleased and shoot people if they do not obey me, and all that sort of thing."[43] That power had once been Sutter's, but he now had to defer to Kern, who doled out rations to him and a stipend of fifty dollars a month. Kern became a prolific recruiter for Frémont. Nearly one-third of the troops that Frémont led south from Monterey in November enlisted at Sutter's Fort, demonstrating the extent to which Sutter's personal empire had been subsumed within the American empire.

Although Bryant was among those recruits and believed that California would flourish under American rule, he did not

---

41. Bryant, *What I Saw in California*, 244; Bancroft, *History of California*, 4:694.
42. Ibid., 247.
43. Kern in Robert V. Hine, *In the Shadow of Frémont: Edward Kern and the Art of Exploration, 1845–1860*, 31, 38–41.

disparage his Mexican opponents and their cause, referring at one point to their "insurrections, if resistance against invasion can properly be so called." The prevailing view among recent American settlers, however, was voiced by crusty old Caleb Greenwood, who had guided William Ide and other emigrants to California in 1845 as an agent for Sutter. "These black-skinned Spaniards have rebel'd again," he told Bryant. "Wall, they can make a fuss, d——m 'em, and have revolutions every year, but they can't fight... They won't stand an' fight like men."[44] Settlers who expressed similar views to Benjamin Wilson had been disabused of those notions when Californios defeated them at Rancho Chino in September. But many of Frémont's recruits had yet to learn the same lesson. In mid-November insurgents led by Manuel Castro, the former prefect in Monterey, advanced on Mission San Juan Bautista. It now served as a garrison for men of Frémont's battalion, who had commandeered hundreds of horses from Californios. Before reaching that objective, Castro's troops seized Consul Thomas Larkin, who helped finance and supply American naval forces and was on his way to visit his wife and ailing child at Yerba Buena. Ordered to write a letter luring the Americans into an ambush, Larkin refused, and his captors took him along as a hostage as they advanced.

On November 16, near Rancho La Natividad, the insurgents collided with Americans who had learned of their approach and come out from San Juan Bautista to meet them. Although lightly armed in comparison to their foes, Castro's men put up a hard fight, feigning flight before turning on their pursuers. "I was in view of the action," Larkin wrote his wife. "One side was my Countrymen, on the other those who I had known and traded with over twelve years—a fall of either appeard sad and disagreable to me." At one point, a Californio who saw a relative of his fall wounded ran at Larkin with a pistol in hand, shouting that "this man caused it all." But no harm came to the consul, who was later released.[45] For an indecisive battle involving fifty Americans and a somewhat larger number of Mexicans, the

---

44. Greenwood in Bryant, *What I Saw in California*, 355–56, 416.
45. Larkin, *Larkin Papers*, 5:310; Bancroft, *History of California*, 5:363–72; Harlow, *California Conquered*, 196–97; Bryant, *What I Saw in California*, 360–64; Hague and Langum, *Thomas O. Larkin*, 150–54.

casualties at La Natividad were steep—nearly a dozen men killed or wounded on each side, making this the bloodiest clash yet in the struggle for California. Mocking comparisons between this uprising and earlier revolutions there, often decided by shows of force that left the contestants unscathed, were no longer valid.

One sign that Americans now realized that they faced a serious threat was the hard line they adopted toward captives seized during Frémont's march southward, which began in late November. Near Mission San Miguel they caught an Indian servant of resistance leader José de Jesús Pico, a cousin of former governor Pío Pico, and condemned him to be shot as a spy. "He was brought from his place of confinement and tied to a tree," wrote Bryant. "Here he stood some fifteen or twenty minutes, until the Indians from a neighboring *ranchería* could be brought to witness the execution." This grim spectacle harked back to Spanish colonial times, when Indians were forced to watch the execution of those who rebelled against Cross and Crown. If the purpose of this demonstration by California's new conquerors was to crush the spirit of resistance, the condemned man did not cooperate. "No human being could have met his fate with more composure, or with stronger manifestations of courage," Bryant remarked. "It was a scene such as I desire never to witness again."[46] A short time later, José Pico was himself captured and sentenced to death by court-martial for fighting at La Natividad in violation of his parole. His wife appealed for clemency, however, and he was pardoned by Frémont, who described Pico as so grateful that he fell on his knees, crossed himself, and pledged himself to his captor: "I was to die—I had lost the life God gave me—you have given me another life. I devote the new life to you."[47] But others, including his cousin Andrés Pico (brother of Pío), refused to bow to the invaders and carried on the fight. Their campaign escalated in December when they challenged U.S. forces arriving from New Mexico under General Stephen Watts Kearny and dealt him a staggering blow.

---

46. Bryant, *What I Saw in California*, 373.
47. Pico quoted by Frémont in Chaffin, *Pathfinder*, 358; Bancroft, *History of California*, 5:374–75.

Reckoning at San Pasqual

Kearny's odyssey had begun back in June when he received orders from Washington to cross the Great Plains and occupy New Mexico before continuing on to California. His Army of the West consisted of more than a thousand volunteers, recruited largely from Missouri, and some three hundred dragoons from the regular army. Their advance went unopposed by New Mexico's governor Manuel Armijo, who like Pío Pico fled south after disbanding his forces. Kearny's proclamations in New Mexico resembled that of Sloat in California. "We come amongst you as friends—not as enemies; as protectors—not as conquerors," he declared. At the same time, however, he threatened to hang anyone "found in arms against me" and required local officials to swear allegiance to the United States "in the name of the Father, Son, and Holy Ghost—Amen."[48]

Some of Kearny's officers found those compulsory pledges of allegiance distasteful. But, like Sloat and Stockton, he was carrying out the policy of his government, which claimed the right to incorporate the inhabitants of New Mexico and California as citizens before this war ended and the occupied territories were confirmed by treaty as American possessions. Kearny's orders called for him to establish "a temporary civil Government" in New Mexico and California.[49] That sounded benign compared to placing the occupied territories under military rule until a peace treaty was signed. To assume as this plan did, however, that that the inhabitants would gladly become part of a nation whose troops invaded their country was asking for trouble. As Captain Philip St. George Cooke of Kearny's army remarked, the "great boon of American citizenship" was being thrust upon people who, however miserable they may have been under Mexican rule, were "still imbued by nature with enough patriotism to resent this outrage of being forced to swear an alien allegiance, by an officer who had just passed their frontier."[50]

---

48. Kearny in Hyslop, *Bound for Santa Fe*, 335–36.
49. Secretary of War William Marcy to Kearny in ibid., 309.
50. Philip St. George Cooke, *The Conquest of New Mexico and California: An Historical and Personal Narrative*, 34–35.

Kearny had neither enough troops nor enough time to secure New Mexico in its entirety. After placing his volunteers under the command of Colonel Alexander Doniphan, who would lead them south to Chihuahua to support the main American offensive, Kearny left Santa Fe for California in late September with his dragoons. On October 6, near Socorro, they were startled by the approach of a small party of mountain men, yelling like Indians. Those scouts were led by Kit Carson, who had left Los Angeles before the uprising began there and was carrying dispatches from Frémont to his superiors back east. Kearny's men were not pleased to learn that Frémont and Stockton had taken California ahead of them. As army surgeon John Strother Griffin wrote in his diary, they were hoping that they "might have a little kick up with the good people of California but this totally blasted all our hopes."[51] Kearny sent two hundred men back to Santa Fe—not enough, it turned out, to prevent an uprising in January 1847 by New Mexicans and Pueblo Indians against the occupied territory's American governor, merchant Charles Bent. Kearny then continued his arduous march to California with barely a hundred dragoons, unaware that insurgents were up in arms there. The presumption of a cheap and easy conquest was not limited to distant officials in Washington. Even seasoned officers like Kearny discounted the possibility that American occupiers would be viewed as enemies and come under attack.

After prevailing on Kit Carson to serve as his guide, Kearny moved west along the Gila Trail that trappers and traders had traversed for decades. He hoped to bring supply wagons with him, John Griffin noted, but Carson declared it "impossible to get wagons through." So Kearny took only two howitzers on caissons and left to Lieutenant Cooke the task of opening a wagon route across the desert to California, an assignment he later fulfilled with a battalion of Mormons who volunteered in the hope that the government would reward them with a homeland in the West. The paths that Kearny and Cooke followed carried them

---

51. John S. Griffin, *A Doctor Comes to California: The Diary of John S. Griffin, Assistant Surgeon with Kearny's Dragoons, 1846–1847*, 20.

through desolate terrain. Skeptics like John Griffin wondered what the United States would gain by annexing this territory, which appeared useless other than as a staging ground for Apache raids on settlements to the south. On October 29 he noted that "we struck the main Indian trace used by the red rascals for going into Sonora, where they plunder the Mexicans to their hearts content, of mules, Horses, women & children." He expressed no sympathy for the victims of those raids, for he regarded Mexicans as "great rascals," who "for a conquered people are treated with a damn sight more courtesy than they deserve."[52]

Yet Kearny and company owed much to some obliging Mexican traders they encountered along the way, obtaining from them fresh horses and mules and news of developments in California. In late November, as the dragoons approached the Colorado River, they spotted what they thought were Mexican troops and brought in four men for questioning. As Captain Henry Smith Turner reported, they proved to be "traders who had in charge some 400 mules and horses which they were taking from California to Sonora." One of them was "quite loquacious" and told of the recent uprising in Los Angeles.[53] The following day Kearny's men detained a Mexican courier who carried letters referring to the defeat of Mervine and Gillespie's forces near San Pedro. That report, Griffin noted, was confirmed by the Mexican traders, who said that Mervine's "Web footed Yankies ran like the Devil." One officer under Kearny had recently remarked that "we all deserved a good trouncing for coming into such a God forsaken country." Soon they would have to reckon with insurgents who had trounced their countrymen and retaken California. They were assured by Mexicans that those opponents were "fiends incarnate," Griffin added, "so I suppose we may expect a small chunk of hell when we get over there."[54]

Kearny remained confident of success, however, and was eager to enter the fight. Crossing the Colorado near the Yuma villages,

---

52. Ibid., 18, 21, 27.
53. Henry Smith Turner, *The Original Journals of Henry Smith Turner: With Stephen Watts Kearny to New Mexico and California, 1846–1847*, 117–18.
54. Griffin, *A Doctor Comes to California*, 37.

he and his men made a taxing trek over bleak desert and barren, boulder-strewn mountains to the ranch of Jonathan Warner, a naturalized Mexican who had lived in California since 1831 and went by the name "Juan José." Griffin noted that Warner, who was not at his ranch at what is now Warner Springs when Kearny's men arrived there on December 2, was "suspected of favouring the Mexicans rather more than his own countrymen" and was being held by Stockton's forces at San Diego.[55] The well-informed Thomas Larkin considered Warner loyal to the United States, however, and had sought his help in encouraging Californios to invite American annexation. Had he been home when Kearny appeared, Warner would surely have welcomed the Americans as did the man he left in charge at the ranch, William Marshall, who had jumped ship in San Diego a year earlier to try his luck in California.

Advancing from Warner's Ranch on December 4, Kearny met the next morning with Lieutenant Gillespie, sent with a cavalry detachment by Stockton to aid the general. Gillespie informed Kearny that insurgents led by Andrés Pico had gathered at San Pasqual, where the road to San Diego descended steeply to the coastal plain. Kearny then ordered Lieutenant Thomas Hammond to reconnoiter Pico's camp that evening, a task that was not carried out with much stealth. According to Gillespie, the clang of the dragoons' swords as they approached on horseback woke the rebels, "who came out, crying *Viva California, abajo los Americanos* [down with the Americans]."[56] As the dragoons rode off, Griffin related, "the Mexicans gave three cheers." Hammond returned around 2 A.M. on December 6 to the American camp, where a cold rain was falling. Kearny's men were exhausted by their long trek that day. They had lost the advantage of surprise, but he ordered them to mount up and attack Pico's force before dawn. In their haste, they did not reload their wet sidearms with dry powder. "Boots and saddles was the word," Griffin wrote, "and off we put in search of adventure."[57]

---

55. Ibid., 41.
56. Gillespie, "Gillespie and the Conquest of California," 341.
57. Griffin, *A Doctor Comes to California*, 45.

Andrés Pico.
Courtesy The Bancroft Library,
University of California, Berkeley
(California Faces: Selections from
The Bancroft Library Portrait
Collection).

Pico's horsemen at San Pasqual were ready for the attack and used the same tactic that their comrades elsewhere had employed successfully in recent battles, firing on the Americans as they charged and then falling back to lure their overzealous foes into a perilous pursuit. Kearny's troopers outnumbered Pico's nearly two to one but became strung out as they advanced. Some were riding tired mules, Gillespie observed, and fell far behind. Leading the way was Captain Benjamin Moore, who chased after the insurgents with thirty-five or forty men for more than a mile before Pico's men rallied and came at them "like devils with their lances," Griffin related.[58] Many of the guns carried by the Americans misfired because the powder was wet, and they had to rely on their sabers, which were no match for their opponents' lances. Moore was among the first to fall dead, pierced numerous times. Some of those with him were lassoed and dragged from the saddle before being lanced.

---

58. Ibid., 46.

Antonio Coronel, who served as a scout for Pico before the battle and spoke afterward with men involved in the fighting, remarked that the Americans "came on rapidly in no particular order, riding half-broken mules and very spirited horses. They were less accustomed than the Californians to managing such animals, and had their hands full just preventing a stampede." Captain Moore, he added, showed "great courage and spirit" in leading that ill-fated charge.[59] Those who went in with Moore and survived Pico's devastating counterthrust were falling back by the time Gillespie came up to join the fray, and he found himself surrounded by Mexican horsemen. "Four lances were dashed at me quick as thought," he wrote. A blow from the rear knocked him from his saddle: "As I attempted to rise, another blow from behind struck me under the left arm upon the ribs, cutting through to the lungs."[60]

Gillespie and Kearny were among seventeen Americans wounded at San Pasqual, by Griffin's reckoning. Eighteen others died at the hands of Pico's men, who suffered around twenty casualties but reported no fatalities in a battle that ended when the Americans finally brought one of their howitzers to bear and drove them off. (The other howitzer fell into Mexican hands after the mules hauling it took fright and ran wild.) Kearny's men remained in dire straits after the battle, hemmed in by Pico's cavalry until a relief force sent by Stockton reached them on December 10 and escorted them safely to San Diego. Kearny claimed victory because his men held the field when the battle ended, but Stockton saw it as a "sad defeat."[61] Griffin, who tended to the wounded, was inclined to agree. "Upon the whole we suffered most terribly in this action," he wrote.[62] Kearny acknowledged afterward that his foes at San Pasqual were among "the best horsemen in the world."[63] But his deceptively easy conquest of New Mexico and his assurance that he was doing Californios a favor by bringing them under the Stars and

---

59. Coronel, *Tales of Mexican California*, 45.
60. Gillespie, "Gillespie and the Conquest of California," 342; Bancroft, *History of California*, 5:341–55; Harlow, *California Conquered*, 181–91.
61. Stockton in Harlow, *California Conquered*, 199.
62. Griffin, *A Doctor Comes to California*, 46–47.
63. Kearny in Bryant, *What I Saw in California*, 397.

Stripes may have led him to underestimate the risks and rush into a battle for which his troops were ill prepared. His miscalculation was not calamitous for his cause, but it prefigured larger debacles for the United States like George Armstrong Custer's defeat at Little Bighorn, where an officer over sure of his might and his right to impose on others paid dearly for his hubris.

Coming to Terms

San Pasqual was the last hurrah for defiant Californios, whose hopes faded as American forces coalesced and brought superior numbers and weaponry to bear. Flores had about five hundred insurgents at his command around Los Angeles to contend with more than six hundred Americans who were preparing to advance north from San Diego under Stockton as Frémont came down from Monterey with another four hundred recruits. Californios who chose to remain in occupied San Diego and Monterey fell back on the time-honored policy of accommodating foreigners, using conventions of hospitality that had long been applied to American traders and were now extended to American officers. "We had a fine ball last night," wrote Griffin after reaching San Diego with Kearny's battered contingent in December, "quite a turn out of good looking women."[64] Walter Colton wrote around the same time that the "ladies of Monterey," who in recent months had been remote and withdrawn, were "gradually coming back into their more gay and social element. The lively tones of their guitars salute you from their corridors, and often the fandango shakes its light slipper in the saloon."[65]

Men as well as women concluded that the Americans were there to stay and that accommodating them now might bring better treatment from them in the future. Some Californios were reluctant to leave their ranches to join the insurgents, for as Agustín Janssens noted, "besides the war against the Americans, we were

---

64. Griffin, *A Doctor Comes to California*, 54.
65. Colton, *Three Years in California*, 126.

threatened by Indian uprisings."⁶⁶ Others sided with the occupiers because they felt no loyalty to Mexico and distrusted the leaders of the uprising. Colton printed a letter in his newspaper from an "old Californian" denouncing prominent insurgents as plunderers of the missions who in order to "secure further plunder, have again hoisted the Mexican flag, which they have long hated and cursed."⁶⁷ Some thirty Californios enlisted as paid recruits under Stockton as he and Kearny prepared to advance on Los Angeles.

Relations between Stockton and Kearny were strained, for they were vying for authority over California. Stockton claimed precedence because he was there first and had commanded occupation forces since July. Kearny cited orders from the War Department instructing him to take possession of California. This jurisdictional dispute would grow increasingly bitter, inviting comparison to past rivalries between Mexican chiefs that American observers had seen as petty and proof that California was in poor hands. For now, however, Stockton retained overall command while Kearny served as his field general, working Jack Tars from the Pacific Squadron into shape as foot soldiers and preparing them to do battle against opponents on horseback. Kearny knew that even the world's best horsemen were no match for tight ranks of well-armed infantry, backed by artillery. In a letter to Frémont, he offered his prescription for victory: "let the enemy do the charging and your Rifles will do the rest."⁶⁸

Marching north from San Diego in late December, Kearny and Stockton approached Los Angeles well ahead of Frémont—whose advance was slowed by rough terrain and bad weather—and did not wait for him to appear before launching their attack. Crossing the San Gabriel River under fire on January 8, 1847, they repulsed several cavalry charges and drove the insurgents back toward Los Angeles. John Griffin watched the following afternoon as California's defenders gathered on horseback near the outskirts of town

---

66. Janssens, *Life and Adventures*, 127; George Harwood Phillips, *Indians and Intruders in Central California, 1769–1849*, 135–39.
67. Colton, *Three Years in California*, 124.
68. Kearny in Harlow, *California Conquered*, 203.

for one last attempt to hold off the invaders. "Finally they made the rush," he observed, "and got most terribly peppered."[69]

Each side lost around fifteen men killed or wounded in these clashes around Los Angeles, which fell to the Americans on January 10. That was a light toll compared to battles elsewhere in Mexico but a heavy one for the outnumbered defenders, involved in what was now clearly a lost cause. Flores and a few other diehards fled to Sonora, hoping to carry on the fight, but most of the insurgents chose to remain in California and reckon with its new masters. Even a staunch loyalist like Antonio Coronel, who had been there only a dozen years, was now so attached to California that the Mexican heartland he once called home seemed foreign and somewhat forbidding to him. He told the men with him that "if we left this country as an army unit, we'd be put in the Mexican army to fight the United States as soon as we got there, where we'd all be under severe discipline in a strange land."[70]

Retreating northward, the insurgents received a peace overture from Frémont, who was camped near Mission San Fernando and sent the reprieved José Pico as his emissary to them. On January 13 they agreed to lay down their arms. Although they pledged to conform to the "laws and regulations of the United States," the terms of this Treaty of Cahuenga specified that "no Californian or other Mexican citizen" would have to pledge allegiance to the United States until a peace accord was reached by the warring nations.[71] This was a significant concession to insurgents who had challenged the presumption that military occupation was equivalent to annexation and relieved them of loyalty to Mexico. Such objections were later sustained by Secretary of War William Marcy, who in pardoning a New Mexican convicted of treason for opposing American occupation forces acknowledged that "territory conquered by our arms does not become, by the mere act of

---

69. Griffin, *A Doctor Comes to California*, 62; Bancroft, *History of California*, 5:385–89; Harlow, *California Conquered*, 203–18.
70. Coronel, *Tales of Mexican California*, 49.
71. Quoted in Bancroft, *History of California*, 5:404–405 n. 26; and in Bryant, *What I Saw in California*, 392.

"Battle of San Gabriel, California," January 1847.
Courtesy The Bancroft Library, University of California, Berkeley (BANC PIC 1963.002:0405-A).

conquest, a permanent part of the United States, and the inhabitants of such territory are not to the full extent of the term, citizens of the United States."[72]

In making this concession, Frémont demonstrated that he was indeed a pathfinder, one who had earlier served as a forerunner of conquest but was now helping to clear the way for peace. Lieutenant Louis McLane, a naval officer who commanded Frémont's artillery, noted in his journal that Stockton was "highly provoked" with Frémont for treating with the insurgents. Stockton felt that he should have been the one to whom they submitted. But McLane, who was not partial to Frémont, observed that unlike the "insulting & unusual proclamation" issued earlier by Stockton, the Treaty of Cahuenga appeared to "satisfy the people and quiet the country."[73] As Antonio Coronel remarked, Frémont "deliberately set

---

72. Marcy in Hyslop, *Bound for Santa Fe*, 400.
73. Louis McLane, *The Private Journal of Louis McLane U.S.N, 1844–1848*, 103.

out to win over the Californians, and succeeded so well that many prominent men declared themselves in favor of the Americans."[74]

Frémont had a personal interest in appeasing Californios, for he would soon be named governor by Stockton. Success in that capacity meant reaching out to people he had done much to antagonize over the past year. But those diplomatic efforts were cut short when the intensifying feud between Stockton and Kearny engulfed Frémont, who sided with Stockton in that dispute and lost out when Kearny prevailed. After ousting Frémont as governor and accusing him of disobedience (for which he would later be convicted by a court-martial), Kearny issued a proclamation to the people of California on March 1, 1847—long before the United States and Mexico concluded a peace treaty—that ignored Frémont's crucial concession to Californios still loyal to Mexico. As if pardoning the populace for past sins, Kearny declared that he "hereby absolves all the inhabitants of California from any further allegiance to the republic of Mexico, and will consider them as citizens of the United States."[75]

Kearny had used the same language in a proclamation he issued in New Mexico in August 1846. Much blood had been spilled since then, but he seemed oblivious to how deeply New Mexicans and Californios resented being incorporated as Americans by force of arms. Fortunately, Kearny did not negate Frémont's surrender agreement with the insurgents by requiring them to swear allegiance to the United States, which could have reignited hostilities. But his proclamation revealed how little he and like-minded exponents of American expansion had learned from recent experience. He persisted in portraying Americans as innocents who intervened here only after "Mexico forced a war upon the United States" (an assertion that Abraham Lincoln and other critics of the conflict regarded as patently false). And he suggested that the wrenching events of the past year—marked by the some of the sharpest battles

---

74. Coronel, *Tales of Mexican California*, 34; Harlow, *California Conquered*, 243; Chaffin, *Pathfinder*, 374–78.
75. Proclamation of Kearny in Bancroft, *History of California*, 5:438–39 n. 5; and in Bryant, *What I Saw in California*, 431–32.

in the recorded history of California—were nothing compared with the turmoil that beset this country earlier under Mexican rule. "California has for many years suffered greatly from domestic troubles," he declared; "civil wars have been the poisoned fountains which have sent forth trouble and pestilence over her beautiful land. Now those fountains are dried up; the star-spangled banner floats over California."[76] In fact, Kearny and his fellow conquerors had ushered in an era of unprecedented strife, an age of discord that would pit Americans against Californios, against Indians, and against each other as their nation divided over the issue of slavery in its newly acquired territories and moved toward a civil war that dwarfed any civil disturbances in California before the American takeover.

Like Spanish conquerors in earlier times, Kearny truly believed that he was redeeming California and fulfilling its promise. In material terms, he had good reason to be optimistic and promise that under American rule agriculture there would improve "and the arts and sciences flourish, as seed in a rich and fertile soil." Yet in declaring that Americans and Californios were "now but one people" and "a band of brothers" who would reap the benefits of this promised land in concert, he was ignoring the cautionary lessons of history and scripture.[77]

The biblical promised land was not a peaceable kingdom. It was a world of strife where God-fearing invaders saw it as their manifest destiny to conquer Canaan and subdue its inhabitants but ultimately fell from grace by betraying the sacred principles that brought them to power. All such holy wars or righteous conquests were ill-fated efforts to regain paradise and reclaim lost innocence, leading inevitably to temptation, transgression, and the bitter knowledge of good and evil. In that sense, California richly deserved comparison to the promised land. As demonstrated by Spanish colonists and American conquerors, doing good there in the name of God or country could have evil consequences, and those who protested their innocence were only displaying their ignorance.

---

76. Ibid.
77. Ibid.

CONCLUSION

The Illusion of Innocence

The distinguishing feature of the American infiltration and conquest of California was the tenacity with which those who carried out that convulsive process maintained their innocence in defiance of contrary views or evidence. With some expansionists that may have been merely a pose, but with others it was a matter of blind faith. Only someone who believed deeply and doggedly in the innocence and righteousness of the cause could speak seriously of Americans and Californios as a band of brothers, as General Kearny did, just months after feeling the fury of the insurgents at San Pasqual. So intent was he on preserving the premise of a peaceful and benign American takeover that he acted as if hostilities had never taken place and delivered essentially the same proclamation that he had drawn up before the uprising began. By absolving Californios of Mexican citizenship and pretending that they were not being forcibly deprived of their distinct identity, Kearny absolved Americans of guilt and preserved their cherished sense of collective innocence.

The Spanish conquest of California was not morally superior to the American conquest, but it had the virtue of recognizing that it was not entirely virtuous. Spanish colonizers brooded over their sins and were well aware of flaws in the moral fabric of their society. What gave American conquerors such an easy conscience? In colonial America, the sense of guilt and imperfection was often as strong among Calvinists and others in the Protestant majority as it was among Catholics. But in times of conflict, such as the fierce wars that New Englanders waged against Indians and their French allies, God-fearing colonists projected all guilt onto their foes and fought with a sense of righteous indignation. That tendency was not unique to Anglo-Americans, by any means, and it was not exhibited by some accommodating Americans who lived amicably among Californios and dealt with them in good faith, even during the Mexican War. But it became a pronounced trait in the character of those who expanded westward across the continent and clashed repeatedly with Indians. They regarded Indians stereotypically as red devils and saw them as evil and menacing even in situations where they were poorly armed and badly outnumbered, as was often the case with the so-called Diggers of the Great Basin with whom emigrant parties clashed on their way to California.

That keen sense of victimization among American emigrants—who were seldom restrained in their attitudes or actions toward Indians by religious scruples of the sort that Catholic priests tried to instill among Spanish colonizers—was soon applied to Mexican authorities, who were seen as racially impure descendants of corrupt Spaniards conspiring with California's red devils against blameless Yankees. Only by demonizing their opponents could Americans of the Bear Flag party maintain their invigorating sense of innocence while acting as aggressors in California. Their attitude influenced officers such as Gillespie and Stockton, whose views were not conditioned by frontier conflicts with Indians but who saw the youthful United States as engaged in a righteous struggle with older and less virtuous imperial powers such as Britain and France and with the rotten Mexican vestiges of the decadent Spanish empire. Kearny invoked that European menace in his proclamation when he claimed that the United States had to take possession of California "to prevent any European power from seizing upon it." Like his assertion that "Mexico forced a war upon the United States," this was untrue.[1] Neither Britain nor any other European power was about to seize California when the United States stepped in. But Kearny and others involved in the conquest needed to believe that they were prodded into taking California in order to maintain their innocence—a belief that Americans clung to ever more tightly as their nation grew stronger and more assertive.

To say that Americans lost their innocence in California is to imply that they were blameless to begin with. It would be more accurate to say that discerning Americans lost the illusion of innocence on which this conquest was predicated as they reckoned with its consequences, including a determined rebellion that challenged their moral authority and a convulsive influx of American prospectors and settlers following the discovery of gold on Sutter's property in early 1848, shortly before the Mexican War ended and the United States officially annexed California. That influx proved calamitous for California Indians and subverted the promise of equal justice for Californios, who were besieged by squatters and whose land claims were considered invalid by the United States unless they could prove otherwise in court, a long and often ruinously expensive process.

A few decades after the conquest, Mariano Vallejo—who had hoped that annexation would benefit all Californians, including those of Spanish heritage—concluded his historical memoirs by asking pointedly if any of the fine promises made by Americans when they seized this country had been kept. "I do not ask for gold, which is only a pleasing gift to abject peoples," he wrote, "but I do demand and I have the right to demand our share of education. In the schools of San Francisco French and German are taught. Why does there not also exist [at least] one class in Spanish?" The Treaty of Guadalupe Hidalgo, which ended the war, had conferred American citizenship on Californios who chose to accept

---

1. Proclamation of Kearny in Bancroft, *History of California*, 5:438–39 n. 5; and in Bryant, *What I Saw in California*, 431–32.

it. Yet Americans continued to treat them "as a conquered people," Vallejo declared, "and not as citizens who willingly became part of that great family which, under the protection of that glorious flag that proudly waved at Bunker Hill, defied the attacks of European monarchs."[2] Not all Americans treated all Californios that way. Vallejo was respected by Anglos living around Sonoma and was elected mayor of that town. But the legacy of conquest was long lasting in California and marginalized most Hispanics and their culture for generations to come.

In time, historians began to grapple with the American conquest and its tumultuous consequences and question the motives of participants and their claims of innocence. Hubert Howe Bancroft, who was often critical of Spanish and Mexican authorities in the monumental history of California that he and his staff compiled in the 1880s, reserved some of his harshest judgments for the Bear Flag rebels, blaming them for poisoning relations between Americans and Californios and ruining what might have been a peaceful takeover by the United States. "Not only did the insurgents not contribute to the American occupation of the country," he wrote in condemnation of the Bears, "but they absolutely retarded it, and increased its difficulties. They were largely accountable for all the blood that was spilled throughout the war."[3] To be sure, those prickly settlers with their defensive frontier mentality and aggressive response to perceived threats antagonized Californios and heightened resistance to the American takeover. But were the Bears the evil force that corrupted an otherwise virtuous conquest? Officers like Stockton and Gillespie brought their own sense of righteous indignation to California that harmonized with the spirit of the Bear Flag revolt but was not a product of that uprising. A defiant frontier mentality was shared by many Americans who went abroad in this expansionist era, including soldiers, sailors, and some merchants who reached California by sea. To blame the Bears exclusively for the misfortunes of the American conquest

---

2. Vallejo, "Recuerdos históricos y personales," 5:189–90.
3. Bancroft, *History of California*, 5:98.

might suggest that Americans collectively were indeed innocent, with the exception of a few bad apples, spoiled in transit as they crossed the wild West and bumped up against its wild Indians.

A broader inquiry into the Bear Flag Revolt and the resulting conquest was conducted by Josiah Royce in his remarkable book *California: A Study of American Character* (1886). "From the Bear Flag affair we can date the beginning of the degradation, the ruin, and the oppression of the Californian people by our own," wrote Royce, the son of emigrants who arrived overland in California in 1849. Unlike Bancroft, however, he did not regard the rebellious settlers as the principal villains here. The overland experience, he argued, "tended to develop both the best and the worst elements of the frontier political character." The Bear Flag Revolt revealed not only unsavory traits in frontiersmen like truculence and prejudice but also redeeming qualities such as "skill in self-government," as evidenced by their awkward but earnest efforts to form a Bear Flag Republic. Royce regarded as hypocritical the attempts of propagandists like Ide to portray this self-serving uprising as "moral, humane, patriotic, enlightened, and glorious." But he saw such rationalizations as evidence that the rebels indeed had a conscience and were trying to assuage it. "The American as conqueror is unwilling to appear in public as a pure aggressor," Royce wrote memorably. "His conscience is sensitive, and hostile aggression, practiced against any but Indians, shocks this conscience, unused as it is to such scenes."[4]

In sum, Royce saw the Bears as representative frontier characters who were capable of good or evil in roughly equal measure but veered toward the latter in their dealings with Californios. But he was relentless in his indictment of the officer who encouraged and ultimately took charge of their uprising, John Frémont. He denied that Frémont had any right as an American officer to interfere in California's affairs before he knew that his country was at war with Mexico and dismissed as fraudulent Frémont's claim that he had received a secret message from Washington, relayed by Archibald

---

4. Josiah Royce, *California: A Study of American Character*, 88, 119, 193.

Gillespie, giving him discretion to take California and deny that prize to the British. Like Bancroft, Royce believed that it was not inherently wrong for the United States to take California if that object could have been achieved without harming the Californios. "With their goodwill if possible," Royce wrote, "and at all events with the strictest possible regard for their rights, we were bound in honor to proceed in our plans and undertakings on the Pacific coast."[5] Frémont dishonored his nation, Royce concluded, when he embraced the unsanctioned Bear Flag Revolt and violated the rights of Mariano Vallejo and other Californios.

Here as in Bancroft's case against the Bears, however, fixing the blame on one or more culprits in California rather than on the nation as a whole or its leaders in Washington suggested that a virtuous conquest might indeed have been possible had the task been entrusted to those who cared more for America's honor than for its selfish interests. Judging by their actions rather than their rhetoric, Polk and his appointees evidently concluded that such an altruistic takeover was neither feasible nor desirable. They paid lip service to the rights of the inhabitants, but the officers sent to California as war loomed, including Frémont, Gillespie, and Stockton, understood that America's interests came first there. Asserting the nation's rights in this way meant doing wrong to others.

Whether viewed as a national transgression or a campaign tarnished by the misdeeds of individuals who exceeded their bounds, the American takeover of California lost its righteous aura when subjected to rigorous scrutiny. By examining the conquest critically, Bancroft, Royce, and later historians worked to dispel the illusion of American innocence and offered in its place knowledge of good and evil as kindred components of the American character. With that knowledge came a reassessment of the cultures that Americans supplanted in California, leading some enthusiasts to invest them with an innocence to which they had no more claim than did the conquering Americans. Those disenchanted with American greed and rapaciousness as epitomized by the Gold

---

5. Ibid., 41.

Rush could look back nostalgically to the supposedly idyllic and carefree Mexican era, ignoring its many stresses and strains, or to the paternalistic regimen of the Spanish padres, whose reconstructed missions looked much like Eden to sympathetic visitors now that they were no longer confines for restless and sometimes rebellious neophytes. Critics of that spiritual conquest, for their part, could seek inspiration in an earlier and simpler time, before Europeans arrived like the serpent in the garden and exposed Indians to shame and strife by luring them away from their presumably peaceful and blameless existence—a notion belied by evidence that Californian Indians, while not avid warriors, nonetheless engaged in raids on rival groups, shedding blood and stealing women.

Searching for lost innocence in an idealized past may be a harmless exercise in the case of societies that no longer exercise authority. But the expansionist impulse that led to the annexation of California and made the United States a world power by the end of the nineteenth century is still with us. From the start that movement, like the expansive efforts of Spanish padres and soldiers on behalf of Cross and Crown, mingled imperialism with idealism. Jefferson's vision of an empire for liberty, spreading democratic ideals across the continent, was refined by liberal expansionists like Frémont, who as a U.S. senator from California and the first Republican candidate for president in 1856 sought to keep American territory seized from Mexico and Indian tribes free of the pernicious slave system that Jefferson and other founders perpetuated. In the early twentieth century Theodore Roosevelt and Woodrow Wilson gave the nation a global mission that combined forceful efforts to project American power overseas with such high-minded objectives as promoting peace, freedom, and self-determination. Americans who saw those generous impulses as defining their character and their role in the world tended to overlook the evils that resulted when they intruded on countries like the Philippines, where Spanish colonizers gave way to American occupiers who waged a brutal war against Filipino insurgents. The conviction that the United States was purely a force for good, free of the impure motives harbored by other great powers, grew stronger when the nation faced challenges from Nazi Germany, imperial Japan, and the Soviet Union under Joseph Stalin and his successors, reinforcing the notion that in defying an evil empire, a role formerly assigned to Spain, Americans could do no wrong or were absolved of any wrong they did.

The illusion of innocence persists, as does the belief that the United States has what expansionist John O'Sullivan called a "blessed mission to the nations of world."[6] But those lofty assumptions have long been challenged by skeptical Americans, including those who saw the Mexican War as evidence that a democratic society could go badly astray when it imposed self-righteously on others. As Josiah Royce observed, the conquest of California was glorified by proponents as a "missionary enterprise, designed to teach our beloved and erring Spanish American brethren the blessings of true liberty." It was not the last time when this dynamic nation dedicated to liberty ended up taking liberties in pursuit of its interests or ideals. The cautionary lesson of California, demonstrated by Spanish colonizers as well as American conquerors, was that pious assertions or pretenses could disguise as just and benevolent actions that violated principles they were supposed to uphold and harmed people they were supposed to help. Royce hoped that Americans would remember this lesson, "so that when our nation is another time about to serve the devil, it will do so with more frankness and will deceive itself less by half-unconscious cant."[7]

---

6. O'Sullivan, "Great Nation of Futurity," 430.
7. Royce, *California*, 122–23.

Bibliography

MANUSCRIPTS

The Bancroft Library, University of California, Berkeley
 Alvarado, Juan Bautista. "Historia de California" (History of California).
  5 vols. Translated by Earl R. Hewitt. BANC MSS C-D 1–5.
 Brown, Charles. "Early Events in California." BANC MSS C-D 53.
 Knight, Thomas. "Statement of Early Events in California." BANC MSS
  C-D 110.
 McChristian, Patrick. "Statement of Patrick McChristian." BANC MSS
  C-E 67:7.
 Sutter, John. "Personal Reminiscences of General John A. Sutter." BANC
  MSS C-D 14.
 Vallejo, Mariano Guadalupe. "Recuerdos históricos y personales tocantes
  a la Alta California" (Historical and Personal Memoirs Relating to Alta
  California). 5 vols. Translated Earl R. Hewitt. BANC MSS C-D 17–21.

Western Americana Collection, Beinecke Rare Book and Manuscript Library, Yale University
 Sully, Alfred. Alfred Sully Papers: Correspondence, 1848–1852.

BOOKS AND ARTICLES
Alvarado, Juan Bautista. *Vignettes of Early California: Childhood Reminiscences of Juan Bautista Alvarado.* Translated by John H. R. Polt. Edited by W. Michael Mathes. San Francisco: Book Club of California, 1982.

Anderson, Charles Roberts, ed. *Journal of a Cruise to the Pacific Ocean, 1842–1844, in the Frigate United States.* Durham: Duke University Press, 1937.

Archibald, Robert. *The Economic Aspects of the California Missions.* Washington, D.C.: Academy of American Franciscan History, 1978.

Atherton, Faxon Dean. *The California Diary of Faxon Dean Atherton.* Edited by Doyce B. Nunis, Jr. San Francisco: California Historical Society, 1964.

Bancroft, Hubert Howe. *California Pastoral, 1769–1848.* San Francisco: History Company, 1888.

———. *History of California.* 5 vols. San Francisco: History Company, 1884–86.

Bandini, José. *A Description of California in 1828.* Translated by Doris Marion Wright. Berkeley: Bancroft Library, 1951.

Barbour, Barton H. *Jedediah Smith: No Ordinary Mountain Man.* Norman: University of Oklahoma Press, 2009.

Batman, Richard. *American Ecclesiastes: The Stories of James Pattie.* San Diego: Harcourt Brace Jovanovich, 1984.

———. *The Outer Coast: A Narrative about California before the World Rushed In.* San Diego: Harcourt Brace Jovanovich, 1985.

Beebe, Rose Marie, and Robert M. Senkewicz, eds. *Lands of Promise and Despair: Chronicles of Early California, 1535–1846.* Berkeley: Heyday Books, in association with Santa Clara University, 2001.

———, trans. and eds. *Testimonios: Early California through the Eyes of Women, 1815–1848.* Berkeley: Heyday Books, in association with the Bancroft Library, 2006.

Beilharz, Edwin A. *Felipe de Neve: First Governor of California.* San Francisco: California Historical Society, 1971.

Bidwell, John. *In California before the Gold Rush.* Los Angeles: Ward Ritchie Press, 1948.

Bolton, Herbert Eugene. *Anza's California Expeditions.* 5 vols. Berkeley: University of California Press, 1930.

Boscana, Gerónimo. *Chinigchinich: A Historical Account of the Origins, Customs, and Traditions of the Indians at the Missionary Establishment of St. Juan Capistrano, Alta California.* Translated by Alfred Robinson. 1846. Reprint edition. Oakland: Biobooks, 1947.

Bowman, J. N., and Robert F. Heizer, *Anza and the Northwest Frontier of New Spain.* Los Angeles: Southwest Museum, 1967.

Bryant, Edwin. *What I Saw in California.* 1848. Reprint edition. Lincoln: University of Nebraska Press, 1985.

Busch, Briton C., and Barry M. Gough, eds. *Fur Traders from New England: The Boston Men in the North Pacific, 1787–1800.* Spokane: Arthur H. Clark, 1997.

Bibliography

Carson, Kit. *Kit Carson's Autobiography.* Edited by Milo Milton Quaife. 1935. Reprint edition. Lincoln: University of Nebraska Press, 1966.

Chaffin, Tom. *Pathfinder: John Charles Frémont and the Course of American Empire.* New York: Hill and Wang, 2002.

Chapman, Charles E. *A History of California: The Spanish Period.* New York: Macmillan Company, 1921.

Churchill, Charles B. *Adventurers and Prophets: American Autobiographers in Mexican California, 1827–1847.* Spokane: Arthur H. Clark, 1995.

Cleland, Robert Glass. *The Cattle on a Thousand Hills: Southern California, 1850–1880.* San Marino: Huntington Library, 1941.

———. *This Reckless Breed of Men: The Trappers and Fur Traders of the Southwest.* New York: Alfred A. Knopf, 1950.

Cleveland, Richard Jeffry. *Voyages and Commercial Enterprises of the Sons of New England.* 1843. Reprint edition. New York: B. Franklin, 1968.

Clyman, James. *Journal of a Mountain Man.* Edited by Linda M. Hasselstrom. Missoula: Mountain Press Publishing, 1984.

Colton, Walter. *Three Years in California.* New York: A. S. Barnes, 1850.

Cook, Sherburne F. *The Conflict between the California Indian and White Civilization.* Berkeley: University of California Press, 1976.

Cook, Warren L. *Flood Tide of Empire: Spain and the Pacific Northwest, 1543–1819.* New Haven: Yale University Press, 1973.

Cooke, Philip St. George. *The Conquest of New Mexico and California: An Historical and Personal Narrative.* 1878. Reprint edition. Albuquerque: Horn and Wallace, 1964.

Coronel, Antonio. *Tales of Mexican California.* Translated by Diane de Avalle-Arce. Edited by Doyce B. Nunis, Jr. Santa Barbara: Bellerophon Books, 1994.

Costansó, Miguel. *The Discovery of San Francisco Bay: The Portolá Expedition of 1769–1770.* Translated by Frederick J. Teggart. 1911. Revised edition, edited by Peter Browning. Lafayette, Calif.: Great West Books, 1992.

Crespí, Juan. *A Description of Distant Roads: Original Journals of the First Expedition into California, 1769–1770.* Translated and edited by Alan K. Brown. San Diego: San Diego State University Press, 2001.

Crosby, Harry W. *Gateway to Alta California: The Expedition to San Diego, 1769.* San Diego: Sunbelt Publications, 2003.

Cutter, Donald C. *California in 1792: A Spanish Naval Visit.* Norman: University of Oklahoma Press, 1990.

———. *Malaspina in California.* San Francisco: J. Howell Books, 1960.

Dakin, Susanna Bryant. *The Lives of William Hartnell.* Stanford: Stanford University Press, 1949.

———. *A Scotch Paisano in Old Los Angeles: Hugo Reid's Life in California, 1832–1852, Derived from His Correspondence*. Berkeley: University of California Press, 1939.

Dale, Harrison Clifford, ed. *The Explorations of William H. Ashley and Jedediah Smith, 1822–1829*. 1941. Reprint edition, with introduction by James P. Ronda. Lincoln: University of Nebraska Press, 1991.

Dana, Juan Francisco. *The Blond Ranchero: Memories of Juan Francisco Dana, as Told to Rocky Dana and Marie Harrington*. 1960. Reprint edition. Arroyo Grande, Calif.: South County Historical Society, 1999.

Dana, Richard Henry, Jr. *Two Years before the Mast: A Personal Narrative of Life at Sea*. 1840. Reprint edition, with introduction by John Seelye. New York: New American Library, 2000.

Davis, William C. *Three Roads to the Alamo: The Lives and Fortunes of David Crockett, James Bowie, and William Barret Travis*. New York: HarperPerennial, 1999.

Davis, William Heath. *Seventy-five Years in California*. 1889. Reprint edition, edited by Harold A. Small. San Francisco: John Howell, 1967.

Dawson, Nicholas. *Narrative of Nicholas "Cheyenne" Dawson (Overland to California in '41 and '49, and Texas in '51)*. Introduction by Charles L. Camp. San Francisco: Grabhorn Press, 1933.

Duflot de Mofras, Eugène. *Travels on the Pacific Coast*. Translated and edited by Marguerite Eyer Wilbur. 1937. Reprint edition. Santa Barbara: Narrative Press, 2004.

Duhaut-Cilly, Auguste. *A Voyage to California, the Sandwich Islands, and around the World in the Years 1826–1829*. Translated and edited by August Frugé and Neal Harlow. Berkeley: University of California Press, 1999.

Ellis, Joseph J., et al. *Thomas Jefferson: Genius of Liberty*. Introduction by Garry Wills. New York: Viking Studio, in association with the Library of Congress, 2000.

Engelhardt, Zephyrin. *The Missions and Missionaries of California*. 4 vols. San Francisco: J. H. Barry, 1908–16.

Essig, E. O., Adele Ogden, and Clarence John DuFour. *Fort Ross: California Outpost of Russian Alaska, 1812–1841*. Edited by Richard A. Pierce. Fairbanks, Alaska: Limestone Press, 1991.

Ewing, J. Andrew. "Education in California during the Pre-Statehood Period." *Historical Society of Southern California Annual* 11 (1918): 51–59.

Fages, Pedro. *A Historical, Political, and Natural Description of California*. Translated by Herbert Ingram Priestly. Berkeley: University of California Press, 1937.

Farnham, Thomas J. *The Early Days of California: Embracing What I Saw and Heard There, with Scenes in the Pacific*. 1844. Reprint edition. Philadelphia: John E. Potter, 1859.

Figueroa, José. *Manifesto to the Mexican Republic*. Translated and edited by C. Alan Hutchinson. Berkeley: University of California Press, 1978.

Font, Pedro. *Font's Complete Diary: A Chronicle of the Founding of San Francisco*. Translated and edited by Herbert Eugene Bolton. Berkeley: University of California Press, 1931.

———. *With Anza to California, 1775–1776: The Journal of Pedro Font, O.F.M.* Translated and edited by Alan K. Brown. Norman, Oklahoma: Arthur H. Clark Company, 2011.

Forbes, Alexander. *California: A History of Upper and Lower California*. 1839. Reprint. New York: Arno Press, 1973

Forbes, Jack D. *Warriors of the Colorado: The Yumas of the Quechan Nation and Their Neighbors*. Norman: University of Oklahoma Press, 1965.

Foster, Stephen C. "A Sketch of Some of the Earliest Kentucky Pioneers of Los Angeles." *Publications of the Historical Society of Southern California* 1 (1887): 30–35.

Frémont, John Charles. *The Expeditions of John Charles Frémont*. Edited by Donald Jackson and Mary Lee Spence. 2 vols. Urbana: University of Illinois Press, 1970.

———. *Memoirs of My Life*. 1887. Reprint edition, with introduction by Charles M. Robinson III. New York: Cooper Square Press, 2001.

Geiger, Maynard J. *Franciscan Missionaries in Hispanic California, 1769–1848: A Biographical Dictionary*. San Marino, Calif.: Huntington Library, 1969.

———. *The Life and Times of Fray Junípero Serra, O.F.M.* 2 vols. Washington, D.C.: Academy of American Franciscan History, 1959.

Geiger, Maynard J., and Clement W. Meighan, trans. and eds. *As the Padres Saw Them: Californian Indian Life and Customs as Reported by the Franciscan Missionaries, 1813–1815*. Glendale, Calif.: Arthur H. Clark Company, in association with the Santa Bárbara Mission Archive Library, 1976.

Gibson, James R. *Imperial Russia in Frontier America: The Changing Geography of Supply of Russian America, 1784–1867*. New York: Oxford University Press, 1976.

———. *Otter Skins, Boston Ships, and China Goods: The Maritime Fur Trade of the Northwest Coast, 1785–1841*. Seattle: University of Washington Press, 1992.

Gillespie, Archibald. "Gillespie and the Conquest of California." *California Historical Society Quarterly* 17 (1938): 123–40, 271–84, 325–50.

Goetzmann, William H. *Exploration and Empire: The Explorer and the Scientist in the Winning of the American West*. 1966. Reprint edition. New York: W. W. Norton, 1978.

Griffin, John S. *A Doctor Comes to California: The Diary of John S. Griffin, Assistant Surgeon with Kearny's Dragoons, 1846–1847.* Edited by George Walcott Ames, Jr. San Francisco: California Historical Society, 1943.

Guerrero, Vladimir. *The Anza Trail and the Settling of California.* Berkeley: Heyday Books, in association with Santa Clara University, 2006.

Guest, Francis F. "Establishment of the Villa de Branciforte." *California Historical Society Quarterly* 41 (March 1962): 29–50.

———. *Fermín Francisco de Lasuén (1736–1803): A Biography.* Washington, D.C.: American Academy of Franciscan History, 1973.

Gutiérrez, Ramón A., and Richard J. Orsi, eds. *Contested Eden: California before the Gold Rush.* Berkeley: University of California Press, 1998.

Hackel, Steven W. *Children of Coyote, Missionaries of Saint Francis: Indian-Spanish Relations in Colonial California, 1769–1850.* Chapel Hill: University of North Carolina Press, 2005.

Hafen, LeRoy R., ed. *The Mountain Men and the Fur Trade of the Far West.* 10 vols. Glendale, Calif.: Arthur H. Clark, 1965–72.

Hafen, Leroy R., and Ann W. Hafen. *Old Spanish Trail: Santa Fé to Los Angeles.* 1954. Reprint edition, with introduction by David J. Weber. Lincoln: University of Nebraska Press, 1993.

Hague, Harlan. *The Road to California: The Search for a Southern Overland Route, 1540–1848.* Glendale, Calif.: Arthur H. Clark, 1978.

Hague, Harlan, and David J. Langum. *Thomas O. Larkin: A Life of Patriotism and Profit in Old California.* Norman: University of Oklahoma Press, 1990.

Harding, George L. *Don Agustín V. Zamorano: Statesman, Soldier, Craftsman, and California's First Printer.* 1934. Reprint edition, with introduction by Roberto Carlos Dalton Matheu. Spokane: Arthur H. Clark, 2003.

Harlow, Neal. *California Conquered: War and Peace on the Pacific, 1846–1850.* Berkeley: University of California Press, 1982.

Híjar, Carlos N., Eulalia Pérez, and Agustín Escobar. *Three Memoirs of Mexican California.* Translated by Vivian C. Fisher. Berkeley: Bancroft Library, 1988.

Hine, Robert V. *In the Shadow of Frémont: Edward Kern and the Art of Exploration, 1845–1860.* 1962. Reprint edition. Norman: University of Oklahoma Press, 1982.

Hurtado, Albert L. *Indian Survival on the California Frontier.* New Haven: Yale University Press, 1988.

———. *Intimate Frontiers: Sex, Gender, and Culture in Old California.* Albuquerque: University of New Mexico Press, 1999.

———. *John Sutter: A Life on the North American Frontier.* Norman: University of Oklahoma Press, 2006.

Hutchinson, C. Alan. *Frontier Settlement in Mexican California: The Híjar-Padrés Colony, and Its Origins, 1769–1835.* New Haven: Yale University Press, 1969.

Hyslop, Stephen G. *Bound for Santa Fe: The Road to New Mexico and the American Conquest, 1806–1848.* Norman: University of Oklahoma Press, 2002.

Ide, Simeon. *A Biographical Sketch of the Life of William B. Ide.* 1880. Reprint edition. Glorieta, N.Mex.: Rio Grande Press, 1967.

Irving, Washington. *The Adventures of Captain Bonneville.* 1850. Reprint edition, with introduction by Anthony Brandt. Washington, D.C.: National Geographic Society, 2003.

Iversen, Eve. *The Romance of Nikolai Rezanov and Concepción Argüello: A Literary Legend and Its Effect on California History.* Edited by Richard A. Pierce. Fairbanks, Alaska: Limestone Press, 1998.

Jackson, Helen Hunt. *Glimpses of California and the Missions.* 1883. Reprint edition. Boston: Little, Brown & Company, 1907.

Jackson, Robert H., and Edward Castillo. *Indians, Franciscans, and Spanish Colonization: The Impact of the Mission System on California Indians.* Albuquerque: University of New Mexico Press, 1995.

Janssens, Agustín. *The Life and Adventures in California of Don Agustín Janssens, 1834–1856.* Translated by Francis Price. Edited by William H. Ellison and Francis Price. San Marino, Calif.: Huntington Library, 1953.

Jones, Thomas ap Catesby. *Visit to Los Angeles in 1843: Unpublished Narrative of Commodore Thomas ap Catesby Jones.* Introduction by Robert J. Woods. Los Angeles: Roxburghe-Zamorano Club, 1960.

Kelsey, Harry. "A New Look at the Founding of Old Los Angeles." *California Historical Quarterly* 55 (Winter 1976–77): 326–39.

Kessell, John L., ed. "Anza Damns the Missions: A Spanish Soldier's Criticism of Indian Policy, 1772." *Journal of Arizona History* 13 (Spring 1972): 52–63.

———. "The Making of a Martyr: The Young Francisco Garcés." *New Mexico Historical Review* 45 (July 1970): 181–96.

———. *Spain in the Southwest: A Narrative History of Colonial New Mexico, Arizona, Texas, and California.* Norman: University of Oklahoma Press, 2002.

Khlebnikov, Kirill. *The Khlebnikov Archive: Unpublished Journal (1800–1837) and Travel Notes (1820, 1822, and 1824).* Translated by John Bisk. Edited by Leonid Shur. Fairbanks: University of Alaska Press, 1990.

Krauze, Enrique. *Mexico, Biography of Power: A History of Modern Mexico, 1810–1996.* New York: HarperPerennial, 1998.

Langsdorff, Georg Heinrich von. *Remarks and Observations on a Voyage around the World from 1803 to 1807.* Translated by Victoria Joan Moessner. Edited by Richard A. Pierce. 2 vols. Fairbanks, Alaska: Limestone Press, 1993.

Langum, David J. "Californios and the Image of Indolence." *Western Historical Quarterly* 9 (April 1978): 181–96.

———. "Californio Women and the Image of Virtue." *Southern California Quarterly* 59 (Fall 1977): 245–50.

———. *Law and Community on the Mexican California Frontier: Anglo-American Expatriates and the Clash of Legal Traditions, 1821–1846.* Norman: University of Oklahoma Press, 1987.

La Pérouse, Jean-François de Galaup, comte de. *Monterey in 1786: The Journals of Jean François de La Pérouse.* Edited by Malcolm Margolin. Berkeley: Heyday Books, 1989.

Larkin, Thomas O. *The Larkin Papers: Personal, Business, and Official Correspondence of Thomas Oliver Larkin, Merchant and United States Consul in California.* Edited by George P. Hammond. 10 vols. Berkeley: University of California Press, in association with the Bancroft Library, 1951–68.

Lasuén, Fermín Francisco de. *Writings.* Translated and edited by Finbar Kenneally. 2 vols. Washington, D.C.: Academy of American Franciscan History, 1965.

Layne, J. Gregg. "Annals of Los Angeles." *California Historical Society Quarterly* 13 (September 1934): 195–234.

Leonard, Thomas M. *James K. Polk: A Clear and Unquestionable Destiny.* Wilmington, Del.: Scholarly Resources, 2001.

Leonard, Zenas. *Adventures of a Mountain Man: The Narrative of Zenas Leonard.* Edited by Milo Milton Quaife. 1934. Reprint edition. Lincoln: University of Nebraska Press, 1978.

Lewis, Oscar, ed. *California in 1846, Described in Letters from Thomas O. Larkin, "The Farthest West," E. M. Kern, and "Justice."* Edited by Oscar Lewis. San Francisco: Grabhorn Press, 1934.

Librado, Fernando. *Breath of the Sun: Life in Early California as Told by a Chumash Indian, Fernando Librado, to John P. Harrington.* Edited by Travis Hudson. Banning, Calif.: Malki Museum Press, in association with the Ventura County Historical Society, 1980.

Lugo, José del Carmen. "Life of a Rancher." Translated by Thomas Savage. *Historical Society of Southern California Quarterly* 32 (September 1950): 185–236.

Bibliography

Lyman, George D. *John Marsh, Pioneer: The Life Story of a Trail-Blazer on Six Frontiers.* New York: Charles Scribner's Sons, 1930.

Mahr, August C. *The Visit of the "Rurik" to San Francisco in 1816.* 1932. Reprint edition. New York: AMS Press, 1971.

Marti, Werner H. *Messenger of Destiny: The California Adventures, 1846–1847, of Archibald H. Gillespie, U.S. Marine Corps.* San Francisco: J. Howell, 1960.

Martin, Thomas S. *With Frémont to California and the Southwest, 1845–1849.* Edited by Ferol Egan. Ashland [Ore.]: Lewis Osborne, 1975.

Maxwell, Richard T. *Visit to Monterey in 1842.* Edited by John Haskell Kemble. Los Angeles: Glen Dawson, 1955.

McLane, Louis. *The Private Journal of Louis McLane U.S.N., 1844–1848.* Edited by Jay Monahan. Los Angeles: Santa Bárbara Historical Society, 1971.

Meyers, William H. *Journal of a Cruise to California and the Sandwich Islands in the United States Sloop-of-War Cyane, 1841–1844.* Edited by John Haskell Kemble. San Francisco: Book Club of California, 1955.

Miller, Robert Ryal. *Juan Alvarado: Governor of California, 1836–1842.* Norman: University of Oklahoma Press, 1998.

———. *A Yankee Smuggler on the Spanish California Coast: George Washington Eayrs and the Ship Mercury.* Santa Barbara: Santa Barbara Trust for Historic Preservation, 2001.

Milliken, Randall. *A Time of Little Choice: The Disintegration of Tribal Culture in the San Francisco Bay Area, 1769–1810.* Menlo Park, Calif.: Ballena Press, 1995.

Monroy, Douglas. *Thrown among Strangers: The Making of Mexican Culture in Frontier California.* Berkeley: University of California Press, 1990.

Montielo, María. "The Colorado Massacre of 1781: María Montielo's Report." Translated and edited by Kieran McCarty. *Journal of Arizona History* 16 (Autumn 1975): 221–25.

Morgan, Dale L. *Jedediah Smith and the Opening of the West.* 1953. Reprint edition. Lincoln: University of Nebraska Press, 1964.

Nidever, George. *The Life and Adventures of George Nidever, 1802–1883.* Edited by William Henry Ellison. Tucson: Southwest Parks and Monuments Association, 1984.

Nunis, Doyce B., Jr., ed. *The Bidwell-Bartleson Party: 1841 California Emigrant Adventure, the Documents and Memoirs of the Overland Pioneers.* Santa Cruz, Calif.: Western Tanager Press, 1991.

———, ed. *Southern California's Spanish Heritage: An Anthology.* Los Angeles: Historical Society of Southern California, 1992.

———. *The Trials of Isaac Graham*. Los Angeles: Dawson's Book Shop, 1967.

Ogden, Adele. *The California Sea Otter Trade, 1784–1848*. Berkeley: University of California Press, 1941.

Osio, Antonio María. *The History of Alta California: A Memoir of Mexican California*. Translated by Rose Marie Beebe and Robert M. Senkewicz. Madison: University of Wisconsin Press, 1996.

O'Sullivan, John. "The Great Nation of Futurity." *United States Democratic Review* 6 (1839): 426–30.

Owens, Kenneth N., ed. *John Sutter and a Wider West*. Lincoln: University of Nebraska Press, 1994.

———. *The Wreck of the Sv. Nikolai: Two Narratives of the First Russian Expedition to the Oregon Country, 1808–1810*. Translated by Alton S. Donnelly. Portland: Western Imprints, Press of the Oregon Historical Society, 1985.

Paddison, Joshua, ed. *A World Transformed: Firsthand Accounts of California before the Gold Rush*. Berkeley: Heyday Books, 1999.

Palóu, Francisco. *Palóu's Life of Fray Junípero Serra*. Translated by Maynard J. Geiger. Washington, D.C.: Academy of American Franciscan History, 1955.

Pattie, James O. *The Personal Narrative of James O. Pattie of Kentucky*. Edited by Timothy Flint, with an introduction and notes by Milo Milton Quaife. 1833. Reprint edition. Chicago: R. R. Donnelley & Sons, 1930.

Perry, Claire. *Pacific Arcadia: Images of California, 1600–1915*. New York: Oxford University Press, 1999.

Phelps, William Dane. *Alta California, 1840–1842: The Journal and Observations of William Dane Phelps, Master of the Ship "Alert."* Edited by Briton Cooper Busch. Glendale, Calif.: Arthur H. Clark, 1983.

Phillips, George Harwood. *Chiefs and Challengers: Indian Resistance and Cooperation in Southern California*. Berkeley: University of California Press, 1975.

———. *Indians and Intruders in Central California, 1769–1849*. Norman: University of Oklahoma Press, 1993.

Pico, Pío. *Don Pío Pico's Historical Narrative*. Translated by Arthur P. Botello. Edited by Martin Cole and Henry Welcome. Glendale, Calif.: Arthur H. Clark, 1973.

Pitt, Leonard. *The Decline of the Californios: A Social History of the Spanish-Speaking Californians, 1846–1890*. 1966. Reprint edition, with foreword by Ramón A. Gutiérrez. Berkeley: University of California Press, 1998.

Polk, Dora Beale. *The Island of California: A History of the Myth*. Spokane: Arthur H. Clark, 1991.

Polk, James K. *Polk: The Diary of a President, 1845–1849, Covering the Mexican War, the Acquisition of Oregon, and the Conquest of California and the Southwest.* Edited by Allan Nevins. New York: Longmans, Green and Company, 1929.

Poole, Jean Bruce, and Tevvy Ball, *El Pueblo: The Historic Heart of Los Angeles.* Los Angeles: Getty Conservation Institute and J. Paul Getty Museum, 2002.

Preuss, Charles. *Exploring with Frémont: The Private Diaries of Charles Preuss, Cartographer for John C. Frémont on His First, Second, and Fourth Expeditions to the Far West.* Translated and edited by Erwin G. Gudde and Elisabeth K. Gudde. Norman: University of Oklahoma Press, 1958.

Pubols, Louise. *The Father of All: The de la Guerra Family, Power, and Patriarchy in Mexican California.* Berkeley and San Marino: University of California Press and the Huntington Library, 2009.

Rawls, James J. *Indians of California: The Changing Image.* Norman: University of Oklahoma Press, 1984.

Revere, Joseph. *Naval Duty in California.* 1849. Reprint edition. Foreword by Joseph A. Sullivan. Oakland: Biobooks, 1947.

Rezanov, Nikolai. *Rezanov Reconnoiters California, 1806.* Edited by Richard A. Pierce. San Francisco: Book Club of California, 1972.

Ripoll, Antonio. "Fray Antonio Ripoll's Description of the Chumash Revolt at Santa Bárbara in 1824." Translated by Maynard J. Geiger. *Southern California Quarterly* 52 (December 1970): 345–64.

Robinson, Alfred. *Life in California before the Conquest.* 1846. Reprint edition. San Francisco: Thomas C. Russell, 1925.

Robinson, W. W. *Land in California.* Berkeley: University of California Press, 1948.

Rosenus, Alan. *General Vallejo and the Advent of the Americans.* Berkeley: Heyday Books, 1999.

Rousseau, Jean-Jacques. *The Social Contract and the First and Second Discourses.* Translated and edited by Susan Dunn. New Haven: Yale University Press, 2002.

Rowland, Donald E. *John Rowland and William Workman: Southern California Pioneers of 1841.* Spokane: Arthur H. Clark, in association with the Historical Society of Southern California, 1999.

Royce, Josiah. *California: A Study of American Character.* 1886. Reprint edition, with introduction by Ronald A. Wells. Berkeley: Heyday Books, 2002.

Sabin, Edwin L. *Kit Carson Days, 1809–1868: Adventures in the Path of Empire.* 2 vols. 1935. Reprint edition, with introduction by Marc Simmons. Lincoln: University of Nebraska Press, 1995.

Salomon, Carlos Manuel. *Pío Pico: The Last Governor of Mexican California*. Norman: University of Oklahoma Press, 2010.

Sandburg, Carl. *Abraham Lincoln: The Prairie Years and the War Years*. New York: Harcourt Brace Jovanovich, 1970.

Sandos, James A. *Converting California: Indians and Franciscans in the Missions*. New Haven: Yale University Press, 2004.

———. "Levantamiento!: The 1824 Chumash Uprising Reconsidered." *Southern California Quarterly* 67 (Summer 1985): 109–33.

Serra, Junípero. *Writings of Junípero Serra*. Edited by Antonine Tibesar. 4 vols. Washington, D.C.: Academy of American Franciscan History, 1955–66.

Shaler, William. *Journal of a Voyage between China and the Northwestern Coast of America, Made in 1804*. Claremont, Calif.: Saunders Studio Press, 1935.

Shapiro, Samuel. *Richard Henry Dana, Jr., 1815–1882*. East Lansing: Michigan State University Press, 1961.

Short, William J. *The Franciscans*. Collegeville, Minn.: Liturgical Press, 1990.

Simpson, Sir George. *Narrative of a Voyage to California Ports in 1841–1842*. 1847. Reprint edition. Fairfield, Wash.: Ye Galleon Press, 1988.

Smith, Gene A. "The War That Wasn't: Thomas ap Catesby Jones's Seizure of Monterey." *California History* (June 1987) 66: 104–13.

Smith, Jedediah. *The Southwest Expedition of Jedediah S. Smith: His Personal Account of the Journal to California, 1826–1827*. Edited by George R. Brooks. 1977. Reprint edition. Lincoln: University of Nebraska Press, 1989.

Snyder, Jacob R. "Diary." *Quarterly of the Society of California Pioneers* 8 (December 1931): 224–60.

Stewart, George R. *The California Trail*. 1962. Reprint edition. Lincoln: University of Nebraska Press, 1983.

Sully, Langdon. *No Tears for the General: The Life of Alfred Sully, 1821–1879*. Foreword by Ray Allen Billington. Palo Alto: American West Publishing Company, 1974.

Sylvest, Edwin Edward, Jr. *Motifs of Franciscan Mission Theory in Sixteenth Century New Spain*. Washington, D.C.: Academy of American Franciscan History, 1959.

Talbot, Theodore. *Soldier in the West: Letters of Theodore Talbot during His Services in California, Mexico, and Oregon, 1845–53*. Edited by Robert V. Hine and Savoie Lottinville. Norman: University of Oklahoma Press, 1972.

Temple, Thomas Workman, ed. "Three Early California Letters." *Historical Society of Southern California Annual* 15 (1933): 32–47.

Turner, Henry Smith. *The Original Journals of Henry Smith Turner: With Stephen Watts Kearny to New Mexico and California, 1846–1847.* Edited by Dwight L. Clarke. Norman: University of Oklahoma Press, 1966.
U.S. Senate. *California Claims.* 30th Congress, 1st Session, Report No. 75 (February 23, 1848).
Vancouver, George. *A Voyage of Discovery to the North Pacific Ocean and round the World, 1791–1795.* Edited by W. Kaye Lamb. 4 vols. London: Hakluyt Society, 1984.
Vecsey, Christopher. *On the Padres' Trail.* Notre Dame: University of Notre Dame Press, 1996.
Walker, Joel P. *A Pioneer of Pioneers: Narrative of Adventures thro' Alabama, Florida, New Mexico, Oregon, California, & c.* Los Angeles: Glen Dawson, 1953.
Walton, John. *Storied Land: Community and Memory in Monterey.* Berkeley: University of California Press, 2001.
Warner, J. J. "Reminiscences of Early California from 1831 to 1861." *Publications of the Historical Society of Southern California* 7 (1906–1908): 176–93.
Weber, David J. *The Californios versus Jedediah Smith, 1826–1827: A New Cache of Documents.* Spokane: Arthur H. Clark Company, 1990.
———. *The Mexican Frontier, 1821–1846: The American Southwest under Mexico.* Albuquerque: University of New Mexico Press, 1982.
———. *The Spanish Frontier in North America.* New Haven: Yale University Press, 1992.
———. *The Taos Trappers: The Fur Trade in the Far Southwest, 1540–1846.* Norman: University of Oklahoma Press, 1971.
Weber, Francis J., ed. *King of the Missions: A Documentary History of San Luis Rey de Francia.* [Los Angeles?:] Weber, [1980?].
———, ed. *The Pride of the Missions: A Documentary History of San Gabriel Mission.* Los Angeles: Weber, [1971?].
Wilkes, Charles. *Narrative of the United States Exploring Expedition.* 5 vols. 1844. Reprint edition. Upper Saddle River, N.J.: Gregg Press, 1970.
Wilson, Benjamin D. "Benjamin David Wilson's Observations on Early Days in California and New Mexico." *Annual Publications of the Historical Society of Southern California* (1934): 74–150.
Winther, Oscar Osburn. "The Story of San Jose, 1777–1869." *California Historical Society Quarterly* 14 (March 1935): 3–27.
Wright, Doris Marion. *A Yankee in Mexican California: Abel Stearns, 1798–1848.* Santa Barbara: W. Hebberd, 1977.
Yount, George C. *George C. Yount and His Chronicles of the West, Comprising Excerpts from His "Memoirs" and the Orange Clark "Narrative."* Edited by Charles L. Camp. Denver: Old West Publishing Company, 1966.

Acknowledgments

I would like to thank Charles E. Rankin, associate director and editor-in-chief of the University of Oklahoma Press, and Robert A. Clark, publisher of the Arthur H. Clark Company, for taking an active interest in this project, providing editorial guidance, and furnishing me with the best possible readers—scholars steeped in the historical literature of California whose publications were as instructive to me as their comments on my work. Albert L. Hurtado reviewed my proposal for this book and encouraged me to broaden its scope and include testimony in translation from Spanish and Mexican sources. In doing so, I benefited greatly from the many such accounts made available to readers in English in recent years by Rose Marie Beebe and Robert M. Senkewicz, editors of the series Before Gold in which this volume appears. The comments and suggestions of Robert Senkewicz were extremely helpful as I revised the manuscript, as were those of David J. Langum.

I would also like to thank other scholars past and present who did not read or approve my work but produced authoritative editions or translations of the primary accounts from which I drew quotations. Among those to whom I owe credit are Antonine Tibesar for the writings of Junípero Serra, Alan K. Brown for the journals of Juan Crespí and the diary of Pedro Font, Frederick J. Teggart and Peter Browning for the journal of Miguel Costansó, Herbert Eugene Bolton for the diary of Juan Bautista de Anza, Malcolm Margolin for the California journal of La Pérouse, W. Kaye Lamb for the narrative of George Vancouver, Richard A. Pierce and Victoria Joan Moessner for the letters of Nikolai Rezanov and the account of Georg Heinrich von Langsdorff, Briton C. Busch and Barry M. Gough for the journal and historical narrative of William Dane Phelps, John H. R. Polt and W. Michael Mathes for the reminiscences of Juan Bautista Alvarado, George R. Brooks for the journal of Jedediah Smith, Harrison Clifford Dale for the diary of Harrison Rogers, Milo Milton Quaife for the narrative of Zenas Leonard and the autobiography of Kit Carson, Francis Price and William H. Ellison for the narrative of Agustín Janssens, Doyce B. Nunis, Jr., for accounts of the Bidwell-Bartleson party, George P. Hammond for the papers of Thomas Larkin, Erwin G. Gudde and Elisabeth K. Gudde for the diaries of Charles Preuss, and George Walcott Ames, Jr., for the diary of John S. Griffin.

In interpreting these and other primary accounts, I drew on many secondary sources, notably the works of Hubert Howe Bancroft and his staff on early California, David J. Weber on the Spanish-Mexican-American frontier, Harry W. Crosby on the Sacred Expedition of 1769, James J. Rawls and Steven W. Hackel on California Indians and their relations with colonizers, James A. Sandos on the Franciscan mission system, Adele Ogden and James R. Gibson on the Northwest fur trade and Russian America, C. Alan Hutchinson and Douglas Monroy on the Mexican era and the Californios, Doyce B. Nunis, Jr., on the American infiltration of California, and Josiah Royce and Neal Harlow on the American conquest. Biographical studies offered me numerous insights into the cultures and conflicts of early California, including Maynard J. Geiger on Junípero Serra, Francis F. Guest on Fermín Lasuén, Edwin A. Beilharz on Felipe de Neve, Louise Pubols on the de la Guerra family, Robert Ryal Miller on Juan Alvarado, Alan Rosenus on Mariano Vallejo, Carlos Manuel

Acknowledgments

Salomon on Pío Pico, Susanna Bryant Dakin on William Hartnell and Hugo Reid, Dale L. Morgan and Barton H. Barbour on Jedediah Smith, Richard Batman on James Pattie, Charles B. Churchill on Alfred Robinson and other American chroniclers of Mexican California, Tom Chaffin on John C. Frémont, Harlan Hague and David Langum on Thomas O. Larkin, Albert Hurtado on John Sutter, George D. Lyman on John Marsh, Werner H. Marti on Archibald Gillespie, Doris Marion Wright on Abel Stearns, Donald E. Rowland on John Rowland and William Workman, and Langdon Sully on Alfred Sully.

Research for this project was conducted at the Library of Congress, the Woodstock Theological Center at the Georgetown University Library, the Beinecke Rare Book and Manuscript Library at Yale University, the California State Library in Sacramento, and the Bancroft Library at the University of California, Berkeley. In quoting from accounts held in manuscript form at the Bancroft Library, I relied largely on editions in print, with the exception of items listed under "Manuscripts" in the bibliography. My thanks to the Bancroft Library for permission to quote from those manuscripts.

Index

References to illustrations are in italics.

Abert, James, 334
Abert, John J., 321, 334
Acapulco, Mexico, 47, 127, 380
Adams-Onís Treaty (1819), 211
African Americans, 17, 24–25, 212, 254
African Hispanics, 96, 103
Agustín (Indian warrior), 185
Alamo (Texas), 343
Alaska, 47, 114, 117, 127, 151–54, 156, 159–61, 163–66, 169–70
Albatross (American ship), 165
Alert (American ship), 313
Aleutian Islands, 151, 161–62
Aleut Indians, 151–54, 161, 165, 168, 170–71
Alexander (American ship), 146
Alta California. *See* California
Alvarado, Juan Bautista, *266*; and Americans and other foreigners, 180–81, 265–79, 281–82, 288, 300–302, 309, 311, 338, 340; early life, 175–82, 184; and Echeandía, 229; and Graham Affair, 273–79, 311; and land grants, 249, 269; and Mariano Vallejo, 175–76, 178–80, 203–204, 268, 272–73, 283–84; marriage, 261; and Micheltorena, 336–39, 342; and Sutter, 281–82, 288
Amador, Rafael, 245
American expansion. *See* United States, westward expansion of
American Revolution, 79, 107
American River, 221, 284, 327
Americans, 13, 139; as alcaldes, 374; American women as pioneers in California, 235, 291–99, 337–38; and British, 167, 211, 349, 372; buildings, 264, 298; and Californios and other Mexicans, 11, 15–26, 29–30; 180–81, 211–37, 240–42, 251–79, 282, 288–91, 298–302, 305–17, 319–20, 324, 328–30, 336–47, 349, 351–99, 401–408; clothing and adornment, 180, 259, 294, 359, 361; crime and punishment, 218, 234, 272, 274–79, 290, 293, 330, 335–36; education and literacy, 265–66, 290, 403; festivities, 368; in fur trade, 140–41, 145–53,

Americans: in fur trade (*continued*), 161–67, 209–32; in hide-and-tallow trade, 187, 251–60; and land grants, 232, 234, 241, 274, 337, 350–51; as maritime traders or settlers in California, 128, 140–41, 145–49, 152–53, 160, 163–67, 180, 187, 205, 214, 217, 219–20, 224, 234, 245, 251–63, 267, 274–75, 286, 311–14, 346, 353–54, 357–58, 391, 404; marriage and intimacies, 215, 220, 229–30, 235, 258–61, 264, 266, 269, 274, 290–91, 293, 298–301, 312, 321, 338, 357–58, 360, 365, 375, 378, 382; and Mexican citizenship, 215, 220, 222, 229, 232, 234–35, 250, 274, 290, 300, 337, 360, 364, 375, 377, 382, 390, 401; as overland emigrants, 215–17, 237, 239, 241–42, 265–67, 273–74, 289–98, 326–28, 331, 337–38, 347, 349–68, 384–86, 404–405; and political disputes, 228–29, 265–69, 273–79, 317, 336–39, 395, 398; population of in California, 299; and race, 205, 219; as ranchers, 232, 234, 290–91, 282; religious beliefs, 217, 269; and Russians, 151–54, 161–65, 167; and slavery, 17, 25, 205, 254; as soldiers, 342–43, 347, 364–66, 368, 371–72, 375, 377, 379–99, 404; and Spanish colonists, 107–108, 128, 140–41, 145–49, 152–53, 156, 160–67, 180, 372; trades, 275; as trappers or mountain men, 209–34, 237–42, 264, 265–67, 273–74, 287, 294, 321, 324, 326, 329–30, 337–38, 346, 351, 389; and War of 1812, 167. *See also* Indians; United States

Andrés (Chumash leader), 198, 200
Andrés, Juan, 41
Anza, Juan Bautista de, 104–105, 107; and Anza expedition, 12, 72–91, 93, 96, 102, 176, 243
Apache Indians, 75, 78–80, 96, 390
Arballo, María Feliciana, 83, 229
Archuleta, Miguel, 179
Argentina, 181
Argüello, Concepción, 155–56, 159–61
Argüello, José Darío, 154, 156, 166, 176
Argüello, Luis Antonio, 154–56, 171, 184, 187, 199, 223
Argüello, Señora (wife of José Darío), 154–55
Arizona, 48, 75, 231
Arkansas River, 334
Armijo, Antonio, 231
Armijo, Manuel, 301, 388
Arrillaga, José Joaquín de, 136, 138, 146, 151–52, 156, 170–71
Ashley, William, 211
Astor, John Jacob, 166
Astoria, 166
Atherton, Faxon Dean, 262–63, 268
Austin, Stephen, 337
Australia, 135; stowaways from, in California, 136, 140–41
Avila, Enrique, 375
Aztec Indians, 80

Bahía San Quintín (Baja California), 152
Baja California, 14, 43, 86, 104, 118, 127, 193, 269, 381; colonization

of, 29; and fur trade, 150, 152–53, 162–64; missions and missionary ventures, 33–40, 64, 77, 124, 150, 202, 226
Bale, Edward, 359
Bancroft, George, 369–70, 372
Bancroft, Hubert Howe, 11, 404–406; and *California Pastoral*, 260
Bandini, Arcadia, 258, 378
Bandini, José, 255, 258
Bandini, Juan, 245–46, 255, 258–59, 271, 378
Baranov, Aleksandr, 152–53, 161–62, 170
Barraneche, Juan, 106–107
Bartleson, John, 293, 295–97
Bear Flag Revolt, 345, 349, 357–68, 370, 372, 374, 376, 381, 384, 402, 404–406
Bear River, 210–12, 222, 294
Belcher, Edward, 275
Belden, Josiah 293
Benicia, Calif., 25
Bent, Charles, 300, 389
Benton, Thomas Hart, 321, 334, 346
Bent's Fort, 331, 334
Berreyesa, José de los Reyes, 365
Bidwell, John, 292–93, 295–98, 300, 327–28, 336, 340, 351, 359, 364
Bidwell-Bartleson party, 292–99, 301, 327, 337, 359
Big Sur, 45
Bodega Bay, 132–33, 165, 168, 288
Bodega y Quadra, Juan Francisco de la, 131–36
Bonaparte, Joseph, 150, 168
Bonaparte, Napoleon, 144, 154, 168, 172–73

Bonneville, Benjamin, 237–38
Bonney, Benjamin, 350
Borboa, María Leonor, 96
Borica, Diego de, 138, 140–43, 178
Boscana, Gerónimo, 44, 188–89, 191, 194, 201, 217
Boston, Mass., 152, 156, 162, 165–66, 227, 256, 336
Botany Bay (Australia), 135, 140
Botiller, María, 96
Bouchard, Hipólito, 181, 183, 187, 196, 220
Brackenridge, William Dunlop, 287
Bradshaw, John, 227–28, 240–41
Branciforte, Calif., 141
British Columbia, 48
Brown, Charles, 357–58, 365
Brown, John, 146–47
Bryant, Edwin, 220, 384–87
Bryant and Sturgis (company), 217, 240, 252, 258
Bucareli, Antonio María de, 64, 68, 70, 77–78, 81, 86, 93–94, 104, 149
Buchanan, James, 340, 346, 376
Buenaventura River (mythical), 211–12, 319–21, 331
Bustamante y Guerra, José, 127

Cabrillo, Juan Rodríguez, 47–48
Cahuenga Pass, 338
Cahuilla Indians, 45
Calafia (mythical queen of California), 27–29
California, as paradise or promised land, 12, 18, 25, 27–30, 72, 75–76, 80, 85, 91, 209, 221, 224, 233, 249, 262, 289, 326, 399, 407
California Trail, 237, 291–99, 350

Californian (newspaper), 385
Californios, 13; alcaldes, 233, 277, 314, 341; and Americans and other foreigners, 11, 15, 18, 20–21, 180–91, 205, 216–23, 226–36, 240–42, 251–69, 272–79, 281–84, 288–91, 298–99, 308–14, 317, 336–47, 349, 352–87, 373–99, 401–408; buildings, 298; clothing and adornment, 182, 185, 254, 256, 259, 261; as creoles, 255; crime and punishment, 199, 241, 266, 274–79, 387; *diputación* (assembly), 184, 227, 246, 248, 268, 377; education and literacy, 176, 178–80, 250–51, 403; equestrian skills, 261–62; 375–76, 393; festivities and pastimes, 259–60, 276, 311, 374, 394; and Franciscan missions, 204, 216, 244, 246–47, 395; hospitality, 219, 222, 227, 264, 291, 311, 315, 361, 394; labor and compensation, 188, 244, 247; land grants and claims, 204, 244, 246, 249–50, 256, 269, 354, 403; marriage and intimacies, 182–83, 186–87, 197, 203, 215, 222, 229–30, 250, 252–62, 264, 266–69, 274, 290–91, 298, 312, 357, 359, 365, 375, 378, 382; and Mexico, 173, 201–204, 243–51, 265, 267–71, 274, 310, 317, 336–39, 354–55, 360, 377–81, 395–99, 401; and New Mexicans, 231, 233; occupations and skills, 243, 248, 250, 256, 261; political disputes, 203–204, 246, 265, 267–71, 317, 336–39, 395, 399; population of, 299; and race, 175, 255; as ranchers, 181–82, 187, 255–56, 268, 285, 375, 394–95;
and religion, 201–202, 213; as soldiers, 185, 192–93, 196–99, 223, 228–29, 246, 255–56, 267–68, 283, 298, 342, 356–57, 373, 381–99; and Spain, 173, 175–79, 201; trade, 185, 227, 231, 246–47, 250, 254–56, 258, 272; as vaqueros, 285; warfare, 185, 196–99, 268–69, 336–39; wealth and finances, 181–82, 187, 204, 249–50, 254–56, 261, 272–73, 354, 377. *See also* Indians; Spanish colonists
Callao, Peru, 306–7
Callis, Eulalia, 121–23
Cambón, Pedro Benito, 65
Camilo (Coast Miwok chief), 283
Campbell, Richard, 225
Canada, 47; and French-Canadians, 212, 224, 270
Cañizares, José, 109–10
Canton (Guangzhou), China, 153, 162–65, 167
Cape Horn, 162, 210, 253, 256
Cárdenas, Juana María, 96
Cardero, José, 128–31
Carlos (Diegueño chief), 69–70, 87, 98
Carlos III (Spanish king), 34, 48, 93, 130
Carlos IV (Spanish king), 130, 138, 144, 149, 168
Carmel, Calif., 65
Carmel River, 64
Carpintería, Calif., 53
Carquínez Strait, 284
Carrillo, Anastasio, 197
Carrillo, Carlos, 271, 274
Carrillo, Francisca, 229
Carrillo, Joaquín, 245–46
Carrillo, José Antonio, 233, 271, 383

Carrillo, Josefa, 229, 246
Carrillo, María, 250, 274
Carrillo, Mariano, 63, 99
Carson, Kit, 233–34, 321, 324, 326, 328–31, 335, 344, 347, 358, 365, 389
Carson Pass, 326
Casa Grande (residence of Mariano Vallejo), 360
Casa Grande (ruins in Arizona), 80
Cascade Range, 345
Castro, Joaquín de, 96
Castro, José, 178–79, 275, 277–78, 311–12, 336–45, 352–59, 364–66, 372–79
Castro, José Mariano, 181–82
Castro, Manuel, 356n17, 386
Catalina Island, 151
Catalonia, Spain, 50
Catalonian Volunteers, 50, 63
Catholicism, 27, 215, 217, 269–70, 282, 286, 290; alms, 197; baptisms and christenings, 33, 36, 39, 59–61, 64, 67, 99, 104, 182, 191, 227, 358; catechisms, 88, 130, 178–79; confession and absolution, 17, 35–36, 81, 84, 156, 190, 197, 218–19; confirmation, 100; convents, 160; conversion to, 99, 107, 128, 156, 160, 186, 220, 222, 227, 229, 232, 357; Cross (Catholic Church), 25, 63–64, 78, 86, 123, 178, 202, 213, 244, 387; crosses and crucifixes, 42, 57, 59, 62, 130; crucifixion, 198; excommunication, 86; fasting, 71; godparents, 21–22, 60, 64, 103, 182; heaven, 109–10, 116; hell, 116, 190, 248; heresy, 179; holy water, 62, 188; hymns, 81, 115, 176–77, 190; last rites, 199; and Latin, 154; Lent, 122, 190; and marriage, 20, 23, 80, 105, 186; martyrdom, 71, 109; Mass and communion, 34, 50, 59–60, 71, 81, 83–84, 86, 91, 176, 189–90, 199; Pentecost, 33, 44, 62; papacy, 58, 100, 156; prayers, 51, 53, 60–61, 81, 88, 116, 137, 148, 177, 180, 188, 256; priests, 17, 23, 26, 34, 53, 70, 80, 84, 87, 94–95, 106–107, 110, 150, 275, 402; purgatory, 36, 71; right of asylum, 86; sacred images, 60, 65, 116, 190, 198, 200; saints, 39, 41, 51, 53, 61, 110; Satan or devil, 38, 72, 80, 84, 188; sermons, 75–76, 84, 89, 176–77; sins, 35–36, 60, 82, 106, 109, 188, 190, 218–19, 401–402; vestments, 115, 219; Virgin Mary, 51, 53, 60, 65–66, 71, 89; Virgin of Guadalupe, 76, 79, 96. *See also* Dominican missions; Franciscan missions; Jesuit missions
Cedros Island (Baja California), 164
Central Valley, 29, 222, 291, 327, 329. *See also* Sacramento Valley; San Joaquín Valley
Cervantes, Miguel de, and *Don Quixote*, 179
César, Julio, 271
Chacón (blacksmith at Mission San Diego), 60
Chalifoux (Charlevoix), Jean Baptiste, 270
Chamisso, Adelbert von, 171
Chapman, Joseph, 219
Charles III. *See* Carlos III
Charles IV. *See* Carlos IV
Chatham (British ship), 135–36
Cheyenne Indians, 294
Chico, Mariano, 265, 267–68

Chihuahua, Mexico, 389
Chile, 185, 229
Chiles, Joseph, 292, 327–28
China, 113, 117, 120, 145, 153
Chinigchinich (Indian deity), 189, 191, 194
Chinook Indians, 165, 325
Choris, Louis, 190
Christianity. *See* Catholicism; Protestantism
Chumash Indians, 45, 52–54, 61, 88, 102, 119–20, 124, 191, 193–202
Chumash Revolt (1824), 138, 196–202
Clark, Orange, 232
Clark, William, 162, 211–12
Cleveland, Richard, 145–51, 228
Clyman, James, 337–38, 351
Coastal Ranges, 43, 326
College of San Fernando (Mexico City), 64, 101, 115
Colorado River, 44, 75, 77–78, 81–82, 102, 104–107, 121, 209, 213, 222, 225–26, 390
Colton, Walter, 374–75, 380, 384–85
Columbia (American ship), 162
Columbia River, 162, 165–66, 211–12, 221–23, 276, 319, 321, 325
Columbus, Christopher, 14, 277
Comanche Indians, 232
Concepción Horra, Antonio de la, 142–43
Congress (U.S.S.), 374, 384
Consumnes River, 285
Cook, James, 48, 113, 131
Cooke, Philip St. George, 388–89
Cooper, J. B. R., 222, 235–36, 312
Coronel, Antonio, 246, 270, 336, 380–82, 393, 396–98

Cortés, Hernán, 27, 29, 177, 277
Cosmopolitan Company, 246–47
Costansó, Miguel, 45, 49–51, 53–58, 119
Coyote Canyon, 84
Crespí, Juan, 34, 41–42, 44, 49–53, 55–56, 61–62, 64–65, 89, 109
Croix, Teodoro de, 93, 95, 100, 105, 107, 109
Cueva, Pedro de la, 158
Cunningham, William, 215
Custer, George Armstrong, 394
Cyane (U.S.S.), 307, 309, 355

Daedalus (British ship), 135
Dana, Francis, 252
Dana, Juan Francisco, 250
Dana, Richard Henry, Jr., 251–60, 266; and *Two Years before the Mast*, 252
Dana, William Goodwin, 234, 250, 274
Davis, William Heath, 20–21, 260–62, 272, 275–76, 283–85, 313
Dawson, Nicholas, 293–94
Delaware Indians, 365, 372
De Smet, Pierre Jean, 294
Díaz, Cristóbal, 109
Diegueño Indians, 42–45, 50, 59–60, 69–71, 77
Discovery (British ship), 133
Diseases and treatments, 42–43, 80–81, 85, 121, 142, 156, 190–91; dropsy, 128; dysentery, 124; malaria, 284, 290, 292; measles, 158, 253, 286; scurvy, 41, 55–56, 128, 134, 154; smallpox, 103, 228, 284; syphilis and other venereal diseases, 124, 158
Dolores, Mexico, 201

Domínguez, Francisco, 108
Dominican missions, 14, 64, 150–52, 164, 202, 226
Doniphan, Alexander, 389
Donner Pass, 335, 337
Don Quixote (American ship), 272
Dorr, Ebenezer, 140–41, 144
Drake, Francis, 139
Drakes Bay, 56
Duflot de Mofras, Eugène, 289
Duhaut-Cilly, Auguste, 168, 227–28, 236
Durán, Narciso, 179, 221, 248, 255, 301

Earthquakes, 51, 193
Eayrs, George Washington, 166
Echeandía, José María, 202–203, 213–18, 221–23, 226–30, 248
El Camino Real (Mission Trail), 102
El Príncipe. See *San Antonio (Spanish ship)*
Emmons, George, 299
England. See Great Britain
Enlightenment, age of, 14–15, 78–79, 115
Ensenada, Mexico, 226
Escalante, Silvestre, 108
Esselen Indians, 45
Estanislao (Indian leader), 330
Estrada, José María, 199
Estudillo, María, 261
Etchinson, James, 135
Eustevan, Manuel, 212

Fages, Pedro, 50, 61–65, 67–68, 90, 94, 99, 113–14, 116–25
Farallon Islands (Farallones), 56, 151, 164, 166, 170

Farnham, Thomas Jefferson, 276–79, 292
Feliz, José Vicente, 104
Ferdinand VII (Spanish king), 150, 168
Ferguson, Daniel, 236
Fernández, José María, 142
Fernández de San Vicente, Agustín, 184
Figueroa, José, 236, 240–41, 244–51, 255, 267; and *Manifesto to the Mexican Republic*, 250–51
Fitch, Henry Delano, 229–30, 245, 381
Fitzpatrick, Thomas, 294, 321, 326
Flint, Timothy, 230
Flores, José María, 381–82, 394, 396
Florida, 107–108
Font, Pedro, 12, 75–91, 93, 176, 229
Forbes, Alexander, 289
Ford, Henry, 364
Fort Bonneville, 237
Fort Hall, 291, 350
Fort Ross, 161, 165, 167–70, 168, 172, 247, 288
Fort Vancouver, 223
Foster, Stephen C., 226–27
France, 138, 144, 264; empire and imperialism, 17, 47–48, 113–14, 289, 402; French language, 155, 270; French visitors and settlers in California, 113–19, 227–28, 282, 289, 361; and Mexico, 278, 355
Franciscan missions, 141–42, 171, 180: alcaldes, 101, 117, 120, 191, 194, 198, 200, 407; and Americans, 26, 217–21, 230, 264–65; *asistencias*, 129; buildings, 59, 65, 176, 192–93, 199; crafts, 116, 139, 190, 198, 250; cultivation and irrigation, 64,

Franciscan missions: cultivation and irrigation (*continued*), 67, 85, 89, 95, 124–25, 192, 263; education at, 68, 116, 129–30, 177, 286; finances and trade, 68, 118, 125, 150–51, 166–67, 169, 186; and Indians, 15, 17, 22, 26, 29–30, 33–45, 50–73, 75–91, 94–95, 97–106, 115–20, 123–26, 129–30, 133–34, 137–39, 141–44, 157–58, 169, 176–77, 183, 187–201, 203–204, 216–17, 221, 244, 246, 249–50, 286, 301–302; livestock, 85, 97, 124, 144, 192; *mayordomos*, 182, 192; and Mexico, 184, 230; *monjerio*, 193; population of, 123–24; and presidios, 33, 64, 67, 69–71, 80, 100, 123–26, 129–30, 133–34, 176; and pueblos, 94–95, 97–98, 105–107, 126, 141; punishments, 64, 68–70, 98–99, 101, 115, 123, 142–43, 196, 213, 218; and ranches, 129, 166, 182, 192; and reform, 94, 100–102, 117, 178; *regidores*, 101; and Russians, 154, 156–58; secularization of, 41–42, 178, 200, 203–204, 216, 244, 246–51, 258, 264–65, 271, 375–76, 395; soldiers as guards at, 59–61, 65, 182, 196–98; and slavery, 26, 99, 115, 216, 218; and Spanish officials, 27, 41, 48, 64–69, 75–91, 94, 98–110, 117–20, 122–26, 128–30, 141–43, 167, 176–77, 184; and spiritual conquest, 17, 26, 33, 36–38, 41–43, 61, 72, 95, 109–10, 143, 149, 195, 198, 224; vows of padres, 70–71, 124, 144. *See also* College of San Fernando; Indians; Spanish colonists; *and individual missions*

Francisco (Diegueño fugitive), 70
Franklin (American ship), 227–28
Frémont, Jessie Benton, 321, 331, 334, 344
Frémont, John Charles, 306, 318; and Bear Flag Revolt, 353, 355–59, 362–68, 370–71, 376, 405–406; expedition to California in 1844, 319–31; expedition to California in 1845–46, 331–36, 339–47, 353; and Mexican War, 371–73, 377–80, 384, 386–87, 389, 395–98; and Sutter, 327–29, 335–36, 363–64, 385; as U.S. senator, 407
French and Indian War, 349, 402
Fuentes, Andreas, 329
Fur trade, 126, 284; in beaver pelts, 209–14, 221–26, 231, 233–34, 237–39, 287–88; in sealskins, 118, 151, 163, 166, 170; in sea-otter pelts, 48, 113, 117–18, 128, 140, 145–48, 150–54, 161–67, 170, 234, 274, 313
Fuster, Vicente, 69–71, 87

Gabrielino Indians, 45, 51, 65–66
Gálvez, Jose de, 48–49
Garcés, Francisco, 77, 79, 81–82, 104–108
Garner, William, 275
Gassiot, Juan, 108
Gavilán Peak, 342–43, 353, 359
Gaviota, Calif., 53
Geddes, Paul (aka Talbot Green), 293
George III (British king), 79
Gila River, 77, 80, 225, 232
Gila Trail, 225, 389
Gillespie, Archibald, 346, 366, 371–73, 376, 380–84, 390–93, 402, 404–406

Gil y Taboada, Luis, 166–67
Godey, Alexander, 329–30, 365
Golden Gate, 89, 133
Gold Rush, 285, 403, 406–407
Gómez, Francisco, 50
Gómez Farías, Valentín, 244–45
Gonzales, Manuel, 96
González, Rafael, 199
Goycoechea, Felipe de, 136, 167
Graham, Isaac, 265–70, 273–79, 281–82, 337–38, 353
Graham Affair, 273–79, 281–82, 291, 353, 358, 361
Gray, Robert, 162
Great Basin, 320, 334, 402
Great Britain, 13, 15, 17, 20; and American Revolution, 79, 107; British visitors and settlers in California, 20, 23, 130–40, 185–87, 212, 222, 228, 236, 249, 259, 271, 275, 283 288, 342, 359, 372; empire and imperialism, 47–48, 113, 117, 126–27, 130–31, 138–39, 288–89, 402; and France, 138, 154, 282; and Graham Affair, 278, 291; and Mexico, 265, 278, 282, 289, 307, 355, 403; rebellion against, 79; Royal Navy, 138, 275; and Russia, 154; and slavery, 288; trade, 48, 113, 117, 212, 228
Great Divide, 294
Great Plains, 26, 388
Great Salt Lake, 209, 211–12, 236–38, 294–95
Green River, 237
Greenwood, Caleb, 350, 386
Greenwood, John, 350–51
Griffin, John Strother, 389–94
Grigsby, John, 362
Grijalva, Juan Pablo, 83
Guadalupe River, 90, 95

Guangzhou. *See* Canton
Guerra, Ana María de la, 259
Guerra, Angustias de la, 20–26, 183, 187, 197, 203, 259, 313
Guerra, Pablo de la, 313
Guerra, Teresa de la, 187, 249–50, 259
Guerra y Noriega, José de la, 20, 25, 183–84, 187, 197–98, 249
Gulf of California, 226
Gulf of Mexico, 369
Gutiérrez, Nicolás, 265, 267–68
Gyzelaar, Henry, 181, 187

Hammond, Thomas, 391
Hargrave, William, 344
Haro, Francisco de, 365
Haro, Ramón de, 365
Haro, Rosalía de, 365
Hartnell, William, 20, 23, 185–87, 222, 236, 249, 259, 271, 342
Harvard College, 253, 290
Hastings, Lansford, and *The Emigrants' Guide to Oregon and California*, 327–28
Hawaii, 48, 113, 135, 162, 164–65, 181, 219, 228, 234, 262, 276, 281, 316
Hawaiians (Kanakas), 135, 162–64, 234, 257, 260–61, 274, 281
Hensley, William, 357
Hernández, Pablo, 329
Hidalgo y Costilla, Miguel, 201
Hide-and-tallow trade, 186, 204, 217–18, 240, 245, 249–50, 252–54, 256–58, 261–63, 313–14
Híjar, José María, 244–48, 250–51, 267
Híjar-Padrés expedition, 243–51, 258, 270, 290, 336, 380
Hill, Daniel, 235

Hinckley, William, 267
Homobono (Indian at Sutter's Fort), 286
Hudson's Bay Company, 212, 223, 233, 283, 287–88
Humboldt River, 236, 238, 291, 294–96
Humboldt Sink, 296

Idaho, 210, 291
Ide, Sarah, 350
Ide, William, 349–51, 353–54, 356–59, 362–65, 368, 386, 405
Il'men (Russian ship), 171
Indians: and Americans, 16, 30, 43, 201, 205, 209, 211–13, 216–19, 221–23, 225, 233–34, 238–42, 282, 289–90, 294, 316, 324–27, 329–30, 337–38, 344–45, 347, 349–53, 365, 372–73, 375–76, 382–83, 387, 399, 402–403, 405, 407; assaults on, 66–67, 88, 102, 233–34, 238–39, 330, 345, 375–76; buildings, 45, 52, 55, 134, 258; and Californios and other Mexicans, 184–85, 187, 195–203, 216–17, 222, 233, 240–41, 244, 246, 255–56, 258, 261–62, 282–87, 311, 316, 327, 329–30, 337–38, 352–53, 365, 375–76, 387, 390, 394; canoes or kayaks, 133, 152, 157, 159, 163–64; ceremonies and dances, 39, 53, 158–59, 165, 176–77, 184, 188–92, 194; chiefs, 65–66, 69–70, 98–100, 121, 137, 191, 201, 222, 226, 238, 283, 316, 352; children, 66; clothing and adornment, 38, 40, 45, 50, 59–60, 66, 81, 94, 157, 191–94, 238, 286; crafts, 52–53, 116, 133, 139, 157, 195, 198; as "Diggers," 52, 239, 326, 402; diseases and treatments, 42–43, 103, 121, 142, 157–58, 190–91, 284, 286, 330; education and literacy, 116, 177, 283, 286; emancipation, 203–204, 216–17, 265; food and subsistence, 38, 52, 54–55, 82, 85–86, 97, 105, 116, 124, 133; as fugitives, 68–69, 142, 158, 169, 195, 213, 233, 264–65, 286; gifts and exchanges, 35–37, 39–40, 50, 57, 59–60, 65, 81–82, 85–86, 94, 105, 116, 128, 212–13, 284, 294; hospitality, 38, 53–55, 114, 120; joyas, 120–21; labor and compensation, 26, 52, 55, 65, 97–98, 101, 105, 118, 125–26, 130, 140, 152–54, 162–67, 169–71, 187–88, 195, 203, 216, 246, 250, 263, 274, 283, 285–86, 300; land, 97, 101, 105, 125–26, 203–204, 216, 244, 246, 249–51, 301–302, 376; languages, 43–44, 60, 88, 116, 130; marriage and intimacies, 36, 40, 66, 100, 102–103, 105, 120–21, 169, 193–94, 199–200, 219, 290; at missions, 17, 22, 38, 43–45, 54, 59–60, 63–73, 77–80, 85–90, 94–106, 109–10, 115–21, 123–26, 133–34, 137–39, 142–44, 150, 157–58, 164, 167, 176–77, 183, 187–203, 213, 216–17, 221, 244, 246, 263–65, 271, 286, 301–302, 407; as pagans, 33, 35–39, 60, 72, 188–90; population of in California, 124, 330; and pueblos, 95–97; punishment, 64, 68–70, 98–99, 101, 115, 123, 142–43, 170–71, 189, 194–96, 199, 218, 265, 271, 285–86, 330, 374, 384; rights of, 14–15, 78, 117, 202, 246,

278–79; and Russians, 151–52, 154, 157–58, 169–70; and slavery, 25–26, 99, 115, 216, 218, 262, 287, 350, 376; as soldiers, 42, 283, 286, 360; and Spanish colonists, 11–12, 43, 50–73, 75–82, 85–91, 94–104, 115–21, 123–26, 129–30, 133–34, 137–39, 141–44, 402; spirituality, 42–43, 51, 62, 66, 72, 76, 79, 96, 116, 184, 188–96, 200–201, 296; testimony of, 13, 188–95; thievery, 59, 195, 200, 223, 233–34, 238, 282, 294, 345, 390; trade, 52–53, 57, 118, 140, 165, 240–41, 284, 294; uprisings and resistance, 29, 59–60, 86–87, 98–99, 104–108, 158, 187–201, 216, 330, 345, 387, 394; as vaqueros, 195, 250, 327; villages, 41, 44, 55–56, 192; warfare, 42, 44–45, 59–60, 66, 94, 120, 163–64, 196–99, 226, 239, 274, 286, 345, 350, 352–53, 357–58, 375, 390, 407. *See also* Franciscan missions; *and individual tribes*
Irving, Washington, 237–39, 242
Islas, Santiago, 105–106
Iturbide, Agustín de, 183, 201–202

Jackson, Andrew, 306, 308, 368
Jackson, David, 211, 232
Jackson, Helen Hunt, 30
Janssens, Victor Eugène August (Agustín), 243–45, 248–50, 270, 338, 394
Jayme, Antonio, 198, 200
Jayme, Luis, 66–67, 69–71
Jefferson, Thomas, 16, 26, 306, 308, 407
Jesuit missions, 34, 68, 77, 93, 179, 294

Jesús, Bernardino de, 64
Jesús, Juan de, 194
Jimeno, Antonio, 22
Jimeno, José Joaquín, 22
Jimeno, Manuela, 21–26, 28, 203
Jimeno Casarín, Manuel, 20, 22
Jones, John Coffin, 316
Jones, Thomas ap Catesby, 305–11, 313–17, 329, 336, 347, 370
José el Cantor (mission Indian), 176
Juno (American ship), 154

Kamehameha I (Hawaiian king), 162
Kamehameha III (Hawaiian king), 281
Kane, Elias, 23
Kane, Mrs. Elias, 23
Kearny, Stephen Watts, 387–95, 398–99, 401–403
Kelsey, Andrew, 359
Kelsey, Ann, 293–94, 297–98
Kelsey, Benjamin, 293–94, 359, 361
Kelsey, Nancy, 293–94, 297–99
Kentucky, 224, 265–67, 278, 331, 361, 384
Kern, Edward, 339, 356, 364, 385
Kern County, Calif., 200
Kern River, 339
Khlebnikov, Kirill, 169
Kimball, Oliver, 165
Kings River, 339
Kinney, Sam, 350–51
Kino, Eusebio, 77
Knight, Thomas, 356
Kodiak (Russian ship), 161
Kodiak Indians, 151, 161, 163–64
Kotzebue, Otto von, 169, 171–73, 190

Kumeyaay Indians. *See* Diegueño Indians
Kuskov, Ivan, 168, 170

Lagoda (American ship), 240–41
Lake Tahoe, 326
Lambert, Jane, 141
Langsdorff, Georg Heinrich von, 153–59
La Pérouse, Jean-François de Galaup, comte de, 112–119, 127–30
Larkin, Rachel Holmes, 235
Larkin, Thomas, 235, 242, 275, 310, 316, 360; as U.S. consul in Monterey, 235–36, 299, 328, 340–43, 354, 369–71, 376–78, 386–87
Las Casas, Bartolomé de, 14
Lassen, Peter, 344
Lasuén, Fermín Francisco de: and Branciforte, 141; and Fages, 119, 123, 125, 134; as father-president of California missions, 99, 115, 119, 125–26, 142–44; and Malaspina, 128; at Mission San Carlos, 115, 129–30; at Mission San Diego, 101, 115; and Serra, 115; and Vancouver, 137
Law, 12; American, 241, 277, 279, 290, 374, 380, 396, 403; international, 315; martial, 368; Mexican, 210, 222–23, 228, 234, 244, 246, 274, 277–79, 282, 286–87, 327, 335–36, 341–42, 359; natural, 15, 78; Spanish, 27, 68, 78, 118, 141, 146, 149, 166–67, 180, 278
Leese, Jacob, 360, 362–64
Leidesdorff, William, 342

Lelia Byrd (American ship), 145–48, 151
Leonard, Zenas, 200, 237–42
Lewis, Meriwether, 162, 211–12
Librado, Fernando, 193–94
Lincoln, Abraham, 366–67, 398
Lincoln, Mary Todd, 362
Little Bighorn, battle of, 394
Liquor (*aguardiente*), 82, 84, 218, 242, 261, 267, 272–73, 311–12, 362, 371–72, 374, 380
Livestock: cattle and oxen, 38, 79, 97, 114, 124, 129, 133, 135, 155–57, 157, 170, 181, 195, 209, 218, 232, 249–50, 256, 262–63, 283, 291, 295–98, 335, 350, 356, 360; hogs, 162, 218, 298; horses, 79, 85, 104, 124, 157, 170, 182, 185, 192, 195, 209–10, 214, 218, 221–22, 224, 226, 231–34, 239–42, 256, 262–63, 267–68, 270, 295, 297, 301, 320, 325, 328–29, 335, 338, 340, 356–58, 360, 363, 371, 374–76, 378, 382, 386, 390, 393, 395; sheep, 97, 124, 133, 135, 194, 218, 263, 301
Loreto, Mexico, 33, 50, 57, 86, 93, 193, 202
Los Angeles, Calif., 51, 102–104, 126, 141, 151, 178, 199, 230, 234, 245, 248, 263, 266, 269–70, 282, 290, 301, 308, 311, 314, 338–39, 356, 366, 373, 377–84, 389–90, 394–96
Los Angeles River, 51, 103
Los Osos, Calif., 54
Louisiana, 48, 108, 144, 264
Lugo, Antonio María, 129
Lugo, José del Carmen, 129, 178, 183, 256, 382
Lugo, María Antonia, 182

Luiseño Indians, 45, 50–51

Machado, José Manuel, 184–85
Machado, Juana, 184–85
Madison, James, 16
Madrid, Spain, 144, 156, 159, 161, 168
Mad River, 163
Málaga, Spain, 158
Malaspina, Alejandro, 127–28
Mallorca, Spain, 33
Manby, Thomas, 135
Manifest destiny, 12, 16, 316
Manila, Philippines, 118
Manila galleons, 47, 127
Marcy, William, 396
Marguerite (companion of John Marsh), 290
Marsh, John, 289–92, 298–99, 352
Marshall, William, 391
Martin, Thomas, 343
Martínez, Encarnación, 301
Martínez, Esteban José, 114
Martínez, Ignacio, 285
Maxwell, Richard, 311–12
Mazatlán, Mexico, 306, 369, 380
McChristian, Patrick, 360–61
McCulloch, Hugh, 185–87
McLane, Louis, 397
Menzies, Archibald, 134–35, 139
Mercantilism, 117–18, 256
Merced River, 240
Mercury (American ship), 166
Merritt, Ezekiel, 359–62, 381
Mervine, William, 383–84, 390
Mesa, Valerio, 96
Mexicana (Spanish ship), 46, 128, 131
Mexican War, 19–20, 220, 300, 346–47, 349, 358, 366–99, 401–408

Mexico, Republic of, 13, 15–18, 20, 27, 29–30, 33, 202–205, 216, 250, 278, 327, 332–33, 407; army, 396; boundaries and territory, 211, 238, 247, 281, 288, 305, 319–20, 331, 366; and Catholicism, 202, 269; Congress, 183, 245–46, 248, 258; constitution of 1824, 202, 244, 269, 271; constitution of 1836, 269, 271; flag, 184, 310, 314, 317, 369, 395; land policy, 244, 249; Mexican trappers and traders in California, 212, 224, 231, 390; Mexican troops sent to California, 309–10, 314–15, 317, 336, 380; Ministry of War, 298, 301–302, 341; political factions and disputes, 202, 204–205, 244–45, 352; population of, 204, 244; and race, 255; rebellions against, 204, 265, 267–68; and Russians at Fort Ross, 247, 288; and slavery, 17, 262; states, 202, 204, 244; trade policies and tariffs, 185, 187, 205, 215, 227, 256, 258, 267–68, 272. *See also* Californios; Mexican War
Mexico: under Spain, 27, 47–49, 76, 80, 96, 117, 156, 159, 171, 175; Internal Provinces of, 93, 107; war of independence, 150, 173, 176, 183–85, 201–202, 204, 362
Mexico City, 64, 68, 73, 76, 100–101, 104, 118, 144, 183, 204, 222, 230, 243–44, 251, 258, 288, 298, 336, 340–41, 352
Meyers, William Henry, 309–10
Micheltorena, Manuel, 302, 309, 311, 313–17, 328, 336–39, 352–53, 361, 377, 380

Mission La Purísima Concepción, 124, 196–97, 199, 250
Mission Rosario (Baja California), 152
Mission San Antonio de Padua, 65, 88
Mission San Buenaventura, 124, 137–38, 193
Mission San Carlos Borromeo, 64–65, 68–69, 89, 109–10, 112, 115–17, 122, 125, 129, 311
Mission San Diego de Alcalá, 45, 67, 69–73 86, 98–99, 101, 115, 119, 177
Mission San Fernando Rey de España, 177, 198
Mission San Francisco de Asís (Mission Dolores), 89–90, 94, 133, 140, 157–58
Mission San Francisco Solano, 222, 247, 283
Mission San Gabriel Arcángel, 29, 45, 65–67, 77–78, 85–87, 90, 97, 103, 129, 177, 193, 213, 217–21, 230–33, 258, 301, 376
Mission San José de Guadalupe, 157–58, 221, 330
Mission San Juan Bautista, 181–82, 240, 343, 386
Mission San Juan Capistrano, 45, 70, 78, 119, 138, 188, 193, 201, 218
Mission San Luis Obispo de Tolosa, 65, 88, 120, 182, 234
Mission San Luis Rey de Francia, 45, 50, 191–92, 227, 264, 271
Mission San Miguel Arcángel, 141, 271, 387
Mission San Rafael Arcángel, 233, 271, 357
Mission Santa Bárbara, 25–26, 124, 136–37, 166, 191, 196–200

Mission Santa Catalina (Baja California), 226
Mission Santa Clara de Asís, 90, 94–95, 97, 123, 133–34, 141
Mission Santa Cruz, 141
Mission Santa Inés, 196–97, 250
Mission Santo Domingo (Baja California), 152
Mission San Vicente Ferrer (Baja California), 202
Mission San Xavier del Bac (Arizona), 52, 77, 79–80
Mission Trail (El Camino Real), 102, 246
Mississippi River, 47–48, 205
Missouri, 224, 281, 290, 292, 297, 301, 321, 327, 388
Missouri River, 211
Miwok Indians, 45, 283, 285, 352
Mohave Indians, 44, 52, 108, 212–13, 221–22, 226
Mojave Desert, 209–10, 214–15, 231, 233, 328–29
Mojave River, 209, 375
Monroe Doctrine, 307, 316
Montalvo, Garci Rodríguez de, 27–28
Monterey, Calif., 20–21, 26, 33, 45–58, 61–65, 73, 75, 80, 86, 88–90, 93–94, 108, 113–19, 121–23, 127–29, 132, 134–36, 140–41, 156, 171, 175–78, 181, 184–85, 199, 204, 220, 222, 235–36, 240–43, 245–48, 258, 262–63, 267–70, 272, 275–78, 291–92, 299, 305–17, 328–29, 336, 339–43, 346, 353, 358, 368–74, 376–77, 382, 384, 394. *See also* Mission San Carlos; Monterey presidio
Monterey Bay, 45–47, 49, 55–56, 62, 114

Monterey presidio, 63–64, 67, 69, 88–89, 95, 97, 122, 125, 128, 131, 176, 180–81, 198, 228, 236, 268
Montgomery, John, 367–68, 371
Montielo, María, 106–107
Moore, Benjamin, 392–93
Moraga, Gabriel, 170
Moraga, José Joaquín, 83, 90, 97
Mormons, 389
Morro Bay, 45, 54
Mount Diablo, 290

Napa Valley, 45, 356–57
Natalia (Mexican ship), 245, 247
Neal, Samuel, 335–36, 357
Neophytes. *See* Indians, at missions
Nevada, 222, 236, 319
Neve, Felipe de, 86, 93–95, 97–104, 107–109, 117, 119
New Albion (British term for California), 139, 163, 169
New England, 79, 160, 162, 263, 276, 278
New Helvetia. *See* Sutter's Fort
New Mexico, 15, 78, 93, 108, 191, 224–25, 231–34, 270, 281, 300–301, 314, 329, 387–89, 396, 398
New Orleans, 48
New Spain. *See* Mexico, under Spain
Nidever, George, 273–74
Nisenan Indians, 285
Noé, Nicolás, 166
Nootka Convention, 126, 131
Nootka Sound, 48, 113, 127, 131–32, 135, 138
Noriega, Matías Antonio de, 122
Noriega, José, 290

Oahu, Hawaii, 162, 164–65
Oak Creek Pass, 329

O'Cain, Joseph, 152–52
O'Cain (ship), 162–65
O'Farrell, Jasper, 365
Ogden, Peter Skene, 233
Ohlone Indians, 45, 55–56
Old Town (San Diego), 59
Ord, Edward, 20
Ord, James, 20, 24
Ordaz, Blas, 194, 197
Oregon, 223, 276, 281, 291, 294, 299, 319, 321, 327, 331, 334, 341, 344–45, 350
Oregon Trail, 224, 291, 294–95, 319, 350
Ortega, Ignacio María, 181
Ortega, José Francisco de, 50, 70, 99
Ortega, José María, 166
Otter (American ship), 140–41
Osio, Antonio María, 121, 178, 197, 265, 269, 272–73, 309–10
O'Sullivan, John, 16–18, 316, 408
Owens, Richard, 353

Pacific Northwest, 48, 113, 118, 126–28, 131–32, 140, 162–63, 165–66, 169, 276, 294, 319
Padrés, José María, 244–51
Paiute Indians, 238–39
Palma, Salvador, 81, 104–106
Palma, Ygnacio, 105–106
Palo Alto, Calif., 56
Palóu, Francisco, 36, 60, 89, 94, 109–10, 125
Papago Indians, 77, 81
Paredes, Mariano, 352
Parrott, John, 306–307, 310
Pattie, James Ohio, 224–30, 240, 242
Pattie, Sylvester, 224–26
Payeras, Mariano, 186

Peacock (American ship), 165
Peña, Tomás de la, 123
Pennsylvania, 237, 293, 364
Peralta, Gabriel, 96
Pérez, Eulalia, 193, 195
Pérez, Juan, 61
Péron, Pierre, 140–41
Peru, 166, 185, 255
Peyri, Antonio, 227, 264
Phelps, William Dane, 162–64, 166, 286, 313–14
Philippines, 118, 407
Philippines Company, 118
Picacho Pass, 80
Pico, Andrés, 387, 391–93, 392
Pico, José Antonio, 226
Pico, José de Jesús, 387, 396
Pico, Pío, 226, 271, 338–39, 356, 372, 376–79, 388
Pilgrim (American ship), 252–54, 258
Pima Indians, 77, 80, 81
Pirates and privateers, 140, 145, 166, 181
Platte River, 294
Poinsett, Joel, 211
Point Año Nuevo, 55
Point Conception (Concepción), 53
Point Loma, 145
Point Pinos, 62
Polk, James, 305–306, 334, 340, 347, 367, 370, 373, 406
Pomo Indians, 45, 169
Popé (Pueblo leader), 191
Portolá, Gaspar de, 33–34, 40, 42, 45, 48–58, 61–62, 88
Portsmouth (American ship), 367
Potts, Daniel, 212
Presidio Hill (San Diego), 59, 67
Preuss, Charles, 324, 326–27, 330

Princesa (Spanish ship), 180
Protestantism, 14, 18, 116, 235, 257, 282, 374, 402; Baptists, 220; Calvinists, 213, 402; and Catholicism, 213, 220, 269
Prudón, Víctor, 361–62
Pryor, Nathaniel, 226–27, 230
Pueblo Indians, 78, 108, 389
Pyramid Lake, 320

Quechan Indians. *See* Yuma Indians
Quintero, Luis, 104

Ragged Point, 54
Ramírez, Angel, 267–68
Ramírez, Nicolasa, 103
Ranches and ranchers, 21, 129, 166, 181–82, 192, 204, 232, 248–50, 254–56, 262–63, 268, 275, 282, 285, 290–92, 301–302, 342, 344, 375, 382, 386, 390, 394–95
Rancho Chino, 382, 386
Rancho La Natividad, 386–87
Rancho La Puente, 301
Rancho Los Meganos, 290
Rancho Nipomo, 234, 250
Rancho Petaluma, 247, 283
Rancho Pinole, 285
Rancho Refugio de Nuestra Señora, 166
Rancho San Antonio, 129
Rancho San Julián, 249
Ransa, John Peter, 212
Reed, James, 218
Refugio Cove, 151, 166, 171
Revere, Joseph Warren, 355
Rezanov, Anna, 160
Rezanov, Nikolai Petrovich, 153–56, 159–61, 165

Ripalda, Jerónimo, 178–79
Ripoll, Antonio, 196–200
Rivera y Moncada, Fernando Javier de, 34, 41, 44, 50, 68–69, 72, 86–87, 90–91, 94, 102–104, 106
Robidoux, Antoine, 292
Robinson, Alfred, 20, 23, 26, 217–18, 258–60, 264–65, 268, 272–73, 275, 278
Rocky Mountains, 211, 297, 314, 320, 331, 334
Rodríguez, José Antonio, 197, 199
Rodríguez, Manuel, 146–49, 163
Rogers, Harrison, 29, 209n1, 212–13, 217, 223
Rome, Italy, 58, 192
Roosevelt, Theodore, 407
Rousseau, Jean-Jacques, 115–16, 179
Rowland, John, 300–302, 338, 379
Rowland-Workman party, 300–301, 375
Royce, Josiah, and *California: A Study of American Character*, 17, 405–406, 408
Rubio, María Petra, 104
Ruiz, Micaela, 96
Rurik (Russian ship), 171
Russia: and Alaska, 47, 117, 151–54; and California, 13, 15, 47, 72, 151–65, 168–73, 228, 247; and China, 153, 167; empire and imperialism, 47, 117, 151, 160–61, 408; and France, 172–73; Russian Orthodox faith, 156, 160, 169; tsar, 153, 159, 172
Russian American Company, 152–53, 161–62, 168–70, 288, 351

Sacramento, Calif., 284
Sacramento River, 223, 282–84, 327, 334, 340
Sacramento Valley, 283, 286–88, 299, 320, 326, 344, 352, 357, 384
Saint Francis (San Francisco), 39, 41, 51, 221
Saint Joseph (San José), 61
Sal, Hermenegildo, 133
Salazar, Isidro Alonso, 126
Salinan Indians, 45, 54, 88
Salinas River, 45, 54–55
Salinas Valley, 342
Sam (servant of Alfred Sully), 24–25
San Antonio (Spanish ship), 33, 41, 61–62
San Bernardino Mountains, 209, 214
San Bernardino Valley, 209, 231, 375, 382
San Blas, Mexico, 61, 146–47, 150, 243, 248, 278
San Carlos (Spanish ship), 33, 41, 45, 137
San Carlos Pass, 85, 91
San Carpoforo Creek, 54
Sánchez, José Bernardo, 217–21, 230, 232
San Diego, Calif., 14, 33–34, 40–45, 49–50, 57–62, 70, 77–78, 80, 86–87, 90, 102, 117, 121, 138–40, 142, 145–49, 151, 163, 175, 185–86, 202, 213, 218, 221, 226–28, 236, 240, 253, 255, 257, 270, 313–14, 377–78, 381, 384, 391, 393–95. *See also* Mission San Diego; San Diego presidio
San Diego Bay, 47
San Diego presidio, 61, 67, 70–71, 87, 138, 146, 245

San Diego River, 67
San Felipe Creek, 83
San Fernando Pass, 52
San Fernando Valley, 52
San Francisco, Calif., 23, 56, 58, 73, 78, 80, 89–91, 94, 102, 133–34, 138–39, 140, 142, 153–61, 165–66, 169–70, 258, 293. *See also* Mission San Francisco de Asís; San Francisco presidio; Yerba Buena
San Francisco Bay, 25, 45, 56, 73, 78, 86, 89–90, 117, 127, 131–33, 137, 157, 162, 165, 170–71, 225, 240, 247, 272, 288, 290, 292, 340, 357, 366
San Francisco presidio, 89–90, 94–95, 97, 123, 133, 154–55, 165, 171–73
San Gabriel River, 395
San Joaquín River, 284, 290, 363
San Joaquín Valley, 45, 119, 199, 214, 221, 233, 240, 242, 297, 339, 341
San José, Calif., 95–97, 103, 126, 128, 141, 158, 179, 264, 291, 339, 341, 352, 356
San José (Spanish ship), 34, 55
San Luis Obispo, Calif., 377
San Miguel de Horcasitas, Mexico, 91
San Pablo Bay, 365
San Pasqual, battle of, 391–94, 401
San Pedro Bay, 51, 151, 164, 170, 266, 376–77, 382–84, 390
San Sebastián (campsite), 83
Santa Ana River, 51, 85
Santa Anna, Antonio López de, 204, 244–46, 265, 268
Santa Bárbara, Calif., 20, 25, 102, 136–37, 151, 167, 181, 187, 235, 249–50, 259, 270–71, 274, 313, 316, 384. *See also* Mission Santa Bárbara; Santa Bárbara presidio
Santa Bárbara Channel, 45, 52, 61, 88, 272, 274
Santa Bárbara presidio, 102, 107, 136, 166–67, 183, 197–98
Santa Clara, Calif., 356, 358. *See also* Mission Santa Clara de Asís
Santa Clara River, 52
Santa Fe, N.Mex., 108, 224, 232, 290, 301, 389
Santa Fe Trail, 224, 231–32, 281
Santa Lucía Range, 54
Santa Margarita, Calif., 377
Santa María, Vicente, 137–38
Santa Rosa Island, 274
Santos, José de los, 135
Sapling Grove, Kan., 292
Sarría, Vicente Francisco de, 177–78, 186, 198–99
Savannah (U.S.S.), 383–84
Scott, Winfield, 19
Sea Otters, 48
Semple, Robert, 361, 385
Serra, Junípero, 15, 32, 79, 88, 195, 198; baptisms performed by, 59–60, 67; and Crespí, 64–64, 89, 109; death, 109–10; early years, 33; expedition of 1769 to San Diego, 33–43, 49; and Fages, 64–65, 67–68, 90; as father-president of California missions, 33, 41, 64–69, 71–73, 93; and Lasuén, 115; missions founded by, 59, 64–65; at Monterey and Mission San Carlos, 64–65, 68–69, 73, 89, 109–10; and Neve, 93–95, 98–102; and Palóu, 36, 60, 89, 109–10; and Portolá, 33–34, 40, 42, 49, 58–59; and

punishment, 68–69, 98–99; and Rivera y Moncada, 68–69
Serrano Indians, 45, 209; Vanyume band, 213
Seven Years' War, 47
Seville, Spain, 108
Shaler, William, 145–47, 149–50, 228
Shawnee Indians, 270
Siberia, 153, 160
Sierra Nevada, 43, 199, 215, 221–22, 233, 237, 239, 242, 291, 295–97, 319–28, 335, 337
Simpson, George, 283, 288–89
Sinaloa, Mexico, 78, 102
Sioux Indians, 290
Sitjar, Buenaventura, 88
Sitka (New Archangel), Alaska, 152–54, 156, 159–61, 163–64, 281
Sloat, John, 368–74, 388
Smith, Jedediah, 232, 234–36, 240, 242, 294, 306, 346; and Southwest Expedition, 209–25, 319–20
Smith, Thomas (stowaway from Australia), 136
Smith, Thomas "Pegleg" (mountain man), 233
Smuggling, 140, 145–50, 166–67, 169, 180, 187, 215, 227–28, 272, 276, 347
Snyder, Jacob, 350
Socorro, N.Mex., 389
Soda Lake, 209
Soda Springs, Idaho, 294
Solá, Pablo Vicente de, 171–73, 176–79, 181, 183–84, 186
Solano (Suisun Indian chief), 283, 316, 357–58, 360
Soler, Nicolás, 122–23

Solís, Joaquín, 228
Sonoma, Calif., 222, 247–48, 251, 275, 283, 316, 329, 353, 356, 358–65, 368. *See also* Mission San Francisco Solano
Sonora, Mexico, 72, 75, 77–78, 82, 91, 93, 96, 102, 107, 390, 396
Sonoran Desert, 12, 75, 245
Soto, Guillermo, 103
Spain, 77, 85, 108, 141, 230; conquistadors, 27, 224, 276–77; constitution of 1812, 179; Crown (monarchy), 14–15, 25, 34–35, 48–49, 62–64, 67, 78–79, 86, 91, 93–95, 99, 101, 105, 117–18, 123, 127–30, 138, 144, 177–78, 181, 185, 188, 387, 407; empire and imperialism, 11, 25, 30, 47–49, 91, 100–101, 107, 110, 126–27, 130, 139, 144, 148–50, 172–73, 216, 242, 402, 407–408; finances, 48, 93, 95, 97, 102, 105; flag, 62, 176; and France, 48, 113, 130, 138, 144, 168, 173; and Great Britain, 47–48, 113, 126–27, 131–32, 138–39, 162; navigation, 27–29, 46–49, 55, 57, 61–62, 103, 113–14, 118, 126–28, 138; rebellion against, 49, 150, 173, 176, 181, 183–84, 201; and Russia, 113, 151–62, 167–68, 170–73; trade policies, 117–18, 127, 140–41, 144–51, 154, 156, 161, 166–68, 170, 172, 185, 256. *See also* Spanish colonists
Spanish colonists, 11–18, 20, 25–30, 212, 399, 401–402, 407–408; artisans, 60, 65, 71, 116, 135; buildings and furnishings, 59, 63–65, 96, 104, 106, 129, 133, 176; California expeditions, 33–43,

Spanish colonists: California expeditions (*continued*), 45–47, 49–58, 61–62, 75–91, 373; childbirth and midwives, 80, 84, 121, 183; clothing and adornment, 154, 172, 177; convicts, 141; creoles, 63, 175–76, 183; education and literacy, 88, 108, 176, 178–80; fandangos and other diversions, 82–84, 91, 134–35, 156–57; food and subsistence, 52, 57–58, 61, 67, 87–88, 95–97, 104–105, 114; hospitality, 114, 134, 136; and independence, 173; labor and compensation, 63, 65, 67, 70, 95, 103–104, 123, 125–26, 129, 138; marriage and intimacies, 66–67, 96, 103, 108, 121–23, 156, 160; medical practices, 80, 121, 183; mestizos, 76, 96, 121, 175–76; *mulatos* and *negros*, 96, 103; navigation, 33–34, 41, 47, 52, 61–62; *peninsulares*, 63, 175; place names, 53; population of in California, 72, 78, 95–96, 108, 124, 136; presidios, 33, 48–50, 75, 77, 79–80, 86, 88–90, 93–95, 105, 108, 122–25, 128, 131, 133–34, 136, 178, 196; pueblos, 51, 80, 94–97, 102–105, 108, 126, 128, 141, 178, 196; punishments, 66–67, 83, 88, 98–99, 115, 123, 179–80; as soldiers, 17, 29, 41–42, 49–63, 65–72, 75, 77–81, 83, 86, 88, 94–95, 99, 102–107, 115, 117, 124–26, 128–29, 133, 139, 146–48, 151, 156, 165, 177–82, 184–85, 373; supply shipments, 67, 94–95, 125, 150, 174, 185; trade, 47–48, 102, 117–18, 127–28, 140–41, 144–45, 150, 154, 156, 159, 161, 166–67, 169–70; uprisings against Spain, 49, 150. *See also* Franciscan missions; Indians; Spain

Spanish Inquisition, 276
Spanish Trail, 231–32, 300
Spear, Nathan, 272, 275–76
Spence, David, 228
Spiritual Conquest. *See* Franciscan missions.
Stanislaus River, 297
Stearns, Abel, 258, 377–78
Stevens, Elisha, 337
St. Louis, Mo., 211, 321, 324, 331
Stockton, Robert, 366, 372, 374, 376–80, 383–84, 388–89, 391, 393–98, 402, 404, 406
St. Petersburg, Russia, 159, 165
Strait of Juan de Fuca, 128, 132
Sublette, William, 211
Suisun Bay, 284
Suisun Indians, 293, 316
Sully, Alfred, 19–28, 203
Sully, Thomas, 19
Suñol, Antonio, 291
Sutil (Spanish ship), 46, 128, 131
Sutter, John, 280–88, 290, 298–300, 327–29, 335–39, 350–53, 363–64, 366, 385–86, 403
Sutter's Fort, 284–87, 299–300, 327–29, 335–37, 339–40, 344, 350–53, 358, 363–64, 384–85
Swift, Granville, 359

Tac, Pablo, 191–92
Talbot, Theodore, 331, 335, 339, 341
Taos, N.Mex., 224, 231, 300
Tapia, Felipe Santiago, 96
Taraval, Sebastián, 77
Tarasov, Boris, 170
Tennessee, 237, 273, 278
Tepic, Mexico, 278, 289

Texas, 48, 93, 108, 265, 268, 288, 300–301, 306–307, 334, 340, 343, 362, 366–67, 369
Thompson, Frank, 253–54, 257, 262
Tlingit Indians, 152–53
Todd, William, 362
Tongva Indians. *See* Gabrielino Indians
Torre, Joaquín de la, 364–65, 366
Torres, Francisco, 248
Townsend, John, 337–38
Toypurina, 29
Traveller (American ship), 180
Travis, William Barret, 343
Treaty of Cahuenga (1847), 396–97
Treaty of Guadalupe Hidalgo (1848), 403–404
Trees: alders, 51; oaks and acorns, 54–55, 189, 213, 297–98, 326–27; poplars, 51; redwoods, 55, 263
Trinidad Bay, 163
Truckee River, 320
Tubac, Ariz., presidio at, 48, 52, 75, 77, 79
Tucson, Ariz., presidio at, 52, 80
Tulares (tule marshes), 199
Turner, Henry Smith, 390
Tyler, John, 306, 316

Umpqua River, 223
United States, 107, 225, 251–52, 281, 290, 351; boundaries, 211, 237, 346; citizenship, 371, 388, 397–98, 403–404; Civil War, 205, 367, 399; Congress, 357; conquest and annexation of California, 20, 204–205, 220, 276, 345, 368–99, 401–408; Constitution, 308, 367; empire and imperialism, 11, 16–18, 26, 148–49, 205, 307, 372, 402–408; flag, 305, 308, 310, 314, 317, 342–43, 371, 379, 399; and France, 306–307, 349; and Great Britain, 79, 107, 104, 211, 216, 237, 276, 289, 306–307, 319, 334, 345, 349, 372, 404; and Indian tribes, 206, 349; Louisiana Purchase, 144; and Mexico, 205, 211, 216, 237, 241–42, 265, 278, 282, 288, 305–307, 310, 316–17, 319–20, 328, 334–35, 339–40, 346–47, 352, 354–55, 358, 366–71, 377–99, 402–406; and slavery, 17, 205, 254–55, 288, 367, 399, 407; and Spain, 107–108, 162, 167, 211, 349; U.S. Army, 225, 300, 381, 387–99; U.S. Marines, 346, 366, 371–73, 376, 380–84, 390–93; U.S. Navy and Pacific Squadron, 262, 305–17, 329, 346, 355, 366, 368–80, 383–84, 386, 388–89, 391, 393–98; U.S. Topographical Corps, 319–34, 346; War Department, 395; westward expansion of, 12, 16, 25, 107–108, 131, 162, 166, 216, 225–26, 230, 237, 242, 288–290, 305–307, 321, 329, 347, 370, 398. *See also* Americans
United States (U.S.S.), 305, 307, 309, 311
Upper Klamath Lake, 345
Uría, Francisco Xavier, 196
Utah, 108, 231

Valdés, María Serafina, 184–85
Valdez, Dorotea, 371
Valenzuela, Francisca, 96
Vallejo, Encarnación, 222, 312
Vallejo, Ignacio, 175, 180, 182–83
Vallejo, Mariano Guadalupe: and Americans and other foreigners, 251, 283, 285, 288, 298, 300–301,

Vallejo, Mariano Guadalupe: and Americans and other foreigners (*continued*), 315–16, 359–64, 403–404, 406; and Bear Flag Revolt, 359–64, 366, 372, 385; early life, 175–76, 178–80, 184, 229; military and political career, 203–204, 247, 252, 265, 268, 271–73, 275, 283, 285, 288–89, 298, 302, 316, 330, 353–57; and Sutter, 283, 285, 288, 298
Vallejo, Rosalía, 360–61
Vallejo, Salvador, 316, 359–62, 364
Valparaíso, Chile, 229
Vancouver, George, 130–40, 145–46, 149, 154, 216, 258, 262
Vancouver Island, 113, 128, 131, 274
Vandalia (American ship), 383
Vasadre y Vega, Vicente, 117–18
Velicatá, 33–35
Ventura, Calif., 52
Veracruz, Mexico, 19, 155, 159, 346
Verger, Rafael, 64
Vergerano, José María, 60
Victoria, Manuel, 204, 236, 246, 248
Vignes, Jean Louis, 282
Vizcaíno, Sebastián, 47–48, 61
Volunteer (American ship), 235

Wagons, 237, 243, 291–92, 294–96, 299, 327, 337, 350, 389
Walker, Joel, 299–300
Walker, Joseph, 236–42, 274, 297, 299, 331, 335, 339, 341, 343
Walker, Mary, 299
Walker Pass, 242, 335
Walker River, 239, 296
Walpole, Frederick, 372
Warner, Jonathan (Juan José), 231–32, 391

Warner Springs, Calif., 391
Warner's Ranch, 391
War of 1812, 167
Washington, D.C., 307, 340, 363, 388–89, 405–406
Watsonville, Calif., 55
Weber, Charles, 337
Western Emigration Society, 292
West Point (U.S.M.A.), 19, 237
Westport Landing, Mo., 324
Wilcox, James Smith, 160, 180
Wilkes, Charles, 262, 287, 299
Williams, Isaac, 382
Wilson, Benjamin, 301, 375, 379, 381–82, 386
Wilson, John, 369
Wilson, Woodrow, 407
Wine and vineyards, 116, 128, 158, 177, 256, 282–83
Winship, Jonathan, Jr., 162–66
Winship, Nathan, 165–66
Wiyot Indians, 173
Wolfskill, William, 231–32
Workman, William, 300–301

Yerba Buena (San Francisco), 261, 263, 272, 275–76, 283–84, 340, 342, 386
Yokuts Indians, 45, 199–200
Yosemite Valley, 239
Young, Ewing, 225, 233–34, 382
Yount, George, 231–32, 234–35, 242, 272
Yuma Indians, 44, 52, 78, 81–82, 102, 122, 390; uprising (1781), 104–108
Yurok Indians, 163

Zamorano, Agustín, 236, 248, 250
Zúñiga, José de, 103